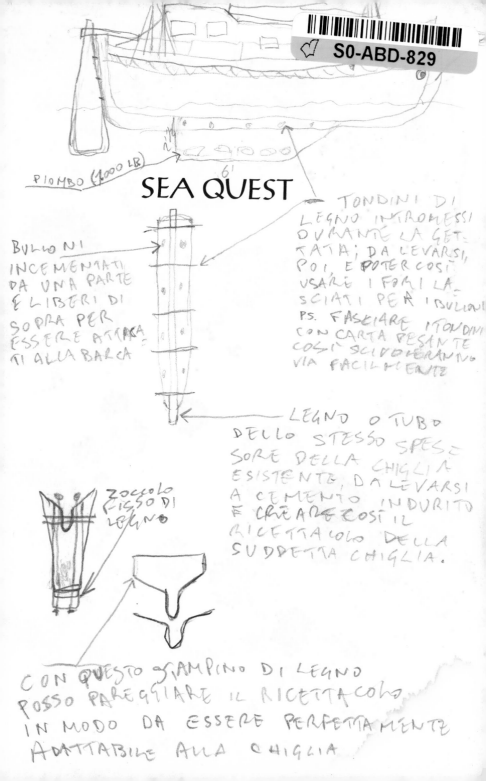

SEA QUEST

PIOMBO (1000 LB)

6'

TONDINI DI LEGNO INTROMESSI DURANTE LA GET-TATA; DA LEVARSI POI E POTER COSÌ USARE I FORI LA-SCIATI PER I BULLONI PS. FASCIARE I TONDINI CON CARTA PESANTE COSÌ SCIVOLERANNO VIA FACILMENTE

BULLONI INCEMENTATI DA UNA PARTE E LIBERI DI SOPRA PER ESSERE ATTRACA-TI ALLA BARCA

LEGNO O TUBO DELLO STESSO SPES-SORE DELLA CHIGLIA ESISTENTE, DA LEVARSI A CEMENTO INDURITO E CREARE COSÌ IL RICETTACOLO DELLA SUDDETTA CHIGLIA.

ZOCCOLO FISSO DI LEGNO

CON QUESTO STAMPINO DI LEGNO POSSO PAREGGIARE IL RICETTACOLO IN MODO DA ESSERE PERFETTAMENTE ADATTABILE ALLA CHIGLIA

SeaBooks in this series:

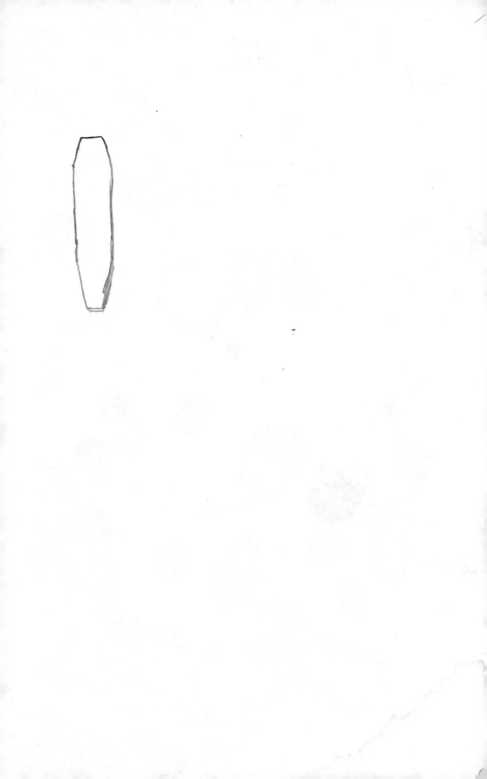

Global Blue-Water Adventuring in Small Craft

CHARLES A. BORDEN

SEA QUEST

DAVID McKAY COMPANY, INC.

New York

To

AL HANSEN, JOSHUA SLOCUM, CHRISTOPHER DE
GRABOWSKI, and all small-boat sailors who have
vanished at sea.

WONG MOW NER of Shanghai who waited with his
ricksha in the rain.

MATIL who waited on the Bir Hackeim long after
Wander Bird cleared the pass.

Ketch *Tiare,* sloop *Confucius,* and the bare oak bones
of *Nancy Lee* that never failed to take the stiffest
blow. (She was a sluggard to windward but I loved
her.)

To those who understand these things.

Spindrift Point—where patches of lichen clinging to the outermost ledges are believed to be as old as recorded history. (Charles Borden's sanctuary may be seen at top of cliff.)

Author's Foreword

Everything can be found at sea according to the spirit of your quest.
—JOSEPH CONRAD

~~~~~~

WRITING these last words at an outermost headland a thousand feet out in the Pacific Ocean, I remember the bag of notes that was carried out along the narrow footpath to this 8-by-10-foot sanctuary on a fogbound day two years ago. Though a part of this book has come out of that seabag, it could not have been completed without the help of many small-ship voyagers, solo navigators, circumnavigators, and others who are scattered widely around the world. Whatever merits it may have belongs in large part to them. Its faults and omissions are my own.

The thought or idea that began a book is seldom remembered correctly. Looking back, it seems to me that the search for all that has meaning is a continuous one, starting at birth, and our individual lives take shape in isolated moments of crisis. If I were to draw up the log of the hours in my life that have really counted, those spent in small ships in the Celebes and in the South Pacific would top the list.

To hold the interest of the general reader without shocking the sailor requires some difficult navigation. A serious effort has been made to present a crosscut of the story of small-ship sailors and the sea. But completeness is impossible and pure objectivity is found only in an encyclopedia. What I have chosen is as highly personal as what I have not included.

If a voyage means no more than ship routine, wind, weather, and distances sailed, then it means very little. It is the individual behind the tiller —his fears, hopes, and achievements—that makes his voyaging of interest. It wouldn't have mattered much if Joshua Slocum had spent the best years of his life ocean cruising in the Atlantic or the Pacific instead of sailing around the world. But it matters greatly that Slocum was Slocum, just as it matters that McMullen was McMullen and that Selkirk was Alexander Selkirk, a man who danced to his cats and goats on lonely Juan Fernández. Slocum did not give up the world, but neither could he find a place in it, so he retired to a small boat and to the sea where he led not a comfortable life but one in which he found meaning. If success must be the criterion, we can say that he was successful in being himself—no small achievement in his or any day.

Alain Gerbault was another who turned from time-filling devices to find purpose and meaning in the open sea. As national tennis champion he could have given up his quest and lived out his years "with bland success," plus security. "But what is security?" he once asked, and answered, "It is death. It is a state in which nothing can happen." Bemused always by a sense of wonder and recognizing what a great gift life can be, Gerbault always took an eagle-eyed view.

Joseph Wood Krutch said of Slocum, "He is one of the small but significant number of American nonconformists who turned their backs on accepted standards and patterns as definitely as Thoreau." Sailors have always been dissenters. In an age when everything is organized from the cradle to the grave and the dull gray glow of the television set prevails, a sailor is never unaware, as Marjorie Petersen of the cutter *Stornoway* recently said, "that the tally of our lives is dwindling and beyond the rim of the hills there lies a broad ocean of wind-cut waves."

The scale of size for offshore caravels has been reduced and out of the centuries-old man-sea relationship has appeared a new breed of sailors who are taking little ships with vane-operated self-steering gear across the Western Ocean and around the world. It is not unusual for the seasoned passage maker with a smart, weatherly, 30- to 40-foot vessel to be out in anything up to a full gale, snugged down to a reefed main and small storm jib.

Advanced techniques, new gear, sophisticated ideas in design and rigging are being tried and new sailing vessels are emerging at an unprecedented rate, but the archetypal cruising spirit remains much the same. Tomorrow's global man, with supersonic planes and satellites at his command, will still need a skin of brine to cross in a small ship, and many of us feel that the future will be not in space, as some would have it, but in the wild, blue sea.

CHARLES A. BORDEN

Spindrift Point
1966

Acknowledgments

~~~~~~~~~~~~~~~~~~~~~~~~~~~~~~~~~~~~

I've been fortunate in having many global cruising friends who sail permanently as a way of life in small vessels and who, while disagreeing with me in some things, have been most helpful. In recording my respect for them I hope they realize how much I value their co-operation. My debt to others extends from Australia and New Zealand through the South Seas to Panama, the Caribbean, and across the Atlantic. Since it is impossible to acknowledge individually shipmasters, port officials, and all those of many latitudes and longitudes who answered queries and gave assistance of various kinds, I thank them here again.

More personally: to Eleanor, sharp-eyed first reader (and bedeviler), corrector of spelling and punctuation, my gratitude for long and faithful devotion.

I am particularly indebted to Harlan Soeten, master mariner and curator of the San Francisco Maritime Museum, for undertaking the route chart of small-ship passages in the Cape Horn area, for drawing the sail plan of *Spray,* and for sketches of small-craft rigs and those that accompany the wind and sea scale. Cordial assistance was received from Mathilda Dring and other members of the staff. Al Harmon supplied documentations and warm encouragement. Unpublished material from Eric De Bisschop and others has been of much use, but gaps in the Al Hansen and Vito Dumas data could not have been filled in without Al Harmon's expediting and the kind help of Mario "Bobbie" Uriburu, skipper of the *Gaucho.*

Deep appreciation and thanks are due to Dr. William Bewley, master mariner of wide experience, for translations from the French and invaluable assistance with early voyaging accounts.

My thanks to Wang Teh Tsing, capable junk master of Aberdeen Anchorage, Hong Kong, for abetting my early interest in junks. And I do not forget an earlier friend, Hsia Ching Tseh, who brought his fishing junk into the Yangtze and up the Whangpoo to Pootung after losing two foresections in a typhoon. Noted junk skipper Dr. E. Allen Petersen of the *Hummel Hummel* helped a lot. G. R. G. Worcester—former editor of *Mariner's Mirror* and British authority on Chinese junks—has been most kind and cooperative. And I'm much indebted to Mike Briant, owner-skipper of the junk *Ying Hong,* for clarification of some points and for a firsthand account of modern junk voyaging in several oceans.

The Royal Western Yacht Club of Plymouth, The Slocum Society of New York, the Seven Seas Cruising Association (Wilmington, California), the Amateur Yacht Research Society of Kent, the Ocean Cruising Club of London, and other world-wide sailing organizations that encourage ocean cruising in small craft have made possible a valuable exchange of information that could not otherwise be obtained.

Maurice Griffiths and Dr. John Morwood, who have done so much to improve the performance of small sailing vessels, and The Slocum Society —its founder Richard McCloskey and the late Commodore John Pflieger, who have done a lot for individual sailors—have my appreciation, as do Lt. Comdr. J. J. Quill, R.N.V.R. of the Little Ship Club, and Ernest Chamberlain, Western U.S.A. Rear Commodore of the Ocean Cruising Club. In recording a personal debt and my deep respect for John Pflieger, it can be said that sailors of many nations dip their colors in memory of a friend who lived with courage and dignity and went out on a tide of his own choosing.

At one time or another I've examined and made notes from old voyaging accounts, letters, personal narratives, and other unpublished material from many sources and express thanks to the following institutions for use of material, advice, or helpful co-operation: The Raffles Library, Singapore;

Carnegie Library, Suva, Fiji; Nassau Public Library, B.W.I.; Musée de la Marine, Paris; National Maritime Museum, Greenwich; Public Records Office, London; British Museum, London; Science Museum, London; Marine Research Society, Salem, Mass.; Mariners Museum at Newport News; Peabody Museum, Salem, Mass.; Division of Manuscripts of the U.S. Library of Congress; The National Archives; The Bishop Museum, Honolulu; The Polynesian Society, Wellington, New Zealand; The Honolulu Public Library; Scripps Institute of Oceanography; California Academy of Sciences.

Acknowledgment is gratefully made to the following publishers, authors, compilers, editors, photographers, sailors, their executors, and agents for permission to use copyright material:

Particularly to John de Graff for permission to quote from *Alone Through The Roaring Forties* by Vito Dumas, *Fight of the Firecrest* and *In Quest of the Sun* by Alain Gerbault, *Trekka Round the World* by John Guzzwell, *The Sea Is for Sailing* by Peter Pye and *The Voyage of the Golden Lotus* by Brian Clifford; Richard Creagh-Osborne, Adlard Coles Ltd. and Rupert Hart-Davis Ltd. for permission to reproduce a photo from *Red Mains'l* by Peter Pye and to quote briefly from *Four Winds of Adventure* by Marcel Bardiaux; Ann Davison Billheimer and *Popular Boating* magazine for extracts from a magazine article; D. Van Nostrand Co., Stanley Smith, and Robert Ross & Co. Ltd. for an extract from *The Wind Calls the Tune;* Arthur Piver for extracts from *Trans-Pacific Trimaran;* Brian Platt of Bothwell, Scotland, for permission to quote from "The Chinese Junk Rig"; *The Rudder* magazine for an extract from "When It's Time to Reef" by Thomas Fleming Day; the Literary Executors of Joseph Conrad and J. M. Dent & Sons Ltd. for quoted material from *Typhoon* and *The Mirror of the Sea;* for much of the text of René Lescombe's ill-fated voyaging and for a photo of same I am indebted to the late Commodore John Pflieger; to one-time shipmate Warwick Tompkins (who helped when it was needed most and in other ways on *Wander Bird's* last trip north from Papeete) my thanks for a quote on Cape Horn.

Acknowledgment is also made to the following for brief quotations in text or appendixes: J. M. Dent & Sons Ltd., London, for material from *Anson's Voyages;* E. P. Dutton & Co. for an extract from *A Daring Voyage* by Capt. William Andrews; Doubleday & Company, Inc., for material from *Alone Across the Atlantic* by Francis Chichester (Copyright © 1961 by George Allen and Unwin Ltd.); the Executors of Harold Gatty and the Grady Press for material from *The Raft Book;* Ted Stokes and Bosun Books for material from *A Sailor's Guide to Ocean Birds;* W. B. Alexander and G. P. Putnam's Sons for material from *Birds of the Ocean;* Stanwood Press for extracts from Thomas Drake's *The Log of the Lone Sea Rover;* Mr. J. B. Morton and A. D. Peters & Co. for a quotation from Hilaire Belloc's *The Cruise of the Nona;* Mrs. Wilfred Noyce and The World Publishing Co. for helpful material from the late Wilfred Noyce's *The Springs of Adventure;* Bruno Traven and Alfred A. Knopf, Inc., for an excerpt from *The Death Ship;* Harcourt Brace & World for a quotation from *Blue Water* by Arthur S. Hildebrand; Simon and Schuster, Inc., for material from *The Voyage of the Heretique* by Alain Bombard; Hill & Wang and Maribelle Cormack for material from *The Lady Was a Skipper;* Cambridge University Press and H. W. Tilman for a plate reproduction from *Mischief in Patagonia;* and Temple Press and St. Martin's Press for permission to quote from David Lewis' *The Ship Would Not Travel Due West.*

My indebtedness to numerous other individuals and maritime organizations will be obvious to those familiar with the subject. All seamen owe much to The Council of the Hakluyt Society for *The Principal Navigations, Voyages, Traffics, and Discoveries of the English Nation.* I acknowledge obligation to them and to the British Admiralty, H.M.S.O. and H. M. Hydrographic Department, and to *Ocean Passages for the World.* Early historical publications, particularly the *Mariner's Mirror,* the *American Neptune,* and *Kedge Anchor,* have been invaluable. I also thank the Nantucket Historical Association.

I received help and owe a good deal to several present and former editors, magazines, and journals. Each of the following have provided assistance or material: John Parkinson, Jr., editor *The Annals of the C.C.A.;* Frederick Franklin, editor *Navigation* —Journal of the Institute of Navigation; William W. Robinson, executive editor, and *Yachting,* N.Y.; John Malitte, editor *Sea Spray,* Auckland; Bernard Hayman, editor, and *Yachting World,* London; Conrad Miller, editor, and *The Rudder* (for a quotation and photo from Thomas Fleming Day), *Boating, Motor Boating, The Skipper* and *Spray* in the U.S.; *Yachting Monthly, Catamaran and Trimaran International News,* the *Journal of The Little Ship Club, The Journal of the Ocean Cruising Club,* and the Amateur Yacht Research Society publications in Britain; *Nautisme* in France; *Till Rors* in Sweden.

In the Pacific area my thanks are due to M. W. Goding, High Commissioner, Trust Territory of the Pacific Islands; the late J. Frank Stimson of Papeete, Tahiti, for interpretations of Polynesian accounts of ancient voyages of discovery; South Pacific Commission Literature Bureau, Sydney; Cecil and Howard Waite, Saipan, Mariana Islands; The Hokuseido Press, Tokyo; Judy Tudor, editor *The Handbook of Papua and New Guinea;* R. W. Robson, publisher, *The Pacific Islands Year Book; The Journal of the Polynesian Society; The Journal of Pacific History; Pacific Discovery; Cook Islands News,* Rarotonga; *The Fiji Times,* Suva; *Le Journal de Tahiti,* Papeete; *Samoa Times,* Pago Pago; *South Pacific Post,* Port Moresby; *Honolulu Star-Bulletin;* Pacific Area Travel Association; and to O. S. Hintz, editor *The New Zealand Herald.*

The courtesy of the New York Public Library, the Explorers Club, the Seattle Public Library Reference Department, and the Fisher Library of the University of Sydney who helped by mail over vast distances is much appreciated. The co-operation of the librarian of the *San Francisco Examiner* and that of Roslyn Sherman and the *San Francisco Chronicle* has been considerable. I am, too, most grateful to the London *Observer, Manchester Guardian, The Times* reference librarian, and the *Irish Times* of Dublin.

Special thanks are due to the Danish Information Service, New York; E. H. Bryan Jr., Curator of Collections, Bishop Museum, and Manager, Pacific Scientific Information Center; Woods Hole Oceanographic Institute; Dr. Lewis Alexander of the Law of the Sea Institute (University of Rhode Island); the Honorable Claiborne Pell; Huey Johnson, and The Nature Conservancy.

It is a final pleasure to give collective acknowledgment direct to the voyaging authors themselves, to photographers, and to others for their fine spirit of co-operation. My sincere thanks to the following for the use of material from their logs and personal journals and, in some cases, for permission to use a photo, a paragraph, or a few words from their own published work: Dr. William Howell, Barbara and Earle Reynolds, Louise Myers, Desmond Nicholson, Warren Roll, Jim Kean, Harry Close, Fiona and David Lewis, Priscilla Cairns, Eileen Ramsay, Sharon Sites Adams, Al Adams, Peter Tangvald, Capt. Ross Norgrove, Peggy Slater, Marjorie and Al Petersen, Axel Petersen, Beryl and Miles Smeeton, Janet and Tom Steele, Rudy Choy, Dick Newick, Ruth and James Wharram, Colin Mudie, Colonel H. G. Hasler, the late Christopher de Grabowski, Ann Carr, Annie and Louis Van de Wiele, Constance Hitchcock, Suttie Adams, Nancy and Robert Griffith, the late Eric De Bisschop, Laila Messer, Jean Gau, Ann and Peter Pye, Douglas Duane, Jean Lacombe, Fred Rebell, the late George Dibbern, Richard H. Dillon, Francis Chichester, Jacques Le Toumelin, Mrs. G. A. Reid Moir and Major H. W. Tilman, Patrick Ellam, Charles Violet, John Guzzwell, Alain Bombard, Richard Maury, Jean Taupin, Kenichi Horie, Eleanor Wilson, Dr. E. Allen Petersen, Olaf Ruhen, David Fifita, and S/Ldr. D. H. Clarke, D.F.C.

If any acknowledgments due to other authors and publishers have been inadvertently omitted I hope they will accept my apologies. In thanking the above authors, publishers and institutions it is fair to add that interpretations and summaries, and in particular any blunders of judgment or direction, are definitely my own for, with all the help received, in the end the writer, like the long-voyaging solo sailor, is self-bailing, sets his own canvas, has the freedom to choose, add, or omit and make his own heaven or hell.

Contents

～～～

SPECIAL CHARTS AND DIAGRAMS

SEA QUEST

CHAPTER 1

Quest

He had but little learning except what he had picked up from the sun and the sea.

—*Moby Dick*

~~~~~~

SAILING into an anchorage at Muir Beach, where wind-sheared cypress, pine, and raw cliffs meet the eye and patches of lichen clinging to the outermost ledges are believed to be as old as recorded history, I've felt more than once the mystery and immensity of our inheritance on earth and how little time we have to enjoy it. Men of the Stone Age witnessed the same sculpturing of the sea, saw the same black cormorants, smelled the same wild fragrance, and heard the same cry of the loon that's heard today at Spindrift Point. Few can behold this promontory of wild earth, with its moods, mists, and roots in the sea, its silences of enduring stone, sage, and chaparral broom, and not be possessed by it. But when a sea wind is blowing, few can behold its ragged cliffs, eroded on the south, east, and west by Pacific gales, and not feel the power and wonder of what lies beyond.

Surprisingly little is needed to change the course of a man's life, and it is astonishing what a part chance plays. I followed many quests and once bought a plantation to—as I then called it—"test the sea severly." The sea always won, and I learned finally that my black sloop *Nancy Lee* was more important than an island in the South Seas, that it's important to find the element to which one belongs and an abiding quality to live by. Outer solutions are forced on us, but the inner ones we must find for ourselves.

For some, a sea quest that has lasted half a lifetime has been for an illusion that never dimmed. Many have pursued another voyage, another horizon, as if some distant landfall would satisfy their deepest longings. It seldom has. Joshua Slocum, circling the world in his broad-beamed, apple-bowed sloop *Spray,* was concerned with a vision—not with the aerodynamics of sailing. Adrian Hayter, world cruising in his yawl *Sheila II,* was "searching for something greater than" his ship or the sea, "and those thousands of miles have given me a clearer idea of what it is I seek and why it eludes me."

The driving power of dreams, the urge of Ishmael, is very little different now than it ever was. The exhilaration of a first landfall after a long and hard first passage is like nothing a desert prospector or a mountaineer may ever know. But the first circumnavigators, the first to complete a westerly girdling of the globe, were eighteen emaciated sailors, who walked barefoot, with lighted candles, through the streets of Triana and wept unashamedly as they intoned the *Laudate Domine* at Magellan's favorite shrine of Our Lady of Victory. Ever since that September day in 1522 when the battered *Vittoria* sailed into Seville with her square foresail, mainsail, and lateen mizzen in patches, her captain-general dead and only eighteen survivors, men have been sailing around the world for one reason or another in small ships. And so long as there is a flow of wind and the salt seas still move in long rhythms, masts and sails will always be a vital part of human questing.

What do we care about one man or several sailing around Cape Horn or across the Atlantic or the Pacific? We care because each solitary voyager is a subtle part of the unquiet spirit of all of us. But for the choice of the gods, that individual beating tooth and nail against the westerlies might be you.

Many times, after spending a night in sea boots and streaming oilskins and going below to a dark, dank, and wet cabin to lie in a nightmarish state of exhaustion, I have wondered what folly could make such hours worthwhile. It takes a long time to learn that life's highest or lowest moments are only moments, that the miracle of change goes on and becomes many things.

Looking at the sky on a clear night, the small-craft man never forgets that he may be hove to in the pale dawn of another day. A few years at sea teaches him not to carry canvas too long and develops his ability to make the best of the worst. If he learns the art of heaving to, lying ahull, or running off under bare poles towing warps, he can bring a staunch little vessel through a gale that may smash bridge and railings and sometimes sink a 10,000-ton freighter or tanker. Again and again it has been proven that seaworthiness has little to do with size; little ships are often safest.

On the afternoon of September 21, 1957, an SOS from the 3,103-ton four-masted bark *Pamir* cracked out over the air: "Listing 45 degrees. . . . In danger of sinking." Bound for Hamburg from Buenos Aires with a crew of thirty-five veteran seamen and fifty-one young cadets, the great steel sailing ship was being battered by the full 127-knot force of Hurricane Carrie six hundred miles southwest of the Azores.

Before the tail fury of the same hurricane, the 30-foot Tahiti ketch *Atom*, sailed by one man and bound from Gibraltar to New York, lay safely hove to about three hundred and sixty miles south of Montauk Point.

As ten vessels of half a dozen nations fanned out into the heavy seas, the *Pamir*, one of the last of the grain ships, was in the last throes of her desperate struggle. Blocks had jammed on the foremast when struck by the force of the hurricane. Torn canvas, rigging, and topmasts crashed down in a spiderwork of flailing steel cables. Cargo shifted as she broached broadside, and she went over until the three port lifeboats were under water. The starboard lifeboats were hit by mountainous seas and hurled hundreds of feet from the ship. Splintered yardarms slashed and battered lifeboats and life rafts to pieces as the crew clung to the starboard nettings.

"Get clear of the ship fast!" bellowed Captain Diebitsch. "Stay together. God bless you!"

All but five of the men not already over the side leaped from the deck and struggled to reach pieces of flotsam.

"The end took thirty seconds," reported Gunter Hasselbock. "With the masts snapped and her sails gone it was impossible to keep her head on to those tremendous seas. She was lying broadside on. Then in the trough of a giant wave she rolled right over and went down like a submarine."

Twenty-two cadets managed to reach a lifeboat that was almost awash. On September 24 the U.S. Coast Guard cutter *Absecon* found Hasselbock alone in that lifeboat with a dead man. Out of the twenty-two that made the boat, seventeen had been washed over and away; "three others jumped over screaming like demons. And if you had not found me today," said Hasselbock, "I would have done the same."

Of the *Pamir's* eighty-six officers, crew, and cadets, only six survived.

The little 30-foot ketch *Atom* sailed by Jean Gau came safely through. Two weeks later, on October 3, 1957, when the *Atom* luffed up to the dock of the Sheepshead Bay Yacht Club in Brooklyn, completing a singlehanded

German bark *Pamir*.

Loner Jean Gau aboard the 30-ft. ketch *Atom* which safely rode out Hurricane Carrie.

voyage around the world that had taken four years and four months, her owner Jean Gau was asked by a *New York Times* reporter: "Well, how was it?"

"What—the world? Very enjoyable," replied Gau, a veteran of four Atlantic crossings.

"Any trouble?"

"No trouble, no sickness, no accidents, only a few gales. The worst was Hurricane Carrie. Before it struck I just furled all sails, lashed the helm down, rigged a can so it dripped oil overside to keep the seas from breaking aboard," said Gau. "Then I closed myself in the cabin and slept, ate, read, and drew pictures."

There is not much difference between a modern small-ship wanderer and those whose ancient quest was to find the islands of the world and the manner of those who lived upon them. Despite all that oceanographers have come to know, there is still enough mystery in the unpredictableness of the sea, in the questing of sea birds, in pelagic perennials, and in the mystery of life contained within a single wave. Man, who cannot swim as well as a fish or fly as well as a sea bird, has nevertheless a tangible relationship with these things and with the moon, the stars, the planetary winds, and the great movements of ocean currents. The stars that guided Tyrian and Sidonian seamen centuries ago are the same today. Early Portuguese and Italians steered by the North Star when troubled by their compasses, and men today still trust to a gleam of sunlight or starlight reflected in the mirror of a sextant.

Navigational ability and seamanly skills, however highly developed, do not in themselves make a sailor. Some who were able to make a quicker splice and work a noon sight in less time than others have made terrible blunders. Some, despite long experience, seem to have endless misfortunes, and others, after long voyages, seem always to arrive shipshape and Bristol fashion. Why is this?

Besides the art of sailing, the sense of pride—the intimate relationship of an individual to his ship—has much to do with the happy voyages. Well planned and executed passages are rarely spectacular. Most exciting experiences are the result of error—which can of course happen to anyone. But the spectacular tales are, more often than not, the result of poor planning, inadequate equipment, or poor seamanship.

Countless venturers have sailed who should never have left port. Vessels aged, rotted, and in no sense seaworthy have carried lubberly individuals who had bravado in place of common sense to a briny grave. To point to those unaware of the line between dream and reality, to the stunters, or to the plain reckless is simply to say that, at sea as ashore, there are men and there are fools.

The sea won't tolerate the inept or pretentious for long. The measure of a man, whether he is an unranked seaman or an ex-admiral of the Blue—his

Beaufort	m.p.h.	Knots	Sailor's Wind Terms
0	0–1	0–1	Calm
1	1–3	1–3	Light air
2	4–7	4–6	Light breeze
3	8–12	7–10	Easy breeze
4	13–18	11–16	Moderate breeze
5	19–24	17–21	Fresh breeze
6	25–31	22–27	Strong wind
7	32–38	28–33	Moderate gale
8	39–46	34–40	Fresh gale
9	47–54	41–47	Strong gale
10	55–63	48–55	Whole gale
11	64–72	56–63	Storm
12	73 or over	64 or over	Hurricane

Wind Force and Sea Scale

(Admiral Sir Thomas Beaufort's Wind Scale of 1806 updated and related to modern ocean cruising vessels under sail.)

THESE figures may only be considered an individual and approximate estimate. Circumstances vary greatly according to the length of time the wind has been blowing, the area and depth of the sea, changes of wind direction, rate of increase or decrease, and other factors, including an individual skipper's variable response to same.

A sound vessel with good gear can thrash into a Force 8 gale and in some instances it may be reasonable to do so for a short time. When passage making, if there is sea room, the seasoned cruising sailor generally finds it prudent and a lot easier on gear, vessel, and crew to heave to in worsening weather.

28

Sea Description	Small Sailing Vessel	
Flat and glassy	Becalmed	
Some ripples (cat's-paws)	Barely under way	
Surface rippled	Light sailing	
Wavelets	Easy sailing	
Moderate waves	Good sailing all points of the wind.	
Large waves forming. Some whitecaps.	Fresh beat to windward.	
Large waves moving. Many whitecaps.	Reefed	
Wind begins to lift off tops of waves.	Reefed down or under storm canvas.	
High waves. Streaks of spindrift.	Hove to. Lying ahull under bare poles.	
Sea lumps up; crests begin to tumble and roll. Dense scud.	Running under bare poles streaming warps. No visibility except on top of each wave.	
Very high waves; heavy, roaring crests. Poor visibility.	Anything is possible.	
	Fighting for survival	
Mountainous long-rolling waves. Visibility almost nil. Small vessels lost to view.	Some have careened or pitchpoled and been dismasted. Many small vessels have vanished.	
Sea completely white with driving spindrift. A sound one will never forget.		

When It's Time to Reef

MEN often ask when it is time to reef? It is always time to reef when you think it is. The moment you would feel easier and your boat handles better by having less sail spread is the time to shorten down. Never mind what anybody else is doing or what anybody else tells you. It is your boat, not some other boat, that is worrying you, and yourself, and not some other person, who is in charge. Never carry sail for the sake of carrying it; the ignorant may praise your recklessness and pluck, but the experienced man will call you either a lubber or a fool.

Never let the action of another guide you in this particular, unless the action agrees with your own judgment. . . . When I was young and fresh I had an idea that if anyone could carry sail on a boat I could do the same. One day I had a lesson that made me think and partially cured me of the habit. I went with a clever old boatman across the Sound to bring home a new cat. We each took a crew, and, to return, he sailed the new boat, and I the one we had come over in. Halfway across it came on to blow very hard . . . my crew wanted me to stop and reef but as the new boat kept on . . . I was afraid of being thought a coward. . . . When at last, after a struggle and half full of water, we reached port, the old man met me with a torrent of invectives. . . . "But you didn't reef," I protested. "Reef!" he exclaimed. "No, for I couldn't; but I'd given fourteen dollars if I could have got that sail down. Do you think I was carrying whole sail for fun?" It seems the halliards, being new, had jammed, and they could not get the sail down, so had to lug it. This taught me a lesson . . . and often times when I see a man struggling along under too much sail, I wonder if he, like the old boatman, wouldn't give fourteen dollars if he could get that sail down.

—Thomas Fleming Day

hopes and fears, the fiber of his temper, facets of character that might other-wise remain hidden all his life behind a web of status and sophistication—are soon known on a long small-ship voyage.

Geologists and oceanographers tell us the sea is always changing, but the small-boat sailor knows that today as yesterday the balances of wind, sea, current, and tide are there to be met. The roll and thrust of graybacks off Cape Horn, the currents and northeasters off Hatteras, the mistrals and tramontanas of the Mediterranean, and the witches' caldron of tides and breakers off the Scillys are no different now than they ever were. Ships that were once the pride of empires greater than any now on earth lie buried beneath the waters of the globe. Great cities like Pompeii and proud countries that based their strength on the power of destruction, as our leading nations do today, have completely disappeared while the sea rolls on. A thousand or ten thousand years of civilization make no difference to Poseidon, whom the Greeks called "the earth shaker." No innovation of the Space Age will ever conquer his titanic rages.

Speaking of strawberries, Dr. William Butler once said, "Doubtless God could have made a better berry but He never did." Doubtless He could have made a greater thing than the sea but was wise enough not to do it. Call the big islands continents, if you wish, but three-quarters of the planet is salt water, and age by age the sea still conquers the land. A gale like that which drowned nearly six thousand people at Galveston, Texas, a tsunami (tidal wave) like the one that killed over twenty-seven thousand people in Japan, or waves of horrendous violence such as those that lifted a World War II destroyer and broke her into two parts with a loss of nearly all hands are mere incidents in the life of the sea. There is always something supremely unruffled; at the peak of the worst blow the depths of the ocean remain undisturbed as ever.

In that greatest voyage of all time, in which 240 hairy, bow-legged, and tattooed men were reduced by hardships and starvation to 18, a bleak chan-nel called the Strait of the Eleven Thousand Virgins was discovered and the Pacific Ocean became a "Spanish lake" for more than half a century. The magnitude of that accomplishment is attested by a tortuous strait that be-came a fulcrum for exploration, in the age of discovery. With the clouds above it, that opening into the western sea still bears a sailor's name.

How many today know the pitch of that other craggy, rock-ribbed cape at the tip of the American continent, which hangs like a pendant into the icy waters at the bottom of the globe, a land of wild moods and screaming ful-mars, jutting out into storm-swept seas that ring the glacial barriers about the earth? That greatest of headlands, known to those of the heroic age of sail as old Cape Stiff, remains unchanged. There was a time when not to have rounded it was not to be a sailor. Never before in the history of sail—and never since—have ships been driven so relentlessly as the tall-sparred clippers in their seventeen-thousand-mile drive around that Cape to San Francisco. In a world that has forgotten the epic voyages of men beating west round the Horn or running to the east past the Isles of Ramirez, few remember the motives that led to the discovery of Cape Stiff and its rounding by Dutch ships from the Zuider Zee, who fought through those icy seas with low decks awash and ropes and canvas frozen hard.

Today the tradition of sail is kept alive by sailors in small sloops, cutters, yawls, ketches, schooners, and multihulls, out circumnavigating or making competent passages across the Western Ocean.

Somewhere along the line the small-craft sailor learns that the sea, which seems to offer the greatest freedom, demands the greatest control. A sailor sewing a sail may be stitching the threads of his life; when he sews a button on a jacket it usually outlasts the garment. In a small boat one learns how little, not how much, he can get along with. It takes many thousand sea miles to know one's self and one's ship. Whether in Slocum's time or in our own, there are always the clear tasks and the same problems, the same fidelity to oneself and to each other.

Every sailor knows days and nights of slogging against heavy seas for the mere gaining of latitude, and most have known longer ones when it seemed he might never again see sunlight and smooth seas. Beyond that he may experience a time when it seems that all the elements are bent on the destruction of his vessel. A good ship comes through most gales in a lifetime whether she lays ahull or runs before. But there is always the possibility of a renegade sea that can destroy much of the quiet assurance a man has gained —a sea that, without luck, a vessel may not come through.

I recall two days and nights with George Trask, a Sitka fisherman: Bound from Monterey to Victoria, B.C., our 30-foot-LOA Bermudian sloop *Nancy Lee* had slogged windward for a week with sheets and weather shrouds straining. A noon sight the eighth day gave us a fix 370 miles W.S.W. of Cape Blanco. The next morning a swell was running; the wind, northerly the previous week, had eased during the night and by breakfast was freshening from the east. The sky filled with low gray clouds, and before noon the wind hauled to south and hardened. It increased to force 8 by 1400 hours, and we hove to under a very small storm jib and trysail. *Nancy* lay on the port tack about five points off the wind, fore reaching slowly and drifting leeward. With deep forefoot and broad beam, she was a stout vessel, well built and—though twenty years old—sound and well found.

There was a brief lull in which the wind fell, but an hour later it rose again and in a very short time was a rising force 9. We were then under trysail only. The sea continued to rise, and with the glass still falling we streamed a cable and sea anchor from the bow. A can of oil was run out with good effect. After a struggle for an effective scrap of riding sail, *Nancy* was balanced with the head of a small storm jib bent to the peak halyard, tack to the end of the

The *Nancy Lee.*

main boom, and clew secured forward. Though she swung to some of the big ones, we were able to ride about four points off the wind. But in the hollow of the deepest troughs, the few feet of riding sail would flog. We were vulnerable during those brief moments but felt there was nothing further that could be done. We were bound to our sea anchor and hoped the thirty fathoms of two-inch Manila warp, chain bridle, and swivel would keep it bound to us. To reduce windage forward, the headsails and halyards were unbent.

The barometer, which had been falling for several hours, continued down to 29.40, and it was blowing a full gale. With the helm lashed amidships, *Nancy* continued to drift slowly down wind, and the moan of wind through the rigging rose to a wail. The seas became gray, toppling cliffs, broken only by great swatches of white. We did what we could and waited.

The barometer fell a tenth of an inch in the next hour. Outward calm is one thing but inner peace is another. We knew that, despite the best fittings and every precaution against chafe or spinning, under certain conditions any sea anchor will break up. All that seemed to matter was the sense of struggle. Though only a few days from land, we felt we were an eternity away.

Everything below was damp and dripping from water that forced its way through the previously waterproof hatches. After a meal of biscuits, hot soup from a thermos that had been made up earlier, and dried fruit, the best we could do was wedge ourselves into our bunks all standing. The motion increased, and the volume of sound rose until it drowned out the slatting of bilge water and we had to shout to hear each other's words. Neither of us could sleep and our nerves were too taut to read.

About 0100 hours, a three-quarter moon shone through a brief cloud break. Soon after George shouted from the companionway, "The oil tin's gone!"

No matter now, I thought. No oil container could last, and it was impossible to keep oil to windward in those seas. Before an oil slick could form it would be blown to lee. Atop the largest crests, the hull groaned and vibrated from truck to keel. Veils of spindrift flung forward from other white tops hit the deck in sheets. We were unable to keep even a slot of the hatch open for ventilation below.

For a long while, each time there was a rumbling roar that was louder than the others we looked toward the hatch. I thought often of the heavy oak ribs and the prime Port Orford cedar planking that had been put into *Nancy Lee* by Lester Stone, the man who built her. Stone, a craftsman of the old school, was one of the best boatbuilders on the Pacific Coast. His fine, honest work was never more appreciated than that night. I dozed off finally and slept fitfully until awakened toward morning by a breaking sea.

Struggling out to the cockpit, we realized we were in seas greater than any we had ever known. Those bearing down on us mast high appeared more than a dozen times that in length. Crouched together, we watched in silence. When our eyes met we seemed to exchange a feeling that the next few hours might call for something bigger than our combined experience.

Though well under control, *Nancy* needed constant watching. In the moments between crests there was that wild slope of water roaring toward us, then the blast from the gale at the top of the crest and the long fall down the roaring lee into the steep shadow of the next sea. The powerful surge and pitch of our sternway put such a strain on the rudder post I feared we might lose it if the pressure increased. There comes a time when a man would have to be a complete fool not to realize that his fate hangs on a particle of time. Should *Nancy* hesitate to rise or rise only a few seconds too late . . .

34

There was fear in our hearts, no denying it. *Nancy* was pitching, rolling, laboring to stay afloat. The dullest man could have felt her pain as she struggled slowly up to each crest. We both knew that no boat can take everything —that there is a breaking point for anything on land or sea. Thinking of past sins, I resolved they would never be repeated if we survived the day.

Soon after the first low, gray light of dawn it began raining. The air was so full of driving spindrift the rain was hardly noticeable. The thumping and pounding of the rudder increased.

"My God, look at this one!" George shouted, leaping from the companionway and slamming the hatch closed.

As he spoke I felt *Nancy* lifting as though starting up the slope of a mountain. An unpredictable cross sea, larger than any other and cresting more than mast high, broke before we had risen fully to meet it. Reeling and staggering under the force, *Nancy* was thrown on her beam-ends. Seconds later she was still down. The awful droning of the wind was drowned out in the rumble and roar of bursting water. I remember well the feeling that this time she might not make it back. Was this the end? George's mouth moved, but I could hear no words. (Later, he said he had spoken to God for our safety.)

Nancy came slowly—falteringly—up, staggering from keel to truck, and began the long rise into the next oncoming crest. The gear was intact, though halyards were overside and the dinghy and port running light were gone. Waist deep in water, with lashings round our waists secured to deck cleats, at a time when we were most exhausted we felt refreshed at the feel of *Nancy* staggering through. We did what we could for her, and that was little enough.

Less than a half hour later, a similar but slightly smaller wall of cross sea broke, leaving us again awash waist deep in the cockpit. Several hours went by with little sign of easing. Three times we were buried by breaking seas. Once we were down so many seconds I thought we were breached, but again *Nancy* came back, water pouring off in a torrent. We lost the sense of time. After the two great seas there were numerous smaller ones when *Nancy* was smothered in white water.

It took most of the day to straighten things out on deck and below. Floor boards were awash; cups gone from their hooks; books, notebooks, charts, and other things had been tossed out of the weather racks. A can of cocoa, onions, five pounds of loose walnuts, dried prunes, and the teapot were floating in the bilges. We bailed first with a bucket and finished with a hand pump that had to be cleared half a dozen times. After that it was necessary to pump once every hour. On deck, crawling forward over the cabin top and foredeck on all fours, secured by a line to the mast, I checked the cable several times. It was taut as a steel rod. We renewed some chafing gear and at 1300 were able to stream two bags of oil out on painters so they floated about twenty feet to windward. During the rest of the day the oil bags were changed twice, and they seemed to help quite a lot. But once, when the bow plunged into a trough, the force of sea and sudden rise nearly hurled us off the deck.

By nightfall the glass was on the rise. The seas remained steep, we still rolled and were occasionally staggered by a breaking crest, but *Nancy* held her own, and the following morning at daybreak we put her on course again. It was a relief to get into dry clothes and have a hot meal. Getting the hawser and sea anchor in and stowed, the trysail and small jib set, and everything in order again took hours. Toward noon a patch of blue sky became visible, the wind was northwest, and at 1300 we were able to set the main, staysail, and jib.

Due to circumstances or mood, a man may call his ship a mean bitch or a wet brute, but as Dave Bone has pointed out he will not stand for such liberties from the beach. If he understands and makes allowances for her shortcomings, then a special relationship exists and a vessel will sometimes give an extra quality that there is no name for.

Whether a boat is the smallest or fastest to cross an ocean is not of much importance, for the man who comes in first is not always the winner. It is more likely to be the one who savors the voyage for its own sake, who perhaps feels that the real reason for sailing is in those values that have to do with the human spirit. As Admiral Sir Lennon Goldsmith, who retired with a knighthood for gallant services on big ships to sail his 30-foot cutter *Diotima* on long voyages, put it, "The object of cruising is to enjoy being at sea, not to crash from one place to another."

I once sailed several thousand miles with a young Polynesian named Tioni who could not read or write but who could navigate expertly by the stars, knew every reef and *motu* (islet) within four hundred miles of his home island, and had as fine a skill with small island vessels as anyone I have ever known. I remember his way of standing sometimes out at the tip of the bowsprit, "catching the feel." He came from a group of islanders gentle and easygoing yet hardened and tough, if need be, and could clap on a Spanish windlass, make a shroud knot, or turn in a mariner's splice without thinking about it and sail long voyages without sextant or chronometer. Tioni had a puckish quality and sometimes would sail a day or more off his course on the chance of exploring a remote island, meeting an oddball trader or an interesting girl. Sometimes he would sail an extra tack to savor a slant of wind.

Hawaiians call a person who "belongs" a *kamaaina*. A man can live in the islands twenty years and never become a *kamaaina*, while the right person becomes one very soon. Unless a cruising man has a natural way—call it sailing instinct or whatever—and the capacity to sense new wind or change of weather, and has feeling for the living things of the salt waters of the earth, he misses much and does not in the fullest sense belong.

"I have never complained of a heavy sea," said Richard Turrell Mc-Mullen, one of the earliest and best small-ship sailors, a man who cruised in small boats for forty-one years. "On the other hand, I have never praised it for anything but its grandeur, which, in a measure, it was compulsory to behold, whether agreeable or otherwise." Hilaire Belloc and Richard Maury were never too cold and miserable and seldom too exhausted to enjoy something about the sea, even when suffering from it. "I was grateful to all the living creatures of the sea and air that I could watch from my boat. They shared my solitude," said Dr. Lindemann, after seventy-two days alone on the Atlantic in a 17-foot canoe. Fred Rebell, who sailed his 18-foot sloop *Elaine* from Australia to California, often talked to sea birds. And Joshua Slocum said, after sailing alone around the world, "I was in touch with nature as few men have ever been. I was aware of it all the time."

Most quests are not as broad or as long as Slocum's and do not need to be. Thoreau found more in a Massachusetts pond than some find in a lifetime at sea. I remember old Col, a fisherman who rain or shine rowed six miles or more out each morning and the same distance back each afternoon to and from a little fish house on the edge of San Francisco Bay. He gave a part of his daily catch to those who couldn't pay and was a friend to wild things, especially birds. Out on the bay in a blow, he was a man who never faltered; when it was time for his final cross bearings he had to be carried, unconscious with pain, from his little 12-foot skiff, the *Dolly*. I met him in the hospital where he was dying.

"I hardly made it back some days," he said, "that damned bite in my chest hit me so I couldn't see sometimes. But you know," he added, "a skiff like *Dolly* gets rooted in a man somehow. I want to get back out on the bay again and just row." He gestured, as if to say: What could be more important? What else is there? For forty-six years Col's questing was always within the salt waters of San Francisco Bay, always near to the mud flats and his unpainted fish house. "A man's alive out there," he said, pointing through a half-opened window toward the bay. "But if I don't make it back this time, who'll caulk and paint *Dolly*?"

Col was a man who belonged—and who was bound to all the skiffs, birds, and salt tides of the world.

What an individual truly stands for too often gets lost in the rush of city living, and the tragedy is not that men perish but that they cease to live, that they forget the real meaning of things. In a smoggy city or suburban subdivision it is easy to become dependent on a television for escape; easy to take a glass of water for granted, lose contact with the wind, grass, trees, rocks, forget the value of a warm blanket or a deep breath of fresh air. To a man at sea any trifle may be of importance: a slight change in the wind force, the sight of a star, a few dry biscuits, a can of beans, a drink of fresh water. In a small boat he cannot ignore the unechoing depths beneath his keel or

ELEANOR F. DIXON

Col, the San Francisco Bay fisherman who belonged—and was bound to all the skiffs, birds, and salt tides of the world.

avoid looking up at the stars any more than he can avoid reflecting on the sun, wind, moon, and trees. Since his mast may be of finest spruce and his hull of long-grain fir, it's not hard for him to understand the aliveness of wood.

Vast areas of thought remain unsurveyed or little touched. The flow of the currents, the motions of the waves, the rise and fall of tides (called by Mohammed "the swelling sea") are known; flora of the shallows and fauna of the depths are classified; and yet much of the mystery remains. There are whole continents still unexplored beneath the seas. Very little is known of the questing of whales or sea birds over millions of square miles of ocean. The whale is a fellow creature with a heart that pumps warm red blood like our own; unlike sea animals, who act entirely from instinct, whales understand much about love and about kindness and the protection of their young. Yet no one knows what guides the herds of whales and seals on their long sea journeys, though they cover as many miles each year as any creature known. And there is the quest of sea birds, who have turned their backs on land for all time (except for brief nesting periods), who forage in the plankton-filled currents and have learned to drink salt water. No one has ever followed them in all their strange wanderings. Their course of flight was shaped before man was on earth, and, if all land were to be submerged, years after the human race became extinct there would still be birds winging about the global ocean, able to live out their life span completely at home in a world of water.

There is no rest for a sea bird in a storm that may last for days or even weeks. I have often seen sooty-brown storm petrels, those smallest of sea birds who have almost lost the ability to use their legs, riding out gales in the troughs of mountainous waves and at other times skimming and scanning in wide circles for plankton. Today sailors still see powerful shearwaters gliding over sea troughs within a few feet of the water or observe the effortless flight of frigate birds with their tremendous sail-like wings that fascinated Columbus and Drake. Fulmars and storm petrels are seen on both sides of the Atlantic and even halfway across, where the great gulf current splits and flows toward the Arctic and toward the hump off Africa.

The impetus of migrating flight becomes so forceful with some birds that only a flight halfway around the world can still it. Besides those masterful navigators, the sooty shearwaters, which sail north each year from Cape Horn or the Chilean Andes, there is the short-tailed shearwater, which nests in islets off the coasts of New Zealand and South Australia and then flies via the islands of Melanesia along the archipelagos of Eastern Asia to the extreme North Pacific, sometimes even passing the Bering Strait, follows the American coast toward Lower California, and crosses the Pacific diagonally to Australian waters, accomplishing a yearly circuit of at least nineteen thousand miles. There's that phenomenal bird, the arctic tern, with its marvelous sense of timing, which flies each year twenty-two thousand miles or more in five months to enjoy more hours of daylight than any other creature. And no one ever forgets the long shrill whistle of the boatswain bird in tropic seas, a swift, long-tailed streak of white disappearing on rapid wings almost as soon as it is seen.

A mariner in the cockpit of a small vessel, a slow-moving fellow without feathers or beautiful wings (Plato's man), must seem a dull creature to the albatross, that greatest of sea birds, which sometimes circles the world in a single year.

So strong is a bird's instinctive directional sense that nothing short of injury or death will prevent every bird from reaching its annual destination. On Laysan Island in the Pacific, a lighthouse keeper discovered an injured western golden plover. He amputated its leg and, after it had recovered, released it. Every winter for five years it returned, across more than two thousand miles of open sea, to the same beach and the same island.

What summons a bird to the same spot, on the same island, at the same time each year? What law of flight, what acute ability, enables it to navigate with such preciseness?

The sky is a bird's compass, and it seems to have an inborn sense of navigation regulated by a precise time-rhythm sense of night and day. One of the late theories is that, though external things affect the annual questing of birds, the restlessness, the urge to fly and migrate, is induced by an internal phase of a bird's physiological cycle. Dr. G. V. T. Matthews of Cambridge University credits birds with the instinctive ability to determine the arc of the sun and differences in time with the accuracy of a sextant and chronometer. With their ability to compensate for varying angles and to predict arc in relation to a few minutes' difference in observation, according to Dr. Matthews, migrating birds can determine their geographical position anywhere on earth from the angular height of the sun at noon for latitude and the difference to "home time" at noon for relative longitude.

Ashore it is easy to flatter ourselves that the world belongs to us, but on a small-boat voyage we know better; it belongs to the creatures of the sea, and we are mere interlopers. From Hatteras to Finisterre and the Horn, the rhythm of great waters, the ceaseless ebb and flow, the balance of the trade winds with the currents and the rotation of the earth remains unchanged. Far beneath the keel of a ship, life still flows from the subtle beginning of things. Unknown mysteries greater than any on earth lurk in the zones of perpetual darkness. Even at ten thousand feet or more, life is abundant; there is quest and the same struggle for existence as elsewhere. Beneath the area of the manta rays, or devilfish, sharks and whales engage in titanic struggles with giant squid, and, still deeper, huge creatures detected by sonar instruments but as yet unseen by man live and engage in mighty combat in the blackness below the three-thousand-foot level. Out on the skin of global waters between the hot and cold edges of the world, past ages and those to come are as one.

We live such a very little time before we have beards as long as Neptune's, and how many find what they are seeking while still able to climb a mainmast? A man can buy a boat easily enough, but he cannot buy a heightened awareness of the night sky or of another human being.

I have never yet met a man or woman who has gone to sea in a small vessel as a way of life who did not have something profound about him. The best are solid individuals who don't believe in taking foolish chances but who also know that there is little of real value that can be accomplished without taking any chance at all. Today most ocean voyages in small ships are carefully planned and executed and require a high order of intelligence to come off well.

Not everyone has the urge toward long sea voyaging. But once it has been felt deeply, one will not again know peace. What is this compulsion? Is it a subconscious rejection of button pushing, an escape from the goading of time consciousness, from the drone of radio and television hucksters? Partly, perhaps. Is it to escape something or to find something? It is not wholly escape, for the intelligent modern person knows that there is no real escape. What then is the answer?

A few noted psychologists believe that the spirit that impels a man to put forth to somewhere dates from early primitive wanderings. Whatever it is, the longings for new experiences are personal and differ as individuals differ. For one man it is to stand on the foredeck sounding the depths, as his vessel heads slowly in to a remote anchorage in a quiet bay where few small ships have ever been before, after the tension and drive of a long passage. For another it is calculated risk and pride in the performance of a well-handled ship. For most it is a need to come to grips with something primitive within them.

A friend who has been offshore cruising for a quarter of a century said a few weeks ago, "All this guff about why a man goes to sea is a lot of malarkey. I just sail for the hell of it." A great many small-boat skippers would say the same thing. But there are many other answers, and no single one can tell it all. "Sailing is an affair between a sailor and his boat, and it doesn't matter a damn what his reasons are," a yachtsman of the hard-facts school said to me recently. "Either you like it or you don't!" Many others have spoken out forcefully, but none have offered watertight answers. "I sail because at sea no man has all the answers," said a forty-four-year-old skipper, bound for Australia in a 30-foot cutter.

Ann Davison, who has "always been a little restless," asked herself one dark night in the cabin of her 23-foot sloop *Felicity Ann*, outbound from Plymouth on a seventeen-month solo voyage down the coast of Europe and across the Atlantic to the West Indies and to the United States, "What am I trying to prove? Cold and lonely and frightened, I wondered why I had let a dream run away with me." Answering her own queries, Ann said, "It's to find out the why, the what and the how at first hand, without taking someone else's word for it. Occasionally you are rewarded by an insight so splendid, you can be satisfied with nothing less ever after, so you go on searching for the rest of your life."

In his *African Tales*, Laurens van der Post reveals a need to move from place to place as a hunger so vital to some African people that, even though the nomadic life is one of incredible hardship, a man forbidden to travel often pines away and dies. And there's the wandering instinct of the Laplanders and the Eskimos, a spirit of restlessness which manifests itself particularly when spring begins. "What can we do?" an Eskimo friend asked the ethnologist Knud Rasmussen. "We were born with the great unrest. Our father taught us that life is a long journey where only the unfit are left behind."

It can be said of most small-ship wanderers that they voyage not to acquire money or status but to accumulate new experience. And beyond that, perhaps, bare points of contact when the beginning, present, and future connect somehow with a ship, sea, sky, and an individual, when for a moment the secret of it all will stand revealed almost within reach. It is these times past and present that give meaning to life.

What I remember most about George Dibbern, Alain Gerbault, Eric De Bisschop, Harry Pidgeon, Christopher Grabowski, and a number of others who made small-ship sailing a way of life is not their courage or seamanship, though they had both in good measure, but their quiet faith, their solid convictions in the face of a doubting world, in the face of some who called them fools. When they were up against the greatest odds, faith in life pulled them through.

Our human rights, Justice William O. Douglas has pointed out, should have "priority over science." And they include the right to breathe clean, fresh air, to have quietness and the time to relax in places where "automobiles and exhaust pipes do not penetrate." Increasingly today, as urban and suburban life gets farther and farther away from the natural world of rocks, trees, wind, and salt water, individuals seek refuge from tensions, noise, political platitudes, and the frustrations of standardized living in overcrowded areas. Some go to sea to forget the land and what is being done to what's left of it.

It is no small thing any more to be able to breathe air that is free of fumes and smog. In what were once quiet bays and coastal anchorages, human forces are exploiting every nook, cove, and hillside, destroying the natural ecology and scarring or obliterating the greenery and contours that attracted them to the seashore in the first place. As Stewart Udall points out, "It is the oceans themselves that now represent the largest remaining frontier." For every crowded acre ashore there are miles of ocean that have not been bulldozed, "developed," and exploited.

The late Dr. Theodore von Kármán, world-famed aerodynamicist, said that there will soon be sailboats that won't need sails, which will sail by an antigravity force that will enable men to cast off from earth at will. But to the true sailor the skin of the oceans of the world still offers adventures enough for any one lifetime. Sailing vessels have greatly increased in number. In an age that idolizes the supersonic pilot and the astronaut, there are more than enough sea-minded individuals who are fascinated not by speed or outer space but by the arched white sails of a schooner making the tide.

The appeal of remote anchorages reached by one's own efforts never dies. Age doesn't seem to matter, for some of the most outstanding voyages have been made by those past fifty. A lifetime is much too short to see it all.

After completing a voyage around the world singlehanded, Joshua Slocum said at fifty-four, "The dial of my life was turned back—my friends all said Slocum is young again." Harry Pidgeon, when past sixty, circled the globe singlehanded and, at seventy-eight, accompanied by his wife, started his third trip around the world. A seventy-year-old retired British admiral, Lennon Goldsmith, crossed the Atlantic twice and cruised twelve thousand miles in a 30-foot cutter with only a young lady for crew. One of the youngest, Dwight Long, was twenty-one when he left Seattle in his ketch the *Idle Hour*, on a round-the-world trip that took six years. Ahto Walters was seventeen when he made his first Atlantic crossing and only nineteen when he completed twenty-five thousand miles of ocean cruising, including five Atlantic crossings, in his sloops *Ahto I* and *Ahto II*, both less than 30 feet LOA.

"Having lived on *Atom* for the last twenty years, I would be miserable had I to spend my remaining old age in a house," said Jean Gau, the American-born French chef and artist from New York, who at fifty-eight was completing his second singlehanded circumnavigation in his 30-foot ketch. In 1966 Major H. W. (Bill) Tilman, a remarkable sixty-eight-year-old British skipper, departed Lymington for the Rio de la Plata and the great Southern Sea, on another of his marathon voyages in his sixty-five-year-old 45-foot Bristol channel pilot cutter *Mischief*.

Though yearning and questing man is still reaching out into lonely space and the spirit of adventure is assuming new forms, we are, as never before, in an era of small-boat voyaging across all seas. Today a small cutter, ketch, or yawl arriving at Las Palmas, Panama, or Tahiti from a port five or ten thousand miles away arouses little if any comment, so commonplace has it become. Tersely written logs, often salty with oilskin drip, tell only the bare-bone facts. Yet everyone who cruises widely in a small sea boat comes to know something that men knew in the beginning.

With the aids to navigation that are now available, it's easy to forget that the first sailors were able to sail over a vast part of the waters of the world without instruments. What first principles did small-boat men know in the beginning that we have forgotten? Who were the first to raise a piece of matting on a pole and move across the sea? What manner of men were they? Where did they sail to, and for what were they questing?

> And his dominion shall be from sea even to sea, and from the river
> even to the ends of the earth.
>
> —Zechariah, IX:10

CHAPTER 2

South Sea Vikings

*Though it is true that the most stupid can go in their embarkations
from a small island to seek a large country—since if they do not hit
one part they will hit another. Yet not for this can it be admitted that
they can, without art, seek small and far distant islands.*

— PORTUGUESE NAVIGATOR PEDRO DE QUIROS
TO THE VICEROY OF PERU, 1597

THOUGH the Mediterranean produced few real seamen previous to Columbus, it is still referred to as the home of the first sailors. The purple sea of
Homer, that Helen among oceans, may well be the most feminine of waters,
but it was not the only cradle of deep-sea questing.

Ages before Magellan, Columbus, and Dias—and several long centuries
before Da Gama ventured fearfully around Africa, hired a Moslem to pilot
him across the Indian Ocean, and became a hero—the Polynesians were
making open-sea voyages in the Pacific that are among the greatest achievements in history.

A proud, freeborn people, the Polynesians were the first to learn how to build and sail deep-sea canoes and were the first transocean canoe voyagers. And what sailors! Their long sea quests, often against prevailing winds and currents, were those of a people who, like the Greeks, loved beauty and life and being free. More so than that of any other early people, the Polynesian language was the true expression of a maritime race, abounding in references to meteorology, oceanography, the building and handling of boats, sails, and the arts of navigation and seamanship. Besides their extensive star language, they had a broad vocabulary of words to denote wind forces and directions and their effect on sea conditions.

For historians they had their artists and voyaging bards, some of whom composed beautiful chants that have been handed down to the present day through genealogical recitations. But they had no Homer to do for their heroic sagas what was done for the Greeks'. Homer's exaggerations of the deeds of heroes spurred the Greeks to attempt to live up to the spirit of those mighty epics. The Polynesians, who were as heroic as Odysseus and incomparably better sailors than the Greeks, received no such impetus.

How then did a stone-, bone-, and shell-age people make great sea voyages over millions of square miles without compass or sextant? Why did they leave the tranquil lagoons of Tahiti and Raiatea to quest for islands thousands of miles to the north and to the south? How did they sail against the prevailing winds and strong currents? What made them better sailors than the Phoenicians, the Greeks, the Vikings, or the early Portuguese and Spaniards?

The Egyptians, who invented the rudder and were among the first to use sails, were so completely under the spell of the Nile they confined their "seafaring" to that fascinating river and to a few coastal trips. Lacking the questing spirit, they failed to feel the lure of the deep sea.

The Greeks, who lived close to the sea, wrote much about it, and conducted great naval wars, were landlubbers at heart, and it was as such that they laid the foundations of science and modern civilization.

Though it was their destiny to use the sea, the Romans heartily disliked it. Their merchant ships were crewed by Phoenicians and other mercenaries, and their war galleys were manned by slaves. The early Romans, whose ships carried catapults to hurl baskets of poisonous snakes and yardarm buckets to pour boiling oil on enemy decks, trained their "sailors" on artificial lakes before crowded stadiums of spectators! To the Greeks and Romans, the best thing about a sea voyage was its end.

"The Phoenicians," Homer says, "care nought for bow and arrow, but for mast and oar and for the shapely ships, in which joyfully they cross the gray sea." A nice sentiment but hardly true. Though the Phoenicians developed their knowledge of navigation and ships far in advance of others and supplied "shipmen" to every nation in the Mediterranean, they were hard-bargaining traders first and seamen second. Like the Greeks, they avoided sailing at night whenever possible and spent as much time in port waiting

Polynesian long-voyaging double canoe with lateen sail, used on voyages to distant archipelagos.

for fair winds as they spent at sea, because they lacked the knowledge and ability to sail to windward. (It took centuries for the lateen rig, which the Mohammedans later brought from the East, to replace the square sail of the Mediterranean.)

Even that greatest Phoenician seaman Himilco, the Greeks Pytheas and Nearchus, and Hanno the Carthaginian, who reputedly sailed around Africa in three years, were always hugging the shore, busying themselves with rituals or setting up altars to placate Neptune, always fearful of venturing out of sight of land. Is it any wonder that the Phoenicians took almost a thousand years to colonize the few hundred miles to the Pillars of Hercules?

Under the standard of the Raven, the raiding inlet men from the fjords of Scandinavia, with their winged helmets—"ax-bearing barbarians" or Vikings, as they were called—were little concerned with the lure of the stars or the true spirit of questing over the sea. Though rapacious at destroying the fabric of Christianity, they feared many things, including coastal fog, and invariably anchored at night wherever they could.

It was no great distance from the Icelandic settlements in Greenland to America. These were comparatively short hops made by men who avoided open water wherever possible. Though they used a few stars for direction finding, the Vikings were never able to develop a system of star navigation. Since they knew nothing of the compass or lodestone, theirs was fundamentally a dead-reckoning system, and when errors occurred, as they often did, landfalls were frequently missed. Iceland was found by a man blown off his course and Vinland (America) was reached accidentally, first by Irish monks who had been terrorized and chased out of Ireland by Norse raiders and later by Bjarni Herjolfsson and his men, involuntarily blown past Greenland, their intended destination. Leif Ericson, who made the three-hundred-mile hop across Davis Strait from Greenland to Baffin Land and coasted south along Labrador, pushed by the strong Labrador current, could hardly have failed to have made a northern Newfoundland landfall even if his crew had been farmers.

The expeditions of Leif and of Thorvald Ericson, that of the Icelander Thorfinn Karlsefni, and of Freydis, the Norse murderess, who killed all the other women of the fourth and last-known Vinland voyage with her own ax, were short-lived and cannot be compared with the centuries of long open-sea voyages, discoveries, and permanent settlements by the Polynesians over fifteen million square miles of the Pacific.

Most Viking chieftains of the eighth and ninth centuries—and others like Eric the Red, who was expelled from Iceland for murder, and Eric's father, who was expelled from Norway for murder—were, according to the Dutch historian Hendrik Willem Van Loon, "a superior sort of gangster leaders." The grim history of Viking settlements in different parts of the world is one of endless hatred, blood feuds, murder, and revenge that in the end exterminated entire colonies—as appears to have been the case in Greenland.

Unlike the Greeks, the Norsemen after two centuries of domination over most of Europe left little but their sagas. A Viking poet was part of an important captain's inner circle, yet in the sagas there is little of the classic sense of wonder, awe, and adventure. All or almost all is of battles, feuds, vengeance, and bloodshed. At a time when the last Viking descendants of Eric the Red were slowly and miserably dying out from malnutrition in Greenland, Polynesian seamen were out sailing to new islands, carrying livestock, food plants, and even flowers over thousand of miles of open ocean in their double canoes.

With all the knowledge and skills that Prince Henry the Navigator made available at his seafaring school at Sagres, the Portuguese, even at that late date (1416–1460), haunted and beset at every turn by terror and superstition, lacked the courage and vision to become more than skilled coast lubbers, always fearful of venturing out of sight of the African coast.

In 1443, when Portuguese ships began reaching around Africa and trading horses for slaves (one horse for ten humans), they began a trade in "black ivory" that dragged twelve million Negroes out of Africa in chains. African natives were, according to the Portuguese chronicler Barros, "outside the law of Christ, and at the disposition, so far as their bodies were concerned, of any Christian nation." With shipmasters more interested in cargoes of black humans, the lands of exploration to the south and the route to the Indies remained undiscovered until 1488—and then only after a gale forced Bartholomeu Dias, a former slaver, far enough seaward to discover that by going on another tack he could drive farther south. After rounding Africa without knowing it, superstitions, fears, and finally terror and threats of mutiny forced Dias to turn back.

When that wily court gentleman Vasco da Gama was ordered by King Manuel to round Africa and reach India, there was no personal vision involved, no love of the sea, no inner urge for adventure or discovery. His great voyage was the cold, calculated task of carrying out orders, motivated by an overpowering greed for gold, rank, and prestige. Inspiring fear and hatred at Mozambique, St. Helena Bay, Mombasa, and wherever else he touched, he followed the course and the sailing directions given to him at Lisbon, reached the Cape of Good Hope, and arrived at Malindi on the east coast of Africa. On that fetid coast Da Gama, who always disembarked and hung his wooden astrolabe on a tree or tripod to take the altitude of the sun, employed his skill at guile to obtain the services of Ahmed ibn Majid, the best pilot and master mariner in the Red Sea, to guide him safely across the Indian Ocean. The Moslem Ibn Majid, an Arab of Julfar, had written many sailing handbooks on stars, navigation, and sea lore, was a cartographer and compiler of sea charts, and was known to every Arab pilot and sailing master in the Indian Ocean. He gave the Portuguese complete detailed maps, showed them the sea road to the Indies, allayed their superstitions and fears, and for twenty-three days after leaving Malindi personally guided them safely across to Calicut.

No sense of fair play ever deterred Da Gama in his quest for power and prestige. Despotic, pitiless, given to mad rages, he laid a foundation of vengeance and hate along the sea coasts of Africa and India. His flat-bottomed flagship *São Gabriel* echoed frequently to the groans of tortured men. By *opingo* (the drops), captives were tortured with boiling oil until they revealed sea lore and coastal information or were killed begging for mercy or "sent home by water"—flung overboard—"to please God and for the honor and glory of Portugal."

After Ibn Majid's guidance to Calicut, Da Gama sailed triumphantly home to Lisbon, leaving a wide wake of treachery, murder, and hatred that was to plague Portugal for the next four hundred years.

A great monument, which still stands, was built as a memorial to the discovery of the route to India. A gold coin was struck commemorating the event. With appropriate ceremonies, Da Gama was dubbed "Admiral of the

Sea of India" and King Manuel assumed the title "Lord of Guinea and of the Conquest, Navigation, and Commerce of India, Ethiopia, Arabia, and Persia."

Just as the Greeks had Homer, the Portuguese in their golden age of discovery had Camoëns to fictionize and glorify the deeds of Da Gama and others into a great national epic, *The Lusiads.*

> Through all the world
> Shall I proclaim in song
> Those who by their valorous deeds
> Hold such a place
> That from death's law
> They are released.

Though the *São Gabriel* and the *Berrio* returned to the Tagus with less than half their men and the *São Rafael* never made it back, no eulogies were pronounced for their long-suffering crews living or dead, no tablets were inscribed with their names, and no official testimonial was ever made to the great services of Ahmed ibn Majid, the Moslem, without whom the Christians aboard the *São Gabriel* probably would not have reached India.

In contrast to the mutinous fears and uncertain gropings of Columbus's and Magellan's crews, the descendants of the first Polynesians to drop their stone anchors in the far-flung lagoons of the Central Pacific had from the beginning and in full measure the true spirit of quest, the passion to see the wonderful things of the sea and the land beyond, that the early Europeans lacked.

Though at first they had no certain goals, the South Sea Islanders brought with them an oceanic culture, and their great canoes heralded the dawn of a new day for even the remotest islands of the great Polynesian triangle. Forty generations before the first European sailed into the South Pacific, at a time when England was being introduced to civilization, Tahiti and Raiatea were advanced cultural and maritime centers. Polynesian seafarers were crossing and recrossing the largest of oceans and taking to hundreds of new islands the heritage of their ancient civilization.

One of the earliest of the epic voyages from Central Polynesia led to the discovery of New Zealand by the Tahitian mariner Kupe, who reported, "I found a great land covered with high mists in Tiritiri-o-te-moana, the open sea that lies to the south." Sailing south from Rarotonga about A.D. 950 to the "land of high mists," followers of the Polynesian sea king had great faith in their captain, their sea gods, and their mighty pahis—sea canoes. They knew no fear. Kupe, who apparently was well acquainted with the yearly migratory flights of the *kohoperoa*—long-tailed cuckoos that fly each year from Polynesia to New Zealand—gave as his sailing directions from Rarotonga, "Let the course be a little to the left hand of the setting sun, moon, or Venus in the lunar month of November–December." Of New Zealand, Kupe reported, "The only people I saw there were a fantail flitting and a bell bird that tolled from the depths of the forest."

Though the Polynesians were the greatest of seafarers, their basic methods of navigation were not much different from those used by the Arabians, Vikings, and Phoenicians. There is no mystery about their powers. They had no magic extra sense of perception. But they did develop their natural senses to an extraordinary degree and used their knowledge to develop and perfect their art of seamanship and navigation to the highest degree. As an oceanic people they were often under compulsion to do so because of economics and trade, but more importantly they were endowed with a venturesome spirit and the urge to know what was over the horizon.

Even the Venetian Zeno brothers, who sailed from the Adriatic to Newfoundland, preceding Columbus by more than a hundred years, had to guess at their distances traveled. And though they steered by a sliver of lodestone floating in a piece of cork in a bowl of water (forerunner of the compass), they, like Columbus, were often hundreds of miles away from where they thought they were because of variation and a lack of knowledge of time.

Polynesians took the rising points of fifteen stars on the eastern horizon, took their setting points on the western sky, plus north and south, and used these thirty-two points as their points of direction, and all their leading mariners knew the cardinal navigation points N., S., E., and W. and the intercardinal points N.E., S.E., S.W., and N.W. Those versed in traditional lore also knew how to put to use all the currents in the Pacific. Besides the prevailing trade winds, they knew the variable winds far beyond their home islands as well as the currents and changing weather conditions.

The skill and knowledge of navigation possessed by South Sea peoples has been much underestimated. They not only understood the positions of heavenly bodies but were able to calculate stellar movements with surprising accuracy. Sky changes north, south, east, and west were studied, and the ability to approximate latitude was acquired. Island astronomers knew that certain stars that belong to what was called the same *rua* (parallel) followed the same curved course through the sky. Besides knowing intimately more than one hundred and fifty stars, the principal navigators knew their time and place of rising, the *rua* to which they belonged, and their movements across the sky for various times of the year. New islands were associated with the stars that were overhead at definite times, because it was known that the same stars passed over the same islands in the same relationship to each other night after night and that they appeared about four minutes earlier each night.

When the sky was overcast, the navigator depended on his dead reckoning and his intimate knowledge of the prevailing wind conditions, currents,

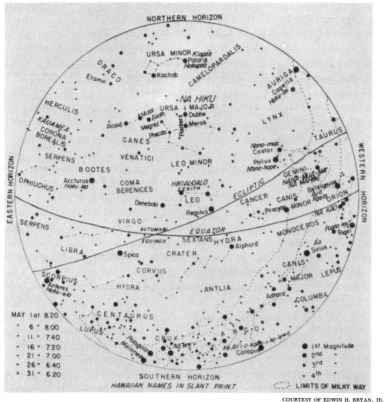

Spring sky over Hawaii, showing many of the Hawaiian names for
stars and constellations.

and sea changes. When the skies cleared during a break in a storm, he would
search for stars that belonged to the same *rua* as the stars he had previously
been following.

Hawaiian astronomers, like the ancient Greeks, regulated their months
by the phases of the moon. Almost every Polynesian island had its own lists
of the "nights of the moon." Measurements of time as well as their calendar
were based on movements of the sun, moon phases, and an annual cycle calculated from known positions of the Pleiades. Mahina, the Hawaiian name

of the moon, was used to indicate the Hawaiian month, and their calendar contained thirty names for various stages of the monthly moon from new to old. By its phases islanders planted crops and defined their activities.

Some planets were given names according to their position in the eastern or western sky; others had distinctive names of their own, such as Jupiter, named Kaawela (because of its brightness), Mars, called Hokuloa (when seen in the morning sky), and Mercury, called Ukali (because it closely followed the sun). When Huihui, the Pleiades, appeared in the eastern evening sky in November (now November 18), it heralded a season of festivity and the official beginning of the Hawaiian year.

When Captain Cook visited Tahiti, he saw 150 large double canoes, 50 to more than 90 feet long, each carrying fifty to one hundred people. A few were as long as Cook's *Endeavour* (106 feet overall). The great canoes seen by European explorers in the seventeenth and eighteenth centuries that were 100 feet or more in length were fair-weather vessels, usually war canoes for protected waters or short coast voyages under favorable conditions. Often they were highly decorated ships of state, used only for special occasions. Polynesian mariners and master shipbuilders knew that a staunch vessel which could be easily handled was preferable to a heavy, cumbersome war canoe on long offshore voyages in variable weather, and as far as can be determined their early double canoes used for long voyage cruising were from 40 to 70 feet overall.

A ship was a means to an end for a Greek, a Roman, or a Phoenician; to a Polynesian it was a living thing, a natural aspect of the life of which he was a part. Special trees for shipbuilding were considered sacred and belonging to the gods. Before cutting one for an important canoe, the island chief (considered directly related to the gods) interceded and obtained permission through proper ceremonies. On the day of the felling, the god Tane was implored to forgive them for cutting down one of his children. Stone tools were used on islands where stone was available. On coral atolls, the shells of the Tridacna was shaped into adzes and chisels. Shark-tooth knives and coral and sea-urchin files were used for shaping and polishing. In some groups, planking was finished off by rubbing with shark skins and with sand held in coconut fibers.

What flax was to the later Maori so the bark of the wild hibiscus was to the people of the high islands of the Central Pacific. Hull planks were made fast with lacings of three-strand hibiscus cord bark and with sennit withes. Seams were caulked with coconut fibers and payed with a waterproof pitch made of breadfruit tree gum.

For lack of long timber, atoll dwellers of the Tuamotus had to build their vessels with patches of short planks ingeniously sewed together. Despite this they were the best canoe builders in Polynesia. Atoll people have always lived a Spartan existence and at best have little food and fresh water. There is always the yearly season of hurricanes, always the threat of heavy seas

In the Tuamotus where lumber has always been scarce ingenious craftsmen built this seagoing vessel of sections of planking shaped to match and sewn together with coconut fiber.

sweeping over and destroying their coralline homes, which rise for the most part twelve feet or less above sea level. Faced from birth with the problems of the sea, is it any wonder that they make excellent sailors?

Some of the earliest vessels, such as the Raiatean *va'a*, had only two strakes built so that in calms they could be paddled easily and with utmost advantage. In contrast to the ancient *va'a*, which was a dugout with bow and stern pieces, a wash strake, and a single outrigger with two booms, the later *Arii* (high chiefs) who raised Polynesian culture to its highest level sailed in plank-built pahis with inserted ribs and V-shaped keels. The two-masted pahis of Tahiti and the Society Islands were similar to the double sailing canoes of the Tuamotus except in the bow, the high curved sterns, and the narrower beam at the gunwales. Marquesan canoes had bird-head prows and sometimes small tikis or human skulls on the stern.

With few exceptions, the sails used on all seagoing canoes throughout the South Seas were triangular and made of plaited coco-palm leaves. The earliest vessels were rigged with simple triangular spritsails, which evolved into the more advanced forms later used in Hawaii, the Tuamotus, and the Society Islands. When the oceanic lateen was given a halyard, this advancement spread rapidly because of the flexibility and facility it gave for tacking and beating to windward. In double canoes the mast was stepped slightly forward of midships. With the underwater shape of both hulls much the same, these early vessels were able to reverse their course without coming about by simply reversing the angle of the mast and bringing the sail over until the tack line became the sheet. As the bow became the stern, the steering *hoe* (paddle) was quickly reversed.

Throughout Polynesia the advanced arts of boatbuilding, navigation, and seamanship were for long controlled exclusively by craftsmen's and navigators' guilds. At one period a guild of tohungas carefully guarded the secrets of navigation, astronomy, advanced seamanship, and meteorology. Men who were able to navigate a double sea canoe on long voyages held power and prestige second only to island chiefs. The high chiefs used the simile of a ship when speaking of their different people. Commoners were represented by the hull, landowners were the rigging, nobles the outrigger, the chief was the mast. And they worshiped the sea god Tangaroa (claimed as their traditional ancestor) in place of Tu, Tane, and the older gods.

In Micronesia, the study of navigation and the art of sailing was more democratic. No young man in the Carolines was allowed to marry until he had given proof of his skill in piloting a proa. Examinations always took place on a day when the sea was running high, and the candidate at the sheet of a vessel maneuvered entirely by sails was expected to bring it in, skillfully balanced, through reefs and breaking seas.

Gilbert Island boys were given a rigorous course of instruction in piloting, navigation, and astronomy. Before being taken offshore and tested under actual stellar conditions, each boy spent long hours in a star-and-sky building, the ceiling of which represented the canopy of the sky. Facing east, students sat at the base of a central pillar whose summit represented the first-magnitude star Rigel, called Taubuki-ni Karana—Ridgepole of Heaven. The heavens were plotted out on the thatch of the ceiling in lines of principal stars and constellations of the Gilbertese sky, according to their angular distance from Rigel and their declinations north and south of the star lines for that time of year. Before completing the course, each student mariner had to know by memory scores of stars and the relative bearings of scores of islands, some of which were more than a thousand miles apart. They associated the rising of Rimwimata (Antares) in the evening with the months of good cruising weather and the ascendancy of Nei-Auti (Alcyone) with the westerlies and "the sea swell from the north." Micronesian cartographs of sea movements are unique among early sailors.

Marshall Islands stick chart made from ribs of coconut palms with shells representing islands and islets.

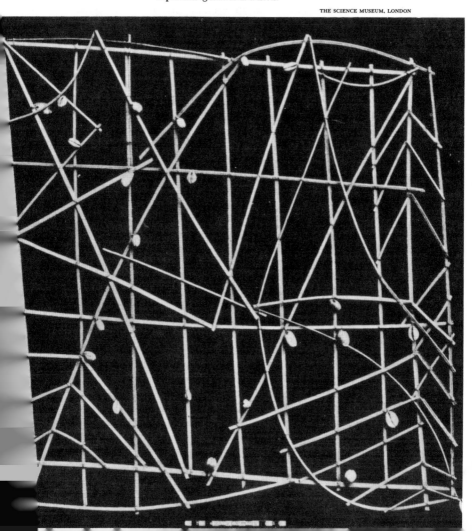

The sailing canoe reached a far higher development in Micronesia than anywhere else in the world. Some of the best features included the flattened lee side of the hull, which reduced leeway drift and compensated somewhat for the outrigger float on the weather side; use of a cantilevered lee platform to greatly increase the vessel's capacity; a pivotal mast located midships to allow "double-ended" vessels to reverse their direction without coming about and thus keep their outrigger on the weather side. The flat of their lee hull and narrow beam enabled them to sail closer to the wind than any other vessel.

Large Gilbertese *bauruas* have been logged at more than 14 knots and the flying proas at sustained speeds up to 20 knots, under favorable conditions. Because of their fine cruising qualities, the flying proas voyaged widely and were once used by the Spaniards to carry fast express and mail between the Carolines, the Marianas, and the Philippines. One flying proa made the 1,700-mile run between Guam and Manila in six days. Explorers were astonished to see the huge flying proas hold a steady course while their own ships had to tack repeatedly. Some runs beating dead to windward that took a European brig or caravel six days were made quite easily by an island proa in one or two days at most.

From Tahiti in the favorable lunar months the great northbound Polynesian pahis and *tipairuas* (double canoes) followed the constellation of Orion's Belt to Hawaii.

The beginning of the season for offshore cruising was always celebrated with a feast. Sacrifices were made and the blessing of the gods assured. On sailing day there was the brave music of drums. The conch sounded in the valleys. Noses were pressed against the noses of loved ones staying behind. Baskets of fresh fruit and vegetables picked late the day before were brought aboard, together with a basket of noisy fowl and a fat pig on a tether, an hour before dawn.

At the hour of sailing we see them before us in their 70-foot two-masted pahi, as island historians once saw them.

After the high carved stern tipped with the image of a god and the steering oar was blessed and the last supplies checked and stowed against shifting in the heavy swells, the pilot took his place at the steering oar. The *kanmoana* (captain), who was a member of the council of Hui Arii (high chiefs), gave the order to make way in the name of Tangaroa, God of the Sea.

"*Ia ora na* (Our love to you)," shouted those who wept and waved from the shore.

Forward in the bow the stroke paddler when given the word slapped three times against the hull, and the crew at their places in the thwarts took up the stroke to the chant of an ancient paddle song. As the great canoe *Mahina-i-te-pua* (the Crescent Wave at the Bow that Bursts into Foam like a Flower) moved slowly out across the lagoon toward the pass, the masts well polished with coconut oil gleamed bright in the strong morning light as did the tamanu-wood gunwales painted black with banana-tree sap and charcoal from the leaf of the pandanus. Long feather pennants called *marouka* streamed out from the masthead the length of the vessel.

When the wind was right the *faatere* (sailing master) gave the word, and the trilateral boomsprit sails were set with the foot of each bent to short curved booms. Only the best of specially selected, long, slender pandanus leaves had been used in making these important sails. The pandanus filled and the ship stood seaward out through the pass before a light offshore breeze and was soon lifting to the sea swell.

Out past the green mountain headland they picked up the southeast trades and were soon bowling along at 6 knots. Scores of *va'as*—small outrigger sailing pirogues—that accompanied them out through the reefs began turning back, and the navigator took his departure bearings. Toward midwatch, standing fast to the north like a great bird, they saw their home island disappear slowly into the sea. The trumpeter blew a blast on his conch shell, and life aboard settled to the duties of cruising routine.

A day and a night aboard this great voyaging pahi was divided into twelve divisions of time, and sea watches were set accordingly. For a log of voyaging time, knots were tied in a length of sennit fiber to designate days that passed. Current changes were noted by differences in the temperature of the sea water observed by hand. The bailers kept the bilge water down and, when not busy bailing, watched the hull seams closely, an important duty aboard a sennit-bound vessel. The masts were stepped on crossbeams, one well forward of midships and the other an equal distance abaft. Each day the *kanmoana* personally checked the hibiscus sennit stays, shrouds, crossbars, and particularly the lashings of the steering oar for wear and strain.

Water, stored in gourds and in lengths of large bamboo joints that contained several gallons each, was issued twice daily. The small galley at the stern of the main hull consisted of a simple imu (native oven) of sand, earth, and stones with a small amount of firewood. Hibiscus rubbing sticks were used by the cook to start his fire, and food was served at ten in the morning and at four in the afternoon. Refreshing young drinking coconuts were used together with sweet potatoes, taro, and bananas, for the first twelve days out. After that, dried taro and preserved (fermented) breadfruit were issued. Yams were a staple that could be counted on to last for two months. Other food included pandanus cakes made from ripe pandanus flour that had been dried and stored in pandanus leaves, dried clams, shrimps, and other shell foods. Chickens and a frigate bird were carried in two cages beside the heathy young pig that was expecting a litter.

At night, when the silent stars came out, the navigator checked the course against his dead reckoning and gave the steersman his orders. At this time of the year there were few starless nights—rarely more than two in succession. In the absence of a compass, true south was determined by observation of the Southern Cross. Unlike modern small-boat navigators, who require a gleam of moonlight and a sight of the horizon to work a position from the stars at night, this Polynesian navigator judged his approximate position from the stars by eye observation at any time of the night. He knew, for example, that the star they were steering for in the sky over Hawaii moved in a definite line a definite distance westward each night and that other stars of the same *rua* (same distance north of the equator) followed in the same rotation. As each star moved on from its position over the island, the next star in the *rua* was used until they arrived beneath the star which was known to be directly over that particular island at that time of the night and year.

When, because of a partly clouded sky or for other reasons, the star over the island for which they were steering was not visible, the navigator selected a secondary or steering star that was in line with their destination. On starless nights his knowledge of winds, currents, and sea changes was used. He could tell from the character of the wind—and from the temperature, humidity, force, and type of accompanying clouds—the direction it came from and could with accuracy set a course in any direction relative to it. When woolly tuffs of trade clouds disappeared before heavy billowing clouds he knew, with other indications, that the wind had very likely gone round through south to southwest or westerly.

During the first week out the weather was fair, the wind varied from E.S.E. to E. to E.N.E. and back to E.S.E., and this great canoe with a sea-wise captain and steersmen averaged 130 to 140 miles daily.

One overcast morning a flight of terns and two long, low, ragged flights of boobies were seen at sunrise flying to the east. Late in the afternoon they were seen again. The inquisitive terns dipped and circled to see the canoe. Low-flying and less inquisitive, the boobies, returning with full bellies of fish, flew steadily, straight as an arrow to the west. The navigator and everyone aboard knew when they saw a flight of frigate birds in the late afternoon that the direction of their flight was almost certain to be the shortest way toward land, usually less than a hundred miles; frigates in this area are land-based birds that fly out to force the boobies to disgorge part of their daily catch.

The captain and crew had sailed to islands in this area (Starbuck, Malden, and Christmas) on previous voyages but this time held their course steadily to the north. It was known that life was hard on these islands, and they were intent on reaching the great fertile valleys of Hawaii, approximately a thousand miles farther north.

In the doldrums, when the sails began to slat, the paddles were manned to give steerageway. Then watch after watch, day and night, the scarcely audible thrust of the broad-shouldered paddlers sent the vessel ahead. Port and starboard paddlers changed positions twice each watch to ease the strain of aching muscles. Coconut oil carried in joints of bamboo was used to rub their arms and shoulders when off watch. In the glassy calm, Portuguese Men-of-War floated on the surface of the sea. Large black porpoises were seen and were heard at night striking the water in their leaps. Occasionally phosphorescent streaks of small fish flashed by as the dorsal fin of a shark cut the water. When the first small puffs of wind gave sign of a rising breeze, word was passed and the paddles stowed as the pandanus sails came alive.

The members of the crew, down to the youngest bailer, were soon seasoned by the passage. With the last of the fresh stuffs gone, the *kanmoana* strictly supervised the allowance of water and provisions. Sailing day after day without sight of land, these island seamen remained in high spirits. All were aware of the vast distance involved, the dangers and uncertainties should the capricious sea god Tangaroa become displeased, but there was no fear, no grumbling, no thought of turning back. Currents were regarded as gifts of the gods. Great stars such as Hoku-paa (the North Star), Newe (the guiding star of the south), Canopus, and others were considered very *tapu* stars, and because of this great usefulness the men sang songs to them. Their belief that the captain, the hull and keel of their canoe, the sails, the steering oar and masts, which came from sacred trees, all had the blessing of their deity made them almost unbeatable, a true oceanic people who looked to the sea to sustain them.

On occasion, island sailors were driven hundreds of miles off their course by heavy gales, and pahis were lost at sea with all hands. When a great canoe failed to return, the word was passed that they had been swallowed by the giant mollusk, Tridacna. And at such times it was said in Tahiti, "Take care of your offspring, that they may replace those who sleep on the pathways of the sea."

When the wind hardened and a heavy swell was running, a pandanus hood was rigged, the steering oar was double manned, and the steersmen relieved twice each watch. In gale-force winds they hove to and rode to double bow anchors. These sea anchors, called *tutau,* were of stone with holes drilled through, to which stout hau fiber and three-strand hibiscus line was bent. Plaited mat covers were battened down over open areas, and the vessel lay head to, taking it on her bows. There were times when all hands labored at the bailers. After a major blow, an offering was made to the sea gods by the navigator, who also was a priest.

Squally weather and intermittent calms near the equator kept the crew on the alert. Waterspouts were seen, and black, ragged squall clouds swept down with sheets of rain. In the calm and slight blow that preceded each heavy rain squall the sails were dropped, *niau* mats were rigged, and in one day enough water was collected to refill several of the largest bamboos. Soon after passing into the easterly countercurrent, meteors were seen bursting out of the black sky trailing fiery tails.

"Greetings from Rongo-mai [a son of Tangaroa, who rode comets and

Long-voyaging canoe that encountered a great storm and was swept far off course.

meteors]," said the *kanmoana*. Part of a captain's duty was to interpret the moods and sense what the sea gods would do in advance. Several, including the captain of the *Mahina-i-te-pua*, were so accurate at predicting sea and sky changes that they were widely known as companions of the gods.

Light winds and squalls were again encountered, followed by strong easterly winds. In the fresh trades, bamboos creaked and the heavy steering oar groaned in its hala lashings at the crossbar steering cleat. Each morning the break of day was saluted by the navigator and another knot was tied in the voyage line. In the early watch of the morning star, he stood forward between the two bows on the sacred miro wood *ahu* (tabu square for discoursing with the gods), clad in a shoulder cape of tapa. After greeting all gods of the sea, including his own *aumakua* (personal god), he offered them a small bamboo of ava, a drink made from roots that they were believed to love.

Sailing full and by, they made the most of the northeast trades. Northerly and southerly bearings were obtained from the circumpolar stars, while the rising and setting points of heavenly bodies gave them their easterly and westerly directions. The westerly set of the equatorial current was allowed for and partly offset by the weatherly qualities of the pahi and by the countercurrent north of the equator. These weather-wise seamen used the sun as a timepiece during the day, and at night, when the weather was clear, the stars and moon.

During the day long withes of sennit from the spare stores were used to strengthen and sometimes replace boom lashings, struts, stays, sennit braces, and fastenings that showed wear. The crossbar hala lashings of the long heavy steering oar had to be replaced twice and strengthened many times after heavy seas. Hour after hour men were busy with the *tatas* (bailers). At the change of watch they doused themselves and sometimes each other with sea water, and those off duty often got out their gleaming mother-of-pearl fish-hooks.

Once a school of sharks appeared to be attacking the canoe. A hundred or more churned the sea with their tails. Some struck the hull with blunt blows, and the men struck out at them with their spears. As quickly almost as they appeared the sharks were gone, and so were the scores of small pilot fish that had accompanied the pahi for the past few hundred miles. Flying fish sometimes broke the surface in silver glitters of flight, closely pursued by dolphins. Often they hit the sides of the *fare oa* (deck cabin) and were grabbed and handed over to the cook. On the day that two yellow and blue dolphins were caught on a lure, the prayer of thanks *"Maui é Ematai tu"* was offered to Maui, the god of fishermen.

Night after night the Southern Cross appeared lower on the horizon and then was seen no more as the polestar and the northern constellations came into view. Knowing that the sea swell runs in the same direction for many weeks and sometimes months, according to the prevailing trades and the time of year, the navigator welcomed and was guided by the northeast swell.

The day came when a shore-sighting frigate bird was released. That great bird with its sail-like wing span of seven feet rose from the masthead in slow widening circles to gain altitude. It hovered a moment over the canoe, circled twice, and then flew off northwest by west. When the bird was no more than a gray speck against the sky, the captain gave the order to the steersman and the pahi was brought to bear in line with the disappearing frigate bird.

The approximate latitude of Hawaii had been gauged the previous night by the altitude of Polaris. Some islanders were able to gauge star angles by eye to within half a degree or less. Whether the navigator of the *Mahina-i-te-pua* used the finger span of the hand (19 degrees) or marked sticks and a short piece of sennit for measuring the elevation of the polestar is not known. We see their arrival as island bards have told the tale:

The *puaa* (pig) becomes restless, strains at his tether, and repeatedly sniffs the air toward the northwest. Late in the following watch the difference between the smell of the open sea and the approaching island is noted by the captain and several of the crew. As darkness rises up from the ocean and the first stars come out, the wind falls and the sails begin to slat with the rise and fall of the swell. Paddlers take their places at the thwarts, and their paddles begin a rhythm of dip and rise that lasts through the long night, to the occasional murmur of a low chant. Before morning the sinews and muscles of their arms and shoulders are aching like sharp wounds, but they never miss a stroke. At sunrise, far off in the sea shimmer of a light trade breeze, a cloud, the first visual sign of land, appears like a shadow on the horizon.

"Behold Hawaii!" the *kanmoana* shouts from the masthead. "An island, a people! The offspring of Tahiti." From the *ahu* at the bow an offering of a sash of sacred red *maro* feathers and a generous bamboo of ava is made to "the great ocean, the great moon, the great sun, and to the wandering stars of Kane."

Songs and shouts of joy go up when the looming mountains come into view. *"Era te fenua O Hawaii-nui!* [There's the land, it's Hawaii!]" All day they watch the distant, shadowy shapes of the purple mountains grow larger. Some speak excitedly of the things they'll do and have ashore. "Fresh, ripe *fara* [pandanus] and a basket of *fe'i* for me," said the youngest bailer.

"Neke [edible octopus]," added the steersman. *"Aue!* with *nato* and *oopu* [shrimp and eels] from the river!"

As the island rises higher the blue shadow of its valley grows clearer, and out of sheer joy a number of the crew leap into the sea and swim beside the slow-moving pahi. The *faatere* runs up the captain's *alii* (pennon of his rank), and *maroukas* (feather pennants) are hoisted to the masthead.

In the late afternoon, as the sea-battered great double canoe stands in toward the shores of Hawaii, the navigator-priest is at the mid-thwart in a short tapa cloak, leading the crew in a prayer to Tangaroa, god of the sea. A bard of wide renown, he greets the island with a chant composed to the land:

> Rising up is Hawaii-nui—akea!
> Rising up out of the night!
> Appeared has the island, the land,
> The cluster of islands
> Stretching to the farthest ends of Kahiki.

Hawaiian tradition records the great voyages of Lono-mai-Kahiki, Kalana, and many others, including Kaha'i, who sailed from Hawaii to Tahiti and returned with breadfruit which were planted on Oahu. On the long voyage south to Tahiti, the great canoes took their departure from a channel between Maui and Kahoolawe called Ke-Ala-i-Kahiki—the Way to Tahiti. Once out of sight of Kahoolawe, the navigators set a course a little to the east of south and were guided during the first part of the voyage by Hoku-paa, the North Star, which was kept directly astern, and by the thirteen "canoe-steerers' stars." After Polaris sank in the sea astern and Te Piko o Wakea, the Navel of Space (Equator), was reached, the star Newe was used as a southerly guide with the constellation of Humu overhead.

Paao, one of the voyagers prominently mentioned in Hawaiian traditions, sailed north from Raiatea in the long path of the migratory golden plover in A.D. 1275. After arriving in Hawaii, he returned to Raiatea and on his next voyage north took with him a chief of high rank, who later became powerful in the Hawaiian Islands. Between the twelfth and fourteenth centuries, other adventurous seafarers who arrived included Puna-nui, who settled in Kauai, Hika-po-loa in Hawaii, Kalana'-nu'u and Hua in Maui, and Maweke and Nela-lani on Oahu, in the second wave of exploration and settlement from Central Polynesia.

These early Hawaiian seafarers from Tahiti were of the *Arii*, the noblest of Polynesians. Their appreciation of beauty was expressed in poetry, chants, carvings, design, boatbuilding, and in the art of sailing. They had no magic sixth sense, as has often been claimed, but their senses of sight, hearing, taste, smell, touch, and an acute knowledge of first principles were developed to the highest degree. They knew and could tell time and sense changes in the wind, sea, and sky almost in the way that offshore birds know those things. During the period of the first great Crusade in Europe and up until the middle of the fourteenth century, Hawaiian sailors were questing south to Samoa, Fiji, and other distant archipelagos. Some voyages were the result of overcrowded islands and disagreements between different groups, but more than a few sailed on voyages of exploration for the sheer love of adventure.

Unlike many European and early American seamen, who often were the dregs of the waterfronts of the world, the products of press gangs or shanghaiing crimps, the crews of the great canoes exploring the unknown waters of Oceania from the end of the eleventh to the fourteenth century were carefully chosen seamen, moved by the same spirit that brought their forefathers across the Pacific before the dawn of recorded history. Like today's astronauts they underwent a long and arduous period of conditioning in endurance and self-control, also in extreme development of shoulder muscles to bear the strain of long hours at the sea paddles. They were trained on concentrated foods and methods of retaining maximum strength under adverse conditions.

At a time when master shipbuilders of the South Seas were building transocean vessels for the express purpose of questing to the outermost reaches of the Pacific, the most common Polynesian voyaging canoes, those used only for voyages of a few hundred miles, were superior in sailing qualities to the long-oared dragons of the Norsemen or the low-bowed, towering-poop ships that the Greeks depended on at the siege of Troy and, for that matter, were superior in many ways to the early Western galleys, barcas, carracks, caravels, and galleons. The transocean double canoes made 7 knots and could come within five or six points of the wind. (Later the Tongan *kalia* could sail even closer to the wind.) And there is ample evidence to show that the best vessels of Micronesia and Polynesia were more weatherly and, despite their matting sails, could outsail the ships of Captain Cook, Bougainville, Kotzebue, and other late explorers. (An average day's run of Cook's *Resolution* was but fifty miles.)

The Phoenicians could not sail their ships to windward. The Vikings, with clumsy square sails that had to be "ridden down" to lower, required large crews of husky bailers and oarsmen and could never go to weather with the efficiency of the Polynesians, though they used beitass poles to stretch the leech of their sails to keep them drawing when on the wind. The first clumsy caravels from Europe, with their towering forecastles and bulky sterncastles "with their arses higher than their noses," as an eminent British mariner put it, had short keels and round bilges, rolled "like barrels in a surf," pitched heavily, yawed as much as six or seven points in a strong sea, and frequently could only be kept afloat by endless labor at the pumps. Under mainsails, square sails, and lateen mizzens, Magellan's five ships could make but 4 knots in a stiff breeze and were unable to tack in any wind; no matter how dire the need, they were unable to come about in a wind and reverse their course. Hence a crew had little chance of being rescued if their ship went down in anything other than light winds and calm seas, even though other ships were close at hand.

Stellar observations were not used effectively by the Portuguese or Spaniards even as late as 1500 to find their way about the ocean, as Samuel Eliot Morison has pointed out, but were employed mainly to determine latitudes of newly discovered coastal lands. Columbus, whose true greatness lay in his fortitude, vision, and sense of wonder, liked to pose as an expert in celestial navigation, but his own journals prove that he was unable to determine latitude from observations of the sun. "I have from our Lord a spirit of intelligence," Columbus once said. "In regard to navigation He made me very intelligent; of astrology He gave me what was sufficient; and also of geometry and arithmetic." Columbus made observations of Polaris frequently enough, but they were of no use because he didn't know the corrections to apply. When the variation of the *Santa María's* compass changed from E. to W., the Genoese sailor told his crew that it was because the polestar was describing a circle in the heavens. Celestial navigation formed no part of the professional captain's or pilot's training in his day or for long after but was practiced mainly by learned mathematicians, astrologers, and doctors.

A ship blown offshore from the southwest of Spain could hardly fail to reach the Americas if she remained afloat long enough. Columbus's caravels, once they had sailed west from the Canaries and picked up the northeast trades and were well into the full grip of the North Equatorial Current, could have sailed or drifted to the Caribbean even if everyone aboard had been tailors. The voyage home was another thing again. The "Admiral of the Ocean Sea" overestimated his daily run by nearly ten per cent. Is it any wonder that on his "glorious conquest for the Cross" he lost his flagship *Santa María* on the very first voyage? Only one of Magellan's five ships returned to Europe. And for nearly a half century after Magellan's death, Spanish explorations failed, either on their westward attempts to cross the Pacific or because they were unable to make the return passage. Poor steering, compass deviation errors, and erroneous charts that misplaced islands and sometimes whole coast lines by longitudinal errors of 1 to 8 or more degrees caused the loss of countless European ships on Pacific reefs.

The navigating aids of the early Portuguese were so crude and inaccurate that these men were dependent on dead reckoning and on natural phenomena. Bird migrations, little changed in thousands of years, played a far more important part in showing Genoese, Spanish, and Portuguese mariners the way to distant lands than has ever been credited. By observing the directions of flights of sea birds, the Portuguese discovered the Canaries, the Azores, and the Cape Verde Islands in the Atlantic. And when Columbus and his fear-stricken crew were groping their way into the east coast of the Bahamas, the sight of booby birds, seaweed, a boatswain bird, and finally phalaropes and terns did more to allay their fears than any confidence in their nightly bearing on the North Star with the astrolabe. One crucial night when flocks of migrating birds flew by to the southwestward, Columbus wrote in his log, *"Toda la noche oyeron pasar pajaros* [All night we heard them flying over]." And it doesn't detract from his stature as the best sailor of his day to say that without those birds some other man at a much later date would probably be credited with the discovery of the "New World."

Sailors have always paid close attention to the flights of birds. The use of shore-sighting birds as aids to navigation goes back to the dove and the raven that Noah sent out from the Ark to find land. The *Dialogues of Buddha* speak of oceangoing ships taking a shore-sighting bird: "When the ship was out of sight of land they would set the bird free. If on the horizon it caught sight of land, there it would go, but if not it would come back to the ship again." Pliny, speaking of the sailors of Ceylon, said, "They take no observation of the stars in navigating. The Great Bear is not visible. But they carry birds with them, frequently liberating them, and following the course they take to reach the land." The Viking explorer Floki took three ravens to help him find Iceland. One raven when set free flew up in the air and quickly returned to the ship, but another, says the Norse *Landnámabók*, "flew forth straightway over the stem in the direction where they found land. They called the land Iceland, because in the spring Floki climbed a high mountain and saw a frith full of drift ice." And in Norse voyages from Norway to Greenland, the pilots were told to keep south of Iceland "so that the sea birds and whales can be seen."

As in other oceans, man's questing in the Pacific has frequently followed the paths of such migrating birds as the long-tailed cuckoo, the godwit, the sooty shearwater, the golden plover, and others whose migrating flights spread their long thin lines across the Pacific yearly. Their importance to ancient South Sea navigators has been acknowledged in traditional island poetry, genealogical recitations, bird cults, and early figurehead carvings, and in a wide range of art motifs on stone and shell. It was partly through the observation of long flights of migrating birds that the Polynesians first received positive indications of land beyond distant horizons. Observing the long-tailed cuckoo taking off year after year in a southerly direction, they knew well enough that the cuckoos, unable to rest on the water, must fly to a distant land. Long-tailed cuckoos in migratory flight to New Zealand fly only a short distance above the sea and can be heard at night and seen throughout the day, reaching southward, for three weeks or more. Each year long flights of Tahitian curlews flow six thousand miles across the Pacific from their nesting quarters in Alaska to Tahiti and other islands. Following an age-old instinct, the Pacific golden plovers and their month-old fledglings arrive annually in Hawaii nonstop from Alaska in forty to sixty hours' flying time and from Hawaii migrate south to the islands of Central Polynesia. A land bird that is unable to alight on the sea, the plover must follow a transocean course that is exact to the nearest degree.

The main Pacific flyways of migrant birds reach out and across to every major destination of the ancient Polynesian voyagers. The sense of timing and of geographical location, the questing spirit and the mystery of birds scarcely a month old striking out for specks of land thousands of miles across open sea, remains one of the wonders of life, a wonder that was and still is closely observed by the Polynesians.

From the Society Islands, explorers and later colonists sailed east to the Tuamotus, south to the Australs, westward to Tonga and Samoa, and thence to Fiji. Tangi'ia, a Rarotongan who lived in the thirteenth century, made known voyages totaling more than eighteen thousand miles. Ru of Havai'i, in his canoe *Te Pua-ariki*, took twenty beautiful young girls of highest rank southwest to colonize Aitutaki, the most northerly of the Cook Islands. In the wake of Ru, others sailed to Atiu, Mitiaro, Mangaia, Rarotonga, and other islands. The mariner Ruatapu in his double canoe *Tuehu-moana* (Sea Spray) brought the first coconuts and the lovely scented gardenia *tiare maori* to Aitutaki.

The great canoe *Aotea*, captained by the fearless Turi and piloted by Te Roku-o-whiti at the steering paddle, left Raiatea in the wrong season and was driven by a prolonged gale west to the Kermadec Islands. After repairing the storm damage and reprovisioning, they sailed again. A week after leaving the Kermadecs the weather turned much colder, and Rongorongo, the captain's wife, fearing the effect of the cold on the precious sweet potato tubers they hoped to plant in the "land of high mists," placed a number of tubers in a wide double belt about her waist and thereafter kept them warm day and night. After a long hard passage, they made a landfall on an inlet on New Zealand's north coast that is now named Aotea. Descendants of the Aotea canoe say, "We can never be lost, for we come of the seed that was sown from Rangiatea [Raiatea]."

Great canoes such as the *Tokomaru, Mataatua, Kurahaupo, Takitumu, Arawa, Tainui,* and others sailed to New Zealand between A.D. 1150 and 1350. And return voyages were made. The *Horouta* and *Mamaru* canoes were among those that brought women and such food plants as taro, yams, and the sweet potato to New Zealand. Sometime in the fourteenth century, the last of the great voyaging canoes that sailed south from Central Polynesia in the path of Kupe arrived in the Bay of Plenty, bringing to an end the long colonizing voyages to the Maori "land of the long white cloud."

"Seamen," said Samuel Pepys, when he was Secretary of the Admiralty, "love their bellies above everything else." But the fare aboard European ships before 1800 was more fatal than hazards of the sea. More seamen died from poor victuals and scurvy than from gales, battles, or shipwreck.

Polynesian sailors in their well-provisioned canoes brought coconuts, taro, breadfruit, yams, plantain, bananas, sugar cane, arrowroot, chicken, pigs, and dogs by one route or another to the maritime centers of Polynesia and are believed to have reached the Peruvian coast and returned with

Maori fleet departing Hawaiki for New Zealand.

AUCKLAND PUBLIC LIBRARY ART GALLERY

kumara tubers (sweet potatoes). Rooted shoots of young breadfruit were packed in earth-filled sections of bamboo for long sea voyages, and highly perishable plants such as sweet potatoes, yams, and taro had to be carefully stowed in earth containers and tended with much care. Livestock, especially young pigs, was carried on long cruises. Early Fijians, in order to maintain their pig-trade monopoly with the Samoans, who had no porkers, only traded dead pigs to the Samoan sailors, until an enterprising navigator from Savaii hid several live young piglets in the carcass of a large sow, sailed back to Upolu, and succeeded in breaking the monopoly and introducing fresh pork to his people.

Tonga and Samoa became important cultural and maritime centers. As late as the sixteenth century the Tongans, who then had the best canoes in Polynesia, were sailing throughout the Central Pacific and navigating north as far as Fanning Island. In the seventeenth and eighteenth centuries they cruised widely among the Fiji Islands, Samoa, the Tokelaus, Gilberts, and Ellice Islands, Rotuma, Tikopia, and other distant groups. Individuals like the Tongan mariner Kau Moala, who cruised for fourteen years before returning to his home port, made long extended voyages on their own. With the *kalia* that replaced the earlier *tongiakis*, Tongans could sail up within four points of the wind. And in the nineteenth century their sailing fleets conquered and settled all the windward islands of Fiji.

As late as the early part of this century, Tongans sailed on long adventurous cruises to Samoa, Fiji, and other more distant islands that took one to three years. Thirty to as many as eighty young men sailed in large Tongan canoes on these extended voyages. Frequent cruises were made to Samoa to get distinctively tattooed and thus improve their status and their chances with the girls of Tonga.

Though willing to take great risks, early Polynesian captains tempered their decisions with seamanly good judgment and sagacity and used the best knowledge available of sea and weather conditions over long cruising routes. In place of our modern Coast Guard, which still lacks authority to stop foolhardy voyages even when they appear certain of failure, the islanders had edicts forbidding long sea voyages during periods when the weather and currents were unfavorable. The November-to-March period of westerly gales and occasional hurricanes was well known by the declination of the sun and ascendant stars, and long offshore cruising was limited mostly to the trade-wind months from April to October. (For ordinary trips, early Tahitians used the southwest wind to go to Anaa. Raiateans depended on a west or northwest wind for voyages to Tahiti. Samoans used a southwest wind for Penrhyn. The Tongans used the southwest or south wind to sail to Samoa.)

Restlessness and the urge to wander has always been viewed with suspicion by wives, politicians, and the clergy. South Sea missionaries in particular took a very dim view of ocean cruising, and more than one bishop complained of the islanders' inherent sense of adventure and "urge to rove about aimlessly." Voyages not for trade or commerce were considered a heathen pursuit and the devil's own workshop. Sermons were preached on the sin of idleness and edicts passed to chasten wandering natures. In exhorting the Polynesians to renounce "sailing about in pirogues and other indolent frivolities," the Calvinists dedicated themselves to creating new desires and to teaching islanders to employ their time in profitable enterprises and in the Lord's work. After one bitter dispute with the missionaries, eleven islanders of Mangareva left their homes in a catamaran and sailed to Sikaiana in the Solomons, 3,700 miles away, a feat that ranks with Bligh's open-boat voyage as one of the greatest small-boat voyages in early South Sea navigation.

The island gods Tane, Tu, Tangaroa, and Rongo are long gone from the island scene. The lays of renowned bards like Ru, the deep-sea poet, and the names of the great Polynesian navigators are rarely heard anymore. The swift flying proas of Micronesia, the Tuamotuan pahis, the Fijian *ndruas,* the *alia* of Samoa, the Tongan *kalia,* the Tahitian *tipairuas,* and the sharp-keel, two-masted, long-voyaging pahis are gone, too.

But canoe traditions remain strong. Just as some Westerners trace their ancestry back to the slab-sided, straight-bowed *Mayflower,* Rarotongans of the Ngatangua or eastern segment of the island of Rarotonga describe themselves proudly as "We of the canoe of *Takitumu."* The Maori people take much pride in tracing their family line directly back to the seafarers and the canoes that sailed to New Zealand in the thirteenth and fourteenth centuries. An old Maori, giving evidence of his tribe's descent in a modern New Zealand court, spoke for three days, naming fourteen hundred people in clan, sept, and family and going back eight hundred years. Each *waka* (canoe division) has handsomely carved replicas of the canoes of the "Great Fleet." And today, when referring to a man's ancestry, the Maoris still ask to what great canoe he belongs.

With their mixture of good judgment, daring, sense of wonder, and hardheadedness, Polynesian sailors brought new life and beauty to the remotest islands of the South Seas. They knew how to get the best out of a sennit-bound double canoe under any conditions, and the "rolling water roads" were as revealing to them as the forests were to the American Indians. Theirs was the human spirit pushing out for the pure raw urge to know the unknown, the spirit of a more-than-Homeric age.

CHAPTER 3

Lone Voyagers

What do we want most to dwell near to? Not to many men surely.
—THOREAU

Woe unto them that join house to house, that lay field to field till there be no place that they may be alone in the midst of the earth.
—Isaiah

"A SAILOR is weeping! Look below," said the Goddess Athena. "That boldest Odysseus is sitting on a rock grieving."

"Oh! Oh! So he is. But why is Odysseus weeping?" asked the nymph Helena.

"For a boat."

"But do heroes weep? Does not the lovely Calypso offer him her favors and the life of a God?"

"Odysseus doesn't want to be a God. His beard is wet with tears because he wants a small boat. He wants to return to his wife and son in Ithaca."

With the help of the Goddess Athena, as everyone knows, Odysseus was soon back on the open sea at the steering oar with his eyes on the Pleiades, voyaging home to his wife and son in the dawn of Greek civilization.

The restless spirit inherited from our nomadic ancestors never dies. Man is still journeying across broad seas toward something or other. He still feels Odysseus's need to know the unknown, an instinctive urge to wander, and an inherent longing for the sea. In the wake of Columbus and Magellan, forty million people have crossed the Atlantic, seeking new life and new experiences. And today human restlessness is greater than ever before.

The wandering spirit came down through the roving people of the Middle Ages. The early craftsmen, sailors, singers, gypsies, teachers, fiddlers, troubadours, artists, bards, traders, conjurers, monks, and vagabond scholars were mostly migrants who wandered far and wide by oxen, ass, camel, dog sled, canoe, and ship.

But the sailors and master shipbuilders were not made overnight. Just as the presence of the Roman army upon the shores of the English Channel brought the sea tides into the general conscience of Europe, it was not for love of the sea or sailing that the French became noted designers of fast sailing vessels. It would be hard to estimate the number of Frenchmen sold into slavery before they began building sharp-modeled luggers and fast frigates that could compete with the swift feluccas of the Moors.

After the "long ships," "round ships," and "great ships" of the Middle Ages, the galleon which came from Italy was quickly adopted by France, England, and Scotland. With galleons and caravels true sailing began to come into its own, and the long-voyaging mariners of Europe were able to rough in the final outlines of Africa, Asia, and the Atlantic side of America.

Bristol seamen were showing their worth in the North Atlantic before the great voyages of John Cabot and Columbus. And long after Portugal and Spain divided the world between them by no less than a Papal Bull of Demarcation, the English and the Dutch were carving out their full share with carronade and boarding pike.

The transition from oars to sails and the growth of English sea power in the sixteenth century prepared the way for the great school of Elizabethan seamen. Gilbert, Drake, the Hawkinses, Frobisher, Davis, and scores like them who fought the ice and fog of the Arctic, doubled the North Cape, navigated the frozen seas of Lapland and the farther East, and struck out at the monopolies of Spain in the New World filled a broad niche in the history of sea questing. When Drake and Cavendish circled the world and challenged Spain for some of her golden eggs they did so in vessels no larger than the Thames barges which ply the London river.

The Dutch, who were fine sailors, were stimulated like the Portuguese and Spanish by hopes of profitably "supplying all Christendom with spices." After England and Holland bested the trinity of Portugal, Spain, and France and Nelson defeated the combined French and Spanish fleets at Trafalgar, British seamanship remained unsurpassed up to the clipper-ship era.

American seamen, harassed by Navigation Acts, debarred from the rich trade of India and the Orient, and excluded by one government or another from every attractive source of maritime trade, developed an early skill at building and sailing swift privateers at a time when fast ships were the order of the day from the fjords of Norway to the Strait of Malacca. Those masters, mates, pig-tailed gunners, and topmen of privateers flying the thirteen stripes had courage, skill, and the highest type of seamanship—qualities that the British also had in full measure. "Rights of search," impressment and seizure by the British Navy, and French piracy during Napoleon's reign increased the need and spurred the skill of down-Easters toward vessels with finer lines and loftier spars, until a fast ship became synonymous with life, liberty, and the pursuit of happiness.

Swift Atlantic packets, Indiamen, and Baltimore clippers brought new life and rivalries to the hustling ports along the Atlantic. A ship's best passage from Canton, Liverpool, or Bristol was front-page news in Philadelphia, New York, and London. The details were discussed with as much interest as is now given to the top performance of champion boxers and football stars.

The lofty, massive-timbered, "reef-an'-turn-'em-out" packets that made record runs between the Mersey and the East River were driven to the extremes of safety at all times to get every last ounce out of spars, canvas, and men. Often they were driven far past limits, and the obituary totals are filled with the names of veteran catlike seamen "lost off the yards" while clawing canvas in freezing North Atlantic gales. Marine notices for the period list scores of ships dismasted and leaking but refusing offers of assistance. (Most, but not all, made it in under their own jury rig.) It took a full generation of the undiluted hell and mad drive of the packets to develop sailors who had the stamina and force that was needed to sail the clippers.

The quest for speed, increased by the threat of steam, hastened in an era that built and sailed the tallest ships in history. It would be difficult to overstate the peculiar glamor and glory of the clippers. The eighteen- to twenty-five-year-old bucko mates and masters who sailed the tea ships home from China were as admired by young boys around the world as astronauts are today.

Like the packets before them, the Cape Horn clippers cracked on canvas until it was worth a man's life to go aloft. Taut, hard-salted men like "Bully" Waterman, Nat Palmer, and Freeman Hatch of the *Northern Light*, who made the passage from Frisco round Cape Stiff to Boston in seventy-six days, set sailing records never equaled.

Never before in the history of sail had ships been rigged so heavily or driven so relentlessly. Built of hard Georgia pine and often of oak or better from shoe to broad teak rail, many new clippers were towed down the harbor with shoreside riggers still setting up shrouds and backstays until the moment when the tug came alongside to take them and the pilot off. Untried rigging and new hemp which would stretch with the first blow required men who knew precisely what to expect. Each one was aware that if he was to make a record passage he had to handle his ship as less than a score of living men were able to do.

It took more than Yankee shrewdness and competence to set steering sails and royals at midnight in squally seas on a sharp-built clipper, freighted heavy, thundering round the Horn for a record run to the Gate. If the skipper was a terror to slow-moving seamen, a driver with a passion for speed and bonus dollars; if he crowded staysails, pounded to windward under steel-bellied topgallants, past prudent craft hove to under a goose-winged topsail; if he cracked on canvas until the spars began to go and the head knees cracked, he occasionally achieved the "impossible."

A small handful of masters emerged who, like the old Magellanic circumnavigators and top Elizabethan navigators, had a measure of the sea-dog spirit that recognized no bounds or limits to what might be done. The stamina and driving force of a handful of such men who sailed with spare spars, "plenty of stuns'l poles," and extra bolts of canvas stood out even at that peak period in the fastest service under sail the world has ever known.

Lofty spars whipping and buckling under a mad spread of taut canvas that drove groaning hulls around to Frisco in record time was a killing drive for men crawling numbly aloft (perhaps to be whipped by a gale, like the hundreds that went that way, from flailing spars)—an agony of endless nights against heavy head gales, of crippled men wracked with suffering, reeling aft across waist-deep seas for another and another trick at the yanking wheel. One master, Judah Baker of the *Flying Dragon*, drove his ship so hard around Cape Stiff he lost her jib boom, sprung her bowsprit, and so exhausted himself that he died "worn out with care and labor" before reaching the Golden Gate. Nearly every American clipper was completely or partially dismasted. Most were old in six years or less and so strained and buckled out of shape they were usually in need of rebuilding.

After the price was paid in twisted spars, wrecked hulls, and scattered human wreckage and long after the glory, split sails, and raw bones, the driving qualities of Cape Horners remained a byword for having produced the toughest sailors the Pacific will ever know.

> They mark our passage as a race of men,
> Earth will not see such ships as those agen.
> —Masefield

A half century before the clipper era, such men as Richard Cleveland, Sir Humphrey Gilbert, John Boit, Jr.—who at nineteen sailed around the world as master of a 60-foot sloop—and a few others were already making long sea voyages in small ships. But it was not until sailors began putting to sea for the simple satisfaction of doing so, for the voyage alone, that little one-man vessels began coming into their own. The records since 1857 are filled with the reports and salt-stained, yellowing logs of small-boat wanderers who have been crossing the seas and sailing around the world. The list of those who have preferred to sail alone includes many of the most competent and some of the strangest sailors of all.

A great gulf exists between people who can accept noise and the lack of any real privacy and those who cannot. "My young days," Joseph Conrad said,

the days when one's habits and character are formed, have been rather familiar with long silences. Beyond the line of the sea horizon the world for me did not exist as assuredly as it did not exist for the mystics who take refuge on the tops of high mountains. I am speaking now of that innermost life, containing the best and the worst that can happen to us in the temperamental depths of our being, where a man indeed must live alone.

When a windship left London in 1877 it was like being launched into eternity, into a boundless silence that swallowed a vessel for 90 to 380 days. During the twenty years that Conrad was at sea in this period he was a solitary, aloof figure, and it has been said that his great books dwell too much on the vastness and sadness of life.

Herman Melville, Henry David Thoreau, Thomas Wolfe, and others of large talents have always regarded loneliness as an intrinsic condition of existence. "The whole conviction of my life," said Wolfe, "rests upon the belief that loneliness, far from being a rare and curious phenomenon, peculiar to myself and to a few other solitary men, is the central and inevitable fact of human existence."

Some individuals require solitude as much as they need water, food, and sleep. When the Greeks said that he who loves solitude is either a beast or a god they meant of course that solitude can be a negative or a positive quest. A man can be a solitary worm or a solitary eagle. When Thoreau went to live in a small hut at the edge of a secluded pond for two years alone he was acting on an impulse that nearly everyone feels at some time or other—the impulse to be oneself. On every seacoast there are people who go in quest of solitude in small boats, who sail and seek out the less-frequented bays and little-known coves and anchorages for that purpose.

Today scores of individuals, about whom little if anything is ever known, arrive and depart in small cruising vessels on some quest or other. Though their number is increasing, men who can spend hundreds of days alone at sea are a rare breed. It takes a special temperament to accept the seclusion of a small boat for long stretches of time.

VITO DUMAS

Modern sailors seldom agree on the merits of small-ship loners, but there are few who would deny that Vito Dumas, the former swimming champ from the pampas of Argentina, qualifies as probably the greatest solitary navigator of all. Dumas was once, as he put it, "chained to the treadmill of today and tomorrow" until he decided to "say goodbye, perhaps forever" in response to his inward vision. Seeking solitude, he "longed to feel at peace with this world that I was about to leave and that I might never find again" and for a quarter of a century sailed on long lonely voyages requiring extraordinary skill and endurance. "Lucky are those," he believed, "who can break loose from habit and escape the dreariness of dying on their feet. But how many reach the end without ever having lived?"

Again and again Dumas made singlehanded nonstop ocean crossings of more than seven thousand miles, repeatedly logging from 103 to 117 days alone at sea between ports; in one year (twelve and a half months) he circumnavigated the world, sailing the "impossible route" through the Roaring Forties and around Cape Horn, 20,420 miles singlehanded in 272 days at sea with only three landfalls. Like a classic few men before him, he proved the "impossible" was possible.

From early youth the sea had always been identified with solitude and freedom in the mind of Vito Dumas. "I once sold my boat," he says, "to buy a tractor. But pushing a plow seemed to put my dreams to sleep. What set me to throw off my normal life and tempt fate? Was it to show that all was not lost, that dreamers propelled by their inward vision still lived?" Whatever it was, as early as 1931 he was sailing a slender international 8-meter-class yawl alone from France across the Bay of Biscay and on across the Atlantic to Buenos Aires (6,270 miles).

In 1942, during the middle of the war, Vito left his home port of Buenos Aires on one of the most extraordinary of his many long ocean voyages. His Bermudian ketch *Lehg II* was a double-ender 31-ft. 6-in. overall, with a 10-ft. 10-in. beam, 5-ft. 8-in. draft, and a 7,700-lb. iron keel.

Sailing out from Montevideo in the teeth of a pampero that had closed the port to shipping, Vito started his long haul to the African coast with a forty-hour stint at the wheel to get safely clear of the coastal shipping lanes. Two days of mountainous waves and winds of 50 knots revealed a serious leak somewhere in a hull that had never leaked before. Forced to shift all his supplies, Vito found that water was coming in from a split plank in the forepeak. Temporary repairs were made with canvas, red lead, and a butt board that greatly reduced but did not stop the leak. While fighting long hours to save the boat, he severely cut his hands in several places, and by the following morning his right arm was infected and useless. Here is Vito's account:

At midday on the 7th of July I took sights and got 35° 47′ S. and 47° W. I was therefore 480 miles E. of Montevideo. The wind chart showed that I was in the zone of

Vito Dumas.

twenty-four days of gales out of thirty. I had both hands bandaged and every bit of work necessary to handle the ship caused me acute pain.

I was heading for a zone in which one storm follows another and which had never been sailed by a lone hand. I knew before I started that it would not be a joy-ride; but imagination always falls short of the truth. I remembered the experiences of other navigators, but all the accounts I had read dealt with less inhospitable regions. That evening I decided to have a feast to boost my *morale*, my first real meal since I set out. The menu: soup and fried potatoes. Not much, but for me, a banquet. So one goes on expecting less and less; and any trifle may become a source of satisfaction. Perhaps that is truly living.

The wind, which had been shifting continually, had unfortunately settled at E.S.E. on the morning of the 8th of July; I was obliged to take a tack to the S. The sky was completely overcast. I had some sleep and at 8:30 tried again to hold the tiller. As I was making no headway and getting very wet, I decided to return to the cabin, where I spent most of the time lying down.

As the day went on, the weather grew worse. It begain to rain and *Lehg II* sailed on alone under the storm trysail, on a south-easterly course.

During the night we had quite a shaking up. In the morning I decided to steer. At midday, when I went below to rest, I was appalled to find that there was a great deal of water in the hull. My summary efforts to master the leak had not been good enough. But the seas were too heavy for me to work on it in that part of the port bow. I should have to wait for better weather in order to make a proper job of it. But, weather permitting, would I still be able to do so? My hand, swollen and misshapen, was a nasty sight.

This hand and the whole right arm continued to swell, making movement impossible. The pain was getting worse and my temperature was rising.

In the evening I decided to give myself an injection to bring down the temperature; I spent an uneasy and feverish night in my bunk.

The next morning (10th of July) the weather was just as bad; on top of that, on this infernal course, the leak was making a great deal of water; and now I discovered that a 5 kg. jar of honey had come adrift and smashed. A disaster: the stuff had run into the bilges and made everything sticky.

Another injection. I sterilized the needle and succeeded in getting l c.c. of the liquid into the syringe; it was not easy to carry out this delicate operation left-handed. The jolting and banging of the boat were so continuous and so violent that I had to be very careful not to inoculate the mattress! An awkward movement, and everything was on the deck. And then—fish the needle out of the bilge, get the apparatus together and sterilize all over again. It took me a whole hour's fidgeting—in great pain, shaking with fever, and sick with apprehension.

The next day I gave myself another injection. The arm was monstrously swollen and my temperature never went below 40° C [104° F.]. I began to wonder what would happen unless I could do something more effective. I could not go on much longer like this, weak with fever, sleepless with pain.

A decision had to be made. That night must be the last with my arm in this condition. Land? I could not reach land in time. If by tomorrow things had not improved, I would have to amputate this useless arm, slung round my neck and already smelling of decay. It was dying and dragging me along with it. It was septicaemia. I could not give in without playing my last card.

There were several suppurating open wounds in the hands, but I could not localize the septic focus in this formless mass. With an axe, or my seaman's knife, at the elbow, at the shoulder, I knew not where or how, somehow I would have to amputate. I thought of the rudimentary material available for my purpose. The boat, her course, the voyage, no longer interested me. Feeble, feverish, and unspeakably depressed as I was, my torments were increased by the endless rolling and pitching.

Slowly they went by, the hours of this long, long night; I yearned to sleep, to sleep for ever.

Amputation was the last hope, but . . . would that be a solution? Was there not a risk of complications, of a more serious and virulent reinfection?

On that unforgettable night was born a fervent prayer—my only hope. I commended myself to little St. Teresa of Lisieux; I asked her help; and I lost consciousness.

I do not know how long it was; but at about 2 o'clock in the night of the 12th of July I awoke. The bunk was damp. Could a wave breaking on deck have got in through the portholes? But I knew that they were shut tight. As I moved, my arm felt lighter. Thank God! There was a gaping hole about three inches wide in my forearm; pus was flowing from it.

That day, as if to celebrate Vito's recovery, the sun rose and the wind veered to south. He began to put things shipshape. The future seemed more promising. On the thirteenth he went back to the tiller, which had hardly been touched for several days. Fresh squalls, characteristic of this zone of the South Atlantic, blew up and continued for a long time. The current was favorable, and *Lehg II* forged ahead under storm trysail, staysail, and mizzen. Vito could not stay on deck for long; his right arm, being protected only by two dressings and a strip of material, soon got sodden.

The wind, which was now aft, required constant attention and obliged him to attend to many other things apart from holding his course. The ketch was heading a little into the current which carried her toward the middle of the Atlantic.

When Vito's arm was well enough he shot the sun and found his position to be 36° S. 41° 50′ W. or about 720 miles E. of Montevideo. As expected he was still in the region of gales prevailing twenty-four days a month! The barometer stood at 780 and the temperature in the cabin at 59° F. Outside the sky was strangely overcast, but he was getting used to this outlook.

The wind changed to N.E. overnight, and Vito was surprised to see that the glass also dropped. The ground swell became heavy, with large masses of water moving toward the N.E.

There were still 900 miles to go before reaching the latitude of Tristan da Cunha. But his arm was better, so he took to setting the mainsail when possible and remaining prepared to lower it immediately in case of necessity.

The weather got worse. A wave breaking over the boat threw her on her beam-ends and got into the cabin through a scuttle which had been left open.

On the twenty-fourth the new storm reached a climax with the west wind gusting to over 70 knots. For thirty hours Vito kept watch, hoping that each blast would be the last, but the squalls followed each other continuously.

The waves appeared over 50 feet high. They came on regularly and shot me down from their crest into the abyss. It was an infernal night; at times the black squall would close round me; and in that blackness one had to feel the wave coming, present the stern to it with a quick thrust of the tiller, then yaw back again. This game continued to the point of exhaustion.

At midnight, taking advantage of a momentary lull, the skipper brought *Lehg II* up into the wind and, leaving her to ride it out alone, went below to lie down on the floor of the cabin, sore and soaking wet. His hands, hardened to the cold, were no longer bleeding; they were as numbed as he was.

On the twenty-sixth of July a lull in the weather allowed sail to be carried again, and in the next twenty-four hours 170 miles were made good under staysail and mizzen, though it seemed at times that the mast was coming down.

After arrival at Cape Town fifty-five days out from the Mar del Plata, Vito soon sailed for the next leg, 7,400 miles to Wellington, New Zealand, which he made in 104 days. Following a brief visit there, he took off across the Pacific nonstop direct to Valparaiso. At the end of seventy-one days, without once sighting land, he stood in to Point Curaumillas and the harbor lights of Valparaiso. "One must always say goodbye to all things—ports, towns, human contacts—and pass on," said Vito. "I only know that I went on again and again with a little spark glowing inside."

A gallant individual and a man of sound judgment, Dumas knew very well what he was undertaking at all times and planned every detail with careful forethought.

Toward the end of May, midwinter in the Southern Hemisphere, he cast off for the imponderables of rounding Cape Horn from west to east. After so many long months of sailing in the Roaring Forties, the heavy seas and recurring squalls encountered between latitude 47 and Diego Ramirez was nothing new to Vito, who rounded Cape Horn under mizzen, storm trysail, staysail, and jib to complete the last leg of his voyage—Valparaiso to the Mar del Plata in forty-one days.

"From the bottom of my heart I thanked the boat, I talked to her with endearments that fled down the howling wind. . . . Perhaps I had the help of those who perished in this trial," Vito said to himself, thinking of the *Pandora* and of Al Hansen, who rounded the Horn from east to west with his dog and cat in the cutter *Mary Jane* but was lost in a hurricane soon after.°

Vito Dumas found it wholesome to be alone much of the time. As the old Quakers say, it centers a man down. More than one lonely Prometheus has paced a heaving poop deck. The satisfactions of distinguished sailors like Joseph Conrad, William Dampier, and Herman Melville, ill at ease in port or ashore, were often incomprehensible to others.

Herman Melville, who was by nature a solitary, a sailor who never in his life was notably happy, said, "Whenever it is a damp, drizzly November in my soul—then I account it high time to get to sea as soon as I can." The deep mystery of the sea tormented the morbid loneliness of young Melville until it forced out of his profound interior aloneness Ishmael the outcast, the lonely men of the *Pequod*, and the solitudes made manifest by that mad Yankee Faust, Ahab. Ahab's fear of the pit of blackness, his "damned in the midst of Paradise," gives something of the central core of despair which every honest man knows to be within him.

In contempt for public taste Melville once shouted, "All fame is patronage, let me be infamous." But if he had not been the great Gloomy Gus of the Pacific that he was and if he had not been appalled by his loneliness almost to the point of madness, *Moby Dick*, one of the world's great sea classics, would not have been written.

Some of the top seamen of all time, Christopher Columbus, Sir Walter Raleigh, Dom Pedro de Sarmiento, and those great Dutch circumnavigators and Cape Horners Jacques Le Maire and Willem Schouten were dishonored, thrown in jail, or worse mainly because they were proud, solitary men and incurred the jealousy and envy of small men in authority.

Surely no man was more alone than Columbus when he wrote to Ferdinand and Isabella:

For seven years was I at your royal court, where everyone to whom the enterprise was mentioned treated it as ridiculous; but now there is not a man, down to the very tailors, who does not beg to be allowed to become a discoverer. . . . The lands in this part of the world, which, by the Divine Will, I have placed under your royal sovereignty, are richer and more extensive than those of any other Christian power; and yet, while I was waiting for ships to convey me to your royal presence I was arrested and thrown, with my brothers, loaded with irons into a ship, and stripped and very ill treated, without being allowed any appeal to justice. I was twenty-eight years old when I came into the service of your Highnesses, and now I have not a hair upon me than is not grey; my body is infirm, and all that was left to me has been taken away and sold, even to the frock that I wore.

Only six years after he had opened the island gateway to a vast new

° See pages 295–297.

continent stretching from California to the Strait of Magellan, Columbus, at fifty-three, broken in health, suffering from *la gota* (arthritis) and from a bitter loneliness, was manacled, loaded with chains, and sent aboard the *La Gorda* at Santo Domingo. When the caravel was at sea the captain offered to remove the Admiral's chains, but Columbus said quietly, "If twelve years of hardship and fatigue, if continual dangers and frequent famine, if the ocean first opened and five times passed and repassed to add a new world abounding with wealth to the Spanish monarchy: if an infirm and premature old age, brought on by these services, deserve these chains as a reward; then it is very fit I should wear them to Spain, and keep them by me as memorials to the end of my life."

Andrew Furuseth, the lonely, hawk-faced grand old man of the Sailors' Union of the Pacific who never quite forgot the feeling of having been hunted down like an animal by crimps and bucko mates, a man of spartan simplicity who did more for seamen than any other man of his generation, once said, when threatened with prison for fighting for sailors' rights, "You can put me in jail, but you cannot give me narrower quarters than as a seaman I've always had. You cannot give me coarser food than I have always eaten. You cannot make me lonelier than I have always been." When asked by Senator La Follette about provision for his old age, the compassionate man who worked all his life for others replied, "I have no provision for old age. When my work is finished, I will be finished." He asked one thing: to be buried as far from land as possible, a request carried out by the S.S. *Schonharie*, hove to in the North Atlantic midway between the United States and England.

In *Mardi* Herman Melville speaks of the "loneliness which overtakes most seamen." He felt that despite the great amount of noise, chatter, and what passes for social life most people "at sea or ashore live in incommunicative cells." In a letter to a friend he pointed out that in the forecastle of a large ship the closest shipmates know little of each other's real self. There are only "the masks," the casual words, the actions that hide the real thoughts and feelings.

One can be lonely in spite of many adventures and many good friends, "but never as alone as in the wilderness of society," said Sir Walter Raleigh. "Of course I am lonely at sea," he admitted, "but one suffers less on the ocean in that respect than in the heart of London."

Columbus, pacing the poop of the *Santa María* and gazing up at the stars, was far less alone than when he faced his persecutors, who bound him like a galley slave.

The world's most famous castaway, that gloomy sailing master Alexander Selkirk, was less lonely in his goatskin suit, dancing and singing to his cats and goats in the enormous solitude of four years alone on Juan Fernández Island, than later in London getting the brushoff from Daniel Defoe, who assured the sick and needy sailor that there was no hope of publishing his narrative (much of which Defoe had already stolen to recast and publish as *Robinson Crusoe*).

Jack London was less alone with his sick companions aboard the *Snark* than he was that day in 1905 at Oakland, California, when newspapers, misquoting him across the nation, blazoned in front page headlines: "JACK LONDON SAYS TO HELL WITH THE CONSTITUTION."

Joshua Slocum, sailing through the Strait of Magellan and feeling the fellowship of the great seamen who had passed that way before, was less alone than when he had to face the charges of his detractors in Sydney, Australia, and that certain Jersey town on the banks of the Delaware River—or in Kingston, Jamaica, in 1907, when he said, "I can patch up *Spray* all right but who can patch up Josh Slocum?

Be the current against us, what matters it? Be it in our favor we are carried hence, to what place or for what purpose? Our plan of the whole voyage is so insignificant that it matters little, maybe, whither we go, for the "grace of a day" is the same! Is it not a recognition of this which makes the old sailor happy even on a plank out in mid-ocean?

JOSHUA SLOCUM

Probably no sailor in history has had a more alluring effect on small-ship men than Joshua Slocum, the loner who sailed with a library of five hundred books but excused himself for writing with "a hand that has grasped the sextant more often than the pen." It is well over half a century since that flinty Nova Scotian hove up over the horizon in his 37-foot *Spray* with the rough notes of a 46,000-mile voyage, *Sailing Alone Around the World*, that will remain a classic thumbed by dreamers and by seasoned sailors of every nation as long as men respond to the sea.

Frank and direct in everything, the bald, thin Captain Josh, at a time when he was broke, fifty-one years of age, defeated ashore, and without any prospects in the eyes of the world, put it bluntly: "I am not the old fossil that some take me for. I am not for old ideas when new ones are better."

In a gaff-rig 37-foot sloop with a 14-foot beam that he had resurrected for $560, with less than $2 in cash in his pocket, the man who had worked himself up "over the bows" to command clipper ships at twenty-six stood out from Boston bound around the world because he thought it was a good idea and no one had done it before—alone.

The high points of the voyage are too well known to repeat here, except for a few words on the aloneness of Slocum's dialogue with the sea. When he was talking to the moon and singing away to the porpoises and sea birds, Capt. Josh reminds us of another lonely shellback—Alexander Selkirk (Robinson Crusoe).

"Good evening, sir," said Slocum, greeting the full moon soon after he had squared away from Yarmouth, Nova Scotia, "I'm glad to see you."

"I'm an old man, and I should like once more to feel a deck under my feet before it is too late," Slocum told a friend shortly before he sailed from Vineyard Haven on his last voyage.

The loneliness of my state wore off [he adds] when the gale was high and I found much work to do. But when fine weather returned, then came the sense of solitude, which I could not shake off. I used my voice often, at first giving some order about the affairs of the ship, for I had been told that from disuse I should lose my speech.

At the meridian altitude I called aloud, "Eight bells."

From my cabin I cried to an imaginary man at the helm, "How does she head, there?" And later, "Is she on her course?" But getting no reply, I was reminded the more palpably of my condition. My voice sounded hollow on the empty air, and I dropped the practice.

It was not long before the thought came to me that when I was a lad I used to sing; why not try that now? You should have seen the porpoises leap as I sang "Johnny Boker" and "We'll Pay Darby Doyl for his Boots."

At Apia, Western Samoa, where solitary ocean voyagers were totally unknown, the gregarious islanders couldn't believe that Slocum had come so far alone.

"*Talofa lee* [Love to you, chief]," said three young Samoan girls who paddled out in a small canoe to welcome the lone mariner. "Schoon come Melike?"

"Yes," answered Slocum, and "Love to you."

"You man come 'lone?"

"Yes."

"I don't believe that. You had other mans, and you eat 'em."

"What for you come long way?"

"To hear you ladies sing."

"Oh, *talofa lee!*"

Once he was accustomed to it, aloneness and singlehanded sailing so well agreed with Slocum that he was able to say at the end of his voyage, "Why, I was at least ten years younger."

A short while after the last of his solitary cruises to the West Indies, fourteen years after his famous circumnavigation, he was again longing for solitude. At sixty-five, lonely and flat broke, with his rigging in need of tarring Joshua Slocum stood out from Vineyard Haven, Massachusetts, and was never seen again.

"I'm an old man," he had told another, "and I should like once more to feel a deck under my feet before it is too late."

ALFRED JOHNSON

The first small-boat voyager to sail across the North Atlantic alone was Alfred Johnson in the *Centennial*, a 20-foot dory rigged as a gaff cutter. Johnson sailed from Gloucester June 15, 1876. A week later he put in to Shag Harbor at the tip of Nova Scotia, restowed ballast, checked his compass, and sailed from there June 25. On August 2, 1876, three hundred miles off Cape Clear on the Irish coast, he had the ample task of unshipping his mast before a rising gale and lashing it down on deck. A few hours later a breaking sea capsized the little vessel. Johnson, clinging to the bottom, had a long agonizing fight trying to right her. After nearly a half hour he managed it with the aid of a breaking sea and climbed aboard to bail. His square sail and stove were gone, drinking water ruined, all his bread and clothing were sodden, and the fog was closing in. But in the next four days of rain and murk Johnson proved that a tough halibut fisherman can carry on against almost any odds.

On August 10 he sighted St. David's Head on the Welsh coast and made port at Abercastle, Pembrokeshire, after forty-six days at sea. The strong-minded, modest Dane, who admitted he "got a little lonesome after the first month," decided he preferred fishing to solitary sailing. Later, as a Banks skipper known to his dory mates and the town as Centennial Johnson, he became part of the tradition of old Gloucester.

BERNARD GILBOY

Bernard Gilboy, deeply impressed by Alfred Johnson's solo voyage across the Atlantic fifty-one years before Lindbergh flew across, decided that he himself would do something spirited and important: he would be the first to sail alone across the greatest ocean of all and would name his vessel *Pacific*. He built a 19-foot schooner with a 6-ft. 6-in. beam in South San Francisco, provisioned with dozens of cans of such things as roast beef, roast chicken, peaches, boneless pigs' feet; took aboard sextant, barometer, charts, and an umbrella; and stood out past the Farallones with official customs clearance for "a voyage of pleasure to Australia."

After broaching to and capsizing in mid-ocean with the loss of his mainmast, mainsail, compass, and watch, after a swordfish pierced his hull and he lost his rudder, 162 days out from San Francisco, Bernard Gilboy was picked up exhausted and starving off Queensland, Australia, having sailed nearly seven thousand miles without touching land. The man to whom "the sea had a peculiar charm" when he sailed out the Golden Gate August 18, 1882, and who was reduced to eating sea birds and finally barnacles, when asked by the master of the schooner that picked him up what he would like, replied, "Some hardtack and molasses."

HOWARD BLACKBURN

Howard Blackburn, that tough Gloucester trawlerman who while dory fishing off Newfoundland had all the fingers of both hands, all of his toes, and half a foot frozen off in a blizzard, was the most indomitable loner of all. Despite his handicaps he had the sloop *Great Western* (30-ft. LOA, 8-ft. 6-in. beam, 5-ft. draft) built in Gloucester, Massachusetts, and sailed from there alone to Gloucester, England, in sixty-one days, much of the voyage against headwinds. He then built the *Great Republic* (24-ft. 8-in. LOA, 7-ft. beam, 3-ft. draft) and from Gloucester, Massachusetts, made a 2,800-mile single-handed passage to the Tagus in the remarkable time of thirty-nine days.

A sailor who preferred lanyards of tarred hemp for his shrouds because he never trusted turnbuckles (feeling they might strip their threads), Blackburn always sailed alone and kept a daily routine of "5 hours below—19 hours on watch" handling halyards, sheets, and gear with the stumps of his fingerless hands. Is it any wonder he became a legend in his own lifetime?

FRED REBELL

Just as sailing the North Atlantic from west to east is a far different thing than beating to windward from east to west, sailing the Pacific from Australia to the California coast is a more difficult thing than sailing across in the opposite direction, because of currents and trade winds.

The voyage of Fred Rebell, who sailed his clinker-built centerboard

Howard Blackburn and the *Great Republic* in Gloucester before leaving for Portugal.

sloop *Elaine* (an open boat with a canvas hood, 18-ft. long overall with 7-ft. beam) 9,000 miles from Sydney, Australia, to Los Angeles, California, was the accomplishment of an extraordinary individual.

Rebell, who learned about sailing in the Sydney Public Library, made his own sextant out of scrap material and did a very skillful job. For a patent log he converted an old alarm clock to record sea miles, installed two cheap watches in gimbals for a chronometer, and for charts made pencil tracings from an old library atlas. His total cost for boat, instruments, and supplies for a year was $225.

With a homemade passport that he issued to himself, Rebell, who preferred bird-watching and Longfellow's poetry to Bowditch, cruised leisurely across the Pacific with calls at Fiji, Samoa, Christmas Island, and Hawaii. On December 27 and 28, 1932, the *Elaine*, already seven months at sea, rode out one of the worst gales of the year off the California coast. A week later land was sighted, and on January 7 Fred Rebell dropped anchor in San Pedro one year and seven days out from Sydney, completing a voyage that was as much a spiritual Odyssey as an extraordinary feat of singlehanded sailing.

Capt. Tom Drake

It was Eric De Bisschop who said, "A seaman is one whose tastes prompt him to live with the sea." Only a small number of small-boat sailors fit this category. Capt. Tom Drake, the "lone sea rover" who roamed the globe in little schooners that he built himself in the Puget Sound, fitted it very well.

Once or twice a year for a quarter of a century, the Cape Flattery lookout at Tatoosh Island, recognizing the familiar scrap of hull and sail coming up over the horizon, would report Capt. Tom bound into the Strait of Juan de Fuca again from Samoa, Honolulu, Panama, and other ports around the world.

Raised in forecastles, Tommy was at sea at thirteen in a fishing sloop out of Grimsby, and most of his training was in the North Sea, the East Indies, and as mate in Aberdeen clippers on the Calcutta run. His last two commands were the bark *Ififia* and the brig *Tartar*.

When a master mariner starts dreaming of island cruising with his own honest deck beneath his feet, he will often be heard humming or whistling to himself and will seem younger than he has been for years, and so it was with Drake. Having decided that a small ship is the only home that enables a man to retain a decent independence and mobility, Tom Drake carved a model of a dream schooner he long had been thinking about during the last of a dozen trips around the Horn in square-riggers. Later at Stanwood on the shores of Puget Sound he selected sound, weather-toughened trees and began milling his own choice planks and timber. Though he knew nothing of the professional yacht designer's curves, series, and differentials or of Simpson's rule, Froude's coefficients, or Dixon Kemp's formulas, he knew what he wanted. In 1915 his first schooner, shaped and fashioned by hand and eye and by instinct based on long experience at sea, was 32-ft. overall, with a 10-ft. beam, inside ballast, and 3-ft. 6-in. draft. Keel, stem, and ribs were of oak; planking and deck were cedar.

Good-byes that stick in the throat were not for Drake. Unassuming, he never thought that he was doing anything unusual. When ready to sail, he cast off for another transocean voyage with less fanfare than a yachtsman shoving off for an afternoon cruise. He often sailed before daybreak and would be missing to his friends until a card arrived from Valparaiso, Balboa, New York, Hamburg, or London.

A battered alarm clock, a barometer, and a beloved sextant were his navigation instruments, and in an oiled case among his charts was a salt-stained ticket that said, "Master Mariner, all oceans, all tonnages." It was part of his

The *Elaine* at anchor at Ala Moana, Honolulu.

destiny to find the simplest things in life and, having once found them, to live with them. Having tired of big ships, he chose sailing alone in small schooners as his way of life.

After sailing *Sir Francis* for many years in the Pacific and in South American and Caribbean waters, he cruised in the Gulf, went north to New York, and visited scores of East Coast ports, from Eastport, Maine, to Norfolk, Jacksonville, and Miami. Poking into a number of the less-frequented anchorages in the Bahamas and the West Indies and logging a total of over 31,000 miles, he sailed again for Panama and from Balboa stood north with a cargo of sea shells, coral, and sponges. On the east coast of Mexico, *Sir Francis* was caught by a sudden, violent norther from the Gulf of Tehuantepec and forced ashore on a wild stretch of coast near Port Angel, Oaxaca. Raided by a gang of Pancho Villa's men, Drake lost everything and narrowly escaped with his life.

Pilgrim, the most widely known schooner that Drake built in the Puget Sound (which replaced *Sir Francis II* lost off Cuba), was another double-ender, 35-ft. overall with an 11-ft. beam and 3-ft. 6-in. draft. After cruising in her on the Pacific Coast, he called at many of his favorite ports in Central America, West Indies, the Gulf, and along the Eastern seaboard, where he visited Harry Pidgeon and the *Islander* at Port Chester. Preferring to avoid the northern winters, he returned to the Caribbean and cruised leisurely for many months. To Tommy, who had more than once spent months beating around Cape Horn, time, speed, or record runs were never important. His decks were coated with tar and sand, his mainsail, foresail, and two headsails were of heavy treated canvas, and many of his fittings were hand carved out of oak.

From Nassau he sailed to Charleston, where he refitted, took on several months' supplies, and added a new dollar watch to his navigation equipment. From the Gulf he had a good passage across the Atlantic, sighted the Azores without putting in, and arrived off the English Channel in a gale that forced him to heave to. Blown back out to sea, he had to beat about off Cornwall for nearly a week before he was able to make Fowey after fifty-two days at sea.

He called at many coastal ports, then sailed on up-Channel and entered the Thames, happy to be again in the river waters he had left over fifty years before. But his fullness of heart on arrival at Gravesend, where he was born, was rudely dispelled. When he luffed up to the mooring of a prominent Gravesend yacht club, the first voice to greet him called out, "You can't berth here."

Not the man to argue over such matters, Drake, who had a lame hip that was bothering him from a previous paralysis, explained briefly that he had come a long way, was very tired, and would appreciate the courtesy of a temporary mooring for a few days. When the club officials still declined and refused to believe him when he said that he hailed from Seattle, U.S.A.,

Drake quietly slipped his lines and sailed across to another less prominent club. Though he was allowed to berth at the second club, all remained skeptical until they cabled Seattle's Queen City Yacht Club for confirmation.

After confirmation arrived from Seattle, many prominent Londoners came down to see the *Pilgrim* and were greeted by Drake with his characteristic smile and hospitable, "Come aboard and gam a bit. I'll make a pot of tea."

Members of the club that had refused him a berth sent a committee to formally apologize. They too were invited aboard. When they asked about his rough tarred decks, Drake replied, "My sanded decks may not be as bright and classy as a yacht but they give an honest footing out at sea." Later the Port of London Authority gave him every courtesy and arranged for him to tie up within a few feet of Westminster Bridge, where many people came to see the man referred to in the London press as a hermit of the sea. Asked if he was a descendant of Sir Francis Drake, he replied, "I really don't know. Never had the time to look it up. Besides, I've been too busy sailing to worry about the dead ones."

Outwardly a warm and congenial man, Drake seldom revealed the deep loneliness that was at the center of his need to wander. But the contradiction of a sailor who loved solitude and at the same time greeted a visitor with a sincere smile is explained partly by a remark he made to a navy man who came up to London to see the *Pilgrim*. "It isn't," Drake told his friend from Portsmouth, "that life ashore is distasteful to me. But life at sea is better."

From Scotland Drake crossed the North Sea to explore the fjords of Norway and visited many ports in Sweden, Denmark, and Germany. En route back to France he was caught in a fierce gale with heavy rain that blotted out visibility and forced him ashore between the River Schelde and the Hook of Holland. He managed to get off in his dinghy and was picked up by fishermen. But the *Pilgrim*, after logging nearly 30,000 miles and calling at 117 ports in four years of round-the-world cruising, was lost, and the sixty-six-year-old skipper was again on the beach.

As soon as he could get back to the Puget Sound, he started building another schooner. One afternoon, while shaping a bent live-oak log for the stern post, he paused to reply to an architect who was asking questions he didn't understand. "Mister," Drake said, "mathematics are Greek to me. Never was any good at figures. When I want a boat I picture her in my mind for a while, make a model, and then go to it." *Progress* when finished was 37-ft. overall, 12-ft. beam, with five tons of inside ballast that increased the draft to 4 feet.

On a three-thousand-mile shakedown cruise down the Pacific coast and across to the Hawaiian Islands, Drake found the *Progress* handled very well. At the end of the twenty-eight-day passage to Diamond Head he was able to say, "She'll ride out anything and she steers well with a lashed helm." And, in a letter to a friend in Monterey, he confided, "*Progress* and I understand each other—she'll never fail me. I don't suppose many of you can understand this craving of mine for blue water, but you get mighty close to something big when you're alone at sea. At times I am lonely all right but probably no more than an albatross or the North Star."

After sailing for several months in the islands, he had a hard passage back to the northwest against heavy head seas and arrived in Ballard Harbor with a painful right arm hanging useless at his side. It had been broken in a ninety-mile gale that smashed his bowsprit, took his triple-reefed mainsail and storm jib, and damaged his rigging. "But I managed all right with my left hand," said Drake. "For twenty of the fifty-three days from Honolulu we were reefed down tight. Had the heaviest seas I've seen in half a century of sailing. First time I've shipped water in the cockpit in twenty-five years. As soon as this right wing is useful again and I can get the ship ready we'll be heading south."

True to his word, soon after he was released from Seattle's Marine Hospital the seventy-three-year-old single-hander refitted, took his beloved sextant aboard in its fine rosewood case, and left the Sound bound south.

Capt. Tommy Drake and *Progress,* the fourth schooner that he built himself.

After ten thousand miles of cruising in *Progress*, on November 15, 1936, Drake stood out the Golden Gate from Sausalito, California, bound for San Pedro, where he planned to leave for the South Seas.

He was never seen or heard from again.

When a mariner like Drake, who sailed 130,000 miles in his own little schooners, disappears at sea, it is a long time before his many friends in seaports round the world accept the fact that he will not be heard from again. Even after he had been gone without a word for nearly a year, his Seattle friends said, "It's hard to realize that we won't see the old captain's cheery smile on Puget Sound again, or hear his hearty, 'Come aboard.' We hope that he has made a landfall at some isolated spot and that one day we'll hear that the lookout at Tatoosh has reported Capt. Tom bound in from somewhere or other."

The differences in the solitudes of men at sea is vast. In the inwardness of each long voyage, where theories and prejudices are easily forgotten, the loner adapts his life to his own temperament. Some, like Thoreau, who never found "the companion so companionable as solitude," simply preferred to sail alone. Others had to.

Ian Nicolson was willing to sail with a companion but had so many failures with those who tried out he decided it was less of a problem to sail singlehanded in his 31-ft. cutter *St Elizabeth*. Two incompatible individuals in a small boat is no small matter on a long voyage. Old and tried friends have been known to refuse to speak to each other after two weeks at sea, where truth is pervading and inescapable. Ideal shipmates are rare. Without them it is better to sail alone.

Marin-Marie, who crossed the Atlantic in a 36-foot cutter and again in a 45-foot motor cruiser singlehanded, said, "The best way to find peace is to sail alone. Taking it all around solitude at sea is not so intolerable as might be thought. Far worse is the case of those who carry solitude in their hearts. For them there is no harbour to look forward to at journey's end. There are many more such people than is commonly supposed."

Some men, like Commander Louis Bernicot, who looked to the sea as a refuge and made one of the most competent solo voyages around the world, were true hermits afloat—ill at ease ashore and avoiding socialities in every port. Bill Weld of the cutter *Pagan*, who cruised extensively in the Pacific in the late thirties and resumed his cruising after the war, was always a little bewildered by life ashore and once out of bitter wisdom said that the sea is still the wildest and the most peaceful place left on earth. By sailing too much alone he found Conrad's "heart of darkness." Olaf Ruhen, competent New Zealand sailor and writer, wrote recently, "I am lonely wherever ocean waters do not reach; but it is the South Pacific to which I am committed as a man loving all women may be faithful to one."

Each year scores of small-boat sailors head for the South Seas. Some go to escape, others "just for the trip" or to see for themselves what it is all about. Occasionally a sailor—often a loner—goes to Atuona, Tahiti, Bora Bora, Suva, or Moresby in search of something.

ALAIN GERBAULT

The most solitary and perhaps the most tragic loner of all was such a man. Nearly all his life, Alain Gerbault found himself essentially alone. Referring to Stanislaus College in Paris, he said, "There shut between high walls longing to escape, I spent the unhappiest years of my life." He was an aviator with the French Army and "after the war could neither work in a city or lead the dull life of a businessman. I wanted freedom, open air, and adventure. Early in life I became my own companion."

The war had taken too many of the men he had known as friends. He wanted none of the competitive madness of business. A civil engineer, tennis star, international bridge player, top football player, and generally a much-sought-after individual, Gerbault was always aware of the hollow ring of public acclaim and of how truly alone and lonely a sports celebrity can be. Always a quiet voice said, "Life must be more than this."

Refusing to squander any more of his life in the pursuit of francs, status, or any of the other things that he felt he didn't need, he bought a flush-deck, gaff-rig English cutter 39-ft. overall with 8-ft. 6-in. beam and 6-ft. 3-in. draft. Narrow, deep, and well balanced with inside ballast and four tons of lead on her keel, *Firecrest* was built entirely of teak and oak.

Gerbault sailed *Firecrest* for two years in the Mediterranean and while living aboard became the tennis champion of France. In spite of much worldly activity, he remained unworldly in the extreme. Feeling always that cities and crowds deprived his life of vitality and meaning, he silently turned his back on the promise of a brilliant future as a world tennis star to cross the Atlantic alone in *Firecrest*.

Without telling anyone of his plans, Gerbault sailed quietly from Cannes April 5, 1924. A week later he put in at Gibraltar to repair a broken gooseneck fitting on his roller reefing gear and sailed from there on June 6.

Having been unable at the time to buy new canvas and rigging, he found his three jibs and large gaff mainsail gave trouble from the beginning, as did his worn running rigging. In heavy weather he was unable to heave to with a sea anchor because of the design and balance of his hull.

After two weeks of gales, of riding to a heavy but worn fore staysail and later to a close-reefed trysail, on the night of August 19:

Sea after sea swept over the little cutter, and she shook and reeled under them. . . . It was a dirty looking morning on the 20th, and the climax of all the gales that had gone before. . . . By ten o'clock, the wind had increased to hurricane force. The seas ran short and viciously. Their curling crests racing before the thrust of the wind . . . bore down on the little cutter as though . . . bent on her destruction. But she rose to them and fought her way through them in a way that made me want to sing a poem in her praise.

Then, in a moment, I seemed engulfed in disaster. . . . The *Firecrest* was . . . under a bit of her mainsail and jib. Suddenly I saw towering in my limited horizon a huge wave. . . . It was a thing of beauty as well as of awe as it came roaring down upon us.

. . . I had just time to climb into the rigging and was about halfway to the masthead, when it burst upon the *Firecrest* in fury, burying her from my sight under tons of solid water and a lather of foam. The gallant little boat staggered and reeled under the blow, until I began to wonder anxiously whether she was going to founder or fight her way back to the surface.

Slowly she came out of the smother of it, and the great wave roared away to leeward. I slid down from my perch in the rigging to discover that it had broken off the cutboard part of the bowsprit. Held by the jibstay it lay in a maze of rigging and sail under the lee rail, where every sea used it as a battering ram against the planking, threatening at every blow to stave a hole in the hull.

The mast was also swaying dangerously as the *Firecrest* rolled. Somehow the shrouds had become loose at the masthead. There was now a fair prospect that the cutter would roll the mast out of her, even if the broken bowsprit failed to stave the hole it seemed trying for. . . . The deck was, most of the time, awash with breaking seas. . . .

First I had to get the mainsail off her, and in trying to do so found . . . that I had to rig a purchase to haul it down with the downhaul; but I finally managed to get it stowed.

It proved a tremendous job to haul the wreckage aboard. . . . The broken part of the bowsprit was terrifically heavy, and . . . several times it nearly jerked me overboard.

The jury sprit was finally set up, a close-reefed trysail was hoisted, and *Firecrest* hove to until some racking seizing could be put around the two port shrouds at the masthead.

Worn sails and rigging contributed to a slow voyage. The skipper's needle, palm, and marlinespike were kept so busy that it might be said he sewed and spliced his way across *Firecrest's* 4,600-mile route from Gibraltar to New York.

After 101 days at sea, badly battered from the tough crossing, Gerbault felt sad to see the land again. In New York City, though he had sailed from France quietly and without announcing his plans to anyone, he was besieged and wildly acclaimed as the first single-hander to sail from Europe across the North Atlantic to the United States.

He received the Blue Water Medal for 1924 and won the Davis Cup in that tennis tournament. After a long stay in New York, *Firecrest* was fitted out with new standing and running rigging, her bowsprit was shortened several feet, and her sails changed from gaff to Bermudian rig.

At the end of the year, Gerbault told a friend he was anxious to get "back out to sea and away from things in New York and Paris that don't really matter." Sailing from Sheepshead Bay bound around the world, he was

Loners Alain Gerbault and Harry Pidgeon on board *Firecrest*.

determined to prove, if only to himself, that life could be lived simply, honestly, and in vital contact with what does matter.

During a three-month layover in Bermuda, *Firecrest* was put on the ways, her copper sheathing removed, and the hull recaulked to stop several persistent leaks.

"I am in no hurry," said Gerbault, "for I'm traveling with my home and hope I shall be able to carry on always. Every man needs to find a peak, a mountain top or a remote island of his own choosing that he reaches under his own power alone in his own good time."

At Panama *Firecrest* anchored two months in Balboa Bay, and the skipper made careful preparations for a long leisurely cruise through the South Seas. From Taboga Island off Panama, where a week was spent in peace and tranquillity, a slow difficult run was made through calms and light airs to Chatham Island in the Galapagos.

There is no point in assuming that sailing ever was the whole thing with

95

Gerbault because it never was, any more than Walden was the whole thing with Thoreau. For Gerbault, sailing was part of a need for islands, remote anchorages, solitude, simple people; part of a positive need to wander and a need for a streaming in through the senses of new vistas and experiences.

During many months of cruising to remote islands in the Gambiers, Marquesas, and Tuamotus he was able to capture for a while the drive and initiative of a simple life lived fully. Later, sailing from Mangareva, one of the loveliest islands in Polynesia, where he was invited to stay forever, he asked himself, "What demon is continually urging me back to sea? I might have laid *Firecrest* up, accepted the offers of young Mangarevan girls and had a family of bronze children who would grow up free and happy beneath the Polynesian sun. . . . But the sea was calling and I could not resist."

Later Gerbault declared he would not wish to have a child by a Polynesian girl because he would scruple to defile so beautiful a race. Referring to the French officials and businessmen of Tahiti, he wrote, "They like exactly what I hated, they and I had scarcely a thing in common, and I lived on board the *Firecrest* at Papeete almost as solitary as if I had been in the open sea." Tahitians and Bora Borans, especially those who remembered and respected the old ways, were always welcome on board.

From Bora Bora, *Firecrest* cruised to Samoa and from Apia sailed to the Wallis Islands. It was while lying off the seldom-visited island of Uvea in the Wallis Group that *Firecrest* met her worst threat in the Pacific:

I was lying half asleep when I was aroused by the noise of the cable dragging against the bottom. The next moment, before I could lift a hand, *Firecrest* had struck against the reef. I had only to haul in a few feet of chain to find that it was broken. The wind had veered to the south and was blowing a gale; *Firecrest* was heeled over and at every wave rose and dropped on the coral with an ugly cracking noise. In the harbor not a boat; not an anchor I could carry out to kedge myself off. Besides, with such a wind blowing it would have taken a steamer to tow the boat clear.

I had been an hour on the reef when suddenly my boat heeled right over on to one side, the deck became almost vertical, and the water began to pour in at the skylight. I had already started swimming toward shore when, to my utter amazement, I perceived that the *Firecrest* was following me; in fact, she reached the beach almost at the same time as I did myself and drove herself hard into the sand. I found she had taken very little water below deck. The night was black and it was half-past one as I made my way sadly up to the residency convinced that *Firecrest* had met her end and my voyage was done.

By daybreak the sea had fallen. I then saw that her lead keel was missing and that the ten bronze bolts that had held it were broken off at the wooden keel. Freed from the weight of four tons of lead she had simply floated ashore.

Gerbault had to locate the eight thousand pounds of lead, drag it off the reef, and float it across the lagoon and onto the beach alongside *Firecrest*.

Ten new bronze bolts a yard or more in length were needed at once. But where to find them on an island that lacked even a forge and was visited from the outside only a few times a year?

Nearly a month and a half later, a tramp steamer put in and offered the use of its forge. Helped by the engineer, Gerbault forged new bolts, *Firecrest* was refloated, and the heavy keel, guided by fifty islanders, was maneuvered into position until the holes lined up and the new bolts were inserted. But later it was found that the new holes were too large and *Firecrest* leaked badly.

Things were looking dismal when the French naval sloop *Cassiopée* dropped anchor in the lagoon. With the enthusiastic help of the naval vessel's officers and men, the keel was unshipped and new bolts were installed during the next three days.

After a stay of four months in the Wallis Group Gerbault was offered the life of a chief and a fine home if he would remain with the islanders forever. But as he wrote in his journal, "I had to go on for the sea was calling me again."

On December 9 he weighed anchor and sailed out through Uvea's narrow channel bound for the Fiji Islands. Never forgetting his first shortages in the Atlantic, Gerbault had ample stores for a long layover. His needs were few and his sea fare plain. Though he could when he had the ingredients make an *omelette bavense,* no small task in a small boat, his staple dinner more often than not was salt beef and rice topped off with a biscuit and tea.

During the six years that he took to sail leisurely around the world, his most memorable days were spent living quietly with island people at seldom-visited anchorages. "I infinitely preferred the slowness of *Firecrest* and the following of my own fancy, calling in at all sorts of little ports." These were months which he knew at the time could never be lived again.

A man who cared, one of the most thoughtful ever to circle the globe in a small boat, Gerbault could do no less than he did. It was his destiny to seek truth and beauty and to find, if only for a short time, profound peace in the splendid isolation of the sea. "As the end of my voyage grew nearer a great sadness took possession of me; the cruise was soon to end and with it the happiest period of my life."

Gerbault brought the battered *Firecrest* into Cherbourg on July 24, 1929, having logged more than forty thousand sea miles during 700 days alone at sea.

As soon as he could escape from the acclaim and publicity he started work at once on another cutter that was 34-ft. overall when completed, with a 9-ft. 9-in. beam and 6-ft. draft. The *Alain Gerbault,* a comfortable and beautiful vessel, was based on his years of cruising in many seas.

Asked where he intended to go, he replied, "Toward the South Seas. I hope to be able to carry on always. . . . Final destination? Who knows? I don't want to know, for I like the unexpected."

The curious personality of Alain Gerbault stands alone. Seeking quietness and seclusion, he sailed about the broad reaches of the South Pacific, anchoring in the remotest bays and lagoons. He shunned most invitations, declined official honors, and came finally to avoid large ports and to spend much of his time with his Polynesian friends. From his own lonely existence he had learned the value of freedom in human life, and most of his writing skill and influence during his final years was used to try to effect a better life for the Polynesians.

Though he arrived too late and saw only the shadows of the lovely past, like Stevenson and Gauguin he sensed and understood the pathos of what others failed to see. He saw instantly the truth about Tahiti and measured the petty-minded officials for what they were. He lamented the disappearance of native arts and crafts, the manufacturing of ersatz "junk for tourists who bring only the gospel of gold," and protested bitterly against laws that forbade many of the old Polynesian songs and dances.

To show his contempt for restrictions against island customs, particularly the law forbidding Tahitians from wearing their traditional *pareus* (one-piece wrap-arounds) in town, Gerbault bought a bright red one with a bold floral design and wore it as he strolled barefooted through the streets of Papeete. As a holder of France's highest honor, the Légion d'Honneur, he used his prestige and considerable standing in Paris to try to awaken the French people to the "reign of mediocrity at Papeete" and the resultant slum conditions, widespread *maladies d'amour* (venereal diseases), elephantiasis, and the increasing ravages of tuberculosis. But like Paul Gauguin he fought alone and in vain.

Part of the price Gerbault paid for his originality and for the privilege of living his life as he chose was a carping criticism of his aloneness, his mistakes, and his seamanship. He has been derided for being an "intelligent idealist, a gifted writer, and perhaps even a mystic"—qualities that one French yachting journalist considers unbecoming in a sailor.

Absorbed in a vision and way of life, Gerbault, like most loners, cared little about the scorn or laughter of those who considered him strange. Though he failed to find happiness after a hundred thousand miles and twenty years of singlehanded cruising, his sea quest never lost its urgency.

Still seeking an ideal, uninhabited atoll that he could retire to with a number of his Polynesian friends, Alain Gerbault was found aboard his cutter suffering from malaria at Dili, Portuguese Timor, where he died December 16, 1941. In 1947 the French Navy returned his body to Bora Bora, where he was buried with naval honors beside the lagoon he loved best.

Loners differ as much as their craft. Some make a specialty of Mediterranean and Atlantic crossings, others circumnavigate, a few have taken up

Valentine Howells in *Eira* departing Plymouth in the Singlehanded Transatlantic Race.

ocean sailing as a full-time occupation and way of life. It is typical of them to spend time, gear, or supplies to help another.

Classic loners like Richard Turrell McMullen, Slocum, Commander R. D. Graham, Louis Bernicot, Harry Pidgeon, Vito Dumas, and others of their caliber, men who never gambled on impossible quests or on a transocean stunt to gain fame or fortune, were concerned mainly with the deep, intimate satisfaction of long voyages well done. Their accounts, devoid of heroics, are filled with common sense, honest facts, and devotion to the sea and small-ship sailing.

R. T. McMullen, who hated slang or profanity as much as he hated a slovenly ship, was the first solid seaman to prove (as early as 1850) that a good small boat properly rigged and handled is as safe at sea as a vessel a dozen times greater in size.

Harry Pidgeon, who had never even seen the sea as a boy, proved that a man of forty-five could start from scratch with little money, build a 34-foot hard-chine yawl with his own hands, and become a first-rate sailor by the age of fifty and a good enough loner to sail it twice around the world.

Bill Murnan proved with his *Seven Seas II* that a sailor who had never before worked with metal could build a 30-foot stainless-steel yawl of his own design in his own back yard and sail it around the world.

They all had their faults. But who has not?

Since England owes her greatness in part to the influence of the voyaging spirit, it is not surprising that her seaports provide an increasing percentage of small-ship sailors. Their developments in the design of small offshore vessels, new techniques and rigs for reefing, easier one-man handling, and advancement in the use of wind-vane self-steering rigs that keep a vessel on its course while the owner eats, sleeps, or does other duties has advanced the popularity and possibilities of singlehanded sailing. Much of the credit for simplifying the work of offshore cruising is due to those who sail single-handed as a sport and make an occasional transocean solo voyage.

The first transatlantic race for loners (1960) from Plymouth's Eddystone Light to New York's Ambrose Lightship was one of the most important events in the history of solo sailing.

The splendid single-handers who participated were: Colonel H. G. Hasler, who originated the idea and sailed in his Folkboat *Jester* (25-ft. LOA, 7-ft. 2-in. beam, 3-ft. 9-in. draft) with an ingenious 240-square-foot Chinese lug sail that rolled up or down like a blind; Valentine Howells of Pembrokeshire, who sailed *Eira*, a modified Folkboat; a London physician, Dr. David Lewis, in his 25-foot Vertue-class sloop *Cardinal Vertue;* Francis Chichester, who sailed *Gypsy Moth III*, a 39-ft. 7-in. LOA, 10-ft. 2-in. beam, 6-ft. 5-in. draft yawl that would normally carry a racing crew of six. The gallant little Parisian-born New York photographer Jean Lacombe (who had crossed once before

Francis Chichester's *Gypsy Moth IV* (54-ft. LOA, 10.5-ft. beam, 7.75-ft. draft, 8,490-lb. lead keel) fitted out in 1966 with alloy spars, four topmast stays, and twin forestays to simplify handling a selection of hanked-on headsails, was designed around the largest sail area the lone sailor felt he could safely handle on his 28,500-mile one-stop circumnavigation.

in his 18-foot *Hippocampe*) was delayed in reaching Plymouth from France by a Channel gale and started five days late in his 21-ft. 3-in. LOA, 7-ft. 5-in.-beam sloop *Cap Horn*.

While Chichester and Lewis took the Great Circle route, Howells and

Lacombe took the flying fish route past the Azores. With the great help of his "Miranda," a 45-square-foot steering sail which controlled the tiller, Chichester, who had headwinds 2,000 miles of the way, arrived off Ambrose in forty days to win the race. He was followed eight days later by Colonel Hasler, who let his wind-vane trim-tab gear guide *Jester* all the way across.

Dr. Lewis lost his 34-foot mast a few hours out, quickly set a jury rig on the 12-foot stump, made it back to Plymouth, and with the help of that fine yard Mashford Brothers was able to sail again two days later and finished third with a fifty-four-day passage from Plymouth. Valentine Howells, flying the Red Dragon (the standard of Wales), was forced to put in at Bermuda for repairs and arrived in New York sixty-three days out. Jean Lacombe in the little *Cap Horn* sailed on north of the 36th parallel to avoid the hurricane area but went too far north and had to buck a strong 1- to 4-knot Gulf Stream current. His sailing time from Plymouth to New York was sixty-nine days.

The logs of loneliness kept by the skippers in the first Singlehanded Transatlantic Race revealed a lot of what goes on in the minds of lonely sailors and proved of much interest to officials of the Psychological Stress Section of the United States astronaut program.

> The competitive aspect of the race was outweighed, for me at all events [said Dr. Lewis], by the struggle between man and natural forces. The adventure itself assumed greater depth and purpose from the clearer understanding gained of a man's reactions when he stands revealed in a struggle stripped of outside support. For a little while I lived intimately with things greater than myself. I knew that I had been subtly changed. A man of deeper calm and confidence perhaps, but above all imbued with profound humility.

Francis Chichester, the fifty-nine-year-old London publisher who won the race in his *Gypsy Moth III*, had this to say of aloneness at sea:

> When I am alone on an adventure I become more efficient and I become vitalized. . . . It seems to me that all one's sensations are magnified, the sensation of excitement, the feeling of accomplishment, of fear, perhaps, and of pleasure. All one's senses are more acute. One becomes so tuned up that the slightest change of conditions, of weather, of noise, or movement will be perceived and, in fact, will wake one up after being alone for a while. Another curious thing about prolonged solitude is that time seems to change its rate. Sometimes there seems a long interval between two words you are thinking, as if you dropped them separately into a pool.

KENICHI HORIE

In Japan, a young sailor from Osaka who admired solo circumnavigators Jacques-Yves Le Toumelin, John Guzzwell, Jean Gau, and Marcel Bardiaux (who rounded the Horn in his 31-foot sloop *Les 4 Vents*) was impressed by the transatlantic race and much interested in the passage of the little *Cap*

Noted solo sailors Francis Chichester, Colonel H. G. Hasler, Valentine Howells, and Dr. David Lewis at Plymouth shortly before start of the classic 1960 Singlehanded Transatlantic Race.

Horn. After eight years of sailing in Japanese waters, twenty-three-year-old Kenichi Horie bought two extra suits of sails for his 19-foot Kingfisher-class sloop *Mermaid,* provisioned her with 88 pounds of rice, 200 cans of fish, 60 bottles of Asahi beer, some saki, songbooks, and a ukelele, and stood out from Osaka, Japan, for San Francisco, 5,300 miles away.

Refused official permission to leave, he sailed sans passport or visa, a very serious thing in the Land of the Rising Sun, where he was given up for dead almost as soon as his sloop was out of sight. After ninety-two days at sea on the Great Circle route and several gales (one smashed his porthole glass), he sighted Point Reyes and sailed into San Francisco Bay August 12, 1962, flying the yellow quarantine flag.

"Like some saki?" asked young Horie with a smile, offering U.S. Immigration officials a swig. Thumbing a Japanese-English dictionary, he explained, "I came here to learn democracy, the frontier spirit, and yachting."

After a pause and another thumbing of the dictionary he added, "Also to ride a cable car."

Curious Coast Guardsmen who went aboard to examine his radio receiver, direction finder, charts, compass, and sextant mused, "Obviously one helluva good navigator."

Vials of liquid vitamin (wheat germ) and beer were given credit for the five pounds that young Kenichi Horie gained in weight during the three months at sea that won him the distinction of being the first Japanese solo navigator to sail the Pacific.

The same need that sent men forth in kayaks and double canoes still sends them forth. "I thrive at sea and in primitive places," says Bill Murnan. "There are no words that can describe the feelings of a sailor at the helm of his own ship bringing her in to an anchorage of his own choice."

Modern loners Edward C. Allcard, Adrian Hayter, Bill Howell, Marcel Bardiaux, Axel Petersen, Jean Gau, and others who make seamanlike passages do so because they plan well, pay close attention to details, and go prepared in vessels well designed and rigged for ocean cruising.

The true small-ship wanderer adheres to no set pattern. He sails with charts but his course is often unchartered—destination unknown. He shuns publicity. At some time or other he will pass through Panama, touch at the Galapagos, Apia, and perhaps Suva, but he follows no beaten path. Some avoid Honolulu, Hilo, and Tahiti in favor of anchorages that have retained their remoteness. (Now that the windship routes are emptier than ever before, hundreds of islands, atolls, and some whole archipelagos are never visited by large commercial ships.)

Right now there are a score of solo sailors around the world whose main purpose in life is to sail somewhere alone. Many are old, but some are young. In 1965 one of the youngest, Alexander Welsh, twenty-two, was reported in Southeast Asia headed west. A graduate of Rennes University in France and an ocean wanderer for several years, Welsh sailed originally from Copenhagen in a 24-foot cutter that took him down the African coast, through the Canary Islands, from Cape Verde across the Atlantic to Panama. Having proven to himself that life stripped of nonessentials can be good, he sailed from Balboa to the lonely Galapagos and from there on to cruise in the remote islands of the Marquesas, then to Ocean Island in the Gilberts. On the last week of a forty-two-day passage from Ocean Island to Yokohama (2,761 miles), Welsh ran low on provisions and had to depend mainly on "beans and philosophy," as he put it, referring to his books on Spinoza, Montaigne, and other philosophers.

Preferring to sail unheralded and unreported, Welsh found it necessary to defend his right to do so and his personal privacy by knocking an American press photographer into Yokohama Harbor and then holing up in his cutter

Loner Alex Carozzo outbound from Choshi, Japan, for a midwinter passage to San Francisco in his 33-ft. sloop *Golden Lion*.

incommunicado. (Presentation of a key to the city and an official civic welcome planned by city fathers, who looked on Welsh as a Kenichi Horie in reverse, had to be hastily postponed.)

'Welsh-san is a serious young philosopher," a group of sympathetic Japanese yachtsmen apologized for him. "It is only natural for him to dislike the press."

While quietly studying Zen, loner Alexander Welsh was able to cruise in Japanese waters and enjoy the serenity of tranquil anchorages. He sailed to Hong Kong and was next reported in Indonesia.

"There comes a time when one must risk something or sit forever with one's dreams," says Venetian sailor Alex Carozzo. Chief Mate Carozzo built his 33-foot yacht *Golden Lion* on a 'tween deck of the *African Lady* when the former Liberty cargo ship was being delivered to Japan for scrap. When completed, the Bermudian-rigged sloop was launched over the side and departed for California. Ten days out of Choshi, the 3-ton *Golden Lion* was dismasted in a typhoon and loner Carozzo made an eighty-three-day midwinter crossing to Midway Island under jury rig. As soon as a new mast was stepped and the boat rerigged, the determined solo sailor shoved off from Midway for a fifty-three-day passage to San Francisco, where he arrived early in 1966. A competent and far-ranging individual dedicated to small-ship sailing as a way of life, Alex Carozzo will represent Italy in the next Singlehanded Transatlantic Race.

In an age of anxiety, men hopefully seek some means of refuge. Solo sailing techniques are being perfected that provide the ultimate in cruising efficiency, and a growing number of individuals feel they can find solace and fulfillment alone in a small ship. But the sea doesn't distinguish between one kind of motivation and another. It makes no distinctions. The rules are the same. Sailors still die.

There is and always will be a bone-to-bone austerity in singlehanded cruising. Whether searching for the golden fleece or to see what is over the next horizon, the aloneness is the same now as it was during Al Hansen's Horn passage to the sailor struggling for a westing beneath fast-moving clouds that hide the stars and darken the earth.

"A man was not created to live on the water nor was he made to live alone," the late Count Christopher de Grabowski, a sailor in the best tradition, pointed out in his last letter from the Caribbean. "Even the best small-ship loner gets sea weary unless a balance is maintained between land and sea, between people and solitude."

The dedicated loner also knows there is a finality about the end of a long sea voyage which he finds impossible to accept.

> *A man who is not afraid of the sea will soon be drownded [said an old seaman from the Blasket Islands] . . . for he will be going out on a day when he shouldn't. But we do be afraid of the sea, and we do only be drownded now and again.*
>
> —JOHN M. SYNGE

CHAPTER 4

Small Ships

The love that is given to ships is profoundly different from the love men feel for every other work of their hands.

—CONRAD

My boat was plumb English, codfish nose and mackerel stern . . . the best sea boat that ever sailed upon the sea. The reason for this was that her lines were of the right sort . . . if you had seen her in any foreign port you would have known at once that you had seen an English thing. . . . She was, overall, 36 feet, she was cutter rig. And she never, never failed. She never failed to raise to a sea, she never failed to take the stiffest or most sudden gust. He who had designed the lines of her approached the power of a creator, so perfect were they and so smooth and so exactly suited to the use of the sea.

—HILAIRE BELLOC

GIVEN an adze, ax, saw, knife, nails, and a few trees, how many modern sailors are there who can build a small boat and sail it around the world? Captain Voss was such a man. So were Joshua Slocum, Tommy Drake, Harry Pidgeon, and a handful of others who sailed without most of the features now considered essential.

There are a few like Marcel Bardiaux, who spent six years (15,000 hours) building his 30-ft. 8-in. LOA jib-headed sloop *Les 4 Vents* and the following seven years sailing her around the world via Cape Horn, and John Guzzwell, who built his 20-foot yawl *Trekka*, one of the smallest boats ever to circumnavigate, at the rear of a fish-and-chip shop in Vancouver, B.C., and sailed her around the globe in four years. There are Dot and Blue Bradfield in *D'Vara*, Jo and Van Vancil in *Rena*, Betty and Dale Nordlund in *Aegean*, and a score of others who have built little vessels with their own hands and are out sailing around the world, but they are rare.

The hand-built gaff-rig schooners, pilot cutters, Quay punts, Brixham trawlers, Tahiti ketches, skipjacks, pinks, and Friendship sloops with fiddle-head bows, bowsprits, deadeyes, and lanyards, once considered the best for cruising by men who practiced the bare-knuckled art of navigation and still considered so by many, have been joined by a breed of light-displacement vessels that are faster, more efficient, and more weatherly than the earlier classic designs.

Under the influence of midget ocean racing, the development of small, easily driven vessels designed to go any place has opened new horizons to the electronic-age sailor. Voyages that twenty-five years ago were feats of seamanship are now common-sense propositions because of improvements in design and rig and new techniques for cruising. Standards and skills are high, and with synthetic fabrics, aluminum-alloy masts, polyester resins, and advanced aids to navigation available the scientific sailor overlooks nothing that will increase the efficiency of his vessel—be it a Block Island-40, Triton, Vertue, or any other of the new compact world cruisers.

Ocean racing is important only to a few thousand participants, but what happens along the courses dictates the trends of modern yacht design. In 1930, when *Dorade* proved to the disbelieving down-Easters of Maine and Nova Scotia that a lightly rigged modern yawl was capable of high perform-ance under a wide variety of conditions and in hard offshore going, she heralded a new concept in ocean sailing as significant as the appearance of John Illingworth's large fore-triangle mastheaded Bermudian rig on *Ortac* and the *Maid of Malham* in 1937.

Later came the small centerboarders from the drawing boards of Phil Rhodes and Olin Stephins that proved extremely fast, sea-kindly, easy on gear and crew, and as capable of taking heavy weather as keel boats.

Finisterre

There was nothing new about broad-beam centerboarders except that ocean racing developed a specialized type in the modern outside-ballasted centerboarder. The elite are vessels like *Golliwogg, Hoot Mon*—and *Finis-terre*, a hull designed for cruising comfort driven by the ultimate in efficient modern racing rigs.

Carleton Mitchell, after cruising and racing his fat (14-foot beam) center-boarder *Caribee* from Havana to Helsinki, through the skerries of Sweden, and along the coasts of France, Belgium, Holland, and Germany for over five years, driving harder and farther than any other boat her size and type, began thinking of a home with a waterline length a lot less than 42 feet, small enough to gunkhole anywhere, comfortable for long passages, and fast enough to win ocean races in any waters. Mitchell's musing and Olin Stephins's lines became *Finisterre*, a shoal-draft jib-headed centerboard yawl of extreme beam and heavy displacement drawing 3 foot 11 inches with the three-quarter-inch bronze centerplate up (in a welded bronze trunk), 38-ft. 7-in. LOA, 27-ft. 6-in. LW, 11-ft. 3-in. beam, and 713 feet of sail (mizzen, main, and genoa) when cruising.

After winning more than her share of racing firsts, *Finisterre* proved in cruising, passage making, and "livability" to be the dream ship Mitchell hoped for—a far-ranging cruiser-racer that has logged a daily average of 154 miles (6.41 knots) for twenty-two and a half days on a Great Circle passage of 3,442 miles from Brenton Reef Lightship to Cape St. Vincent.

Finisterre has a system of four #6 Nevin winches flanking the cockpit, roller-reefing main and jib, radio telephone, depth finder, two generators and dockside charger, radio direction finder, wind indicator to tell wind direction on a cockpit dial, barograph, two heads, an ice maker, and a portable fireplace that can be removed in the tropics. Feeling he has an extra hand aboard in "The Ape" (a Bendix automatic pilot with remote control to anywhere on deck), Mitchell says he wouldn't sail without it.

The cost? Reputedly $2,000 a foot or $76,000 total—probably the most expensive 38-foot yacht ever built.

The sleek ocean racer with lofty alloy masts and a precision-trained crew carrying canvas long after it is prudent to do so is one thing, and the loner running with the wind on the quarter or the cruising family snugged down making a westing or running in the trades with twin spinnakers set and main hatches open, bound to a remote island anchorage, is quite another thing again. The ocean racer-cruiser is more than a handful for those who sail alone or with children too young to wrestle with the latest in racing techniques and gear.

Right now there are more Tahiti ketches, ex-trawlers, pilot cutters, and other small craft with traditional lines than there are Vertues, Folkboats, and modern ocean cruisers out circumnavigating or making major ocean passages, due partly to finances but largely because there will always be those in the Pacific and on both sides of the Atlantic who prefer the older thoroughbreds of time-tested design and special character.

Nearly every cruising man with his own special preferences (and prejudices) hopes someday to build a "perfect offshore vessel" for transocean passages to out-of-the-way places. For one it may be a converted Leigh bawley, an ex-Colchester oyster smack, a Hastings lugger, a Chesapeake bugeye, or perhaps an Atkin-designed double-ender. For another it's a mastheaded Bermudian sloop, cutter, yawl, or ketch with corrosion-resistant alloy-steel hull and deck, cabin, and cockpit of molded fiberglass.

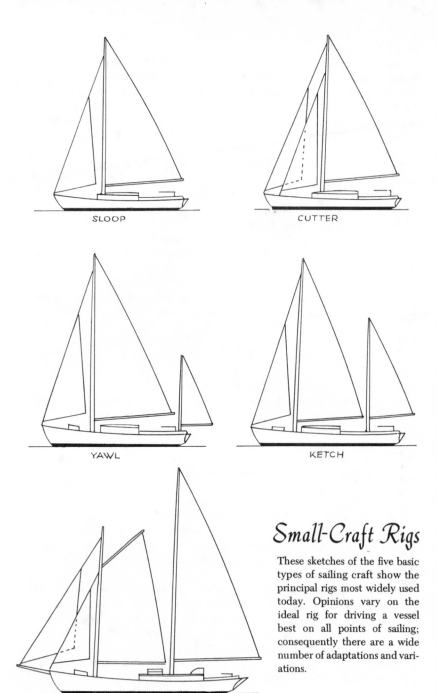

SLOOP

CUTTER

YAWL

KETCH

SCHOONER

Small-Craft Rigs

These sketches of the five basic types of sailing craft show the principal rigs most widely used today. Opinions vary on the ideal rig for driving a vessel best on all points of sailing; consequently there are a wide number of adaptations and variations.

The perfect boat probably does not exist and has never existed. Gaff, staysail, and Bermudian-rig schooners, ketches, yawls, cutters, and sloops all have made remarkable voyages in safety. Each is a compromise, and often it is their handling rather than their design that is the determining factor in a successful long voyage. Two recent surveys of small ships currently cruising in many parts of the world reveal that 30- to 40-foot-LOA ketches are the most popular size and rig, with yawls and cutters second and third respectively. Another survey conducted among hundreds of Ocean Cruising Club members, each of whom had sailed an average of 17,000 miles, showed that wooden construction is still much preferred to plastic, composite, or metal; counter sterns are favored over transom or pointed; medium overhangs are chosen nearly three to one over short; and conventional fin keels are overwhelmingly preferred to twin bilge or centerboard.

The designer-scientist analyzing and defining details over his drafting board sees a small ship as a complex of forces and motions; the builder sees her as an example of craftsmanship. But the character of a small boat, generally defined in the run of her sheer line and the amount and type of overhangs, evolves one way or another out of the vision and instinct of a man who knows what he wants, a designer with the ability to create it in lines, and the builder long devoted to the art who can form, shape, and build a beautiful hull.

Designers and builders vary in their opinions as greatly as ocean sailors. Once or perhaps twice in a lifetime a designer or builder turns out a masterpiece such as a *Dyarchy, Dorade, Finisterre,* or a *Vertue.* But for the modern or traditional-minded who like simple, practical seagoing boats there are a half dozen top designers on both sides of the Atlantic who can be depended on to design a capable small ship with simple gear and comfortable quarters for global voyaging. The art of tank testing goes on seemingly day and night, but there are still and perhaps always will be unexplored realms, for there is no more finality in small-boat designing than in any other art.

Opinions differ so greatly that one man's "perfect boat" for ocean cruising is generally perfect only for himself. With all the advancements in materials, techniques, and new skills there are those who still admire the seamanly ease and precision of men who sailed without most of the features now considered essential.

Spray

The most famous small ship of the past century—that classic example of a heavy shallow-draft boat—is, of course, Joshua Slocum's sloop *Spray,* with her 14-ft. 2-in. beam, 4-ft. 2-in. draft, and 36-ft. 9-in. length overall, a comfortable vessel that weathered her share of Cape Horn gales without any outside ballast. Rebuilt at a total cost of $556.63 and thirteen months' labor, *Spray* was that rare thing, a perfectly balanced hull arrived at without the complex techniques of modern yacht design.

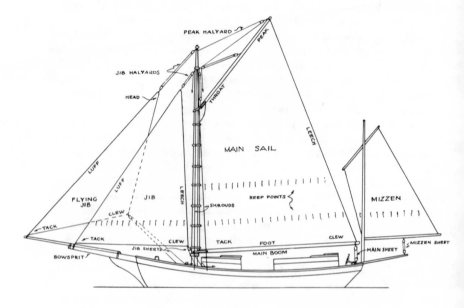

PEAK HALYARD
JIB HALYARDS
HEAD
PEAK
THROAT
MAIN SAIL
LEECH
LUFF
LUFF
LUFF
JIB
LEECH
REEF POINTS
MIZZEN
FLYING
JIB
CLEW
SHROUDS
TACK
TACK
CLEW
TACK
FOOT
CLEW
MIZZEN SHEET
JIB SHEETS
MAIN BOOM
MAIN SHEET
BOWSPRIT

Sail Plan of the "Spray" as a Yawl

For a simple description of a basic sail plan the general reader is referred to the *Spray*, most widely known small sailing vessel of all time. Joshua Slocum, when less than half-way around the world, adopted the yawl rig as an improvement on *Spray's* original sloop rig because it "reduced the size of a rather heavy mainsail and slightly improved her steering qualities on the wind."

Today the four-sided sail of the traditional gaff rig, as shown above, with head secured to a spar (called a gaff) and the luff (forward edge) secured to a mast, has been generally superseded by tall-masted triangular sails, called the Bermudian or Marconi rig.

In the tradition of Thoreau, the flinty nonconformist who rebuilt the skeleton of a hundred-year-old Delaware oysterman in a Massachusetts pasture out of whatever was handy and he could afford said, "I did not know the center of effort in her sails, except as it hit me in practice at sea, nor did I care a rope yarn about it. As a sailor judges his prospective ship by a 'blow of the eye' . . . so I judged the *Spray*, and I was not deceived."

At Fairhaven, finishing a stem piece from "the butt of the smartest kind of a pasture oak," Josh found time to rest on his adze among the blossoming apple and cherry trees to gam with arctic whalers, who inspired him "to put a double set of breast-hooks in *Spray*, that she might shunt ice" if necessary. Adding some freeboard, he increased the sheer until it was hard to say at what point the old died and the new began.

"Yachtsmen pleasuring in the 'lilies of the sea' will not think favorably of my craft," warned Slocum, anticipating the criticism of those who juggle with coefficients. "They have a right to their opinion, while I stick to mine."

Iconoclast-designer John G. Hannah, known as the sage of Dunedin but perhaps better known as the designer of the Tahiti ketch, said of *Spray*, "I hold that her peculiar merit as a single-hander was in her remarkable balance of all effective centers of effort and resistance on her midship section line." Hannah nevertheless felt it necessary to warn prospective circumnavigators looking for a suitable vessel that "*Spray* is the worst possible boat for anyone lacking the experience and resourcefulness of Slocum to take offshore."

When Commodore John Pflieger pointed out in *Spray*, the journal of The Slocum Society, that a long keel is harder to tack or go about in and that a boat similar to *Spray* foundered on a lee shore on this account, Peter Tangvald, competent ocean sailor who circumnavigated in his 32-foot cutter *Dorothea I*, promptly replied, "How much more should Slocum have done to demonstrate that the boat was seaworthy? I would not hesitate to claim that if one *Spray* was wrecked on a lee shore it was because her crew needed a few more hours of sailing lessons."

Cipriano Andrade, Jr., engineer and yacht designer, said of *Spray:*

After a thorough analysis of *Spray's* lines, I found her to have a theoretically perfect balance. Her balance is marvelous—almost uncanny. Try as I would—one element after the other—they all swung into the same identical line. I attacked her with proportional dividers, planimeter, rotameter, Simpson's rule, Froude's coefficients, Dixon Kemp's formulae, series, curves, differentials, and all the appliances of modern yacht designing, and she emerged from the ordeal a theoretically perfect boat. For when she is underway every element of resistance, stability, weight, heeling effort, and propulsive force is in one transverse plane, and that plane is the boat's midship section. I know of no similar case in the whole field of naval architecture, ancient or modern.

One of the most remarkable things about *Spray* was her ability to run before the wind under her regular fore-and-aft rig with the helm lashed. She was able to hold a true course on her own on all points of sailing and in the Indian Ocean sailed 2,700 miles in twenty-three days with no one at the helm. Other details of extraordinary sailing ability in the course of her 46,000-mile voyage are too well known to readers of *Sailing Alone Around the World* to recount here.

Bound from Samoa to Australia, Slocum encountered gales and heavy seas that foundered the American clipper ship *Patrician* running a course south of *Spray*. A French mail steamer blown off course reported seeing *Spray* at the height of the storm and wondered what sad fate had befallen the little ship. Slocum's log records that at the time that passengers of the steamer were up to their knees in water in the big ship's saloon *Spray* was lying snug under a goose-winged mainsail and arrived safely at Newcastle in the teeth of a gale.

Leaving theory and controversy to others and devoting himself to enjoying the first singlehanded circumnavigation of the world, the uncommon Yankee who became known to mariners of all nations as a classic sailor and a forthright, honest man said simply, "I have given in the plans of the *Spray* the dimensions of such a ship as I should call seaworthy in all conditions of weather and on all seas."

Moonraker

Moonraker of Fowey, the ex-Cornish fishing boat that Dr. Peter Pye and his wife Ann bought for £25 ($100) and have sailed on long ocean voyages for the past three decades, is an example of what can be accomplished with an old working hull.

Like E. F. Knight's famous yawl *Falcon*, *Moonraker* was built in the West Country by craftsmen of the old school, who built with well-seasoned pitch-pine planking on honest oak frames. Bought and converted to a gaff-rig cutter by the Pyes in 1932, her waterline and overall measurements are both 29 feet, with 9-ft. 8-in. beam and 6-ft. draft. With bulwarks 9 inches high, a bold 10-foot oak bowsprit, a considerable sheer, and a fine transom stern, she is a unique example of her type and, according to the Pyes, a happy ship—sea-kindly and safe when running before a strong wind and sea.

Launched at Looe in 1896, *Moonraker* was fifty-three years old when Peter and Ann Pye sailed her across the Atlantic for the first time. Seventy years old in 1966, she was still making notable passages in safety and comfort.

A modest couple with a considerable knowledge and an intimate feeling for the sea and sailing, the Pyes were singularly devoted to their well-found little cutter and kept her in fine shape with the help of an occasional volunteer crewman. In return, *Moonraker* has shown her worth on numerous Atlantic crossings and established an outstanding record of what a very old vessel of character can still do on long passages in the North and South Pacific, the Mediterranean, the North Sea, and other distant parts of the

FROM *Sailing Alone Around the World*, 1900

"There the *Spray* rode, now like a bird on the crest of a wave, and now like a waif deep down in the hollow between seas; and so she drove on."—Joshua Slocum

world. During one thirteen-month voyage she crossed the Atlantic twice, sailing a total of 11,600 miles. A weatherly little vessel that looks like it to an experienced eye, she "sails like a witch," has logged 150 miles in 24 hours, and on long stretches in the Pacific and the Atlantic averaged better than 120 miles a day.

The sea is a great destroyer of false values. "Ships, like women," according to Dr. Pye, "sometimes have an aura round them; some are just plain dull, others have the spice of life, while some you take your hat off to and offer up a silent prayer."

Few mature married couples can be said to love a little ship more than Ann and Peter Pye loved *Moonraker*. "To contemplate a voyage in another ship," Peter once said, "would be almost as impossible as to look for another wife."

Seven Seas II

Seven Seas II, the unique little stainless-steel Bermudian centerboard yawl that Bill Murnan spent two years welding and building by hand in a Los Angeles back yard to sail around the world, was taken from the lines of Thomas Fleming Day's famous 26-foot yawl *Sea Bird*.

An unconventional boat 30-ft. LOA, 28-ft. LW, with a 9-ft. 8-in. beam and 3-ft. draft, *Seven Seas II* has no room for a conventional cockpit because her cabin extends aft to a few inches from the mizzenmast. For practical purposes and his own particular brand of extended cruising, Bill sacrificed many customary features and a point or two of beauty. With the ship's wheel mounted inside the cabin, the helmsman steers from a position half in and half out of the main hatch on a seat over the lower companionway slide.

Never a man to hurry, Bill believes in seeing and fully enjoying the places along the way. Besides a six-year supply of dehydrated foods he took an abundant stock of canned meats, vegetables, and fruits aboard. When topped off with 120 gallons of fresh water and 150 gallons of fuel for her two Universal 25 h.p. auxiliaries (a hollow stainless keel holds 40 gallons), *Seven Seas II* floated eight inches below her lines.

Sailing from San Pedro with his wife Ceice, Bill visited Hawaii, Tahiti, and Samoa, with many stops en route. At Pago Pago, Ceice became ill and was advised by doctors to return to a cooler climate. At the end of the hurricane season Bill sailed on alone to the Fijis, New Hebrides, Solomons, New Guinea, Australia, and up through the Arafura Sea to Timor.

Seven Seas II was at Christmas Island in the Indian Ocean when the advance winds of a hurricane hit that tiny harbor. Though still weak from a local illness, Bill put out from Christmas and rode the heavy weather out at sea. A truck tire, bridled so it towed upright, was used effectively as a drogue. The seas and gale-force winds of the hurricane season made it impossible to put in at Cocos-Keeling or at Rodriguez. Sailing at times under bare poles,

Bill Murnan's stainless steel yawl *Seven Seas II* outbound across the Indian Ocean en route around the world.

Seven Seas II averaged nearly one hundred miles a day for the 5,100-mile passage to Africa. A final gale whipping down the Mozambique Channel drove the steel yawl toward Durban, where she arrived nonstop fifty-three days from Christmas.

In Durban and four hundred miles south in Port Elizabeth, bets were wagered that the *Seven Seas II*, heavily laden and many inches below her lines, would never make the "Cape of Storms" at the southern tip of Africa. (Besides two 25-pound Northill service anchors, Bill carried twice the usual amount of ground tackle, an ample supply of spares of all gear, and much special equipment for explorations into primitive native areas.) In fourteen days of gales, less than four hundred miles was logged. Bill reached and safely passed Cape Agulhas, only to be hit with strong northwesterly winds off Danger Point that forced *Seven Seas II* to lay hove to for five days and nights.

At Cape Town, with fierce gales reported, the press put Murnan and his vessel down as another casualty of the Cape of Good Hope. But Bill's wife, waiting at Cape Town, refused to give up hope. "Bill knows the ocean," she said, refuting the press, "and he knows his boat. If any man can make it, he can."

When the *Seven Seas II* passed in between the breakwaters and stood slowly up the harbor, Cape Town came alive with horns and whistles and with sirens from ships at anchor in the bay. A case of champagne was brought out by two Australians, one of whom admitted that the arrival of the little yawl would cost him a ten-pound note he had bet that Murnan would never make it.

For most of her 25,000-mile voyage around the world, *Seven Seas II* steered herself. With a seven-to-one worm gear and an improvised brake on her steering wheel drum, she held course well on any point of sailing. In fair winds Bill used his spinnakers much of the time. The hollow stainless-steel poles were attached on goosenecks to the mainmast and the spinnakers hanked to jackstays that secured to ring bolts on deck a few feet from the mast, with the clews bent to the out ends of the poles before the sails were hoisted. Rigged thus and sheeted aft, they effectively kept *Seven Seas II* on her course many thousands of miles.

In 1952, when *Seven Seas II* arrived back in Miami, Bill Murnan became the fourth man in history to circumnavigate and the first to do so in an all-stainless-steel boat. After spending the largest part of a lifetime at sea, Bill said recently, "When I leave a harbor and hoist my sails a big load seems to slide away and I feel like a new man."

With the aura of tar and hemp and the day of the foredeck musclemen gone, modern mastheaded sloops, cutters, yawls, and ketches built to today's light-displacement, no-maintenance standards—tough, durable little vessels of metal alloys, resins, and glass fibers that continue racing in winds up to gale force and carry as many as a dozen headsails, including genoas, Yankees, triangular or quadrilateral jibs, and spinnakers large enough to wrap the hull in—have more wonders than Slocum ever thought of.

Hoods, dodgers, Plexiglas blister domes, and other devices keep the helmsman dry, and self-steering systems from mechanical to hydraulic to wind vanes to the direct utilization of sails include more than a dozen methods designed to allow small yachts to steer themselves in any weather on any course. Chrome pulpits and guardrails make it seem longer ago than it was when Claud Worth apologized for putting a single wire round *Tern II*.

The use of reinforced plastics is probably the most striking single rapid development in modern boating. The change from natural to synthetic fibers (Nylon and Dacron) brought a revolution in sailmaking, with new techniques in cutting, finishing, and cloth preservation. Nonabsorbent foam plastics that can be mixed in a bucket and poured boiling into the bilges to fit the hull shape have advanced buoyancy. And tomorrow will see updated techniques in the use of fiberglass, steel, aluminum, foam flotation, synthetic sealants, and weather-resistant finishes.

At one time jambing cleats and halyard winches were considered gadgets and the Marconi rig considered a "crazy thing," so there is a good chance that self-steering vanes, fire-resistant resins, and alloy masts will be accepted as standard equipment for the cruising loner of 1975. Just as Roman sailors were amazed to find that the pre-Britons who inhabited England stained themselves all over blue with woad, the solo sailor of the distant future will perhaps be amazed to learn of *Spray's* 34-foot boom that extended 6 feet astern and of McMullen "clapping on luff tackles" to flatten his double-canvased sails.

The modern ocean cruiser-racer with small inboard rig and speed under almost all conditions has developed a type of hard-bitten offshore skipper who continues to windward when others are running or lying ahull. As Colonel Hasler, veteran authority on small-ship rigs, puts it, "The fanatical offshore racing man . . . may have an inherent need for a different and more difficult boat than the ideal offshore cruiser."

For most of us a small blue-water vessel capable of going anywhere from the Bahamas to Tahiti, Bali, or the Scandinavian skerries and designed to be sailed by one or two people will do. There certainly is a considerable difference between a man who spends most of his time and thought getting the ultimate speed out of a yacht, driving hard for a record, and striving continually to improve on a previous day's run and a man who takes things as they come, sails his vessel efficiently, but is more concerned with enjoying life at sea than in proving something or winning a goblet. The completely devoted cruising man or the skipper sailing around the world with his wife is usually not in a hurry and is not interested in racing rules, ocean or otherwise. Unhurried and unworried, he is more concerned with the care of the gear than with cutting a few hours from a twenty-five-day passage.

Stornoway

The smooth lines and seaworthiness of the Norwegian double-ender, as perfected by Colin Archer for the North Sea, has been the dream ship of many besides Ralph Stock, Erling Tambs—and Sten and Brita Holmdahl, who circumnavigated with *Viking* in two years.

Al and Marjorie Petersen's salty-looking *Stornoway*, a modified Colin Archer type gaff-rigged cutter 33-ft. LOA, 28-ft. 6-in. by 11-ft. beam, and 5-ft. 10-in. draft, has taken the eye of many sailors during the two decades that she has been making ocean passages and gunkholing in many parts of the globe.

Before marrying Marjorie, Al Petersen sailed *Stornoway* around the world singlehanded and was awarded the Cruising Club of America's coveted Blue Water Medal in 1952.

Al and Margie Petersen aboard *Stornoway*.

Fitting out and sailing from Oxford, Maryland, in November, 1948, Al cruised through the West Indies to Panama, the Galapagos, and on across the Pacific to the Marquesas, Tuamotus, and Society Islands. For many thousands of miles in the Pacific, *Stornoway* sailed herself under twin staysails with the sheets rigged to her tiller. After visiting New Zealand, Australia, and New Guinea with many pleasant stops, *Stornoway* sailed up through Torres Strait to Timor and on to Bali, Surabaja, Singapore, Colombo, and other ports en route. For many years, while saving up money to be able to do so, Al had dreamed of cruising in the Mediterranean and had planned to circumnavigate via the Red Sea rather than the well-worn sea tracks around the Cape of Good Hope. So, from Ceylon *Stornoway* sailed across the Indian Ocean to Aden.

Like Susan and Eric Hiscock on their second circumnavigation (see next section), loner Petersen had but one serious mishap in his four years and four months of globe girdling. And his, like theirs, was almost disastrous. In the Strait of Bab-el-Mandeb, after long hours at the helm, Al was sailing reefed down in the northeast monsoon when *Stornoway* struck a reef off the fetid, desolate Yemen coast of Arabia. When the tide ebbed and his vessel lay in a few feet of water, Petersen, seeing that he'd never get her off without help, made his way ashore, then up the coast seven miles to the sweltering town of Al Mukha. As soon as he was out of sight, Arab pirates plundered *Stornoway* of nearly everything of value, including chronometer, compass, bedding, stores, and spare sails.

At Al Mukha, Petersen, unable to speak Arabic, drew pictures of his boat on the reef to convey the idea to town officials in an effort to get help. Instead of getting it, he was confined and held captive for four days. Upon his release, finding *Stornoway* still on the reef, Al hired a fishing vessel and started at once the tremendous task of moving inside ballast, fuel, water, and everything else of weight. With the hired help of twenty Arab policemen and pirates, *Stornoway* was floated free and anchored off in deep water on the eleventh day after she had struck.

Sailing slowly across the Strait to the Eritrean town of Assab after two of the toughest weeks of his life, Petersen dropped anchor in a quiet anchorage, settled up his salvage bills, and took stock of what needed to be done. Later he sailed up the coast to Massawa, where facilities were available to put *Stornoway* back in seagoing shape. By the time she was ready, he himself was in a weakened condition from strain, overwork, terrible heat, and painful sores that now covered his body. In this state he carried on nine hundred miles to Suez.

At Cyprus and again at Gibraltar, Petersen took time out to help the Englishman Ed Poett with his heavily rigged 13-ton cutter *Kefaya*. These considerable delays plus his own difficulties and slow passages to Malta and Las Palmas set his sailing schedule many months behind. Leaving Malta in November, five months later than he had planned, he ran into a succession of westerly gales that kept him thirty-four days at sea to Gibraltar. Saying goodbye to his friend Poett at Dakar, French West Africa, Al Petersen and *Stornoway* sailed to New York in fifty days nonstop—completing a circumnavigation of four years and four months.

Ed Poett, in a letter to *Yachting* magazine, said:

If you peruse the Atlantic weather charts, you will observe that by helping me Petersen was seriously handicapping his own voyage with respect to the seasonal hurricanes. But that was Al Petersen, a gentleman by heart and by instinct. Your readers and yourself are too experienced to not fully realize that what has gone into the handling of his small boat is real first class seamanship. Good sailors are usually fine men. Don't you find it so?

Since 1953, when Al gave up lone seafaring in favor of sailing with his capable mate Margie, a good sailor and navigator in her own right, their rugged little cutter has cruised widely in the Atlantic, coasted the Côte d'Azur in December, gunkholed the western coasts of Corsica and Sicily. And in the course of many passages they've had their share of Levanters, tramontanas, squalls, headwinds, adverse currents along the coasts of Tunisia and Morocco, plus a few transatlantic gales and mistrals in the Gulf of Lions. Much of the time, whether driving to windward under jib, staysail, and main, bowling along with twin staysails in the West Indian trades, or riding to a storm trysail, *Stornoway* has proven capable of looking after herself.

Having a well-balanced vessel that handles herself well is not without danger even in mid-ocean under the best of conditions. During a passage from New York to the Azores when the Petersens were both below and *Stornoway* was sailing herself down wind under twins in a fresh breeze, Al came on deck to check the course and, looking forward, shouted and leaped to the tiller barely in time to avoid a large barnacle-encrusted derelict metal pontoon that was floating a few feet above the surface directly across their course.

Much planning, hard work, and good judgment have gone into the Petersens' many long cruises, and whether they are tied stern to the quay in the ancient city of Siracusa in the Ionian Sea or snugly at anchor at St. Lucia in the Windwards dining on fresh bonito, plantains, limes, rum, and sugar apples they are never tempted away for long from their home aboard "Stornie."

To be able to live decently without dependence on button pushing is a deep satisfaction to Margie and Al, who often seek out the quiet, less frequented spots, prefer the soft glow of cabin oil lamps, and are not above priming their pressure kerosene stove with West Indian rum in lieu of alcohol when necessary.

Beamy, but graceful and easy in a sea way, "*Stornoway*," says Margie, "is the kind of boat that seems to like being at sea." And the Petersens, man and wife, admit to having no dream ship other than "our dear *Stornoway*."

Wanderer III

The cutter *Wanderer III* and the names Susan and Eric Hiscock have become almost a byword among modern nautical readers for long, well-done voyages. Now on their third circumnavigation together, they have sailed farther than any other man and wife in a vessel 30 feet LOA or less.

In 1963, when *Wanderer*, with the ensigns of seventeen countries she had sailed to flying from her starboard crosstree, slipped into her home port of Yarmouth in the Isle of Wight, she had been away three years and three weeks, had sailed 30,190 miles, and had visited 150 places in the course of her second voyage around the world. "She looked as fresh and ageless as the Hiscocks," said the *Yachting Monthly*.

"With her water tanks refilled and food lockers replenished, *Wanderer* could, no doubt, have set out next day on an equally long voyage," said Eric. "Susan and I are very proud of her."

Wanderer III is a traditional British cutter of heavy displacement (16,000 pounds) and narrow beam with modern jib-headed rig. Her measurements are 30-ft. 3-in. LOA, 26-ft. 4-in. LW, 8-ft. 5-in. beam, 5-ft. draft. Eric regards a 30-foot waterline length as the minimum for a comfortable oceangoing yacht, with preferred beam of about 9-ft. 6-in. He also prefers a short sawn-off counter for a vessel with a moderate forward overhang, especially if intended for long passages of running before a strong wind and big seas as so often prevail in the trade winds. After twelve years of sailing with a tall jib-headed rig, the Hiscocks have not been converted from a long preference for gaff, and if they build again they say it will be gaff rig.

All sailing and island cruising is adventure. There are few bodies of salt water that the Hiscocks have not sailed on and shown on many occasions that gales, adventures, and an occasional tight situation are merely incidents in a well-planned voyage. Nevertheless, despite long experience and the best precautions and care, accidents do happen even to the best.

During their last circumnavigation, *Wanderer* struck a shoal off the west coast of Croker Island about 150 miles northeast of Darwin, Australia. Unable to sail off or kedge off when the tide dropped, *Wanderer* lay at an angle of 55 degrees. Pumping the tanks and shifting as much weight as possible, they anxiously awaited the next high tide, which lifted but failed to float *Wanderer* by inches.

Fearing another tide would break up their little ship, they rowed ashore thinking they might never see her again. Making their way across the island to the mission station, they were given encouragement and help by the capable Australians in charge. The superintendent made radio contact at once with the mission ship, which happened fortunately to be nearby. At high tide in the early morning hours of the next day, *Wanderer* was dragged off the reef in the cold light of the moon with the help of the captain of the mission ship *Larrpan*, aided by sixteen aborigines, two schoolteachers, and the Australians who run the mission.

From Darwin, *Wanderer* sailed to Christmas Island, making the 1,512-mile passage in the good time of twelve days and six hours. The next 534 miles to Cocos-Keeling was made in four days and two hours, and the long passage to the Seychelles in twenty-six days. From Aden they took the Red Sea route to the Mediterranean. After many stops in the Balearics and along the coast of Spain, they sailed through the Strait of Gibraltar and on to Studland Bay and Yarmouth.

Wanderer's 600 square feet of sail, with mainsail and genoa set, give her a good speed under fair conditions, and in the trade winds her twin spinnakers (125 square feet each) have given her many of her best days and highest speeds. However, Eric points out that *Wanderer's* twins were used only 38 out of 400 days of ocean cruising, because more often than not the wind was too far out on the quarter or on the beam for her self-steering rig to work. At the other extreme she has run for days at a time under bare poles, had stretches of more than a week of high seas with never a glimpse of sun or stars, and at times has had to lay ahull.

A Laurent Giles design, *Wanderer* has probably visited more places and logged more blue-water miles than any other small yacht of her size. Her best day's run on her first circumnavigation was 157 sea miles, and 169 on her second time around. Eric readily admits that greater beam would have made *Wanderer* more comfortable and longer overhangs more suited to his purpose, but in 1952 when she was built at the fine yard of Messrs. William King of Burnham-on-Crouch the cost would have been more than they could then afford.

Though Eric and Susan admit to dreaming on occasion of a larger vessel, Eric said after 90,000 miles of deep-water cruising in *Wanderer III*, "We know of no yacht that satisfies us as well as our own little ship. To us she is a personality and we understand her."

The husky little double-ended Tahiti ketches designed by John G. Hannah that have been proving their ability on long voyages over the past quarter of a century were planned for simplicity, ease of handling, and cruising comfort. Well-balanced under full sail or almost any combination of sails, they have proven the designer's contention that they would sail well with the tiller lashed. Not meant for speed, though they have won a few tough races, including the Trans-Tasman Ocean Race, they were intended to take sea conditions that might prove disastrous to craft of less stability. Like Colin Archer of Narvik, Hannah felt and often pointed out that for offshore cruising a boat with a sharp stern, with bow and stem much alike, commonly called a double-ender, is the most seaworthy hull possible. Intended for the man with a limited income, early models cost $1,000 to $1,500 to build. The cost now is seven to ten times that, but the design remains popular. Among the many out cruising or at anchor in various parts of the world in 1966, Jean Gau's *Atom* and Tom and Janet Steele's *Adios* are fine examples of what can be done with Tahiti ketches when handled by able and efficient circumnavigators.

Adios

Early in 1964, when the Blue Water Medal for outstanding amateur seamanship was presented to Tom Steele of the 32-foot Tahiti ketch *Adios* for two voyages around the world, the award was made in strife-torn Panama where Tom and Janet, his wife, after almost six years of steady cruising, were anchored and living aboard at Balboa while Tom ran an electric canal mule for a short while to replenish the ship's strongbox.

On *Adios's* first circumnavigation, while attempting to round South Africa's "Cape of Storms," Tom and Ray Cruickshank, his inexperienced companion at that time, were rolled completely over in what Cape Town and Durban papers called the worst storm in years.

Between Durban and Port Elizabeth, where the hundred-fathom line of the continental shelf lies ten to little more than twenty miles from shore, the

Adios at Moorea.

current runs from fifty to a hundred miles a day, paradoxically obtaining its greatest strength when the wind is opposed to it. A few days out of Durban en route to Cape Town, *Adios*, knocked on her beam-ends in a confused sea, lost her pram and had her main boom splintered. Two days later, trying to make Port Elizabeth, they were caught in an eighty-mile-an-hour southeaster. Blowing at right angles to the current in the relatively shallow coastal depths, the wind raised mountainous seas that appeared to be coming from all quarters. After thirty freezing hours at the tiller without food or relief, Tom, nearly exhausted, turned the tiller over to Ray and went below to attempt a pot of tea. The water was boiling when *Adios* went on her beam-ends and a moment later was flung completely over. Hot water, mattresses, and bunk boards flew through the air to the starboard side of the cabin as *Adios* righted again. Opening the hatch, Tom found the mizzenmast and sail gone and the mizzen shrouds holding Cruickshank bound to the deck. The rudder was gone and the vessel lay broadside with the mizzen banging alongside, threatening to punch a hole in the hull. Cutting the lanyards from the shrouds and setting the mast adrift, Tom set a sea anchor out over the stern on a heavy wire cable secured to the stump of the mizzenmast. The wire cable soon parted, and *Adios* came close to rolling over again. A spare twenty-five-pound anchor was then shackled to 150 feet of 3-inch Manila line, and the heavy little ketch came around again stern to the sea as the line tautened out and the anchor lay near the surface astern. Still pooped by an occasional green sea, they were driven W.N.W. in the direction of a reef off Cape Recife, twenty miles out from shore.

Around midnight a change was felt in the motion of the sea. Looking out the hatch, Tom saw Cape Recife light less than two miles to starboard. The current had set *Adios* far enough south to just clear the reef and Cape Recife, and she now had sea room to the westward. On October 3, Tom managed to get the auxiliary to run, and *Adios* motored and sailed to an anchorage on the western shore of Plattenburg Bay 120 miles west of Port Elizabeth.

After Tom Steele completed his first circumnavigation, *Adios* acquired a permanent mate in Janet, Tom's attractive wife, and the little 12-ton ketch, bound north up the Red Sea, had a memorable meeting at Aden with the Hiscocks and *Wanderer III*, two well-proven 30-footers each making a second voyage around the world.

On arrival in port the Steeles look for a dock or spot where they can tie up alongside to disembark the motorcycle which is carried on one of the side decks and put to use for shopping and sightseeing. Wherever there is a supply of fresh water, a washing machine in *Adios's* forepeak is put to work. While at anchor off the Club Nautico at Algeciras, Spain, the Steeles made a land trip on their seagoing motorcycle to Malaga and Granada, the first time in over four years they had spent a night off the *Adios*.

During a long Atlantic passage from Spain via Las Palmas to Barbados they caught up on their sleep, owing to head winds, light winds, and sometimes no winds at all, and Janet was able to bake fresh loaves of bread in their pressure cooker "bake shop." From Barbados they cruised through the Grenadines to Grenada—anchoring off many green islands and cays, including lovely Bequia and Tobago, followed by other stops—and then had some fine sailing with the square sail up in the roar of the trades to Cartagena and on to Cristobal.

After a slow cruise up from Panama with stops at Golfito, Costa Rica, and Acapulco, Mexico, when *Adios* quietly slipped into San Diego in 1964 she had been away seven years, made good 55,472 sea miles, and visited 286 ports and anchorages. While planning their next cruise in *Adios*, the Steeles felt like foreigners trying to adjust to the amplitude of supermarkets and the somewhat hectic pace of an American urban center. "Strange," says Tom, "when you're always on the move you look forward to an anchorage, but once you have stopped you look forward to sailing again."

Atom

Jean Gau, the elusive and retiring French-born American single-hander who finished his first solo voyage around the world in *Atom* in 1957, left New York in 1962 for the Azores, en route to his homestead in the Midi, Valras-Plage, on the first leg of his second circumnavigation.

"Now alone again in the midst of this isolated ocean," Gau wrote in the North Atlantic, "I feel happy to have left behind the bustling civilization, happy to be free and my own master." One hundred days out of New York he arrived at Sète near Valras-Plage. After spending the winter in the Mediterranean, *Atom* sailed the old windjammer route from Madeira to the Antilles. Completing his sixth singlehanded crossing of the Atlantic, Gau arrived in San Juan, Puerto Rico, on September 12, 1963, sixty-two days from Funchal. At the end of the hurricane season he sailed to Panama and out from Balboa to the Galapagos and on to lonely Pitcairn. Finding it impossible to anchor in safety in Bounty Bay, Gau exchanged flag greetings with the hilltop radio station and headed west via the southern edge of the Tuamotus to Tahiti, where he arrived April 26, 1964—102 days from Panama.

In December, 1965, Jean Gau wrote from South Africa:

Here I am in Durban since November 6. I sailed from Thursday Island in Torres Strait in one stretch covering 7,000 nautical miles. It took me 113 days and was my longest stretch without stopping.

My most gruesome experience came a few months ago when I ran aground on a coral reef in Torres Strait at 5 A.M. I was high and dry and got out of my boat to walk along the reef. There I found parts of masts and spars with rusted iron rope and blocks still attached to them and tangled crazily in heaps of seaweed. It was an old wreck imbedded in the coral with skeletons on board. Human bones were spread all over. To think that my fate would probably be the same made it even more depressing. Luckily, after 19 hours in a critical situation, at high tide I was able to get my boat off the reef. Then I sailed across the Arafura and Timor Seas and the Indian Ocean to South Africa.

Early in 1966 the wiry Frenchman who safely rode out the 1957 hurricane that sank the German ship *Pamir* was capsized by a rogue sea in a hurricane off the wild southern coast of Africa 180 miles from Cape Town, with *Atom* losing both her masts, bowsprit, sails, and dinghy. Gau cut away the rigging and was able to make it in to Mossel Bay for repairs.

Here we have a classical deep-sea single-hander, a man who never married, who has been sailing for three decades, who does not take passengers or crew, shuns publicity, and is not interested in week-end sailing, racing, or establishing records. He has had adventures enough for any one lifetime, but they were not the kind that denote lack of experience. His departures and arrivals are made quietly. His preparations are thorough. Like anyone who has cruised for the largest part of a lifetime, Gau is proud of the little ship that has carried him on so many long passages. He is respectful of the might of the oceans and grateful to those who have helped.

"One must make a long sea voyage to realize the immensity and solitude of the sea," says this modest, capable single-hander, who has experienced its unbridled rage more times than he cares to recall.

A successful landfall is the small-boat sailor's greatest moment. As Jean Gau and Eric Hiscock both point out, it never stales no matter how often you do it. On completing his second world voyage, Jean Gau looks forward to retiring to Tahiti and making his future landfalls in the South Seas.

Marco Polo

Marco Polo, a Bermudian-rigged ketch 28-ft. LOA, 8-ft. beam, 4-ft. 6-in. draft, and one of the smallest to circumnavigate, has well earned a place in the records of small ships that have proven their worth in many seas.

Built and skippered by New Zealander Anthony Armit and crewed by Brian Loe, *Marco Polo* was sailed to Australia in 1955 and from there across the Indian Ocean to Durban. Like *Adios*, *Marco Polo* was hit by a black southeaster between Durban and Port Elizabeth and took a severe battering for nine days. After stops at St. Helena and Ascension Island, they sailed to Barbados and on to Miami, where skipper and crew went ashore to replenish the strongbox. Later they sailed to Panama, the Galapagos, and across the Pacific to New Zealand, becoming the first New Zealanders to circumnavigate.

Axel Petersen, a Danish immigrant to New Zealand who had dreamed of sailing his own small ship home to Copenhagen, bought *Marco Polo* and with only a few weeks' sailing experience set out from Auckland in the 1958 midwinter down under. Avoiding the well-worn sailing routes for the 7,500-mile voyage to San Francisco, *Marco Polo* had a hard passage up through the Roaring Forties, with rain, hail, and squalls most of the way to Rarotonga. West of Tahiti she "ran off under bare poles before a gale that blew up to 70 knots."

En route from Papeete to the Marquesas, the vessel struck a submerged reef in the Tuamotus on the south side of Arutua. By the time the sails were got in, *Marco Polo* had broached and was lying broadside on her bilge with the waves crashing over. "This is the end, my little ship is gone," thought Petersen. But after four days of back-breaking work, with the help of islanders, coconut logs, and an island trading schooner, *Marco Polo* was pulled free and towed to the village for temporary repairs to her cracked ribs and damaged planking. She then continued on to the Marquesas and from there sailed 3,000 miles to Hawaii, to be hauled out and have seventeen cracked frames repaired.

On the 2,300-mile passage from Honolulu to San Francisco, Axel pegged the tiller and the ketch sailed herself much of the way across the calms of the Pacific high. Cruising south, he spent Christmas at Catalina Island and from

Loner Axel Petersen aboard *Marco Polo* at Sausalito, California.

San Diego sailed to Panama, with stops at Acapulco, Mexico, and Golfito, Costa Rica. From Jamaica Axel sailed singlehanded direct for England, weathered the near center of Hurricane Cleo one thousand miles west of Lands End, "the worst storm I ever met," and arrived at Plymouth sixty-eight days from Kingston. From England, *Marco Polo* sailed to Belgium, Holland, and home to Denmark.

After a notable voyage from England to Seydisfjördur in eastern Iceland, to climb a couple of mountains and sail down the west coast of Scotland to Stornoway and back to Plymouth with Dr. David Lewis in the catamaran *Rehu Moana*, Axel Petersen returned again to Denmark and began preparations to enter the 1964 Singlehanded Transatlantic Race.

On May 6, 1964, *Marco Polo* sailed from Copenhagen up through the Hunfjord and departed Thyboron direct for Plymouth, arriving at that port on May 23, a bare half hour before the start of the race. The ketch was put on the ways for some work and a coat of antifouling, and Axel Petersen sailed May 26, three days after the race began, for the long haul across the Western Ocean to Newport, Rhode Island. Setting out for a northerly route, *Marco Polo* encountered fourteen days of succeeding gales, and Axel set a course farther south toward the Azores, where he found no wind at all for many days. Between longitude 50 and 60 degrees west, better winds were encountered. Hoping and planning to hit the Labrador Current south of Halifax, he crossed the Gulf Stream and ran into thick fog off Nova Scotia.

Last to arrive off Newport's Brenton Reef Light Tower, *Marco Polo* sailed into Brenton Cove on July 26, 1964, and at 6 P.M. dropped anchor off the Ada Lewis Yacht Club—sixty-two days from Melampus Buoy, Plymouth.

"So many things can happen at sea," said Axel.

Temptress and *Sea Wanderer*

Edward C. Allcard, the English single-hander who gave up a career as a naval architect and marine surveyor to cross the Atlantic a half-dozen times and cruise many coasts, is by now the dean of that small handful of solo sailors who have been making major ocean passages in small vessels for more than a decade. Whether they sail a Swedish or Norwegian double-ender, a stainless-steel yawl, or a Vertue, all seem to have something from the days when sea questing was central to man's survival.

In 1947, Allcard was out single-handing in the 20-ton cutter *Content*. Finding her unsuited for his purpose, he acquired the *Temptress*, a short-ended, canoe-stern yawl rigged with gaff mainsail and a small jib-headed mizzen. Built in 1910 in Cornwall, her dimensions were 34-ft. LOA, with 10-ft. 2-in. beam and 6-ft. 3-in. draft. After cruising to La Coruña and Lisbon, Allcard, during a long layover at Gibraltar, hand-adzed a new 41-foot mast from a "Corsican pine" log shipped down from Hampshire in the south of England.

Sailing the route that Alain Gerbault had taken, *Temptress* made the crossing from Gibraltar to New York in eighty days. On the return voyage from America, Allcard was delayed by circumstances from starting until well into the hurricane season and encountered severe gales that carried away his mizzenmast, broke the main boom, fractured two of the skipper's ribs, and forced him to put into Horta sixty-four days after departing Long Island, N.Y.

Following his return to England with *Temptress* in 1951, Allcard set out in the cutter *Catania* with Norman Fowler early in 1952 to take delivery of *Sea Wanderer*, which he bought in the United States, sailed to the Bahamas, and from there had an austere, seventy-six-day passage to England. A Bermudian-rigged ketch built in 1911 at Lubeck on the shores of the Baltic, *Sea Wanderer* is 36-ft. LOA and 30-ft. LW, with 11-ft. beam and 5-ft. 4-in. draft, and a 16-horsepower Lister diesel auxiliary. After spending some time in Europe and the Mediterranean, Allcard made another Atlantic crossing in *Sea Wanderer*. Sailing from Las Palmas November 20, 1957, the same time as Peter Tangvald in *Windflower*, he made English Harbor, Antigua, in thirty-three days, two days after the arrival of Tangvald's 45-foot yawl. For the following four years, *Sea Wanderer* sailed and cruised on charter to islands and anchorages of the Windward and Leeward Islands.

Unresponsive to what yachting advertisements call progress, Edward Allcard values simple living, liberty of choice, and freedom from adherence to a pattern as highly as did the late Christopher de Grabowski. "Sailing for me is practically a religion," says Allcard, who knows very well that the satisfaction he gets out of solo cruising cannot be measured by standards commonly applied. When necessary he has lived happily enough (rice and Scotch oats) on fifty cents a day. (Thoreau, John Muir, Slocum, and other loners have lived at times on much less than that.)

Tiring of noisy tourists, water skiers, and the increasing roar of outboard motors, and haunted by the spirit of adventure, Allcard departed Antigua November 29, 1961, to sail around the world via Cape Horn. On March 9, 1962, *Sea Wanderer* arrived off La Paloma at the entrance to the Mar del Plata one hundred days nonstop from the Leeward Islands. Dividing his time between charter work in the Rio-Uruguay and refitting *Sea Wanderer* for future passages, the competent loner, who dislikes modern coach roofs and chrome fittings, wrote from Montevideo: "Beware of 'yachty' fittings—strive for simplicity. I am weeding out all the 'yachty' junk and putting on gear which works, but would not look pretty at the Boat Show. Also tearing out the cockpit completely before I continue for Tierra del Fuego. To Hell with comfort; it's greater fun to stay afloat."

Dorothea I

Dorothea I, a 32-foot cutter with no motor, no electricity, no transmitter, no winches, no cockpit, no head, no skin fittings—a true wanderer with no home port (Peter Tangvald always listed her home as the Seven Seas)—completed a five-year voyage around the world at Brixham, England in 1964.°

Copper fastened and heavily built in 1934 of teak, pitch pine, and ironwood, *Dorothea I* is 32-ft. LOA, 30-ft. LW, 9-ft. 8-in. beam, 5-ft. 10-in. draft, Bermudian rigged with 660 square feet of canvas. With confidence born of years of reliance on sails alone, Peter Tangvald, who differs sharply from many current views, generally sails "when I please and not necessarily when the season is at its best," placing his reliance on sound gear, adequate ground tackle, and a thorough knowledge of his boat under all conditions.

Sailing from Falmouth, England, in 1959, *Dorothea I* made a twenty-nine-day passage from Las Palmas to Antigua. After some months of cruising in the Caribbean, *Dorothea I* sailed from Martinique to Panama, went on to the Galapagos, and arrived at Tahiti in March, 1961. After five months in French Polynesian waters, Tangvald made a twenty-eight-day singlehanded passage to Honolulu, where *Dorothea I* was redecked with two layers of laminated plywood and fiberglass. Also her mast was moved aft eighteen inches and rerigged from sloop to cutter to increase the fore triangle.

Scheduled to leave for San Francisco, Peter found himself irresistibly drawn to Papeete and one morning with a "Tahiti wind" blowing from the west abruptly decided to sail back. Before anything could change his mind, he provisioned at once and sailed that same day at 1600. The seductive west wind lasted only a few hours and his new rig was given a more than adequate test by a violent east trade wind. Close-hauled on a single tack he made Moorea singlehanded in twenty-four days. After several months in Tahiti, his petite mate Simonne arrived back from Martinique and they sailed for Europe via the New Hebrides and New Guinea, where Peter recoppered and refastened *Dorothea's* bottom and at the same time threw the head overboard to prevent electrolysis. From Darwin they made Christmas. After much illness in Red Sea ports, they were glad to get to Rhodes and on to the Greek Islands, the Riviera, and Cannes.

Tangvald firmly believes that a good sailor can sail anywhere in the world without an engine. Convinced that the advantages of auxiliary motors and the disadvantages of not having them are overstated, he backs up his opinion by numerous facts and points out that the expenses of a good auxiliary, fuel tanks, and incidentals can pay for more than a year of cruising for the deep-water man short of funds. Perhaps his most convincing argument: engineless *Dorothea I* had a daily average on her round-the-world voyage of well over one hundred miles a day, for five years got safely in and out of the many ports he desired to visit, cruised through the difficult Tuamotus and the dangerous archipelagos of Southeast Papua, and never once missed a tack in 40,000 miles, part of which was sailed solo.

° Peter Tangvald's *Sea Gypsy*, one of the best cruising accounts published in 1966, tells of this voyage.

An original and a competent individual, Peter Tangvald is as good an example as Slocum of the innate independence of the devoted small-ship sailor.

In summation, Tangvald feels that vessels with auxiliaries and "pure sailing boats" are two different things, appealing to different types of people with different tastes and training. The fact that boats with auxiliaries are more popular in this push-button age doesn't mean that sailing boats without motors are unsafe. The only lack of safety—if there is lack of safety—as Tangvald sees it is a skipper's lack of skill in handling an all-out sailing vessel. It has been proven more than once that a skipper with the finest auxiliary engine and all the electronic equipment and other gear his small boat could carry has got into more trouble on a voyage around the world than the sailor equipped mainly with seasoned seamanly know-how. Dr. Peter Pye of *Moon-raker,* who met many American ocean-cruising boats and was surprised at the number of those with large engines and small sail plans, commented, "We are filled with admiration at their putting to sea with little but their engines to rely on."

Peter Tangvald much prefers small boats.

All my crossings have been done much faster in my 11-ton *Dorothea I* than in my 21-ton *Windflower* [a 45-ft.-LOA gaff yawl he sailed singlehanded from England to Los Angeles]. While the maximum speeds of larger boats are obviously higher than that of the smaller ones, they do not necessarily reach port faster. The smaller one will go faster in light airs, and unless there is a large crew on the big ship she will generally be under much shorter canvas than the little one, which is so much easier to handle.

Peter Tangvald was stricken with a severe heart condition at Cannes, France, spent six months in a hospital in 1965, and was scheduled by doctors for one full year in a "maison de repos" to convalesce when he decided instead to get back to his boat and some sunshine and sea wind. On August 4, though still so weak he could stand on his feet only a few minutes at a time, with the help of Simonne, mooring lines were cast off, sails hoisted, and *Dorothea* left Cannes under easy canvas bound for Spain.

By heaving to at night so that Peter could regain his strength, and with the help of sailors at ports along the coast of Spain, who hoisted the anchor for them when they were ready to leave, they reached Gibraltar, where, as Peter put it, he felt "strong enough to get married." From the Canaries they crossed to South America, with Peter slowly regaining much of his former strength during the passage.

"Had I listened to all the people who advised me to remain ashore," he wrote in a letter to his friends, "I would still be in the same dreary office, which I left against the advice of everyone many years ago. The heart is a tricky organ and I have dragged this infection too long to expect my heart not to have permanent damage. But even with limited activities, life can be very pleasant."

In the course of her circumnavigation *Dorothea* had well proved her worth on countless passages, but during those years Peter had, little by little, designed a dream ship based on his lifetime of experience. After checking with boatyards all over the world he decided to build *Dorothea II*—a modified Atkin design—at the mouth of a river in French Guiana with the help of Simonne. Without touching the original *Dorothea* lines he has added a clipper bow to balance off a low castle where the helmsman can steer and trim sheets in cold weather. Her rig, designed as a gaff cutter, is set up with deadeyes and lanyards. "She does not have the usual snug rig but on the contrary spreads a huge amount of sail like all sailboats should do when not equipped with motors. I am not installing electricity, heads, winches, or other gadgets."

A former loner, an original, and a competent individual, Tangvald is as good an example as Slocum of the innate independence of the devoted small-ship sailor.

Kurun

One of the best of the round-the-world voyagers, Jacques-Yves Le Toumelin, a sailor who always took time to help others and who circumnavigated in the traditional gaff cutter *Kurun* (33-ft. LOA, 11-ft. 8-in. beam, 5-ft. 2-in. draft), felt the same as Peter Tangvald about auxiliary power and said, "*Kurun* is a pure sailor, and I would have considered it a sacrilege to have allowed an engine within her beautiful oaken hull, even if I could afford to. It is hard to become a true sailor if you get into the habit of using a motor."

Today many fiberglass hulls are retaining old rigs, and there are still many in the Pacific and on both sides of the Atlantic who prefer traditional designs. This is seen on Dutch waterways and in the sailing and racing of thoroughbreds with classic proportions in Britain on the Blackwater, Medway, Clyde, and Solent, and in the Bristol Channel.

Replicas of old-style working craft with broad sterns, decorated taffrails, bowsprits, and gaff mainsails are being built in several parts of the world. Small Nova Scotia schooners have been completed recently; also Maine Friendship sloops, sharpies, Block Islanders, and, in Britain, luggers, unpretentious gaff cutters, and others. On the Eastern Shore of Maryland, neat little Chesapeake skipjack schooners with clipper bow and hand-carved trail boards are being turned out by hand in a few small boatyards. Except for minor changes, they still retain a solid, hefty 12-foot beam on a 34-foot-LOA hull and the distinctive raked masts of their hard-working ancestors. Some are used for pleasure, and a few still work the oyster bars. In Japan and Hawaii, several types of traditional sampans for fishing are constructed that are little different from those of a quarter-century ago, and in China ocean junks are hand-crafted much the same as they were fifty years ago. Many of the more colorful and less practical models are exported from Hong Kong to yachting centers around the world. In Holland, the cradle of yachting, a country where every town can be reached by boat, many original Dutch sailing craft—hoogars, batterjacts, tjalks, boeirs, and others—are built, and an annual sail meet is held by owners of such craft.

Honest shipwrights, sparmakers, and joiners who know the hand woodworker's art are still around, but their numbers are diminishing with the increasing number of mass-produced fiberglass and metal hulls coming down the assembly lines. Though the plastic and metal boat salesmen point out that wood just won't last, there are mighty fine examples around to the contrary. Some men still hew and adze their own stem and keel, steam-bend their own frames, splice all their rigging, cut and sew their own sails, and do a good enough job to circumnavigate or make major ocean voyages. But such individuals are rare.

Skipper L. H. Roberts of Nelson Island, British Columbia, a man well past seventy with sixty years' experience in Northwest Pacific waters and three previous cruising vessels to his credit, completed his ketch *Chack Chack*

III in 1964 on the shores of Cape Cockburn, sixty miles up the coast from Vancouver. Designed for permanent cruising for skipper Roberts and his wife Marjorie, *Chack Chack III* (Chinook for bald-headed eagle) is 40-ft. LOA, with 10-ft. 6-in. beam, and took six years to build. A confirmed do-it-yourselfer with a fine disregard for what others think, Roberts designed his own plans, made the lumber by hand at his own simple saw mill, forged his own ironwork, and made his own sails by hand, aided by his wife on a treadle. Preferring to work alone, he ripsawed the long one-and-a-quarter-inch cedar hull planks by hand from a red cedar log of sixty rings to the inch—a tree two thousand years old.

Viator, a 32-ft.-LOA, 10-ft.-beam, 6-ft.-draft schooner hand-built in two and a half years by Harry Close and handsomely maintained and sailed by him for thirty-two years, returned to the California coast late in October, 1964, from another of her many long Pacific voyages. Rigged with Bermudian main and gaff foresail, *Viator* made the passage from Papeete, Tahiti, nonstop to San Francisco in forty-five days.

Te Matangi, a 35-ft.-LOA Block Island ketch built in Nevada, hauled two hundred miles overland, and launched at Sacramento, California, in 1955, has been out sailing the Pacific for ten years. Builder-owner-skipper Jack Ferguson and his wife Daisy have cruised extensively among the islands of Hawaii, French Polynesia, Cooks, Tongas, Fijis, Lord Howe, New Zealand, and Australia. They departed Queensland via the Barrier Reef to cruise in the South Pacific until some future date, when they will return to San Diego, California, to make new plans for future sailing.

Aegean, an Atkin-designed double-ended ketch 37½-ft. LOA, 11½-ft. beam, 5½-ft. draft, took Dale and Betty Nordlund two and a half years to build near the north end of Vancouver Island, British Columbia. Sailing from Vancouver in August, 1962, the *Aegean* made stops at San Diego and Ensenada before crossing to the Marquesas in thirty-one days. After visiting many island groups, the Nordlunds with their two daughters Jule and Shelley sailed to Brisbane. During nine months on the Australian coast they waited out the cyclone season at Maryborough, left Brisbane at Christmas, cruised north with many stops and a few adventures along the Barrier Reef, and sailing out Cook's Pass, north of Cooktown, ran straight across the Coral Sea to Port Moresby. From New Guinea, *Aegean* cruised to the Orient and from Japan made a forty-five-day North Pacific passage home to Vancouver.

Others, like Allen and Sharon Farrell of Pandor Harbor, who took 20,-000 hours to build their 44-foot ketch *Ocean Girl* while clamming and salmon fishing for a living, selected and sawed their own logs, beachcombed for natural crooks, and did all their own work by hand. Believing that the way to get a perfect boat is to build one, sail it awhile, then build another, the Farrells, after several years of chartering *Ocean Girl* in the West Indies, went back to Victoria, B.C., to complete a new 39-ft.-LOA, 10-ft. 2-in. beam

Harry Close's 32-ft. LOA schooner *Viator*.

double-ender with a small hold, a live well for codfishing amidships, living quarters forward, engine, and a small stern cabin aft.

D'Vara

The 30-foot-LOA canoe-stern, main-trysail-rig ketch *D'Vara* from Fremantle, Australia, built there in two and a half years by Blue and Dot Bradfield to a Harrison-Butler design, began cruising in 1958 to out-of-the-way ports and anchorages around the world.

Beautifully built, the 7-ton *D'Vara* with red sails and white masts has evoked admiration in Mediterranean and European ports, and her unusual rig has aroused keen interest among sailors and fishermen. Under a main-trysail rig designed by Frederic Fenger, *D'Vara*, according to Blue Bradfield, "maneuvers well and is so balanced that she will sail to windward with the tiller free."

Taking a tack from old shipmasters, who reduced yaw when close-hauled by bracing their yards less sharply on the mainmast than on the fore and less sharply on the mizzen than on the main, the Bradfields made *D'Vara* self-steering on all courses, from close-hauled to directly downwind, by trimming her 104-square-foot weather twin so that a reverse flow from leech to luff canceled out the rounding-to effect of her after sails. The spinnaker sheet is led through a quarter block and attached to the tiller, with the pull of the sheet counteracted by shock cord.

With only an occasional adjusting of shock cord by the Bradfields, *D'Vara* sailed herself most of the way across the Indian Ocean, averaging over one hundred miles a day in winds of varying strength and direction.

Departing Vigo in late June, 1964, the Bradfields gunkholed slowly down the Portuguese coast, calling at Viana do Castélo, Lexioes, and Belem, the yacht harbor for Lisbon; *D'Vara* made the 540 miles to Madeira in four and a half days, with the steering sail doing the work. From Funchal they sailed to Las Palmas and on to the Cape Verdes for a month among those seldom-visited islands, before heading west to Antigua in the West Indies.

Typical of the older seafarers sailing small ships that have cut a lot of salt water in the past few years is Buck Taylor from Seattle, a Navy veteran who said that "sticking around home is not for me." Buck, sixty-two in 1966, and his wife, sixty-one, have been voyaging in the Pacific for the past several years with their 30-foot ketch *Koae*. Leaving Suva, Fiji, September 14, 1963, they cruised to Auckland and on to Russell in the Bay of Islands, then across the Tasman Sea to Brisbane, Mackay, and Townsville. Mid-April, after the cyclone season, they sailed to Cairns and arrived in Port Moresby with John Burgess as crew. Buck and his wife, who state bluntly that "a retired couple are better off dead than sitting in a rocking chair watching television," sailed from Port Moresby bound for Indonesia, India, the Mediterranean, the Carribbean, Panama, and the west coasts of Central America and Mexico.

Seventy-two-year-old John Goetzcke, who sails solo much of the time, is a one-time windjammer sailor and businessman who sold his property to buy the 32-foot-LOA ketch *Valkyrie* of Charlotte Amalie, Virgin Islands. John cruised the eastern seaboard, Gulf of Mexico, the Caribbean, and sailed from Panama to Hawaii, where he arrived in April, 1963. Aften ten years' cruising in the Atlantic, Caribbean, South Seas, and the Southwest Pacific, John left Brisbane in 1965 at the end of the hurricane season for New Guinea and the Philippines. Crossing the South China Sea from Manila to Malaya, he was held by pirates at Pilau Linang for thirty-nine days but arrived safely at Singapore, unharmed except for loss of $300, and headed west across the Indian Ocean to Durban, where he arrived late in 1966 on a ten-year round-the-world voyage.

Sixty-two-year-old Frank Casper cruised in the Mediterranean and made two singlehanded crossings of the Atlantic in 1961 and 1962 in his 29-ft. 6-in.-LOA Bermudian cutter *Elsie* (ex-*Liberia IV*). Deciding to spend his senior years by sailing leisurely around the world, Casper departed Melbourne Beach, Florida, in December, 1963. On arrival at Tahiti via Panama, *Elsie* remained two months for repairs before sailing to Bora Bora and Rarotonga. She called at Pago Pago after visiting the Cook Islands and departed for Auckland, New Zealand, late in 1964 en route to Timor and the Indian Ocean. A former engineer who prefers ocean cruising to any other way of life, loner Casper left South Africa for the West Indies early in 1966 en route to the United States.

As coastal bays, anchorages, and inland waterways around the world become more and more overcrowded, sailing a small boat offshore—whether a modern Vertue, Bermuda-40, Chinese junk, Red Sea dhow, bugeye, billyboy, or an Irish hooker from County Galway—is still one of the few measures of independence available to twentieth-century mid-sixties man.

Never before has there been such a variety of designs and such a wide group of specialized small craft, from cup defenders to circumnavigating cockleshells. The variance in types and individual vessels that have completed sea passages of ten to fifty thousand miles is equally broad, and some are as different from the conventional as those who sail them. Since 1960 hundreds of transocean passages have been made in everything from a converted Falmouth quay punt rigged as a gaff yawl, a French pilot ketch from Brittany, a 60-year-old lapstrake-planked, trunnel-fastened, double-ended Swedish trading cutter, a Tollesbury smack, catboats, Noank sloops, and other hallowed hulls and rigs to modern fiberglass Seawind ketches, Folkboats, and Dutch-built Northeast-38's. A few small ships are out making voyages that even in this day are extraordinary. In 1966 one was in the Strait of Magellan with a mountain climbing mate and skipper, three were exploring Arctic waters, and four were rounding Cape Horn.

Mischief

The gaff-rigged Bristol Channel pilot cutter *Mischief,* 45-ft. LOA, 13-ft. beam, 7-ft. 6-in. draft, built at Cardiff in 1906, is one of the oldest small vessels to make remarkable annual passages. Since 1954, sailor-mountaineer Major H. W. (Bill) Tilman, who combines sailing with climbing because he likes both and refuses to give up either, has sailed *Mischief* over a hundred thousand miles. Generally avoiding the trade-wind ports where "one might get bogged down and lose one's crew," he has cruised widely in both hemispheres from the Southern Ocean to Arctic days and nights among pack ice, fog, and icebergs, beating up fjords to climb unscaled peaks.

In 1955–56 *Mischief* logged 20,000 sea miles. Departing England June 26, 1955, she called at Montevideo, went on through the Strait of Magellan to Punta Arenas, where she arrived November 9, and proceeded to an anchorage in Peel Inlet for three weeks while her skipper and friends climbed the unexplored Patagonian icecap. From Tierra del Fuego they cruised the South American coasts to Valparaiso, Callao, Panama, Bermuda, and back to Lymington on July 10, 1956. The following year, 1957–58, 21,000 miles was logged to Las Palmas, Cape Town, Comoro Islands, Aldabra, Aden, Malta, and home again to Lymington. The next year it was Cape Town again and from the African coast to the remote Crozet and Kerguelen islands in the Indian Ocean, then to St. Helena, and home to England with another 20,000 miles under the counter.

In 1961 *Mischief* sailed to Belfast, Ireland, and from there nonstop to Godthaab, West Greenland, in forty days, and north to Umanak Fjord and other anchorages inside the Arctic Circle, where Tilman scaled unclimbed mountain peaks before returning to England. Again crossing the North Atlantic in 1962, she made landfall on Cape Farewell and sailed up the Greenland coast, dodging the ice floes of Julianehaab Bight. From Godthaab she went north to Evighedsfjord in north latitude 65° 50' and on to an anchorage beneath the 6,995-foot icy peaks of Agssaussat. Tilman and a friend climbed to the top of Agssaussat and several other glacier tops before sailing on to Kangamiut, a rocky, hillside town of three hundred Greenland fishermen, and on through much fog, rafts of pack ice, and south-flowing icebergs of the Labrador Current to Exeter Sound on the desolate east coast of Baffin Island just inside the Arctic Circle. Nineteen-sixty-three saw *Mischief* sailing northern waters once more—this time to Baffin Bay in the Arctic Circle. While anchored off Upernivik glacier, Tilman and friends scaled its summit peaks before departing for Lancaster Sound, Bylot Island, Godthaab, and back to England. In 1964 *Mischief's* first stop after departing Lymington River and the Needles was Reykjavik, Iceland, where she waited for the ice to break up before sailing to Angmagssalik, where she was caught in ice floes and damaged several planks. In 1966 the mountaineer-skipper took the cutter that had logged 90,000 miles under his command on a South Atlantic crossing to Montevideo and the South Falkland Islands.

In his quest for remote mountains reached by sea in a small boat, seasoned sailor Bill Tilman has a distinct preference for desolate places. The three geographical features that have been named by Canada and France after his rugged little pilot cutter—Mount Mischief in the Northern Hemisphere near the pole; Cap Mischief and Mont du Mischief in the Southern Ocean—are a well-earned part of her long career.

As long as compass needles point north there will always be men who scorn "tin masts" and prefer the feel underfoot of a wood deck, and there will always be character boats with lots of right sheer. Of eighty-one small vessels ranging in size from 18 feet to 45 feet LOA that had made notable ocean passages or were circumnavigating in 1966, only thirty-nine were of modern design and rig.

When "sailors" in space suits land on the moon, the lug sail, the lateen, and the gaff will still be out sailing the salt waters of the globe, and among them will be Vertues, gaff cutters, and Tahiti ketches with baggy wrinkle.

CHAPTER 5

Midget Ocean Voyagers

*There was room to lie and sleep, and room to sit . . . what more does
any man want?*

—ARTHUR RANSOME

*I have sailed my own vessels, from the tiniest up to seventy-tonners,
upon many seas; but have got the most delight out of a little yawl
(5 tons) with which I cruised for thousands of miles along the shores
of several European countries, visiting remote islets, fishing havens,
shallow straits, and windy fiords, inaccessible to larger yachts.*

—E. F. KNIGHT

IN THIS day of miniatures and compact cars, boats are no exception. And now
that the urge to go sailing has increased beyond anything envisioned by
Thomas Fleming Day, trends toward smaller hulls have produced many
classes of midget ocean craft less than 26 feet overall.

Good seamanship, hard experience acquired in the making of long and
sometimes difficult passages, and soundly established principles have evolved
a breed of very small craft designed to go anywhere. Class boats such as the
Vertues, Folkboats, and individual miniature cruisers like *Nova Espero*
(20-ft. LOA), *Sopranino* (19-ft. 8-in. LOA), *Trekka* (20-ft. 6-in. LOA), and
others have performed well at sea, taken anything they met in the way of
weather, and safely completed many long ocean passages.

Today's difficult crossing by a seasoned single-hander in a sailboat 19 to 25 feet overall that may seem to the landsman a "damn fool stunt" is usually a carefully planned and well executed job of precision sailing. The Atlantic, Las Palmas to the Caribbean, is frequently crossed, and presently two midget cruisers are in the Indian Ocean, several are crossing the Pacific, and five are bound around the world.

Only a few years ago, light-displacement craft 19 to 25 feet overall were considered unsuited for transocean cruising. Competent modern sailors, including Patrick Ellam and Colin Mudie, Stanley Smith, Charles Violet, John Guzzwell, H. G. Hasler, Captain John Illingworth, that keen champion of midget ocean racers, and others, have had much to do with changing such thinking.

Thomas Fleming Day, the crusading editor who initiated the Bermuda Race in 1906 and made his fine 1911 passage in his gaff yawl *Sea Bird* (26-ft. 3-in. LOA, 8-ft. 6-in. beam) from Providence, Rhode Island, to Gibraltar, driving hard all the way to Horta, averaging 101 miles daily with a best day's run of 163 miles, spoke out scornfully against officials in the hallowed halls of yachting who belittle ocean cruising in small vessels.

"What do those miserable hulks who spend their days swigging booze on the front stoop of a clubhouse know about the dangers of the deep?" asked Day, two years before the first Bermuda Race. "If they ever make a voyage in a ten-knot breeze it is the event of their lives. . . . What does the average yachtsman know about sea sailing? Absolutely nothing!"

The early voyages were far more than outstanding feats of endurance. John Buckley, Thomas Crapo, Frederick Norman, William Andrews, Josiah Lawlor, and a few others who sailed midget vessels across the Western Ocean before the turn of the century were fine sailormen.

Red, White & Blue

One of the first west-to-east North Atlantic crossings in a small boat was made over a century ago by the all-metal *Red, White & Blue* (26-ft. LOA, 6-ft. 1-in. beam, 3-ft. depth). A full-rigged three-masted little ship with clipper bow, bowsprit, jib boom, and martingale, *Red, White & Blue* was square-rigged on each mast and had a 10-foot main yard and a total of twenty-two sails, including stunsails, flying jib, topgallants, and royals.

Skippered by William Hudson with Frank Fitch as crew, *Red, White & Blue* sailed from New York July 9, 1866, was sighted by the schooner *Pequonneck* of Bridgeport while hove to in a heavy sea, later spoke the bark *Danish Princess*, and arrived off the English Channel on August 14. This thirty-five-day passage with an average of 85 miles per day was very good, considering the unsuitable rig and the fact that she was riding to a sea anchor part of the time.

City of Ragusa

The tiny yawl *City of Ragusa*, a lifeboat converted and decked over by her owner John Buckley, an American, and Pietro de Costa, an Austrian, departed Liverpool June 3, 1870, intent on sailing the tough northerly route across the Atlantic from east to west. They put in at Cork, Ireland, sailed from there on June 17, and soon found that sailing against the prevailing westerly winds with a 20-foot-LOA hull, broad-beamed, with no real keel, and yawl rigged with jib boom, three headsails, square sail, and a topsail over the main, was slow, hard work.

Between July 28 and September 1 a number of ships were spoken, and Buckley was given supplies by several. On September 4 the *City of Ragusa* was hove to in a "fearful gale" under a few feet of canvas (storm staysail). Following is a brief excerpt from the skipper's log:

11 PM: Gale still increasing with frightful heavy sea, the glass still falling, being now at 29.20.

12 Midnight: Blowing a furious gale. I assert, and am not ashamed to do so, that I felt for the first time fearful that our last moment had come, and that the next wave would be our destruction.

But the little yawl rode it out and two days later spoke the schooner *Emma L. Rich*, who reported her boat had been swept over and lost in the same gale. On September 9, 1870, they were met off Boston by a government tug and on arrival in port received the reception they well deserved as the first to sail a midget vessel from Europe to the United States. Superb seamanship, endurance, and courage, rather than the right hull and rig, can be credited for this outstanding eighty-four-day passage.

New Bedford

The year after Alfred Johnson's solo crossing in his 20-foot dory *Centennial*, described in Chapter 3, Thomas Crapo, an experienced seaman, designed *New Bedford*, a little 19-ft. 7-in. LOA, 6-ft. 2-in. beam, schooner-rigged Bermudian dory that was built at Fish Island near New Bedford. With his wife Joanna aboard, Crapo departed Chatham, Massachusetts, for a fifty-one-day gale-swept 2,815-mile passage across the Atlantic to Newlyn, Cornwall, where they arrived July 21, 1877. (Crapo was lost in 1899 attempting a passage from Newport to Cuba in the 9-foot boat *Volunteer*.)

Nautilus

The Andrews brothers, anxious to beat Thomas Crapo's record, sailed from Boston June 7, 1879, in *Nautilus*, a 19-ft. LOA, 6-ft. 7-in. beam, 2-ft. 3-in.-depth vessel completely decked over except for hatches amidships and

The *City of Ragusa* (the windmill, originally intended for becalmed areas, was discarded later for hand power).

aft. Lateen rigged, with a yard longer than her overall hull set on a short unstayed mast, *Nautilus* made a forty-six-day passage to the Scilly Islands.

Little Western

Thirty-six thousand people and several hundred small vessels assembled at Gloucester, Massachusetts, to see the departure of *Little Western*, a 16-ft.-LOA cutter with 6-ft. beam and 2-ft. 6-in. depth. Departing Gloucester on June 12, 1880, *Little Western*, sailed by Frederick Norman and George Thomas, made the 3,000-mile passage to Cowes in forty-six days, an achievement that received the salute of American warships off Gravesend.

The following year, on her return passage from London to Gloucester, *Little Western* was approximately seven hundred miles west of Bishop Rock when caught by a breaking sea and thrown on her beam-ends. Norman and Thomas were tossed overboard. When the cutter righted, both men managed to get back aboard and continue their passage. Several vessels were spoken, and on August 28 land was sighted. *Little Western* arrived at Halifax, Nova Scotia, September 2, 1881, one of the smallest boats to cross the Atlantic from east to west before the turn of the century.

Mermaid and *Sea Serpent*

Eighteen ninety-one stands out in the history of great voyages in midget vessels as the year of the first singlehanded transatlantic race, with William Andrews and Josiah "Si" Lawlor racing from Boston to England for the satisfaction of doing so with no prizes or trophies at stake.

After sixty-one days at sea, Andrews's 15-foot-LOA gaff sloop *Mermaid* capsized while laying to a sea anchor about six hundred miles from her destination. Andrews was able to right her after a long struggle but was picked up by the steamer *Ebruz* in an exhausted condition the following day.

Si Lawlor, driving hard in his spritsail-rigged 15-foot-LOA *Sea Serpent*, was thrown overside twice. On July 18, twenty-eight days out from Boston, *Sea Serpent* was running before a heavy sea when flung over on her beam-ends. Lawlor, heavily clothed with three coats and long heavy hip boots, was flung into the sea. Coming in on his life line, he had a hard struggle to get back aboard. The second time the little vessel went over she partly filled, and Lawlor had a long struggle out on the keel before she righted again. Despite this and much more he went on to arrive off Land's End forty-five days from Boston.

Sapolio

The following year the veteran William Andrews, sailing solo across the Atlantic in his 14-ft. 5-in. gaff sloop *Sapolio*, made a most remarkable passage from Atlantic City, New Jersey, to Spain in eighty-four days, the smallest boat to make the crossing.

Nova Espero

In 1949 Stanley and Colin Smith built the 20-ft.-LOA, 6-ft. 3-in. beam *Nova Espero* in the basement of a chapel in Halifax. Lacking funds to build a cabin, they securely lashed their 7-foot pram dinghy over the cockpit for

Little Western.

William Andrews arrives in Spain in the 14-ft. 5-in. LOA sloop *Sapolio*.

a cabin and sailed across the Atlantic from Nova Scotia to England in forty-four days. A one-tonner, sloop-rigged with a long fin keel and 800 pounds' outside ballast, *Nova Espero* would not lay easily to a sea anchor on her first voyage. In 1951, when Charles Violet and Stanley Smith were planning an east-to-west crossing in the little clinker-built vessel, alterations were made to the keel and she was given a small mizzenmast, a solid cabin, a sliding gunter lug mainsail, and other improvements.

Smith and Violet departed Dartmouth May 24, 1951, crossed the English Channel, encountered strong west and southwest winds off the French coast, and had a narrow escape weathering Ushant. A few days later, hove to in a rising gale, they wrote:

How miserable and small we felt, as we watched the seas climb higher and higher and heard the relentless whine of the wind in the rigging . . . we could hardly hear each other speak inside the cabin. As the day progressed the seas got bigger until, during the afternoon, they towered considerably higher than our mast. . . . *Nova Espero* is not much affected by such seas. It is the little ones on the big ones' backs that throw her.

Later, as they lay with the sea anchor streamed from the bow, the strain

147

on the rudder broke the blade loose on the stock, well underwater, where it couldn't be repaired at sea. A graphic description is given by Smith and Violet in their book *The Wind Calls the Tune*. Following is a brief excerpt:

> The wind seemed, if anything, to have increased and had backed a little to the south-west. The seas now tumbled more heavily and heaped up in stupendous confusion. When we looked out of the little portholes we saw only the blue sky above or a foaming valley stretching away below us, as we pitched for a moment across the backbone of some huge monster of a sea. . . . Suddenly in a weird hush, we heard a slight warning hiss high above the boat. The cabin darkened. . . . We remember only a fantastic roar and a stunning bang. Charles was hurled out of his bunk on the port side into the cabin roof opposite, together with the radio, loose clothing, cans and bedding.
> Everything went dark as night and water seemed to fill the cabin. We remember thinking only, "This must be the end," when we found ourselves in a heap in the starboard berth. A second later, with a loud sucking noise and another tremendous bang, we saw light again. We watched the water fall from the cabin roof drenching everything. We heard it swilling about heavily from side to side. The little boat had righted and resumed the old familiar dance on the surface of the sea.

A few hours after their knockdown by the freak wave that nearly turned them completely over, the wind moderated. A jury rudder was rigged, and *Nova Espero* got under way again for the Azores under jib, trysail, and mizzen.

Repairs were made at Horta. On July 3 they sailed from there and had a spell of easy weather followed by squalls, variable winds, and a succession of gales that were with them much of the way across.

Nova Espero's yawl rig proved a considerable improvement for balanced sailing and for lying to in heavy going. Aided by the mizzen, with helm lashed amidships, she rode well to a sea anchor, handled well under mizzen and foresail, and when the wind was forward of the beam sailed herself under mizzen and a full or reefed main. To save space and weight no fresh water was carried. Smith and Violet had arranged to test the Permutit salt-water conversion process during the crossing. A half hour daily was spent changing salt water into fresh water. Though expensive if they had had to pay for the chemicals used, the process worked very well and for two and a half months they drank desalted sea water and depended on it for their other needs.

After passing from the Gulf Stream into the Labrador Current, they spoke two vessels and spotted a white whale. On August 6 cod and sword-fishing boats were seen, land was sighted at 2 P.M., and by nightfall *Nova Espero* was moored to a buoy off Shelburne, Nova Scotia, thirty-three days from the Azores. A heavy crop of goose barnacles was removed with scrapers and wire brushes at Shelburne, the bottom was repainted with antifouling, and the little yawl sailed on to Buzzards Bay and City Island, New York.

Sopranino

"Two good dry bunks, two stoves, toilet, chart tables, plenty of stores. What more could any sailor want?" asked Patrick Ellam as his 19-ft. 8-in.-LOA sloop *Sopranino* slipped down the English Channel bound for Plymouth and the start of the Santander Race. Departing Plymouth Sound August 8, 1950, in driving rain and a hard blow from the southwest, *Sopranino* drove hard all that day and night for the French coast.

"For the next three days and nights we sailed straight on to the south, towards Spain," wrote Ellam, after they rounded Ushant at the western end of France. "It was a thrill to come up out of the tiny cabin in the middle of the night to find her racing across the seas."

An unofficial entry in the important Santander Race from Plymouth across the Channel, around Ushant, and on across the Bay of Biscay, tiny *Sopranino*, sailed hard by Patrick Ellam and Tony Needham, closed the Spanish coast in good time, rounded the headland into Santander with Red Ensign and quarantine flag showing, and stood across to the yacht anchorage. Arriving only a few hours after the last of the large official entries, she was given a resounding welcome by the crews of the thirty-four ocean racers that completed the strenuous 1950 race.

A year after the return passage to Lymington and the end of her 1,200-mile maiden ocean voyage, *Sopranino*, having proven a safe and efficient sea boat, was made ready for a 10,000-mile voyage from Falmouth out over the ancient route of the trade winds. Three months were spent by Patrick Ellam and Colin Mudie, another experienced small-boat sailor, in trial runs and careful preparations and adjustments to *Sopranino* before starting this next voyage that was to take three hundred days.

Designed by Laurent Giles as a light-displacement Bermudian cutter 17-ft. 6-in. LW, 5-ft. 4-in. beam, 3-ft. 8-in. draft, *Sopranino* (a name referring to the smallest musical wind instrument), was clinker-built with a round canoelike midsection and a weighted fin keel by Wooten Brothers of Cookham Dene on the Thames. Self-righting and made unsinkable by buoyancy compartments filled with flotation rubber, she was built to come through most anything likely to be encountered on a long sea passage.

Getting away from Falmouth September 6, 1951, later than planned, she encountered calms and much fog west of Ushant. A deep depression coming in over the Atlantic two days later brought a southwest gale, and *Sopranino* with all canvas removed lay hull to while her crew rested below in their bunks. Pushing on south they approached the steep cliffs of the Spanish coast (known locally as the "Coast of Death") in the night, picked up the Tower of Hercules Light at 1 A.M., and by late afternoon were berthed at the Club Nautico de La Coruña, eleven days out of Falmouth.

Dipping her ensign to warships and ocean liners and dipped to in return,

Sopranino departed El Ferrol, the Spanish naval harbor, and sailed south down the Portuguese coast before a strong northwest wind and sea. After several weeks up the Tagus at Lisbon and Belem, *Sopranino* cruised south to Cape St. Vincent and from there set a course for Casablanca, North Africa.

Though less than 20 feet long, *Sopranino* was registered with the Board of Trade as a British merchant ship, flew the Red Ensign of the British Merchant Marine, carried a complete set of ship's papers the same as an ocean liner, and was reported regularly in the shipping news.

While sheltering at Casablanca behind the great sea wall from a succession of African gales then pounding the coast of Morocco, Ellam was swept from the wall by a mountainous sea and had a narrow escape that laid him up and delayed the voyage a week.

Well out from the Barbary Coast and squared away for the Canary Islands, they put their twin spinnakers to work before a light northerly. Rolling and sometimes drifting in calms, they had a slow passage to the Agadir Line and southward to the Canaries.

A long stay was made at Gran Canaria. After many weeks of careful preparation for the 3,000-mile passage to the West Indies, the little ship cleared officially from Las Palmas for Barbados. In the bright moonlight of January 11, the harbor lights were left behind and *Sopranino*, bowling along past the shipping lanes, sailed south until well into the northeast trades. After a few adjustments were made to the twins and the Braine steering gear adaptation, the crew got down to a sea routine. Regular watches were still kept but spent mainly with odd jobs, cooking, cleaning up, navigating, and repairs.

Running before strong trade winds and heavy seas, *Sopranino* began to log more than 90 miles a day, and over the westward side of the ocean better than 130 miles were logged from noon to noon on many days with a top day's run of 134 miles approaching Barbados. Twenty-nine days out of Las Palmas, with the ship in good shape, crew in fine fettle, and "basic stews," Ryvita biscuits, tea, cocoa, and porridge still in good supply, *Sopranino* rounded Needham Point into Carlisle Bay and, dipping her ensign in salute to the port, sailed across to Bridgetown to await customs and health clearance.

After a stretch ashore and rest from the continual bracing against the motions of ship and sea, they sailed from Barbados south to Tobago and on to Venezuela and Port of Spain at the mouth of the Orinoco. From there they cruised up through the Caribbean.

While at the Isle of Pines, Colin Mudie had to return quickly to England; Patrick Ellam went on to complete the last 1,700 miles to Havana, Miami, and up the Intracoastal Waterway to Cape May. *Sopranino's* 40-mile run up the Jersey coast to New York was made on January 6, 1953. "It may be reasonably said," Ellam observed on arrival, "that she was one of the safest vessels that has ever sailed on the sea."

Meticulously planned and executed, theirs was a fine record of small-craft seamanship and precision sailing accomplished by experienced sailors who prepared well and knew what they were doing.

Though men have crossed the Western Ocean in dories and other boats less than 15 feet overall, we are concerned here mainly with sizes and types that can cruise anywhere in safety and a reasonable amount of comfort. Vertue-class Bermudian sloops (25-ft. 3-in. LOA, 7-ft. 2-in. beam, 4-ft. 6-in. draft), considered by some the best of their size for offshore passage making, have made a remarkable number of transocean voyages, have performed well, and have proven able to stand up to the toughest going. Descendants of the Falmouth Quay Punt and the Bristol Channel Pilot Cutter, Vertues are heavy-displacement 21-foot-LW little vessels that have averaged 70 to 100 miles a day on offshore passages.

Andrillot, a gaff cutter built in 1936, was the first of the little 5-tonners, but it remained for Humphrey Barton to show what they could do in 1950 when he sailed *Vertue XXXV* from Falmouth to New York in forty-seven days through twenty-four days of headwinds, several depressions, and a hurricane.

In 1952 Joseph Cunningham sailed *Icebird,* another Vertue, from Ireland out to Barbados, Bermuda, and up the east coast to Newfoundland. In 1955 he cruised from St. John's back to the Caribbean in *Icebird* and later crossed from Bermuda to Ireland in thirty days. Dan Robertson, sailing solo in *Easy Vertue,* dodged two hurricanes crossing from England direct to the Bahamas in 1954.

Speedwell of Hong Kong and Salmo

Commander Peter Hamilton, R.N., sailed his 25-foot Vertue *Speedwell of Hong Kong* from Singapore to England in time that nearly equaled that of the old square-riggers. Two years later Hamilton sailed *Salmo,* another Vertue, singlehanded and without any self-steering device, from Scotland to Quebec in fifty-six days. On this tough course from the Clyde to Belle Isle, Newfoundland, north of the Great Circle route, *Salmo* was hove to in four gales and the tail end of a hurricane, averaged 70 miles daily, and had seventeen days on the wind and twelve days reaching.

Joined by his wife Jill, Peter Hamilton sailed down the St. Lawrence River in the spring of 1957, cruised the Atlantic and Gulf coasts to Hatteras, and went on through the West Indies to Panama. From Balboa *Salmo* had a leisurely passage to the Galapagos. Two days after departing Elizabeth Bay on Isabella Island, the southeast trades were picked up, and daily runs of 130 miles or more were logged for the remaining twenty-two days of a 3,000-mile passage to Pitcairn. Several days were spent in Bounty Bay before *Salmo* took off to Oeno and from there swung off westerly to Mangareva.

From the Gambiers en route to Tahiti, calls were made at Rapa and Tubuai in the Australs.

When the Hamiltons were informed by a doctor at Papeete that they could expect to be the parents of a child in a few months, they quickly decided to forego plans to circumnavigate and sailed at once for the Marquesas. From Nukuhiva *Salmo* was driven nonstop to Los Angeles in forty-six days.

John Goodwin, bound for South Africa, sailed Hamilton's former Vertue *Speedwell of Hong Kong* from Yarmouth to northern Spain and to Gibraltar. From there the little 5-tonner was single-handed to the Canary Islands and from Las Palmas to Barbados in twenty-six days. After some time in the Caribbean, Goodwin, with Campbell Odlum as crew, sailed *Speedwell of Hong Kong* to Cape Town with calls at Recife, Brazil, and Tristan da Cunha.

Folkboats, one of Scandinavia's most popular cruising vessels, have a considerable record of ocean voyages, including Atlantic crossings. Valentine Howells made several solo ocean passages in *Eira* before his crossing from Plymouth to Bermuda en route to New York. Adrian Hayter, single-handing in his Folkboat *Valkyr* and dodging three hurricanes, had a notable forty-eight-day passage to Trinidad from Las Palmas. Commander Mike Bales, R.N., sailed his 25-foot Folkboat *Jellicle* from England to New Zealand via the Caribbean and Panama in ten months, making part of the voyage singlehanded.

Jester

Jester, H. G. Hasler's modified, carvel-built Folkboat (25-ft. LOA, 7-ft. 3-in. beam, 4-ft. draft) has proven her seagoing abilities on many ocean passages.

In choosing the lines of the Scandinavian Folkboat, Hasler wanted a boat in which one or two people could make long open-sea passages in reasonable comfort and could cope with strong winds, rough seas, and cold weather without, as he put it, "calling on their last reserves of endurance." Convinced that "no small boat can sail fast to windward without throwing a lot of spray over herself," Hasler eliminated the cockpit and handled everything from a small circular hatch located amidships at the forward end of the cabin. For singlehanded sailing *Jester* was given a Lapwing rig (a development of the pre-war Ljungstrom). Twin cantilever booms were added, allowing her to go to windward with the twin wing sails closed together, to reach or run with them open, and reef by rolling both sails up on a rotatable unstayed mast.

For the 1960 Singlehanded Transatlantic Race, *Jester* was given a Chinese lugsail (240 square feet) set on an unstayed hollow spruce mast. With a yard at its head, a light boom at its foot, and five full-width battens dividing it into six panels, this single sail handled and trimmed on all points of sailing

Colonel H. G. Hasler's *Jester*—a modified, carvel-built Folkboat with Chinese lugsail, departing
Plymouth in the Singlehanded Transatlantic Race.

as a fore-and-aft sail. Without moving from the forward central hatch opening, Hasler could hoist, lower, or trim the sail, take sextant sights, or adjust the wind-vane steering gear. Both rigs reefed in seconds without touching the sail itself and both were tacked or jibed without touching anything but the tiller.

Twice reduced to five reefs on the 1960 Transatlantic Race, Hasler did so in seconds without leaving the center hatch. *Jester* sailed the far northern route up to the 57th parallel and, except for about an hour of manual steering off Land's End, steered herself at all times during the forty-eight-day passage that won second place.

In *Jester* Hasler developed one of the most unusual small modern vessels designed for offshore passages by one or two people—a combination that gives good ocean racing results with a minimum of expense and hard work at sea.

Trekka

This 20-foot yawl built by John Guzzwell is another thoroughbred light-displacement hull designed by Laurent Giles.

She was ridiculously small to be sailing around the world," said John, "but she was home to me and, once aboard, I felt completely independent."

A one-and-a-half tonner 20-ft. 6-in. LOA, with 6-ft. 5-in. beam, *Trekka* has amply proven that a well-found modern midget vessel competently handled can cruise anywhere in safety and modest comfort.

John Guzzwell, who began making long transocean passages at the age of three on his father's gaff ketch, laminated the keel of *Trekka* in a basement boiler room of the Y.M.C.A. and under far less than ideal conditions did the lofting, planking, finishing, and fiberglassing of the deck in a small storeroom at the rear of Bell's fish and chip shop in Victoria, B.C.

After nine months of building and nearly a year's careful preparation, John and *Trekka* departed Victoria September 10, 1955, bound around the world. Out of the Strait of Juan de Fuca, edging offshore from Cape Flattery, *Trekka* was approached by a Norwegian fisherman who came close to hail, "Vere de hell you tink you are going in dat ploody little pisspot?"

"Honolulu," Guzzwell called back.

"You're crazy!" shouted the fisherman, rolling off astern. "Put goot luck!"

Soon after this hearty farewell the sea started to build up, the barometer went down, and with the wind beginning to moan through the rigging *Trekka* was made ready for her first gale. Finding that she wouldn't lie comfortably or safely to a sea anchor, John put her beam on to the sea and with the helm lashed down to leeward and everything on deck secure went below. By the time the wind veered off to the southwest, John had his sea legs and his confidence in *Trekka* had increased a peg or two.

John Guzzwell en route to Hilo, Hawaii, with *Trekka* under self-steering trade-wind rig.

During two and a half days of fair weather, the twin-staysail self-steering rig was tried out, sights were taken, positions plotted, and *Trekka* rolled along toward San Francisco. South of Cape Mendocino, *Trekka* lay ahull for the second time since leaving Cape Flattery. After a few hours conditions eased enough to get under way, but soon the wind increased to a full gale.

Judging the wind force at 70 m.p.h. and the height of some of the seas to be 25 to 30 feet, Guzzwell stayed in the cockpit "not daring to leave the tiller." With her 24-square-foot storm jib sheeted flat and every warp aboard streaming out astern to help keep her running dead before, the little yawl encountered what was later judged to be the worst gale of her 30,000-mile voyage around the world. When an occasional roaring sea burst over the quarter, half filling the cockpit, John—cold, soaked, struggling to stay awake and alert—wondered, "Whatever possessed me to leave the earth for this madness?" By noon the next day, unable to remain awake any longer, he pulled down the storm jib, lashed the tiller to leeward, and went below. When the weather eased, landfall was made on Point Arena.

Eight days after sailing in through the Golden Gate, *Trekka* put out to the southwest for Hilo with a fine westerly breeze to send her bowling along. A few days later, when the wind went round to east of north, Guzzwell lost no time getting the twin staysails set. On most courses *Trekka* steered herself very well, especially when running free with the twins boomed out wing and wing and the sheets led back through quarter blocks to the tiller.

After many weeks of cruising in Hawaii, *Trekka* departed Honolulu for Fanning Island and from there sailed down through the Pacific to Samoa, Tonga, and Russell, New Zealand. Guzzwell left *Trekka* in New Zealand to help the Smeetons sail their 46-foot ketch *Tzu Hang* around Cape Horn. A thousand miles from the Horn they were pitchpoled and dismasted in the Roaring Fifties, and *Tzu Hang* made the Chilean coast under jury rig.

Returning to New Zealand, Guzzwell set out again in his 20-foot yawl across the Tasman to Australia, up through the Timor Sea, and on across the Indian Ocean. Her 2,000-mile westward passage from Cocos-Keeling to Rodriguez was made in seventeen and one-half days for a daily average of 111 miles. With a favorable current adding 20 miles or more to her noon-to-noon position, a day's run of 155 miles in 24 hours was recorded off the east coast of Madagascar. From Durban *Trekka* rounded the Cape of Good Hope and sailed up through the South Atlantic to Barbados and the Panama Canal.

While devoid of lurid incidents that denote lack of experience or forethought, John Guzzwell's circumnavigation had adventures enough for anyone. Going through the Panama Canal, he felt that his $2.16 toll was a very good value for not having to go around Cape Horn.

Trekka had the usual slow beat out to the Galapagos but in the course of her 5,400-mile passage from Panama to Hawaii had a day's run of 175 miles, aided of course by the strong flow of the Equatorial Current. Several days of 150 miles or more were recorded, and in the full grip of the southeast trades she made 1,101 miles in one week. A small spinnaker set from the masthead above the twin staysails, with the sheets led through blocks on the end to the twin poles, helped to make the fast trade-wind passages and was Guzzwell's favorite rig when the wind was right because it cut down some of the roll. On the afternoon of July 22, 1959, *Trekka* passed Makapuu Point, rounded Diamond Head, and tacked up the Ala Wai Channel sixty-two days from Balboa.

Anxious to get back to Victoria before the winter gales set in, Guzzwell departed Honolulu for the 2,600-mile passage north to British Columbia on August 8. Three weeks later on September 3, north of latitude 42, he wrote: "I knew again the lonely feeling of a gale at sea. All sail was down and *Trekka* was riding the white-crested swell as buoyantly as the big gooney birds." Exactly four years from the day she departed, *Trekka* arrived back in Victoria, British Columbia.

For his singlehanded circumnavigation and for a voyage well done, John

Guzzwell and *Trekka* were awarded the Cruising Club of America's Blue Water Medal—the smallest yacht ever to be honored with the award. The following year Guzzwell was married, and in 1961 John and his wife Maureen sailed *Trekka* to Hawaii and back to California. Speaking of future voyages and of an ideal little ship for ocean cruising, Guzzwell said: "The most important requirement of all would be that this little vessel be constructed with my own hands, for I would want to know every nail and bolt in her and have handled every one of her timbers; perhaps then I would also know the confidence that *Trekka* gave me during her trek around the world." John now has that boat—a Laurent Giles designed 20-tonner that he built in three years and sailed to the Caribbean for a shakedown cruise early in 1966 with his wife and their twin sons.

JEAN LACOMBE

The gallant Frenchman Jean Lacombe, who sailed the smallest boats in the last two transatlantic singlehanded races, made his first Atlantic crossing in the 18-ft.-LOA, 6-ft. 3-in.-beam Bermudian cutter *Hippocampe* (Sea Horse). Departing France in April, 1955, he sailed via the Canaries and the trade-wind belt to Puerto Rico in sixty-eight days. From there he was twenty-four days to Atlantic City, where he put in for repairs en route to New York. In 1960 Lacombe's crossing in *Cap Horn*, a light-displacement, fiber-glassed, centerboard Bermudian sloop (21-ft. 3-in. LOA, 7-ft. 5-in. beam, 2-ft. draft) equipped with servo-type wind vane, was made from Plymouth north of the Azores to New York. In 1964 in *Golif*, his 21-ft. 3-in.-LOA Bermudian sloop, despite difficulties with a sea anchor, a broken boom, and a very wet forty-six-day passage, Jean Lacombe arrived ninth among the fourteen loners who raced from Plymouth to Newport, R. I.

Mermaid

Kenichi Horie, the ebullient, self-confident Japanese skipper who crossed the Pacific solo from Osaka, Japan, in his self-righting 19-ft.-LOA, 5-ft.-beam hard-chine Kingfisher class sloop *Mermaid*, encountered five gales on his 5,300-mile passage from Nishinomiya Harbor to the Golden Gate. Sailing the northern route, Horie-san made his first landfall on Point Reyes, ninety-two days from Osaka, and two days later brought his little sloop into San Francisco Bay. A reverse-sheer 1-tonner and one of the smallest vessels to cross the Pacific, *Mermaid* made 90 miles per day for one week and had an over-all daily average of 56.5 miles for the 1962 crossing.

Wanderer II

Bill Howell's 16,000-mile cruise—and especially his singlehanded passage from Tahiti to Hawaii and on to British Columbia—in the Hiscocks'

Kenichi Horie arriving at San Francisco from Japan.

former 24-foot-LOA *Wanderer II* deserves a place in the records of outstanding solo voyages in very small craft.

Wanderer II, a miniature Bristol Channel pilot cutter without an auxiliary (24-ft. LOA, 7-ft. 1-in. beam, 5-ft. draft), had been sailed to the Azores and back to England by the Hiscocks. Howell, an Australian, and his crew Frank McNulty sailed the little gaff-rigged $4\frac{1}{2}$-tonner from Falmouth to Gibraltar and Algeciras late in 1951. From Las Palmas they crossed to Bridgetown, Barbados, in twenty-four days and cruised on through the Caribbean to Panama. After a beat in heavy seas out to the Galapagos, they made the 4,200-mile run to Tahiti in thirty-four days, a hard-driving passage with an average of 124 miles daily.

"Tahiti is an earthly paradise," wrote Howell, "but like any paradise it has its serpents." On March 3, 1953, he departed Papeete for Hawaii singlehanded in a heavy rain squall.

The first night was, as always is, the loneliest of the passage. I have found when singlehanded that the longer I am at sea the less I feel the loneliness and the more company I find in the sky, the wind, the waves, my boat and even in myself. But this night the sense of aloneness was accentuated by the weather, by periods of calm and slatting canvas punctuated with gale force squalls and icy rain. The dawn, thin as it was, was welcome.

The first week was much the same as the first night. Forging north in the hurricane season, *Wanderer II* crossed the equator on the nineteenth day at 149° 40', more than a hundred miles west of where the skipper would liked to have crossed. After another twelve days fighting for easting, the 12,000-foot snowy peak of Mauna Kea was sighted, and the following morning *Wanderer II* ran into Hilo before a fresh trade breeze thirty-two days from Tahiti.

A pleasant few months were spent cruising among the Hawaiian Islands before Howell waved a reluctant farewell to his friends on the Kona coast and sailed north in mid-August for Canada. Five weeks later, coming in to Juan de Fuca from the southwest, Howell had four frustrating days of sleepless maneuvers with pea-soup fog, rain, and floating logs between the Lightship, Tatoosh Island, and Race Rocks before *Wanderer II* made it up the strait to Victoria forty-one days from Hawaii.

Stardrift

In 1962 Bill Howell, single-handing from England in his 30-foot 8-ton cutter *Stardrift*, crossed the Atlantic to Barbados from Vigo and Las Palmas and cruised through the West Indies to Panama. Two years later, using one of Hasler's self-steering rigs, he brought *Stardrift* from Plymouth to Newport, R. I., in thirty-eight days for sixth place in the 1964 Singlehanded Trans-

DR. W. B. HOWELL

Wanderer II at Honolulu shortly before shoving off for a 41-day singlehanded passage to Victoria, B.C.

atlantic Race. On the return crossing, Howell made a 2,000-mile passage to the Azores in twenty-three days and from there 1,500 miles to the Channel and up to Dover in thirteen days.

The details of some of the best midget ocean voyages are not available because the individuals involved quietly arrived and departed from various ports and anchorages as inconspicuously as possible and without caring to write accounts of their passages. Following are a few that are perhaps typical of the smallest craft making major ocean voyages or circumnavigating in 1966.

Thalaloca, a 20-foot-LOA sloop built and sailed by Hein and Sigrid Zenker from Vancouver, B.C., began to cruise in the Pacific in 1962. After crossing from San Francisco to New Zealand and up through Timor to South Africa with many calls en route, *Thalaloca* sailed from Durban on across the South Atlantic to the Caribbean, Florida, and Canada in 1966.

Trekka, John Guzzwell's former 20-foot-LOA yawl, with new owners Cliff and Marian Cain, bound around the world from Monterey, California, made calls at Samoa and Fiji en route to New Zealand in 1965 and in 1966 left South Africa bound for European ports. "We are the first to admit that we began our voyage as novices," writes Cliff Cain. "That we've had such good sailing we owe in part to our preparations, but mostly to our fine little boat."

Geneve, 25-foot-LOA Marconi sloop (a converted lifeboat) with Michel Mermod, departed Callao, Peru, early in November, 1961, following a year of conversion work and careful preparation for extended cruising in the South Pacific and a voyage around the world.

Mermod, a Swiss sociologist and experienced ocean navigator, had completed many thousands of miles of solo canoeing in Alaska, Canada, and South America, including a 2,000-mile canoe trip from Pucallpa, eastern Peru, to Belem at the mouth of the Amazon in Brazil. Flying the Swiss flag, Mermod sailed to the Galapagos, Marquesas, Tahiti, Cooks, New Hebrides, Solomons, New Guinea, Carolinas, and the Philippines. Late in June, 1964, loner Mermod departed Manila in *Geneve* for Europe via the Red Sea and Africa.

Gannet from London, a 21-foot-LOA Hillyard sloop single-handed by Ron Russell across the Atlantic in 1963 via Las Palmas and from there to Barbados in thirty-four days, went on to Panama and from Balboa to the Marquesas, where Richard Pohe joined as crew. *Gannet* cruised up through the Tuamotus to Tahiti, Bora Bora, across to the Cooks, Tonga, and on south to New Zealand, where she arrived late in 1965 en route around the world.

Several of the smallest boats ever to have crossed the Atlantic single-handed completed their voyages in 1965 and 1966.

Sjo Ag, six-foot four-inch sailor John Riding's 12-ft.-LOA French-built

Bermudian-rigged sloop (5-ft. beam, 3-ft. 6-in. draft, $\frac{1}{3}$-ton displacement) sailed from Plymouth in July, 1964, cruised to Spain, crossed later to Flores in the Azores, and from there made a sixty-seven-day passage to Bermuda. "You don't set out in the first place if you do not have an instinct for the sea, which today, is perhaps, an instinct for survival," said the loner who sailed the hard way, east to west, in one of the smallest boats ever to cross the Atlantic.

In August, 1965, a day after John Riding arrived at Newport, Rhode Island, in *Sjo Ag*, Robert Manry completed a 3,200-mile voyage from Falmouth, Massachusetts, to Falmouth, England, in seventy-eight days aboard his 13½-foot clinker-built sloop *Tinkerbelle*.

Another smallest-ever Atlantic solo crossing was made in 1966 by Irish-American William Verity in his 12-foot-LOA home-built sloop *Nonoalca* to prove "that seafaring monks from Ireland came to America in the fifth and sixth centuries." Verity sailed from Fort Lauderdale, Florida, on May 8 "with the blessings of St. Brendan" and had a sixty-eight-day passage to Tralee, Ireland. On arrival in County Kerry the *Nonoalca* and skipper were in good shape and had enough food and water aboard to last another two weeks.

Two hardy English oarsmen, John Ridgway and Chay Blyth, rowed their 20-foot red-and-white Scotch fishing dory *English Rose III* across the Atlantic from Cape Cod to Galway on Ireland's west coast late in 1966. After ninety-two days of rowing, the red-and-white dory made landfall on the northern tip of Inismore in heavy seas and gale winds. Two weeks after their arrival, skipper Ridgway reported he was still tired.

Though Scotsman Paul Johnson's double-ended, seventy-one-year-old ketch *Venus* is but 18-ft. 6-in. LOA (6-ft. beam, 3-ft. draft), he finds room aboard for a library of fifty books. Having been raised on a 43-foot ketch, Johnson bought the former Shetland fishing boat in 1960 when he was twenty-one, converted her from an open gunter sloop to an oceangoing ketch, and crossed the North Sea to cruise a year in Scandinavia followed by many years of passaging in Europe, the Atlantic, the Caribbean, and in North American waters. Johnson's use of Fritz Fenger's Weather Twin system for self-steering has provided him with much time for reading in the trade winds. On a thirty-nine-day passage from the Canaries to Martinique (2,760 miles) he spent only ten hours at the helm.

With improvements in the design of small craft and new ideas on stowage, self-steering, navigation, victualing, and simplified gear and sail handling, the modern midget cruiser provides a lighter, different kind of performance and seaworthiness. For the loner unable to afford a large vessel, the 20- to 25-foot-LOA hull costs comparatively little to maintain, can be easily careened or lifted out, can go where deep-draft hulls cannot, has minimum port charges, and when entering or leaving crowded harbors can

Christopher de Grabowski's 25-ft. cutter *Tethys* tying up at Bizerta, Tunisia, before departing for an 84-day passage to New York.

maneuver quickly under sail and get around in close quarters without difficulty.

It should not be forgotten that the advanced pocket cruiser of the mid-sixties evolved out of the important early voyages of men like William Andrews and "Si" Lawlor, two of the best small-boat sailors of all time. Richard Turrell McMullen, single-handing a 3-ton cutter for his "health's sake and from a natural love of the sea," showed as early as 1850 that his little 20-foot-LOA *Leo* was as safe in a Channel gale, or safer, than many of the great yachts in Cowes Roads and was the first to prove that it is not the size of a vessel that counts but her efficiency and handling.

Modern sailors, including the late Chris Grabowski in his 25-foot-LOA cutter *Tethys*, a fine little ship with an outstanding record, Humphrey Barton and Kevin O'Riordan in the little 5-tonner *Vertue XXXV*, Guy Cole in *Galway Blazer*, and Vito Dumas with his 103-day and 117-day nonstop passages in the 21-foot-LOA sloop *Sirio*, have shown what really can be done in a small boat with careful preparation, good judgment, and first-rate seamanship.

Lorin Smith, who cruised the South Pacific for eighteen years in his Tahiti ketch and in larger vessels, brought the Cook Islands' trading schooner *Te Taveuni* into Rarotonga late in 1963 after an ordeal that made news across

Polynesia. After turning the larger vessel over to her owners, he returned to his own little *Tahiti*. "In the future," Smith said, "I sail in nothing bigger than twenty-five feet. They are far the safest for the Pacific."

Ocean voyaging in small craft is no longer an endurance contest, and for the modern midget ocean cruiser with Bermudian rig a 25-mile-an-hour wind is no longer a small-boat gale. Beating to windward across the Atlantic, Vertues and Folkboats have made as good and frequently better time than many of the big barques, brigantines, and full-rigged ships of the last century.

Without the really small boat we would have no new sailors. Now that the smallest vessels are racing across the English Channel and the Junior Offshore Group (as small as 16 feet LW) are scudding away between England and France and down to Santander, Spain, as the twentieth century rockets along we can expect that an increasing number of loners and others will be out proving that tough, functional little vessels are best. Many will contribute to the development of new hull forms, special equipment, and safety at sea.

CHAPTER 6

Strange Quests

Many things are strange, none stranger than man.

—SOPHOCLES

Ah, who shall soothe these feverish children?
Who justify these restless explorations?

—WALT WHITMAN

~~~~~~

SEA life has always attracted unusual people. Here we have the audacious, eccentric, and sometimes heroic individuals.

There are enough records of singular quests and uncommon voyages that have been made in the Atlantic, the Pacific, the Mediterranean, and the Indian Ocean to make a large book in itself. Since it is impossible to list more than a few, the following accounts in one way or another are typical of many others.

Sturdy and *Sturdy II*

Edward Miles, who made the strangest solo circumnavigation on record, spent over $50,000 and thirteen years of his life building and sailing around the world from west to east in his schooners *Sturdy* and *Sturdy II* in an attempt to prevent World War II and save civilization from future wars.

After years at sea as a young man, Miles settled in Memphis and accumulated a small fortune as a building contractor so that he could cruise the seven seas spreading friendship and understanding among all people.

A lean, wiry individual with a message of hope, Miles found strength in the inwardness of his venture—his positive conviction that fundamentally most people are friendly and kind. As a sailor before the mast, he had studied men and women in many ports of the world and concluded that people of different colors and creeds get along well together if given a fair chance. "Prejudices," he said, "are unnatural and are stirred up by so-called patriots who thrive on racial prejudice."

Sturdy, a Bermudian-rigged schooner, 37-ft. LOA, 11-ft. beam, 8 tons net displacement, was completed at Thunderbolt, Georgia, in 1928 after two years of hard labor, with Miles doing everything including the casting of his own 5,000 pounds of lead ballast. When friends offered to help Miles thanked them but declined, explaining that in the spirit of his quest he felt he should do all the work himself.

Following a 700-mile trial run from Charleston up the coast to New York, Miles had enough confidence in the boat and his plans to tell his wife, who was hotly demanding a full explanation.

"She exploded, completely blew up," on hearing his future plans to circumnavigate, declared that "women couldn't trust men," and went to stay with friends in California.

Sturdy sailed from the Pilgrims Yacht Club, New York, August 31, 1928. As he waved farewell to the Statue of Liberty, her forty-nine-year-old skipper felt fully confident that his mission would be firmly established in many parts of the world before he saw the torch again.

Very few details of the schooner, her rig, and seamanly incidents of sailing and passage making are available, as Miles in his speaking and writing preferred to subordinate them to the motives and principles of his quest.

I felt [he said] that a goodwill voyage would give people of other countries a better understanding that each others' problems are the same. I knew that the knowledge I would gain by increasing my understanding of other nations, I could share with less fortunate Americans at home.

In steady weather I lashed the helm and let her sail herself. But if the weather was heavy, I had to take in everything and let her drift broadside to it. I usually tried to get my sleep between midnight and five A.M.

Many people think I might have got lonesome, but lonesomeness comes of an idle mind. I was too busy to get lonesome. Besides, with the birds that can live indefinitely at sea and with fish so close, I was never really alone.

Sturdy made the crossing to Gibraltar in forty-five days, cruised on to

Tangier, Algiers, Tunis, Malta, and on up to Constantinople. All through the Mediterranean Miles and his schooner were given a big welcome. Trips inland were made to visit officials of many nations to study people and talk brotherhood.

After a long stay at Alexandria, Egypt, *Sturdy* passed through the Suez Canal and was three days out into the Red Sea when an accident with gasoline enveloped the vessel in sudden flames. Miles miraculously escaped in the dinghy, managed to reach a nearby lighthouse, and was picked up by a supply tender and returned to the Suez Canal.

En route back to the United States by steamer, the tenacious sailor and boatbuilder completed a full set of drawings for another vessel to carry on his good work. In Memphis, while building it, he was divorced and soon remarried.

Sturdy II was also a schooner, 36-ft. 9-in. LOA, 10-ft. 10-in. beam, 4-ft. 9-in. draft with a 20 h.p. diesel auxiliary. When completed, Miles's third vessel was shipped on a steamer to Port Tewfick near Suez, and in September, 1930, Miles sailed again into the Red Sea.

Unaccustomed as he was to extreme heat, the following month of light breezes or sometimes no wind at all and the necessity for running the diesel almost continually was "plain hell," wrote Miles, as he perched day after day at the wheel under a big umbrella with a stream of water from an auxiliary hose spraying the umbrella during the hottest hours of the day. Cold, heavy weather and all other cruising conditions he could take, but the fetid, killing heat of the Red Sea nearly did him in.

Sailing out through the Gulf of Aden, *Sturdy II* crossed to India, where much time was spent meeting people from all walks of life.

On down the Malabar coast, *Sturdy II* went aground on a coral reef at the entrance to the port of Galle, Ceylon. Mohammedan and Buddhist fishermen promptly helped to get her off, and the people of Galle helped to make repairs. Christians, Buddhists, and Mohammedans all working together to help an unknown fellow human being greatly strengthened the captain's convictions that he was on the right course to a better world.

He crossed the Bay of Bengal, sailed up the Strait of Malacca to Singapore, and from there went on to Manila, Hong Kong, and Japan with considerable success in his mission.

Departing Yokohama, *Sturdy II* had the longest single passage of her circumnavigation—fifty-two days to Honolulu—and Miles became the only small-boat sailor to go straight across the Pacific through the westerlies, the horse latitudes, and the northeast trades.

During a month on Oahu and the other islands, Miles was much in demand as a speaker by schools, clubs, and luncheon groups. The spirit of aloha was much in evidence among the islanders of mixed colors and backgrounds who came to listen and ask questions at Honolulu, Kahului, and Hilo. This heartened the skipper. He felt more confident than ever that his message of brotherhood among men was making an impact in places where it counted most.

Crossing to San Francisco in eighteen days, *Sturdy II* cruised down the Pacific Coast with many stops and from Panama proceeded to Cuba and on up the Atlantic Coast. On June 17, 1932, approximately six years after he started building *Sturdy* in Georgia, Edward Miles arrived back in New York, broke from his years of voyaging and the tribulations that beset his personal life.

American audiences were interested in the account of his voyage around the world but little interested in his appeals for understanding among men. His story found no takers among New York publishers, magazines, and lecture agents. In order to live and continue to spread his message of good will, he was forced to sell his navigation instruments, tools, and sails. Finally he had to sell *Sturdy II*, a seasoned, well-built schooner with a fine record, for $1,000 less than a fifth of the cost of the materials that had gone in to her.

In February, 1933, Miles formed an organization to fight against racial and religious prejudices and promote peace and co-operation among all men. But the time wasn't right. The Americans he was able to reach were not interested in reading or hearing about tolerance and understanding. The second man in history to sail a schooner around the world was called an impractical dreamer and worse.

Funds got so low he slept on the floor of his little office and often went several days at a time without eating. Despite the cold shoulder and sometimes the scorn of those who passed him by, Miles never became embittered. He felt the lack of response was mostly due to ignorance and misunderstanding.

In 1944 Edward Miles ran for president of the United States as an independent. As a candidate he was defeated by Franklin D. Roosevelt, but as a sailor-crusader he never was defeated and never regretted sailing 32,000 miles singlehanded in the interest of friendship and understanding among people of the world.

R. K. Fox

As an extreme test of what can be done in very small craft, men have ridden out winter gales in the North Atlantic in inflatable dinghies, and oarsmen of incredible stamina have rowed 3,250 miles across the Atlantic in open boats.

When George Harbo and Frank Samuelson rowed the *R. K. Fox* from New York to France, Harbo was thirty and Samuelson twenty-six. Harbo had a master's ticket and had been a pilot. Both knew well what they were doing, had a good boat, were accustomed to rowing dories weighted with a half ton or more of fish, and were as hard and able as men could be for the long crossing.

The two Norwegian immigrants spent many years at sea before they joined the fishermen and clammers of Fish Row at Branchport on the New Jersey shore. For two years, working and living aboard their fishing sloop, they spent their spare time planning to cross the Atlantic, but they lacked funds for the right boat and for gear and provisions until R. K. Fox, a New York publisher, offered to back them.

The dory R. K. Fox, built by William Seaman, whose family had built fine skiffs and dories since before the Civil War, was a clinker-built, cedar-planked double-ender, 18-ft. 4-in. LOA, 5-foot beam, with watertight compartments in the bow and stern for dry storage space and reserve buoyancy. Two runners were fitted below the waterline to be used as handrails in case of capsizing, and for heavy weather a canvas cover was made that secured to the gunwales with openings for the rowers.

Sailors shook their heads when the dory was rowed to the Battery, but Harbo and Samuelson paid little heed to remarks and banter as they finished fitting out and stowed provisions that included 250 eggs, 100 pounds of sea biscuits, oatmeal, and 60 gallons of water. A compass, octant, Coston flares, sea anchor, six gallons of fish oil for heavy weather, and five pairs of oars were among the last to come aboard. All clothing except oilskins and what they had on was discarded.

On June 6, 1896, a quiet crowd of over two thousand gathered along the Battery sea wall to see their departure on what some felt was suicide and others said openly was at best an "impossible voyage."

"We'll see you in Havre," shouted Harbo to a friend on the dock as they cast off and swung quickly out, four oars flashing in the late-afternoon sun. Harbor whistles and a few sirens blew as the Fox skimmed down the bay and out through the Narrows in the full sweep of the ebb.

The first night they held off to the south of the steamer lane, rowing all night in accord with a carefully planned routine that called for $15\frac{1}{2}$ hours of rowing every 24 hours for each man.

Their course was eastward by way of the Gulf Stream and the North Atlantic drift. They hoped for a daily run of 50 to 55 miles and with the help of the drift expected to make the passage from New York to France in sixty days.

No one had ever rowed across the Atlantic Ocean before. There were no rules. They made their own. During the day both men rowed from 8 A.M. to 8 P.M. with a one-hour rest at noon and at dinner. From eight at night until seven the next morning they stood $3\frac{1}{2}$-hour watches, with one man always at the oars while the other slept.

On the fourth night out Harbo was lying under the canvas cover in the stern. Sitting up suddenly, he called out, "Something bumped us!"

As they both listened the bumping came again and was followed by a scraping across the hull. Something white flashed and broke the surface in the water alongside.

"A shark," said Harbo.

For a day and a night the shark swam with the boat. The oarsmen kept their stroke, paying it little attention.

A week out they spoke the Canadian schooner *Jessie* bound to New York with lumber.

"Come alongside," hailed the captain of the *Jessie*. "We'll take you aboard."

"Thanks," Samuelson replied, "but we're on a voyage."

"Where bound?"

"France."

"A good passage, then"—and the schooner fell away.

Mile after mile, day and night, it was oars and oars alone. Cooking was difficult and the fare plain. Their oil stove refused to function soon after leaving, and they ate their food cold. Everything—sleeping, eating, writing up the log—had to be done in a cramped position. With only nine inches of freeboard they were wet much of the time.

On the morning of June 16 they spoke the *Fuerst Bismark*, pride of the North German Lloyd.

"Are you shipwrecked?" queried the captain.

"No. Bound for Europe."

"Do you need anything?"

"Nothing. Thanks."

Passengers at the rail cheered as the *Fox* pulled away.

A strong south wind drove them north toward the Grand Banks, where they had some fog and twice had to lie hove to with their sea anchor before a heavy sea.

On July 1 they were sighted by the Banks fishing schooner *Leander* of Lunenburg, Nova Scotia, which ran down to see if they were castaways.

For the next week they had fair weather and made good progress. Backs were sore, legs stiff, and they had painful sores from sitting almost constantly on the hard thwarts, but the pace was kept, 30 strokes to the minute, 1,800 to the hour—a rhythm, pull, and endurance that had been developed in a hard school. It equaled 50 miles daily, more or less.

On July 7 a gale blew up out of the west and they hove to with their sea anchor again. When everything was secured, the two oarsmen put on life jackets, made their life lines fast, and lay hunched together on the floor boards amidships. Though partly sheltered from rain squalls, they had to bail regularly. By the ninth the sea anchor could no longer be depended on. The tops of some of the crests were breaking aboard, and one man bailed almost constantly while the other did what he could at the oars to keep her headed to the sea.

At nine the following morning Samuelson saw a huge sea bearing down. "Look out!" he called.

"This is it!" shouted Harbo, a moment before it broke and caught them quartering on the bow.

The *Fox* started to lift, was swept round, and in an instant capsized with the two men struggling beneath the surface of the icy water.

The life lines held, and when their heads broke the surface they pulled clear, fought back to the hull, and secured a hand hold on the runners that served as bilge keels.

The compartments in the bow and stern helped to keep *Fox* afloat, but some oars and much gear were floating away. Harbo and Samuelson watched their chance and after several attempts righted the boat, climbed back aboard, and began bailing.

It was difficult work balancing to keep the dory from capsizing again while bailing furiously against the water that came over the gunwales. Though it seemed hopeless at first, they bailed doggedly.

When she was clear they stripped, each in turn while the other rowed, wrung out their clothes, and put them back on again. During the rest of the night they stayed at the oars for warmth, to keep the stiffness from their swollen joints and to keep headed to the sea.

In the morning the weather improved and they continued to row. Their hands were raw, and the chafing of their oilskins made it worse. A large portion of their provisions were gone, with the sea anchor, signal lights, and several oars. Some raw eggs, sea biscuits, and a little rice had to be rationed carefully, as they were still less than halfway to Europe.

Five days later the dory was sighted by the full-rigged bark *Zito,* bound from Quebec to Pembroke, England. The bark came up, backed her yards, and hove to. *Fox* drew alongside, and the two men went aboard for their first hot meal in over a month.

The *Zito* was from Larvik, Norway, and several of her crew came from the same town as the dory sailors. They were given a warm welcome, clothes were dried, and water, provisions, and material for a new sea anchor were lowered to the dory. Much heartened, Harbo and Samuelson took up their oars with renewed strength and spirit.

At six weeks out, despite their best efforts, *Fox* was still only halfway across the Atlantic. It was decided to increase the pace. But how? For weeks their stroke had been the maximum for men who rowed steadily all of the day and most of the night. The few hours they slept could not be cut, so it was agreed to do away with the hour of rest after lunch and dinner.

Stroke after stroke, mile after mile, hourly, daily, nightly it was oars and oars alone. Sores increased from sitting on the hard thwarts, backs ached, legs swelled, but for the next nine days they averaged 65 miles a day.

Four hundred miles west of the Scilly Islands, they spoke the bark *Eugen* bound from Halifax to Swansea.

"You have done enough," they were told and were urged to give it up, to allow their sore hands to heal, regain the strength to stand on their feet, and recover the use of their joints. Lesser men would have yielded. But the two steady, single-minded Norwegians shook their heads and took up their oars again.

Hour after hour, mile after mile, day and night, it was four oars rising and falling in unison, 1,800 strokes to the hour—a torture to hands, back, and buttocks broken only by a few hours of sleep. The Viking galleys, thirty-two men to a long ship, with the men changing sides every two hours, averaged but 3 knots in fair weather—no better than Harbo and Samuelson.

On Saturday morning, August 1, fifty-five days out from New York, the obdurate dorymen made an accurate landfall on Bishop Rock lighthouse in the Scilly Islands, the southwestern tip of Britain. Shortly before noon both were helped ashore at St. Marys, and within the hour a cable dispatch went out:

> ROWBOAT FOX PASSED IN ELEVEN A.M. TWO OCCUPANTS WELL
> BUT EXHAUSTED.

Except for sea sores, boils on their buttocks, chafed raw skin, and the condition of their hands, a doctor's examination showed both men to be in good condition. However, on their first day ashore they developed bad colds.

After a few days' rest, *Fox* was rowed out from the Scillys and on up the English Channel 250 miles to Le Havre, where they arrived on the seventh of August to the cheers of a large crowd. From there they rowed up the Seine to Paris.

Barely enough was made in France and England to pay their living expenses, and the two men returned to New York with the dory on a steamer. Harbo went back to harbor piloting and Samuelson to Fish Row and oyster dredging and clamming with his sloop in Sandy Hook Bay.

In their later years both men returned to Norway, where Samuelson died at the age of seventy-five in a home at Farsund.

"The world will not soon see his like again," wrote a prominent Norwegian paper. "Ours is an effete age."

There have been many experimental craft and others devoted to unusual and sometimes novel rigs and gear. One of the earliest was the *City of Ragusa*, which had a two-blade windmill on her mizzenmast rigged to a propeller and later to a hand gear by which the skipper hoped to be able to produce his own wind. (See picture on page 145.)

The schooner-rigged raft *Nonpareil*, one of the strangest craft to make an ocean passage, was thought by her owner to be the perfect lifesaving vessel. Built mainly from three large rubber "sausages" (each 25 feet long by 2½ feet in diameter) with a wood decking and a small shelter tent amidships, *Nonpareil*, skippered by her builder John Mikes with a crew of two, departed New York June 4, 1868. Dependent mostly on dead reckoning, they made heavy weather of it, were hove to seven times, but arrived at Southampton safely after a forty-three-day passage.

In *Vraad*, a virtually unsinkable steel egg (18-ft. long, 8-ft. beam, 8-ft. deep with four watertight compartments and a single standing lugsail), Captain Ole Brude also thought he had invented the perfect ship's lifeboat. With three paid hands Captain Brude crossed the stormy North Atlantic late in 1904 from Alesund, Norway, to St. John, New Brunswick. From there in fierce squalls and gales that tied up New England shipping, *Vraad* was sailed down to Boston where they arrived January 16, 1905, 162 days from Norway.

Captain Walter Westborg, a Danish master mariner, sailed his 23-foot metal lifeboat *Dana Rescuer* with a 46 h.p. Perkins diesel (and a small mainsail and loose-footed square sail) from Esbjerg to England, France, Lisbon, the Canaries, and from the Cape Verdes to Panama in thirty-three days. Westborg had an automatic pilot and spent his spare time at sea reading books on agriculture in a cabin completely enclosed with a perspex dome.

Ian Major's (25-ft. LOA, 7-ft. 1-in. beam, 2-ft. 6-in. draft) turtle-decked sloop *Buttercup*, with an unstayed cantilever mast and a streamlined blister completely enclosing the cockpit, was one of the most unusual modern cruisers designed for ocean sailing.

An extensively rebuilt twenty-year-old vessel with a mahogany hull, edge fitted with no caulking, *Buttercup* was rigged with a small foresail and a loose-footed sliding gunter-type mainsail with a hollow yard sharply curved to increase the width of the sail at the head. Twin keels with 800 pounds of lead in each enabled her to sit upright when aground.

After a shakedown cruise from Port-Vendres, France, to Gibraltar and on to the Canaries, Ian Major with Gordon Sillars left Las Palmas May 5, 1956, and under a headsail set from a head yard with the foot free had a very good twenty-nine-day trade-wind crossing to Georgetown, Barbados.

Buttercup's wind-vane-operated rudder, the first trim-tab gear ever fitted to a transocean sailing vessel, did all the steering for the Atlantic passage. Her unstayed mast and square sail eliminated chafe, and a trysail set right to the masthead and sheeted hard aft curtailed much of the rolling when under her square sail in the trades.

For their serious attempt to improve gear and equipment for ocean cruising in small craft, Major and Sillars were given the first Voss Award of The Slocum Society.

Half-Safe

Ben Carlin, an Australian, felt that a "man is not made to go about being safe and comfortable and well-fed and amused. Almost any man if you put the thing to him, not in words but in the shape of opportunities, will show that he knows as much. Against his interest, against his happiness, he is constantly being driven to do unreasonable things. Some force not himself impels him and go he must."

A trip around the world in an amphibious jeep was dismissed by most people who heard about it as a harebrained stunt that couldn't possibly succeed.

They were wrong.

To Carlin, an ex-British Army major, an intelligent individual, and a skilled automotive engineer, the idea became an obsession. The problems encountered by Ben and his wife Elinore, who accompanied him during the first years of the jeep *Half-Safe's* voyaging, would have ended the venture a score of times for most adventurers; first during three frustrating years of preparation and later during mechanical setbacks at sea, including the difficulty of towing enough fuel so that *Half-Safe* could have its approximate one gallon per hour day and night crossing several oceans. There was the unique problem of laying to a sea anchor in heavy weather in an 18-foot jeep heavily laden with fuel, gear, and supplies. Like most circumnavigators, the Carlins were short of funds most of the time.

After a very hard thirty-one-day voyage from Halifax, Nova Scotia, across the North Atlantic, the Carlins drove their war-surplus jeep safely ashore at Fayal in the Azores late in August, 1950.

A warm welcome was extended by the Portuguese to the sturdy couple and their "zheep amfibic," as the islanders called it. "Horta simply closed down for the day," said Elinore, "and proclaimed a Festa da Jeep."

Crossing from Fayal to Funchal in the Madeiras late in November nearly put an end to *Half-Safe* and the Carlins. That they survived can be attributed to courage and stamina of a very high degree.

Half-Safe rode out the first day and night of gale-force winds very well with oil bags and a sea anchor streamed out from astern. But a second gale that swept down on the night of November 30 parted the warp of their sea anchor. An improvised drogue proved of little use and was soon in ribbons. After three days of strong winds and heavy seas, it was necessary to keep the engine turning over to prevent *Half-Safe* broaching to.

On the evening of December 4 it was blowing 70 m.p.h. when a trailing line fouled the propeller. A second later *Half-Safe* was broadside on to the sea. Despite the wind force and long-sweeping waves, Carlin stripped, went over the side, swam under the wildly pitching tons of steel, and, slashing out with his sheath knife, cleared the propeller, fought back to the surface, and crawled aboard, naked against the icy blast. The engine was started, and for the next forty hours they ran before a huge sea and a wind that reached hurricane force at times.

During the night of the fifth the weather improved, though a blocked fuel pipe and a jammed starter added to their problems. For the rest of the passage they bucked a S.E. wind and were twenty-three days at sea from Fayal when their battered craft crept slowly into the harbor of Funchal on December 12.

The crossing from the Madeiras to Cape Juby on the North African coast was uneventful, and *Half-Safe* went on from there across deserts, mountains, and other ocean waters. Visits were made to many countries, including Holland, Belgium, Germany, Denmark, and Sweden.

After 61,000 engine miles, much of it under corrosive and very arduous conditions, the 18-ft. 3-in. LOA by 5-ft. 3-in. beam ocean jeep that had survived a hurricane needed and got a refitting and rebuilding during a long stay in London.

Half-Safe's steel fittings were replaced with aluminum and plastic until she was 600 pounds lighter. Her fuel capacity was beefed up and her neoprene waterproofing thickened before she left London to cross the English Channel and visit Paris. From France the Carlins went over the Simpler Pass into Italy and on through Yugoslavia and Greece. From Zagreb they journeyed to Ankara, crossed the high, arid plateaus, and went down through the Taurus Mountains and across Syria to Baghdad.

After crossing the Atlantic under her own power with calls at many countries in Europe, the *Half-Safe* visits London and the Strand with Elinore and Ben Carlin.

In Iran *Half-Safe* was mistaken for a Russian tank and received a military escort to the Pakistan border.

The rainy monsoon season was spent in India, much of it in Calcutta making repairs. It was here that Elinore, a woman of courage far above the average, remembered her continual seasickness across the Atlantic and, thinking of the sea passages ahead to Japan and Alaska, made other plans.

Carlin crossed the Bay of Bengal alone and was joined by Barry Hanley in Akyab for the run through Burma, Thailand, Cambodia, and Vietnam.

On the 500-mile passage across the South China Sea to Hong Kong they lived mostly on fruit, bread, and canned beans. Leaded gasoline that fouled the engine made it necessary for Carlin to do a complete valve job at sea. In Hong Kong, thinking to avert that problem on the long transpacific passages, he converted the engine to run on kerosene, only to find out later that none was available in the area.

In Formosa they were welcomed with fireworks, a military escort, and all the free watermelons they could carry for the passage north across the East China Sea to Okinawa and Kyushu.

Arriving in Japan too late in August, 1956, for a Pacific crossing to Canada, Carlin and Hanley enjoyed a few months of sukiyaki and rice wine before heading out over the North Pacific in the spring of 1957.

A 1,300-mile voyage from Hokkaido Island in the north of Japan brought the bearded and bushed amphibious jeepsters chugging slowly into Shemya, an Air Force base in the Aleutians, on July 7, 1957. At sea the lightly constructed steel hull dripped steadily, and nearly everything was damp most of the time from condensation.

Shoving off from Shemya after a short rest, Carlin and Hanley pressed on to Cold Bay on the western tip of the Alaskan peninsula, completing another 1,000-mile ocean passage on the homeward stretch to the Yukon, British Columbia, and across to Montreal.

Ben Carlin, the first to circle the world by land and by sea in an amphibious jeep, spent $36,000 and ten years of his life on *Half-Safe* and his 40,000-mile circumnavigation.

Though the oceans have been crossed for many reasons in a variety of craft from dugout canoes to a combination sea sled and balloon, almost every year there are new ventures—like the full-scale replica of a ninth-century Viking drakar sailed by seven Norwegians in 1963 from Norway to New York in twenty days. (The Viking drakar was powered with diesel motors!)

Some plans, like that of thirty-five-year-old London College lecturer Geoffrey Ashe, who intends to sail a "dark ages" boat across the Atlantic to prove that Saint Brendan of Ireland, the Abbot of Clonfert, sailed to the New World in the sixth century hundreds of years before Leif Ericson, have many followers.

Lehi IV and *Lehi V*

De Vere Baker, a Mormon elder who skippered his rafts *Lehi I, Lehi II,* and *Lehi III* out to sea from San Francisco Bay, is determined to prove it is possible to drift from the Middle East to America in support of evidence that a white civilization existed there over two thousand years ago.

The Prophet Lehi, according to Baker, used rafts to get some of the ten lost tribes from the Holy Land to Central America in 600 B.C. Following his successful drift in *Lehi IV* with a crew of four from Redondo Beach, California, to Hawaii in sixty-nine days, Baker built *Lehi V,* a 40-ft. by 20-ft. raft. To his followers who helped raise the $50,000 to build *Lehi V,* Baker's theories are no more fanciful than those of Thor Heyerdahl of *Kon-Tiki* fame.

In 1963 the forty-nine-year-old Mormon raft skipper, his wife Nona, and a crew of five departed San Diego on *Lehi V* for a five-year 14,000-mile drift to trace the voyage which the *Book of Mormons* relates that the Nephites took as one of the lost tribes of Israel.

Lehi V was lost off Lower California. But Baker still plans to drift across the Indian Ocean to Ceylon, through the islands of the Far East to Manila, and north along the east coast of Japan to the Japanese Current that he expects will take his final *Lehi* raft across the Pacific to Central America.

One of the earliest Westerners to make a major ocean crossing without a sextant or chronometer was Captain William C. Newman, a professional seaman who made the first power-boat crossing of the Atlantic in the 39-foot-LOA *Abiel Abbott Low* to prove a small motorboat could make a transatlantic passage using only kerosene for fuel. Accompanied by his sixteen-year-old son, Newman departed New York July 2, 1902. Though the *Abiel Abbott Low* ran into a series of gales and laid to her sea anchor more than once, Captain Newman, navigating with only a compass and a barometer, had an over-all average of 86 miles daily for the thirty-six-day passage to Falmouth, England.

Another who sailed without a sextant was Paul Muller, a German, who departed Hamburg July 6, 1928, in *Aga,* an 18-ft. LOA, 6-ft. beam open boat with a single sail. Equipped with only a compass for navigation, Muller voyaged to Holland, France, Spain, and Africa and crossed from Santa Cruz in the Canaries to Barbados, where he arrived April 22, 1929.

The mystery of the disappearance of that strange sea wanderer Ira C. Sparks of Indiana and Honolulu, who sailed his 16-foot *Dauntless* out from Hawaii toward Mecca in 1924 and never was seen since, though his empty punt arrived in good shape at Zamboanga in the Philippines several months later, has never been solved.

There will always be men and boys of restless imagination, and the records are filled with accounts of frustrated voyagers. Take, for example, the apprentice in the Swedish schoolship who stole the captain's portable bathtub and sailed ashore in it in the Torres Strait Islands. The government soon picked him up and after an official hearing deported him, because he did not have proper papers or visas and did not bring his craft to a port of entry. And there was the crew of the *Rieko Maru*, who crossed the Pacific in 1953 with a cargo of saki (rice wine) to make their fortunes but ran short of water and had to breach their cargo—with very odd results on their landfall.

In this modern day of instruments, when every pawnbroker has sextants and chronometers, a few wanderers still put to sea without so much as an astrolabe. Others sail without charts, with an uncompensated compass, or with none at all. Some get by for a while though many do not, and occasionally tragedy is shipmate on these voyages.

Jan and Al, two young men from Holland sailing their way around the world on a shoestring in *Harry*, a converted, ex-Morecambe Bay prawner, arrived at Vigo, Spain, under jury rig after an encounter with a steamer in the Bay of Biscay. Repairs were made, and they pushed on to the Canary Islands. The *Harry* departed Las Palmas for San Francisco with four compasses aboard but no sextant and ended up ashore on a beach in Brazil.

Twenty-one-year-old Wolfgang von Schwarzenfeld left his studies of Oriental philosophy at Cologne to build *Seepfeil* (Sea Arrow), a steel catamaran 25-ft. LOA and 15-ft. beam, rigged as a Bermudian ketch. Sailing solo from Veer, Holland, Von Schwarzenfeld was hit by a ship that failed to stop, southwest of Ushant. With a stove-in port hull, *Seepfeil* limped across the Bay of Biscay but was prevented from reaching Coruña by strong headwinds. Rounding Cape Finisterre she ran before a northerly down the coast of Portugal. At Safi, Morocco, repairs were made by Wolfgang, who then sailed on to the Canaries where he was joined by his brother Heinz.

With no log, no sextant, no chronometer, and an unadjusted compass (on an all-metal boat!) the brothers Von Schwarzenfeld departed Las Palmas early in 1955 in their craft (renamed *Gerümple*) and had an uneventful thirty-day passage to Barbados using a system of their own for determining latitude from the shadows cast on a board.

Olaf Aken, a Swede, and Dan Mulville, an Englishman, found the abandoned thirty-year-old Camaret crabber *Aventurier* in the Canary Islands and put her back in condition for an ocean voyage. By the time they were ready to sail they were flat broke, but they were determined to get to the West Indies as soon as possible and pushed off from Las Palmas in the summer of 1956 with inadequate provisions and no navigating instruments. Expecting a fair-weather run in the trades, they encountered contrary trade winds and had to beat most of the way. About midway across a leak in the water tank was discovered, and a few days later the *Aventurier's* fresh-water supply was gone. Provisions were low, and after the fortieth day fluids pressed from raw dolphin flesh were drunk. Navigating by dead reckoning, Aken and Mulville made English Harbor fifty-nine days out from the Canaries.

Another thing again in the way of navigating without instruments was the voyage to freedom of three Polynesians over 2,360 miles of the South Pacific in an open boat with only a fifty-cent compass to navigate by.

Though their blood has been diluted by two centuries of Western voyagers, the Polynesians of Easter Island have not entirely forgotten the odyssey of Hotu Matu'a and the long-voyaging canoes. Drawn by a strange longing for the Polynesian heartland 2,500 miles to the northwest that most Easter Islanders have never seen, a few still sail out in the middle of the night toward Tahiti. Of nine small boats averaging less than 20 feet overall that have attempted the voyage in recent years, four have made it safely in twenty-nine to thirty-seven days. Five boats and thirty-one islanders have been lost at sea somewhere between Rapa-nui and the Tuamotus.

Though Easter now has an airport, it has always been and for its present 1,100 inhabitants still is one of the most isolated places on earth. No commercial ships call, and native islanders are not permitted to leave without special permission from the Chilean Navy, which rules the outpost. A harsh, rocky, lava land dependent mostly on the raising of 40,000 sheep, Easter lacks a single fresh-water spring or stream. Every drop of rain and brackish well water has to be carefully hoarded. Is it any wonder many have longed to escape during the past quarter century?

Late in 1956 Pedro Tepihe, long dissatisfied with the rule of the Chilean Navy, felt that he couldn't take it any longer and, accompanied by Aurelio Hill and Filipe Teao, decided to sail west to the Tuamotus to ask the French government to add Easter Island to France's other Polynesian possessions.

To avoid alerting the naval authorities in Hanga Roa, their preparations had to be made in strictest secrecy. Others who had tried to escape from Easter had been returned and punished. (Pedro's father, a teacher who had been haunted by the restless spirits—aku-aku—that islanders believe still inhabit their lava slopes, had built a small cutter and set sail one night with two friends in an attempt to reach the outside world. None of the three was ever heard from again.)

Pedro borrowed an open boat 24 feet overall with a 4½-foot beam from friends, and Filipe quietly made a mast for it from the limb of a tree, while Aurelio cut and sewed a crude mainsail from an old awning and a jib from some heavy burlap. The night before sailing, two sacks of corn, some salted mutton, sugar cane, bananas, and a small cask of murky water were secreted aboard.

Two hours before dawn on November 7, 1956, the trio sailed quietly out from the lee of the island of outsized stone images into the sweep of the long-rolling seas from Antarctica.

A course was kept, according to Pedro, "so the sun always rose behind us and was ahead at setting. At night *Matariki* [the Pleiades] and *Tue* [Orion] guided us."

"The days were long," said Filipe, "and sometimes wild. At times we would disappear in the great waves and could see only mountains of green water and the sky."

Soaked much of the time, they bailed frequently during the early part of the voyage. When the last days of November slipped by without sight of an island, Filipe began to think they had missed the Tuamotus and that a *moai kavakava* (evil spirit) was guiding them to a slow death at sea. Twice a little rainfall helped their depleted water supply, but it wasn't much. Scooped up from the bottom of the boat, it tasted salty but they drank it anyway.

"We steered steady to the north of where the sun set in the direction of the star *te Ura Ahi-ahi* [Venus]." By the twenty-third day, food and water were gone. Aurelio, sick and badly blistered from the scorching rays of the sun, lay in a delirious coma on a bed of sorts made across two thwarts by his mates, who doused him and each other occasionally with sea water.

On the morning of the thirtieth day, Filipe at the helm thought he saw the faint outlines of a ring of palms. Twice he saw it and then he didn't. He felt perhaps it was a mirage; perhaps he was getting delirious. On seeing it for the third time he called out "land!" and pointed ahead over the bow.

Without food or water for seven days, Aurelio was too far gone to move or speak. Pedro, unbelieving at first, looked hard, nodded, and mumbled a prayer.

Hours later they entered a small pass in the reef at Kauehi Atoll. Coming in to a deserted beach, Pedro and Filipe had enough strength left to pull the boat up and to drag Aurelio out and up the beach to the shade of a coconut tree, but both men were too weak to climb the tree for a drinking nut. Sinking to the sand for a brief rest, they arose shortly to stagger to a village where they were given help and their presence reported to a missionary, who notified the governor at Tahiti. Later they were taken in the government schooner *Tamara* to Papeete, where Aurelio was hospitalized and slowly recovered.

The Chilean government was notified but showed no interest in returning the men to Easter Island, and they were allowed to remain with Polynesian relatives under French rule.

Early in 1965, following a brief rebellion against naval rule on Easter Island, reforms were granted, an election held, and the native islanders given a larger measure of self-rule.

A natural craving for the simple life manifests itself in many strange

("Only step out of my sunlight," said Diogenes.) An audacious mid-sixties craft from Sausalito, California, designed for ample sunlight and "getting away from it all."

ways. Some have fled to the desert, to a remote mountain, or to a monastery, and a few who chose the sea became as devoted to solitude as Diogenes who, tiring of looking for an honest man, went to live in a tub and, when Alexander the Great asked what he might do for him, replied, "Only step out of my sunlight."

René Lescombe

Wounded as a paratrooper in Indo-China, René Lescombe was permanently lame. "On land I am ugly, at sea beautiful," he once wrote, attempting to explain his strange obsession with the ocean. "Like a forgotten creature from the beginning of time I seek a silence that towers above the world of noise."

Soon after his wife left him in 1957, Lescombe built a 13-ton raft of seven pine trunks and, with scanty provisions, departed France for South America June 28 minus official clearance and most other requirements for an east-west crossing of the Atlantic.

"My bitterness is called Babette, but not my hopes, not any more," wrote Lescombe. "I have no more hope. Do not hasten to put a label on my solitude."

After twelve days of uncertain navigation, the lonely Frenchman found himself off the African coast, taking a bad pounding in the breakers. His life was saved by a native fisherman, who, after pulling him from the heavy surf, became his friend and took him to live in the small Negro village of Canon.

Mimi Teschoueyre, the fisherman, and another African helped René Lescombe to start building another raft, and for the next six months when not working on it he studied navigation and spent long, pleasant evenings with his African companions. Nights he preferred to sleep out under the stars.

When the second raft was completed it was named *Pot-au-Noir* (Black Pot). To a friend who wrote urging that he give up this second venture and return to France, Lescombe replied, "There are girls who have knitted me sweaters. That's very nice, but, you understand, these amount to strait jackets. The constant 'happiness under pressure' which young girls dream about is as unbearable to me as an iron lung. House walls are prison walls."

Sailing westward on his second attempt to cross the Atlantic, Lescombe practiced his newly acquired knowledge of navigation, watched his gear closely, fished, and for the first week out lived entirely off the sea.

A second gale quickly put an end to his westerly progress, and a day and a night of heavy seas reduced *Pot-au-Noir* to a barely floating wreck that Lescombe clung to for five days and was again tossed up on the African coast.

Making his way back to Canon and his African fishermen friends, the lame Frenchman started at once to construct *Pot-au-Noir II*. Putting all of his savings from a meager Air Force pension into materials for his third raft and refusing to sponge on his friends, Lescombe occasionally went several days at a time without eating and slept out under the stars.

Restless, lonely, and anxious to be free of the land, as the time approached for his departure he wrote, "I'm ugly as soon as I'm leading a normal life, like an old stuffed bird. But I'm beautiful when I'm alone and risking my life on the sea. Stupid maybe, but beautiful. Nothing is simple. Therefore, when I am asked why I do this or that—with or without authorization, with or without favorable winds, I can only reply, 'I leave in eight days.'"

With very few supplies, makeshift gear, and almost no navigation equipment, Lescombe again said farewell to his African friends and started his third attempt to cross the Atlantic.

Four days after departing, *Pot-au-Noir II* picked up the trade wind and had a full week of clear weather and fair winds. On the twelfth day out the sky turned ominous. There was lightning on the horizon, and by noon large swells were sweeping the raft.

Taking what precautions he could, Lescombe secured everything movable, "checked every knot, lashed the sails double to the boom," and a few hours later from the meager shelter of his tiny cabin wondered if he was in the center of a hurricane. He had never before experienced anything like it. In heavy weather there was always danger, but this was different. For two days and nights there was no sleep, no certainty of survival or of anything other than "mad winds and wild seas crashing down and over." After forty-eight hours, Lescombe was physically exhausted.

The battered raft proved sturdy enough to survive, and after the depression passed the sense of having survived the worst storm he had ever known put Lescombe in a mood of solitary elation. "I go to sea for what I will not find there," he wrote, "noise, crowds, cities."

Much work had to be done in the fair days that followed. There was damage to be repaired, trouble with the steering, frayed and loosened lashings to be renewed. There were records to be kept; there were fish to be caught. To a man who depended on fish and seaweed to survive, days on end without wind in the Sargasso became a grim menace.

After two weeks without a breeze the raft moved on, and the gaunt, black-bearded Frenchman became alert again to the creaks and strains of the rigging and lashings.

Fifty days from the Canary Islands, *Pot-au-Noir II* struck an outcropping of rocks on the east side of the island of Barbados and sank to the bottom of the cove. Lescombe, reduced in weight to a skeleton, got safely away and stumbled ashore at Fall-in Cove.

Weak as he was, Lescombe managed to salvage parts of the raft and later, with money obtained from teaching French, went to Pointe-à-Pitre, Guadeloupe, and began work soon after arrival on his next and last raft, the 26-by-9-ft. *1000 Bornes*.

Plagued again by poverty and endless disappointments, in addition to bad weather, he was unable to depart from Guadeloupe before May 25, 1963, bound for the Bay of Biscay and Arcachon.

"This life I have chosen," he wrote, "isn't really human. I sail to the limits of the possible. Afterwards, if there is an afterwards, I will be wiser, because I believe the sea has taught me humility."

An admirer of the poet Rilke, Lescombe held a master's degree and, if he had not been obsessed with the sea, might have lived a long life in a remote monastery.

Late in May, 1963, René Lescombe spoke a Greek cargo ship, and later he was sighted by a Russian freighter. On the seventh of June, a Portuguese fishing vessel from the Azores sighted the *1000 Bornes*. The mast and sail were gone and the raft was breaking up in a bad gale. The Portuguese fishermen tried twice to reach Lescombe, but the seas made it impossible. Later the wreck of *1000 Bornes* and the remains of René Lescombe were found washed up on the island of Flores.

"Life and solitude are full of pain," Lescombe wrote in one of his last letters from Guadeloupe. "I prefer the sea."

"Do not hasten to put a label on my solitude," said René Lescombe, who was last seen by a Portuguese vessel fighting to save his foundering *1000 Bornes* in a gale off the Azores.

Pipe Dream

Somewhere in the South Seas "to get away from a material civilization visibly crumbling away at the seams" is Al Wolfson, who built his dream ship—the 34-foot-LOA trimaran *Pipe Dream*—from three 24-inch-diameter water mains filled with styrofoam and added a 32-foot steel lamppost for a mast.

A former aircraft engineer and a vegetarian who prefers the spartan life, Wolfson provisioned *Pipe Dream* mainly with coconuts, dried fruits, several sacks of sun-dried bread, dried vegetables, and many gallons of honey and peanut butter (which he mixes half and half).

Departing Sausalito, California, in August, 1963, he crossed to Hawaii in thirty-eight days. After a year in the fiftieth state, Wolfson found the main islands too much like the concrete jungles he had sailed 2,300 miles south to get away from. With his young island bride Yoshiko and Larry Appleton for crew, he put out from Waipio Stream, Hawaii, bound for the remote Marquesas.

"I am like a dead man," said the forty-nine-year-old skipper as he cast off. "I fear nothing."

Nearly two months later, on October 8, 1964, *Pipe Dream*, in need of repairs, put in to Tabukinberu in the Southern Gilberts 3,500 miles off course!

"I knew very well where we were going even if my calculations were off," said Wolfson, who prefers no definite destination, and added, before leaving the Gilbert Islands, "our direction and next island will always be determined by wind, sea, and chance."

An herb doctor who subscribes to Thor Heyerdahl's migration theories, Al Wolfson plans to study Polynesian and Melanesian medicinal lore and is looking for an island that he once saw in a dream with "red rocks, low coconut trees, and lots of fruit."

L'Hérétique

Why should an intelligent and successful doctor (a former sufferer from tuberculosis and jaundice) give up a good position as a medic and researcher to cross the Atlantic alone in a 15-foot rubber dinghy without food or water beyond what he could get from the sea?

In 1952 Alain Bombard, a young French physician, was determined to prove that the shipwrecked mariner can live for months on plankton and fish. As a student of the nutrient qualities of the sea he had worked in the laboratories of the Monaco Oceanographic Institute, and his many researches convinced him that raw fish and plankton could provide the essential food elements for sustaining life and that adequate quantities of fresh water could be obtained by eating raw fish if taken in small amounts for a limited time.

"What I remember most about you, Alain," wrote Percy Knauth in the *Saturday Review*, "is your courage and faith in the face of all who, early or late in your venture, decried you as a fool. Faith in life is what we need so much today, when faith in death appears to be man's answer to his problems."

Because he was widely laughed at and ridiculed for attacking the prevailing belief that it was impossible to live on the resources of the sea alone, Bombard named his craft *L'Hérétique*. Fifteen feet long with 6-foot beam, *L'Hérétique* was a horseshoe-shaped rubber life raft with a short mast, a few feet of sail, and leeboards for maneuverability. Its floats were divided into five sealed compartments.

Following a difficult trial run in the Mediterranean with a companion, Bombard departed Casablanca alone on August 24, 1952, made Las Palmas in ten days, and departed the Canaries October 19 for the 2,900-mile voyage to the West Indies.

A three-masted training schooner of the Spanish Navy hove to off Las Palmas and dipped her colors as *L'Hérétique* sailed out toward the south of Gran Canaria, her tiny Tricolor taut in the breeze.

Bombard intended to take advantage of the N.E. trade wind between latitudes 10° N. and 25° N., a course that would take him past the Cape Verde Islands to the Antilles. As an amateur navigator, he told himself he at least knew as much about navigation as Columbus.

With a makeshift spear fashioned from his knife and an oar, he soon caught a dorado, made a natural bone hook from its gill cover, and "from then on had all the food and liquid I needed every day."

At the end of the first week he logged, "If I am where I think I am, I should be at Latitude 21° North by Wednesday, changing course to the west on Thursday, after covering seven hundred miles in ten days."

Flying fish chased by dorados that hit the sail, mast, or rigging were welcome additions to what he caught with his line. One day it was sea perch, another day dorado, once it was a snake mackerel, and another time barracuda. Dorado were the easiest of all to catch, by using a bone hook baited with a flying fish.

Convinced that a man can survive for thirty days without food but less than eight days without water, Bombard was dependent most of all on the 50 to 80 per cent of fresh water found in the average fish. For food value the fish were eaten raw or partly dried in the sun. To prevent scurvy, a hundred grams, or two cups, of plankton were consumed daily. A fine mesh net was used to catch plankton, as was his sea anchor on occasion. "Dried in the sun it tastes like cooked shrimp," said Bombard. For a change of diet he ate a shearwater raw and compared it favorably to steak tartare.

Tragedy was narrowly averted in mid-ocean when he went overboard to swim and retrieve a cushion that had fallen over and was fast drifting away. Acting quickly he left *L'Hérétique* lying to a sea anchor but failed to notice that, instead of submerging, the light cloth sea anchor formed an air pocket and, together with the rubber craft, moved away before a light breeze. When Bombard, an expert swimmer, noticed *L'Hérétique* gone he tried to overtake her but could barely keep pace. It took an hour of the hardest going, gaining foot by foot, before he was able to crawl back aboard, nearly exhausted.

Day after day he ate his raw fish and fish juice with an occasional spoonful of plankton. When not writing in his log, sewing his sail, or catching and preparing the fish and plankton, Bombard read Nietzsche, Spinoza, and Montaigne. He enjoyed going over his favorite musical scores, the two Passions of Bach and the Quartets of Beethoven. (Halfway across, when paper ran short and he was forced to sacrifice a book "for purposes of my natural functions, I decided the most appropriate was Rabelais.")

Fifty-three days out, Bombard spoke the British freighter *Arakaka* bound from Liverpool to Georgetown. Invited aboard he ate an ounce of liver, an egg, and a spoonful of cabbage and was strongly urged by the captain to give up the venture, stay aboard, and be landed in British Guiana.

"I have to admit," said Bombard, "I very nearly stayed."

But he declined, knowing full well that he was still nearly seven hundred miles from his destination.

"Then what can I do for you?" urged Captain Carter. "You must let me do something."

Thinking of his devotion to Bach, Bombard asked him to request the B.B.C. to play the *Sixth Brandenburg Concerto* on Christmas Eve.

Soon after his visit aboard the *Arakaka*, Bombard found the bit of liver and cabbage severely upset the fish-and-plankton diet balance that he had become accustomed to and gave him severe cramps and other complications.

During the last ten days *L'Hérétique* leaked increasingly and had to be bailed and watched closely. It was during this period that the resolute French physician became convinced that the state of mind and morale of a castaway are more important than food. Sustained by the strength of his convictions, he made a landfall on Barbados on December 23.

"For 43 days I drank only fish juice and for 65 days lived exclusively on what I could catch from the sea. I lost 55 pounds in weight," Bombard admitted, "and it is true, I was somewhat shrunken on arrival, but I got there."

Captain Carter of the *Arakaka* spoke for seamen everywhere when, hearing of Bombard's safe arrival, he cabled:

> CONGRATULATIONS TO A GALLANT GENTLEMAN—WHO HAD SO MUCH COURAGE IN HIS CONVICTIONS TO CARRY ON WHEN SAFETY AND LUXURY WERE OFFERED.

Visitors to Paris may now see *L'Hérétique* in the Naval Museum.

JACINTO BELDA

Jacinto Belda, a one-legged fisherman of Alicante, Spain, who spent nearly half of his sixty years aboard a 10-foot rowboat, said early in 1965, "Here I will live until the Lord calls me."

The story goes that Jacinto lost his leg to a shark while on a strange sea quest, but he tells inquirers, "The truth I only know and will tell nobody.

"I promised myself to live aboard my rowboat to the end of my days and I am well on my way. Many think I am crazy. But I do not care. I feel completely independent and happy."

Town officials offered to buy the crippled fisherman an orthopedic leg, but he declined the offer. "I do not need it," he replied. "Please spend your money on someone who may need it more than I do." Cigarettes and an occasional bottle of wine are the only gifts he welcomes.

"The sea left me disabled and it is the sea that should provide me with the necessary means to get along," says Jacinto, who spends six to eight hours a day catching bait which he sells to pole fishermen.

"Profits are low, but they permit me to live on my own effort. A broth, some fish or meat, and a cup of black coffee I cook myself are all I need to survive. Believe me," says Jacinto Belda, "I would not trade my humble rowboat for a palace. This has been my home for half my life, and I would like it to be my coffin when I die."

CHAPTER 7

Small-Ship Women

It was not the beauty alone of Helen of Troy which launched a thousand ships.

~~~~~~

FOR many years now modern blue-water women have been making major ocean passages and circumnavigating in able, well-found little vessels. With modern gear there is no reason why women who like sailing cannot be as good at it as men. All of us know a few who have put aside high heels and hairdos for jeans and a real share of ship's work.

Long-experienced deep-water cruising mates like Beryl Smeeton, Brita Holmdahl, Susan Hiscock, Ann Pye, Margie Petersen, and many others can plot a course as well as anyone, have earned their status as competent sailors and navigators the hard way, and in an emergency can tackle any job aboard.

One sign of a mature civilization, according to ocean sailor H. G. Hasler, is that men actually enjoy the companionship of their women. For years women have been civilizing the insides of sailing vessels, and, "It is a pity," says Hasler, "that seagoing women have not raised their voices more loudly."

Long before Columbus and Magellan, women of spirit were leading sea voyages and shaping a tradition of seafaring that goes back to the Viking Age and the Norwegian *Vestervegen*—"western way" voyages. At the time that Leif Ericson made his 300-mile hop across Davis Strait to a New World, tenth-century women were sailing open boats under a square sail on expeditions across the northern sea. The fourth and last known Vinland voyage included many women in the crew and, as leader, the fierce Norse seawoman Freydis.

Alivelda, daughter of a Gothic king, held command in a man's world, and Anne Bonney was another who more than held her own wielding a rapier, swinging a cutlass, or sailing a ship.

"Love is not what you think," Mary Read told Captain Calico Jack Rackham a few hours after she killed a buccaneer in a sword duel to save the sailor she loved. Asked by Rackham why she continued to follow the sea and a life almost certain to lead to the hangman's noose, Mary replied, "As to hanging, I think it no great hardship, for were it not for that, every cowardly fellow would turn pirate, and so infest the seas that sailors of courage would starve."

In a losing sea battle between Calico Jack and Captain Barnet of the Royal Navy, when Rackham and the rest of the crew deserted the deck, Anne Bonney and Mary Read fought on alone until overcome and put in chains. Whatever else they may have been, Mary Read and Anne Bonney were skilled sailors and in times of crisis displayed a greater degree of valor than their male followers.

Hsi Kai Ching Yih, who commanded her own flagship, was a fine junk sailor, but it was her capabilities as strict disciplinarian, efficient shipmaster, and keen tactician that gained her the command of more than five hundred Chinese pirate junks on the South China coast.

Among seagoing whaling women there were remarkable individuals like Abigail Jernegen of the *Eliza F. Mason*, the first white woman to spend a night on Japanese soil. Others, like Mary Carlin, married whaling masters while still in their teens, sailed out of Martha's Vinyard, New Bedford, and San Francisco to Talcahuano, Hakodate, Paita, Rarotonga, and Masafuera, went humpbacking off the African coast, and sought barrels of sperm from the Gulf of Anadyr and the Sea of Okhotsk to the Indian Ocean.

Almira Dexter of the whaler *Emily Morgan*, Ethelinde Lewis, and a few others like Mrs. John Heppingstone of the *Julian*, proved their mettle in the great disaster of 1871 when their entire whaling fleet of thirty-three ships was lost in an Arctic trap and they had to fight through pack ice in open whaleboats to reach Icy Cape and beyond.

Whaling wives like Gertrude West, one of the first white women to land at Point Barrow (a voyage in which the bark *California*'s anchors "were raised and dropped repeatedly to cut through pack ice"), outdid many of the male whaling mates in their ability to plot a course and take difficult star sights. They were good sailors with a keen knowledge of whaling and ship maneuvering under difficult conditions. In a typhoon off Japan when "we sprang the main topmast and twisted the rudder head off—and the lower main topsail, main spencer and foresail carried away" and the *Horatio* was so badly strained Gertrude and her husband thought she wouldn't weather the gale, she wrote, "Somehow I managed to put on four dresses over my bloomers—knowing without question that I was preparing for an open boat in that awful sea."

MARY PATTEN

Mary Patten, a beautiful young woman of refinement who sailed with her husband, Captain Joshua Patten of the *Neptune's Car*, became an accomplished navigator and at the end of her first trip around the world was given her own small micrometer-type Husan sextant.

On their next long voyage in *Neptune's Car*, Mary and Joshua sailed from New York in June, 1866, bound for San Francisco. On the long leg to Cape Horn, an incompetent first mate neglected his duties. After repeated warnings, when Captain Patten found the man still sleeping on watch and sailing under reefed courses contrary to orders, he took over the first mate's duties in addition to his own.

In the Strait of Le Maire, Captain Patten contracted an illness brought on from exhaustion and worry that soon developed into brain fever. Second mate Hare was advanced to first mate, but as he was unable to navigate Mary Patten took over as master, took her own observations, made up the reckonings by chronometer, laid the ship's courses, and commanded the officers and crew.

At a time when Mary had her hands full handling the ship off Cape Horn and doing her utmost to relieve the agony of her husband, who was close to death, the former first mate attempted to start a mutiny when she refused to reinstate him.

Acting decisively and at once, Mary called all hands aft, forthrightly gave them the facts straight from the shoulder, and asked for their allegiance to the ship and support for herself as master.

The second, third, and fourth mates respected her competence and proven ability, and the entire crew stood by her to a man.

Nearing the latitude of Valparaiso, the former mate was given another chance to return to some of his previous duties, but when Mary found him steering the ship off course and heading for the coast of Chile he was formally reduced to the rank of seaman.

Joshua Patten's condition became worse, and for the last twenty-five days of the passage from the Horn to California he was totally blind.

Between Mary Patten's duties as master of a 216-foot, 1,616-ton extreme clipper ship and her constant efforts to keep her husband alive, she had only brief snatches of sleep. In her report on arrival at San Francisco, 134 days from New York, it was noted that she had not had a full watch below for fifty nights previous to bringing *Neptune's Car* into the Golden Gate.

For her skill as master and devotion to the best traditions of the sea, Mary Patten was presented with $1,000 and a document of commendation by the underwriters.

ELEANOR WILSON

Eleanor Wilson, ordained minister and island pilot whose skill with a ship is known from Guam in the Marianas to Ebon in the Marshall Islands, became "Lady Skipper" in 1950 when the former captain was suddenly called home and no one else was available to take the missionary schooner on her regular run.

A small woman with white hair who kept a Bible beside her nautical almanac and set of *H. O. 214 Navigation Tables,* Miss Wilson was fifty-nine when she took command of the *Morning Star VI* (ex-*Norseman* of Boston) and in the following years cruised widely through the islands of Micronesia, bringing passengers and supplies and conducting christenings, marriages, funerals, and conferences with island leaders.

After learning navigation from a Navy captain, seamanship from the islanders, and pilotage from years of sailing in the Caroline and Marshall archipelagos, Eleanor Wilson found that a woman captain went against the grain of the Marshallese male. In their long tradition of priest-astronomer-navigator there had never been a woman to whom the secrets of a ship and the sea had been entrusted. The navigator was always a man of high rank and prestige.

But Eleanor Wilson, with her many years of experience in Micronesia, was not to be done in by island tradition. When orders came through from Beacon Street, Boston, to take over the *Star,* she quietly assembled the crew on the afterdeck.

"The ways of the Lord," said she, "are past understanding. He means for us—you and me together—to sail the *Star* and do His work. When Jesus began his ministry on earth he had only twelve disciples. Many were fishermen as you are. They set out to carry the gospel to the whole world. They did not despair. Nor did they question their orders. Our task is much simpler than theirs. We have only to carry on the work here in these islands."

Surprised, the men looked at her with respect and were silent.

"We will pull together with a will," she added. "So, come now. Let us all turn to at once."

"Praise the Lord," said Luckabudge, an ordained minister and spokesman for the Marshallese sailors. "We will sail the ship." To the islanders he added, "Since there is no man to be our captain, Mother Wilson will read the stars."

After her freight was loaded, the 64-ft.-LOA, 19-ton vessel carried up to twenty passengers on a first-come-first-carried basis. No charge was made for passage. The islanders brought their own food and slept on deck, and their baggage sometimes included coconuts, stalks of bananas, a few live chickens, and occasionally a pig or two on a tether. As the lady skipper put it, "The islanders consider the *Star* their ship, and of course they are right."

On one passage from Majuro to the Carolines, the schooner was approaching Mont Pass off Ponape in the middle of the night. Two men were on watch as usual. Below in her cabin the skipper felt restless and, deciding to have a look above, found the mate stretched out in the cockpit sound asleep. His watchmate was below and the helm was lashed. Without waking the man she quietly took over the wheel.

When the mate awoke he stared at the skipper and leaped to his feet. "Mother Wilson," he said, "I will take the wheel. Steering is not woman's work."

"No," she replied. "You go forward. I am *toban* [the man on watch] now."

When the lookout who had been sleeping below appeared, he too was sent forward.

At daybreak she took the *Star* in through the pass to Kolonia. When the anchor was down, she told the men in no uncertain terms what she expected of them in the future and from that day forward had an alert, dependable crew who could be counted on in any emergency. More effective than her words was the shame that they would never live down had it become known among the islands that they had been caught asleep on watch and the helm taken over by a woman.

Sailing the rounds of her 500,000-square-mile parish, Skipper Wilson slept on a plank bunk, ate rice and beans with fish and an occasional can of bully beef, and ran a taut ship—one that "the Lord wouldn't be ashamed of." Morning prayers were held daily at sea, and no smoking, drinking, or trifling with the Seventh Commandment was permitted.

Over the years she taught many of her crew members how to use a sextant, take a star sight, and plot a course. In return she learned local piloting and sea lore from men whose grandfathers and great-grandfathers knew over a hundred stars, could plot a course by wave patterns, and navigated by cloud formations, flights of birds, and bearings on the sun, wind, and waves.

Like most interisland schooner skippers, she had her share of heavy weather and a few close calls among the coral atolls and the more than eleven hundred reefs and motus of the low, windswept Marshall archipelago. Scores of ships have been lost in the tricky currents, unmarked reefs, and sudden squalls of Micronesia, but in the years Eleanor Wilson skippered *Morning Star VI* and *Morning Star VII* all of her passages were made safely without loss of life or injury to passengers or crew. Ironically, when she went home on a long-overdue leave in 1954, *Morning Star VI* foundered in a gale between Ponape and the Marshalls while under the command of a veteran Canadian master mariner.

When a suitable replacement schooner was found in Japan and Eleanor Wilson took *Morning Star VII* on the old run with passengers, freight, and the blue pennant with the white dove at the masthead, there was rejoicing in the many ports of her parish from Majuro and Ailinglapalap to Ponape and Kusaie. Most of today's leading Micronesians remember and some have sailed with the "Lady Skipper" in what is now the United States Trust Territory of Micronesia.

A few former small-ship sailing women like Danuta Kobylinska, who sails out of the Polish port of Gdynia on the Baltic, have gone on to command big ships as professional sailors with four stripes on their sleeves. Attractive thirty-three-year-old Danuta Kobylinska, captain of the 10,000-ton *Kopalnia Wujek* with a crew of thirty-eight men, is one of a small number of German, Polish, and Russian women who have earned unlimited master's papers for any ocean. Danuta learned much of her early seamanship as a small-boat sailor, became a pilot, advanced to marine inspector, and during ten years at sea skippered ocean tugs before she was given command of merchant ships on the transatlantic run.

Gwen Tompkins

Gwen Tompkins is one of the few women to make a Cape Horn passage as mate in her own small ship. In addition to many hard-driving record passages, she has made thirteen North Atlantic crossings and cruised the length and breadth of the Baltic, the Mediterranean, the coasts of South America, and the South Seas in the schooner *Wander Bird*. Gwen has sailed through Woods Hole, beat to windward through Stockholm's Skargaard, and passed through the slender Great Bras d'Or of Cape Breton.

"Good helmsman and best of shipmates, Gwen is more vital to this ship than its spars," said Warwick Tompkins of his attractive wife and full-fledged mate of *Wander Bird*.

With her two babies aboard Gwen stood her full watch, shorthanded with but two in the crew, from Stockholm to the Bahamas and cruised in mid-December from the West Indies to icebound Boston with only one other than her husband to sail the half-century-old German gaff-rig pilot boat ex-*Wandervogel* (76-ft. LW) that they bought in Hamburg for $1,500.

(It cost many times that sum to clean, scrape, and paint her hull and spars—fidded topmasts—and to provide new gear.)

Of their two children Ann and Commodore, both raised aboard, Gwen had this to say after their east-to-west passage around Cape Horn: "The children have missed a lot but they gained much more in individuality, real values, and fundamentally sincere and straight thinking."

After 70,000 miles of ocean sailing together in the *Bird*, Warwick Tompkins affirmed, "My wife's unflagging and quiet faith, courage, and good humor kept me going ahead many times when another single step forward seemed impossible."

"If you want a crew, marry one," said Conor O'Brien, who sailed around the world in his 42-foot ketch *Saoirse* with an all-man crew. Many sailors have taken O'Brien's advice. A recent world survey revealed that husbands and wives who sail together have less than one per cent of the divorce rate of those in other activities, perhaps because they were pre-tested and knew what they were getting into. Some, like Julie Tambs, Gwen Tompkins, Maurine Fisk, and Fiona Lewis, have raised quite young children aboard who became at a very early age self-reliant shipmates on their own.

Mrs. McMullen, one of the earliest sailing wives, accompanied her husband on many of his notable cruises, including that of 1869 in their heavily sparred and canvassed yawl *Orion* (19½ tons), but the first small-boat wife to make a major ocean passage was Joanna Crapo, who sailed across the Atlantic in 1877 with her husband in their 20-foot clinker-built Bermudian ketch *New Bedford*.

Julie Tambs

Julie Tambs, one of the earliest of the sailing wives who have had children born while voyaging, sailed on her honeymoon from Oslo, Norway, into sixteen days of North Sea gales en route to Le Havre and around the world in the 40-foot-LOA Norwegian pilot cutter *Teddy*. Her first son, a thirteen-pound boy, was born less than a year later at Las Palmas in the Canaries. At the age of six weeks, Tony Tambs started across the Atlantic well provided with powdered milk.

"Life at sea is good for the boy," said skipper Erling Tambs en route to Curacao in the West Indies. "There is no one here to worry him or to poke needless pills into his small but smoothly operating interior." Their biggest problem was diapers.

While his mother stood watch and helped work the stout vessel with her twin-halyard mainsail of nearly 600 square feet of canvas, young Tony stayed below in his canvas bunk. At ten months he could manage the companion ladder without help and was given a canvas harness when on deck.

"I have a good wife, a dependable mate, and a good boat," Erling wrote

Mate Julie Tambs and family aboard cutter *Teddy* at Papeete.

in New Zealand, where they had their second child and were flat broke. "Therefore I am rich."

"To hell with sailing," the wife of a well-known sailor said at the end of their first long Pacific Ocean passage. "I don't care who knows it, I'm just plain scared of this goddam ocean." A year later she had "adjusted" and now, ten years later, loves offshore cruising as well as her husband.

"Love," said St. Exupéry, "is not looking into each other's eyes, but looking together in the same direction." Many small-ship women spent their honeymoon on a transocean passage, including Eleanor Bradley, Dr. Allen Petersen's bride, Taní, Bernadette Dupret, Benita Pachernegg, and others.

KWAILAN LA BORDE

Kwailan La Borde, who cruised widely in the Atlantic with her husband in *Humming Bird*, was introduced to sailing long before they were married. To gain her permanent interest in the mate's berth aboard the 27-foot gaff ketch he was building at Trinidad, Harold wrote to Venezuela where Kwailan was working, "If you don't come soon, I shall set off alone like Joshua Slocum."

Kwailan came, liked the ketch, and they sailed to Grenada on the first day of their honeymoon.

EDITH STROUT

Edith Strout, who sailed around the world (37,000 miles) as mate of *Igdrasil* (a gaff sloop that was similar to Slocum's *Spray* and, like *Spray*, had her rig changed to gaff yawl during the voyage), shared fully in the navigation of the 37-foot-LOA vessel and in the planning, hard work, and seamanship necessary on a voyage of this type and duration.

Edith and her husband received the first of six Blue Water Medal Awards by the Cruising Club of America to wife-and-husband combinations, in four of which the wife was sole crew.

MARGUERITE GRAHAM

Commander R. D. Graham's daughter Marguerite already had years of deep-sea experience when she sailed as mate with her noted father on the 7-ton cutter *Emanuel* to the Faeroe Islands, the Hebrides, and on other long ocean passages.

In 1938 she was his capable mate in their 35-foot gaff yawl *Caplin*, voyaging from England to Bantry Bay, Ireland, and on to Madeira. From Funchal they had a good crossing to Bermuda, arriving there sixty-seven days from Bridgewater, England, a voyage that earned them that year's Blue Water Medal. After the hurricane season was over, Marguerite and her father sailed *Caplin* south through the Caribbean and later to Panama and across the Pacific to New Zealand.

Some women have a natural reserve of strength that occasionally enables them to outlast men when the issue is one of patience, courage, and fortitude. As Edward Allcard says, they have some queer reserves of bravery.

Take Jane Allison Mitchell of Surrey, who reached St. Hélier, Jersey, in the Channel Islands to report the foundering of the 50-foot yacht *Maricella* in very heavy weather. She was below when the yacht "turned right over" but managed to get out through a port. When she surfaced, the wheelhouse and superstructure were swept away as were her four shipmates, none of whom was ever seen again. Clinging to wreckage, she was swept along the coast in the gale. After being in the water for fifteen hours, bruised and nearly blinded, she swam many miles through heavy seas to reach the north coast of Jersey Island.

There are many accounts of women who survived hardships that proved too much for their husbands. Some, as in the *Wing On* tragedy, were partly sustained by a maternal urge to return to their children. When the 28-foot converted lifeboat *Wing On* departed San Pedro, California, for the Marquesas and the Tuamotus August 15, 1939, Chester Thompson, a deep-sea diver, Dalton Conly, a professional seaman, and their two young wives expected to make their fortunes diving for pearls in Polynesia.

Before reaching the equator they were caught in a hurricane that dismasted the sloop and disabled her rudder beyond repair. With a jury rig of sorts made from torn sails and the short stump of the mast, *Wing On* started a long, westerly drift-sail that took her north of the French Polynesian archipelagos and several isolated islands that lie below the equator. At first they fished to supplement their dwindling provisions. Later, when the sea diver and the ex-boatswain became too weak to catch enough fish to stave off starvation, the two women took over.

By the end of October their water, doled out a few mouthfuls at a time and finally drop by drop, was finished.

November 7, Fern Thompson, who was striving to keep the others alive, wrote in the log:

"Chet has died. What next? Help us, oh God."

After a brief service the body was disposed of over the side and the facts logged on November 8. "Buried Chester Thompson, age 21 at 8:10 A.M. Died of starvation. He was too far gone to stand any of the remaining can of apricots."

Conly lasted four days longer. Before he lost the strength to move or speak, he showed the two women how to steer by the stars toward the Lau Group in the Fijis or the New Hebrides—"depending," as he put it, "on wind and current."

November 12, the death of Dalton Conly was recorded in the log by Fern Thompson, but the two women lacked the strength to lift his body over the side.

Ten days later Conly's young widow Eve died of thirst, mumbling the name of her year-old child.

Left alone with two dead shipmates whom she was unable to consign to the deep, Fern Thompson continued to make observations and to steer the sloop toward Fiji.

November 24, ninety days from San Pedro, having sailed and drifted 6,000 miles, Mrs. Thompson brought *Wing On* in to a barrier reef a half mile from Vanua Levu, Fiji.

Badly emaciated, half delirious, and mumbling to her children, "Don't worry I'll be home," Fern Thompson was taken to a Suva hospital, where she slowly recovered, to return later to her two children in Oakland, California.

MARGARET PIDGEON

Margaret Pidgeon, who was bound around the world with her noted husband on his third circumnavigation when caught in a hurricane and driven ashore in the New Hebrides, was a capable sailor in her own right long before she married the man who had already circumnavigated twice singlehanded in the 34-foot-LOA hard-chine gaff yawl *Islander* that he built "near a lumber yard for a thousand dollars."

Born at sea aboard a square-rigger commanded by her father, Margaret began sailing her own boats in her teens and was devoted to small sailing craft all her life.

Following their marriage, Margaret and Harry made *Islander* their permanent home and after several years of offshore cruising together sailed from

Los Angeles to Hawaii in 1947. Departing Honolulu in November for Torres Strait, *Islander* experienced much bad weather and broke her main boom on the sixty-seven-day passage to the New Hebrides. The night that the thirty-year-old V-bottom yawl (a veteran of 50,000 miles of ocean sailing) put in at Hog Island on the Island of Santo, the first hurricane the area had had in nine years came up suddenly, swept her ashore, and damaged her beyond repair on a ledge.

After returning to California, Margaret and Harry, who then was seventy-nine, built a small Sea-Bird-type yawl, 25-ft. 6-in. LOA. They were planning another long voyage when Harry died in 1955.

BRITA HOLMDAHL

Brita Holmdahl and her husband Sten received the Blue Water Medal in 1954 for circumnavigating in their 33-foot double-ended ketch *Viking*. Brita worked as a seamstress to help save every last dollar of the hard-earned money that went to buy the twenty-year-old little fishing cutter that they converted to a Bermudian ocean-cruising ketch. Besides working as a seamstress, Brita helped her husband do all the work with their own hands. On their voyage around the world, Brita was mate of *Viking* in the fullest meaning of the word.

ANN DAVISON

As pointed out in Chapter 3, singlehanded ocean sailing appeals only to a rare breed of individual. Ann Davison, who lost her husband and their fishing ketch *Reliance* in a gale in the English Channel and decided to carry on alone, is such a person.

"Sailing, particularly ocean sailing has given me much," says Ann.

I've had to resort to oil bags in force ten gales and I've been so nearly run down in fog that the drumming of the liner's engines still throbs in my dreams. . . . But when I look back the experience that stands out above all others did not at first seem destined to be exciting at all.

It began rather drearily on the eve of my sixtieth day at sea after leaving Las Palmas in the Canary Islands bound across the Atlantic for the West Indies and America. The ship, my 23 ft. sloop *Felicity Ann*, was running under double reefed main and storm jib and had been yawing all day, bearing on the tiller like a hard-mouthed horse. The clouds were low and the seas were monumental. The wind was easier than it had been for the past two weeks, but was still blowing more than 45 miles an hour. I had been at the helm for nine hours without a break, except for taking a navigational sight in the morning when there was a fortuitous gap in the clouds, and I was dead beat. For two months the strain of single-handed sailing had been accumulating and by sundown that evening I couldn't take it any more. There was no margin for error in those seas; an involuntary jibe could be serious, so I hove to and went below.

I had reckoned on the voyage taking about 35 days, and might have made it in that

Ann Davison with *Felicity Ann* on the ways in Florida after an 18-month solo voyage from England via Spain and the West Indies.

time if I hadn't run out of the trade winds in the doldrums, where I was trapped for 23 days. The conditions of calms and squalls were harder to bear than the gale force winds that had blown since I had picked up the trades again two weeks ago. Now with the sixtieth day at sea coming up, it seemed as though the voyage would never end, as though I'd become a modern Flying Dutchman, doomed to sail on forever.

For two months I had been making little marks on the chart without any tangible assurance they were right. There had been no way of checking my sights. There had been no intermediate landfalls to give assurance. The fact I had made accurate landfalls in the past was no comfort now. Every passage stands on its own, and I had never made such a long one before. In three thousand miles one could build up a considerable error.

Towards dawn awakened by a vicious squall I rolled out of the berth and climbed into the cockpit to see how we were making out. Another tough day, I thought, no sextant observations either, and my gaze wandered round the ragged horizon towards the west in the direction we would take when under way again.

Dead ahead, on the horizon of our course was a thin grey line. A line such as might be made by distant hills. There was a peculiar definition to the outline that couldn't belong to anything so ephemeral as a cloud. Yet, I remained incredulous, not daring to believe. The long grey shadow did not alter shape.

I went below and lit the stove for coffee. If it is still there and still the same after I've had coffee, I told myself, it is Barbados, and there'll be time enough to think about what that means then.

Too filled with emotion to make any further efforts at breakfast, I drank my coffee slowly, and when I looked out again, the shadow was still there on the far horizon, unchanged. Irrefutably Barbados, on time and in place.

It was the most rewarding experience of my life. But there is a lag between undergoing an experience and the full appreciation of it. At first my reaction was the simple one of pleasure at having crossed the Ocean.

Now it means much more than that. And when doubts assail me, when goals seem unattainable, I think back to the joyous sight of that thin grey shadow on the skyline. It took a long time to turn up, but it did, in the end.

I was very tired by then physically and mentally. We could not make Carlisle Bay before night and having no charts of the island I didn't want to go in in the dark so hove to. But during the night it blew up. Swept across to St. Lucia we sailed round to leeward of the island and made north for Antigua.

The alluring description in the West Indies Pilot book proved too much for me and I dropped the hook in Prince Rupert Bay. It is sixty-five days since I sailed out of Las Palmas and last set eyes on a fellow being.

Two islanders from a native schooner lying at anchor came over to give me a hand anchoring. They thought it strange and unnatural for a woman to be sailing on her own, and right away offered to abandon their own ship and join mine.

Cruising up through the West Indies to Nassau with many calls en route, *Felicity Ann* sailed across to Florida and on north to complete her seventeen months of solo voyaging at New York City.

"Most people come by it naturally, but I had to sail across thousands of miles of ocean to find out that courage is the key to living. For courage," said Ann, "is the will to face every day of your life and every humdrum trivial little detail of it, and realize that you don't amount to much, accept the fact, and not let it deter your efforts."

RUTH MERSEBERGER AND JUTTA SCHULTZE-RHONHOF

Ruth Merseberger and Jutta Schultze-Rhonhof, the two German girls who helped Jim Wharram build *Tangaroa*, were as capable at ocean cruising as they were at planning, building, and fitting out. After Ruth and Jim sailed the 23-foot catamaran on a shakedown cruise from England to Germany and up the Rhine to Düsseldorf, the two girls sailed back with the skipper and cruised the south coast of England. With Ruth as mate and navigator and Jutta as crew they departed Falmouth on a seventeen-month voyage across the Bay of Biscay to Spanish and Portuguese ports. From the Canaries they sailed *Tangaroa*, the smallest catamaran to make a major ocean crossing, across the Atlantic to Trinidad.

From scraping to painting, steering, rigging, and navigating and to "providing an adequate and interesting diet for seven dollars a week," the girls did their full share at sea and in port.

On a beach in Trinidad, under three giant mango trees, Ruth, Jutta, and Jim built *Rongo*, a 40-foot catamaran. From Trinidad they sailed north to St. Thomas and from there 1,500 miles up to New York and on across the Atlantic to Liverpool (3,100 miles), the first round-trip crossing of any ocean by catamaran (westward in *Tangaroa* and eastward with *Rongo*). Ruth

Merseberger and Jim Wharram made two more Atlantic crossings in *Rongo* before building *Tiki Roa,* a fast 38-foot-LOA double outrigger with black hulls and red sails.

PHYLLIS CROWE

Phyllis Crowe spent part of her honeymoon caulking a 34-footer. After that it was a 19-foot skipjack, then a 25-foot yawl that she and her husband built in California and sailed to Hawaii.

"It was a wonderful feeling," said she, when they sold their business, most of their possessions, "and left the complicated system of modern living —lawn-mowers, smog, washing machines, telephones and multiple taxes behind."

For more than a quarter century, since she helped build the 39-foot schooner *Lang Syne* on a beach under the algarroba trees near Waikiki and sailed as mate on her 10,000-mile shakedown cruise, "Billie" Crowe has been making deep-sea passages.

Billie and her husband were awarded the Cruising Club's Blue Water Medal for a "most meritorious example of seamanship" after a three-year circumnavigation in their Block Island double-ender. Still offshore cruising as mate of *Lang Syne,* Billie Crowe has logged over 60,000 ocean miles.

SUTTIE ADAMS

Petite, thirty-seven-year-old skipper Suttie Adams, who took her schooner *Fairweather* around the world, sailed first on a leisurely voyage from the Gulf of Panama and up the West Coast to San Francisco.

With the Adams children—Rick, seventeen; Jon, sixteen; Sue, eleven; Patrick, seven—and two friends as crew, the 58-foot-LOA gaff schooner cruised from California to the Marquesas, Tahiti, Samoa, and Fiji en route to New Zealand.

Five months were spent in New Zealand, and the ship was put on the ways for a bottom job. From Auckland, where Mate Suttie took over as skipper, *Fairweather* departed Waitemata May 19, 1962, for Noumea, New Caledonia.

"On the afternoon of the seventh day out the wind was light, a strong swell was coming from the North and before sunset," said Suttie Adams,

I noticed a small black cloud on the distant horizon.

During the night the wind and sea built up and by morning we were hove to under storm canvas. At 10 A.M. *Fairweather* had her rail under in a sudden hard gust when the cleat of the stays'l sheet broke free, pulling two three-inch lag screws.

The glass was falling and the speed with which the wind increased was hard to believe. Realizing we were in for something big we took down and furled the heavy trysail with double lashings, sent the working jib below, secured ports, battened hatches and put extra lashings where required. In coming round to run off downwind the ship

Skipper Suttie Adams and the crew of *Fairweather*.

took two cross seas that crashed down, burying the deck and cockpit under solid water. She felt sluggish, wallowed heavily, heeled, and finally came through with us up to our waists in water. *Fairweather* responded to the helm and we were able to hold her to the course dead before it with every hawser aboard out as stern warps along with a heavy tire and three beefy planks. The warps effectively slowed us several knots but with all our drags we were still running about four knots under bare poles.

No one can judge positively but based on what we observed: tops blowing off the tumbling crests and the confused white sea, I put the wind speed down at 90 to 100 m.p.h. The noise was terrifying.

Since it had come up so suddenly I felt it would blow itself out in a few hours. But I was wrong. At 1500 it was worse. By night the seas were white phosphorescent cliffs that roared down and swept by on either side. Anxiety increased though my confidence in the ship was unshaken.

Conditions remained severe. The wind never slackened. Wheel watches required the most careful steering with close attention to each crest before it broke and passed under us. Watches were shortened to an hour each as watch by watch we ran before that awful wind and sea.

The storm seemed to reach a peak and keep it—shifting slightly from a few degrees east of North to North, then to North-by-West.

Little was said when we gathered in the cabin. No one cared for food. The bilges were watched and kept dry. Sue and Pat, the two youngest children, unworried with everything snug and secure below, slept and read in their bunks much of the time.

At 1400 I wrote in the log: "Wind still hurricane force."

We tried to run the auxiliary in reverse during the worst of the gusts but it didn't help. Oil that was drained slowly out through the self-bailing cockpit helped some. With the oil and the warps out only a few waves broke on the stern. Several big ones broke on the quarter. Every tenth or fifteenth seemed like a mountain.

A driving rain lashed us and in the black night the water close around was white with spindrift blowing flat off the confused seas. With warps out *Fairweather's* movement downwind remained under control even at the worst of it.

One huge sea greater than the others rolled up late the second day. Higher and higher it came until the first slope lifted our stern until we were well down by the bow. Had we been moving downwind under bare poles without warps the increased forward movement could have forced the stem down and pitchpoled us stern over bow. But *Fairweather* started to climb the long slope until the crest passed beneath and we fell off into the following trough.

I was proud of the way the ship responded as hour after hour each watch kept her keel in line with the direction and push of the sea. But I would be a liar if I said I was not afraid. . . .

Six weeks were spent in Noumea. We then beat out to the New Hebrides and from there to New Guinea. From Port Moresby we sailed to Torres Strait via Thursday Island and Darwin, then across the Timor Sea to Bali, Java and Singapore.

As veteran small-boat sailors know the Torres Strait, Arafura Sea, and the Timor Sea never fail to give some anxious moments. But being a woman in this area has some advantages. In Indonesia, for example, where several yachts have had difficulties in the past, we were treated well. The Indonesians were most kind, harbor officials were cooperative and helped with papers without charge.

We stayed seven months in Singapore and worked on the schooner while Chinese craftsmen carved by hand panels, doors, chests and cabinets of teak including a symbol of *Fairweather* in Chinese for our main cabin.

May 13th we departed for the Nicobars and took 13 days to sail 390 miles because of the very strong currents and short, choppy seas between Penang and the Nicobars caused by the aftermath of a typhoon in the Bay of Bengal. At one point I thought we might have to return to Singapore and go south of Sumatra.

Much has been written about crew problems. Aboard *Fairweather* shared enthusiasms and understanding helped greatly. Everyone had their duties and responsibilities, including Pat, the youngest. No one complained or hesitated at an order. The good will, stamina and loyalty of the crew determined the safety and happiness of the voyage.

Leaving the Nicobar Islands we were pursued by local craft off Great Nicobar who seemed determined to overtake us, probably to obtain some of our gear and supplies. Our auxiliary was disabled and in the light winds that prevailed they were coming up on us for a while. The boys set every spare foot of canvas we had and we slowly pulled away for the Chagos Archipelago where due to gales we were unable to enter and pushed on another thousand miles to the Seychelles, one of the loveliest islands of all.

Fairweather had a fair downwind sail to Zanzibar, then on to Mombasa, Kenya. We remained one month in Africa. My son Rick was married there to Melanie, who had joined the crew in New Zealand, and we all went on a honeymoon safari to the Tsavo Big Game Reserve.

From Aden to Suez took a month with three days at Port Sudan and four calls in Egypt. During a five-month stay at Rhodes, Greece, I became a grandmother with the birth of a daughter to Melanie and Rick.

Our longest stays were in New Zealand, Singapore and Rhodes. A good layover was enjoyed at Tahiti and we took time to gunkhole along the coast of Corsica. Though it is true we stayed longer than most voyagers in ports we liked best my eyes and thoughts were always on distant horizons. When the newest member of the crew was three weeks old we cruised through the Greek Islands and headed west to Italy.

While *Fairweather*, with her heavy spars, rigging and 29 net tons, is not as "yachty" as the cruisers with lofty Bermudian rig and light displacement she has proven again and again what she can do—slogging to windward in wild blue water, ghosting in to a remote anchorage in light airs or lying to in a gale. Never once has she failed to lift or respond to the wheel.

She may not tack with the speed of a racing machine but comes about smartly as a well-balanced schooner should. Running or reaching she can show her wake to most ships her size. In 40,000 miles under our flag, whether sailing through the reef-strewn Tuamotus, threading the Torres Strait or picking her way in and out of crowded harbors, she has proven she can do most things well and some things better than any ship her size I know of.

From Las Palmas *Fairweather* cruised 900 miles south to Portugal's lonely Cape Verde Islands and from there, without help from the northeast trades, had a twenty-one-day Atlantic crossing to Barbados. Many calls were made in the West Indies en route to Panama.

On the long haul up from Balboa to Mexico and the California coast a Tehuantepecer off Guatemala kept *Fairweather* hove to for forty-eight hours. "The strongest winds of our four-year voyage," said crewman Vern Hansen, "except for the hurricane in the Tasman Sea. Fortunately we had plenty of sea room."

On arrival in San Francisco May 18, 1965, Mate Rick Adams reported the boys liked the idea of a woman skipper and there was no crew trouble on the voyage. Vern Hansen and crewman Ray Pettigrove agreed, adding, "The skipper has been fair to us and we have no bitches."

"The boys have developed not only as sailors," said Suttie Adams, "but as young men. Strict school hours were maintained aboard for the youngest children, Patrick and Sue, and during long stays in Auckland, Singapore, and Rhodes they went to school ashore while the ship was in port. Patrick, now eleven, has become a proper sailor like his older brothers Jon and Rick. Weaned on H.O. 214 Tables, he soon was taking noon sights; next he was plotting a position and perusing *Ocean Passages for the World.* He can hand, reef, and steer with the best.

"By watching expenses closely, costs for the world voyage averaged about $300 a month. We did all of our own work and lived cheaper than you can live ashore," Suttie Adams pointed out and, speaking of her next cruise, said, "I look on ocean sailing not as a sport but as a way of life because I'll never live on shore again."

CONSTANCE HITCHCOCK

Constance Hitchcock can hardly recall a time when she was without a boat. Sailing ten years on inland waters in small craft, Connie, who learned her navigation at a waterfront school and practiced on a roof top, started off-shore cruising in 1946, the first woman to skipper a small yacht from California to Hawaii. She planned the voyage, did the navigating, and with her daughter and a friend as crew sailed *Makai*, her 38-foot-LOA gaff-headed ketch to and through the Hawaiian Islands and back to San Francisco Bay. In 1954, after thirteen years of cruising, Connie retired from newspaper work to devote the rest of her life to sailing and with Eric, her cruising partner, has sailed *Makai* over 30,000 miles.

"At sea," says Connie,

I stand my watches as do my crew, write every day in my log and also do my share of the cooking and other chores. But the thing of which I am most proud is my navigation—for I have never missed a landfall.

It still seems miraculous to me after 35 days at sea without sight of land, or plane or ship or even flotsam, to be able to put a pencil point on our big Pacific Ocean chart and say, "We are there. Tomorrow morning at dawn we should see the island of Ua Huka on the horizon"—and the next morning at first light, there is the faint line of the island to the west.

All at once a load falls from my shoulders and I am hungry once again.

In 1966, with twenty-five years of sailing experiences to recall including countless island landfalls in the South Pacific and many transocean passages, Constance Hitchcock lives permanently aboard and sails her thirty-two-year-old ketch out of Sausalito, California.

PEGGY SLATER

Peggy Slater of San Pedro sails her own K-43 (43-foot-LOA Kettenberg sloop) *Valentine II* and is equally at home at ocean racing or as cruising skipper. Her early training and long experience in sail is typical of a number of small-ship women around the world who have devoted a lifetime to off-shore cruising.

With a commodore for a father and many years of early crewing aboard the family 40-foot gaff cutter *Jolly Roger*, Peggy was sailing a 14-foot boat

PEGGY SLATER

Skipper Peggy Slater, an exponent of the hard-sail school, has beaten some of the best men in offshore racing.

when she was eleven, a 26-foot sloop at fifteen, and has since owned and sailed her own K-32 and K-38 sloops.

Already winning races as a teenager and later with *Seventh Heaven,* a 26-foot sloop, Peggy won thirty-seven consecutive races and was Pacific Interclass champion several times. It was not unusual to see her offshore cruising singlehanded with her Irish setter. An exponent of the hard-sail school, with over sixty cups and trophies to show for it, she has bested some of the best men in offshore racing.

"Peggy gets no special consideration from the rest of us," a competing male skipper said at the end of one rugged ocean race. "We give no quarter. She expects none."

A few years ago, when Peggy was sailing master of the 72-foot sloop *L'Apache* and running in second place in the Transpacific Race, crewman Ted Sierks went overboard in a heavy sea in mid-ocean at a time when *L'Apache* was boiling along at 10 knots before half a gale wind under her mainsail and balloon spinnaker.

"Man overboard!" went the cry, as a life ring with smoke attachment was thrown out.

Peggy was on deck in a flash. They were unable to jibe without dismasting, and it took some time getting the big spinnaker in and coming to the wind. She put a man on the lower spreaders and beat back but was unable to sight the missing crewman because of the eight-foot sea then running. They searched the rest of the day and throughout the night and were joined by planes, yachts, and naval vessels. Their position was approximately 840 miles from Honolulu.

By morning the prospects of finding the man looked grim. Veteran seamen among the searchers felt they would never find him alive. But the search went on.

At noon the second day, after twenty-nine hours of continuous searching, the captain of the naval escort vessel said he had orders to proceed with the racing fleet to Honolulu and that L'Apache must also proceed.

Peggy Slater refused to sail on and stated bluntly that L'Apache would continue the search, alone if need be.

The Navy captain argued that any further search was hopeless. But Peggy held firm to her conviction that the man was still alive and might be found if they searched more to the east of where they had been looking.

The captain finally agreed to continue the search until 1400 and moved off in the direction the L'Apache's navigator calculated the missing man might be.

Two seamen aboard the destroyer escort sighted a bobbing head at 1315 and shortly after the man was brought aboard alive!

As a cruising skipper and Corinthian sailing master, Peggy has probably sailed more ocean miles than any other small-ship woman. Her accomplishments as top helmswoman in major races and cruises in Pacific waters from Alaska to the Gulf of Mexico would require a full chapter. Here we can only say briefly that her many passages as sailing master of thoroughbred ocean craft include the 52-foot yawl Dorade, the 60-foot schooner Dirigio, the 73-foot schooner Nordlys, the 66-foot ketch Nam Sang, and many others.

Small-boat cruising has taken her through the Mediterranean in the 30-foot sloop Easterly and cruising Hawaiian waters in the 36-foot sloop Westward Ho. She explored the Caribbean for many months in a 14-foot native sloop and made eighteen cruises through those waters in a 31-foot sloop, in the 42-foot schooner Mektaub, and in other small yachts. Ventures in distant waters include long cruises to Central America, the Greek islands, and the South Seas. When not ocean sailing she has taken time to run the Grand Canyon rapids in an 18-footer.

I asked Peggy about her plans for the future.

"A cruise without end in many waters from Tahiti to Australia to the Bahamas," she replied. "I'd like to spend my winters cruising the Caribbean and my summers sailing the Mediterranean. And since there will be a lot of singlehanded sailing in the future. I may put wind-vane self-steering gear on *Valentine II.*"

In 1965 Peggy was at sea on another ocean voyage to Honolulu and beyond as sailing master of the 50-foot-LOA Kettenberg sloop *Irish Mist.*

MARJORIE PETERSEN

A seasoned sailor in her own right, Marjorie Petersen has handled the tillers of many craft from racing dinghies to oceangoing yachts. One of the few women to pass the U.S.P.S. four-year celestial navigation course, she can snatch a star sight and work out and plot a line of position while running before half a gale on the slopes of the trade swells, no easy task in a 30-foot-LOA hull.

"Whether slogging windward under jib staysail and trysail or bowling along under twin staysails, the mate of a small offshore cruising cutter has to be prepared for anything," says Margie. "Sailing in dense, drifting fog in the steamer lane approaching San Francisco I once wrapped the ship's papers, plus our passports and traveler's checks, in plastic and buttoned them snugly in my shirt.

"Living afloat," Margie points out, "requires a decent routine." As mate she keeps a master list of everything aboard and knows where to find a snatch block, chain swivel, and chafing gear, a sail needle, ball of marline, or the makings of a heavy-weather stew or her husband Al's favorite dish, "Hash Stornoway": a savory mélange of corned beef, onions, garlic, dried potatoes, and a dash of red pepper fried to a crisp and served with stewed tomatoes.

Marjorie's touch is apparent in their comfortable, homey cabin. "*Stornoway* may not be up to the times with her gaff rig, which we prefer, and lack of radio direction finder and depth sounder, but we are no deliberate reactionaries. Our oil lamps are dear to us for their coziness and soft, warm glow —also because they save running the generator."

After more than a decade of creditable passages to widely scattered ports and anchorages around the world, Marjorie Petersen says, "There is a deep satisfaction in the personal accomplishment of basic needs in a seamanly manner when it can be done in a floating little world ready for exploration and for encounters with other people who share the deep waters of the earth."

BERYL SMEETON

What can one say of veteran blue-water sailor Beryl Smeeton, mate of the 46-foot-LOA tall Bermudian ketch *Tzu Hang* and one of the most capable small-ship women of our generation?

When swept overboard in the Roaring Fifties while running before a gale under bare poles 900 miles west of Magellan Strait, Beryl kicked off her sea boots, treaded water, and despite oilskins swam back aboard the dis-

MILES SMEETON

Beryl and Miles Smeeton and a visitor aboard *Tzu Hang* in Japan.

masted teakwood vessel. How many men in her place, with a broken collar-bone and deep scalp wounds, could, without attention to personal injuries, continue working for twelve hours without rest to repair gaping holes in the doghouse and hatches of the waterlogged ketch (both masts were lost at the deck, the bowsprit was in two pieces, dinghy and rudder gone, and the deck nearly swept free of everything)?

With her head still bleeding, a painful, injured arm, and a sprained ankle on which she could barely stand, Beryl bailed steadily with a bucket all day and part of the night. She cooked, sewed sail, and did her full share of deck work to save *Tzu Hang* and work her 1,350 miles under jury rig from 98° W. and 52° S. up to the Chilean port of Coronel, where they arrived eighty-seven days from Melbourne under circumstances where less capable sailors would have perished.

Since then Beryl Smeeton and her husband have crossed many oceans and for fifteen years have been cruising in *Tzu Hang* to more than a score of countries in Europe, the Mediterranean, Africa, Southeast Asia, and the Orient.

SUSAN HISCOCK

One of the few small-ship mates who has circumnavigated twice, Susan Hiscock in 1966 was outbound from Yarmouth, Isle of Wight, on another round-the-world voyage with husband Eric in the 30-foot 6-ton cutter *Wanderer III*, rolling along averaging 120 miles a day with their new Hasler self-steering vane. Susan very likely will soon be the only blue-water woman to have circumnavigated three times as mate in her own small ship.

ANN PYE

The mate of *Moonraker* of Fowey is another all-around sailor who has made long sea voyages and countless landfalls in many parts of the globe. Ann is one of a competent foursome of noted ocean-cruising mates referred to by skipper T. H. Carr as "The Long Range Annie Club," which includes Annie Van de Wiele, Anne Worth, and Anne Carr—all circumnavigators devoted to sailing as a way of life.

ANNE CARR

"I have lived afloat all my married life, 33 years now (except for brief periods of war service)," Anne writes from Bermuda. "And we have spent the last 18 years cruising in *Havfruen III*." Besides her duties below, Anne takes care of the upper deck, all painting and varnishing, and is a full-fledged navigator in her own right.

"She is one of the best," says Annie Van de Wiele, speaking of the capabilities of Anne Carr, the mate of *Havfruen III*, who has eight Atlantic crossings, a round-the-world voyage, and more than 100,000 miles of sailing to her credit.

Havfruen III, the Carrs' 60-foot-LOA gaff ketch, designed personally by Colin Archer of Narvik, was built of teak in Norway in 1897. Rigged by skipper Carr to be sailed by the mate and himself, her standing gaff with mainsail running in on a track under the gaff and brailing to the mast enables the topsail to be set alone. This they often do.

Cruising extensively in Europe, including the Baltic, charter sailing in the West Indies, and passage making in many other parts of the world, mate

Anne Carr and her husband live an ocean-cruising way of life that many people dream about but very few achieve.

Fiona Lewis

Of Fiona, his seagoing wife, Dr. David Lewis says, "It is not surprising that even before we were married we had begun to plan a voyage across the world. The circumstances that, after two years of marriage, we had two little girls, in no way affected our preparations—the catamaran would have ample room for them too."

With Fiona as mate, the Lewises' 40-foot catamaran *Rehu Moana* has sailed over 25,000 miles in the past few years, including a passage through Magellan Strait to cruise the Patagonian channels and the ironbound coast of Tierra del Fuego between Punta Arenas and Cape Horn.

Priscilla Cairns

Priscilla Cairns, English yachtswoman and member of the Little Ship Club of London, sailed many small craft in Britain before world cruising with

As a navigator and cruising mate quiet, modest, first-rate sailor Ann Pye has contributed her full share toward *Moonraker* of Fowey's 18 years of successful deep-sea passage-making.

PETER PYE PHOTO FROM *Red Mains'l*, COURTESY RUPERT HART-DAVIS LTD.

Auckland Weekly News PHOTO BY JACK TAYLOR, RAROTONGA
Fiona Lewis, circumnavigating mother, wife and capable mate of *Rehu Moana*,
with Vicky and Susie.

the David Lewises in *Rehu Moana*. After crossing as watch mate from Valparaiso, Chile, to Easter Island, Mangareva, and Tahiti, Priscilla took over as conventional instrument navigator aboard and, keeping her daily positions to herself, navigated by modern sun, moon, and star sights while the skipper and Fiona navigated to Raiatea, the Cook Islands, and on across the Pacific to New Zealand without instruments in an attempt to throw new light on early noninstrumental navigation in the South Seas as practiced by the ancient Polynesians. A competent yachtswoman who won an award in London for her ability as a navigator, Priscilla expects to make many more long ocean passages.

SHARON SITES

Sharon Sites, the first woman to sail solo from California to Hawaii, made the 2,300-mile passage in her 25-foot Bermudian-rigged, lapstrake Folkboat *Sea Sharp* in thirty-nine days.

Having worked as a dental secretary to save enough money to buy the

Sharon Sites aboard *Sea Sharp*.

modern sloop, Sharon, a thirty-four-year-old Los Angeles widow, declined to take a radio because "I wanted to be alone. And I didn't particularly want to talk to anyone."

Sea Sharp cleared San Pedro June 12, 1965, with provisions aboard for two months and fresh water for ninety days. To avoid the extra weight, no fuel was carried for the sloop's auxiliary. Skipper Sites reported she was becalmed with flat seas and almost no wind at all for over a week. Six hundred miles out a depression was encountered. And June 24 to 29 she noted in her log "heavy seas with winds gusting to 65 m.p.h." The trades were picked up on July 2, and *Sea Sharp*, with a twin genoa rig that raised, lowered, and was controlled from the cockpit, averaged 80 to 90 miles daily for the rest of the passage.

Annie Van de Wiele.

During the night of July 20, Sharon passed Diamond Head and was spotted off Barber's Point, Oahu, shortly after dawn, weak and weary from lack of sleep and from codeine she had taken to dull the pain of a broken wrist sustained the previous night.

Why did Sharon Sites sail solo? For the same reason Ann Davison crossed the Atlantic singlehanded in her 23-foot sloop *Felicity Ann.*

"Because I wanted to," said Sharon. "I take very little personal credit, most goes to friends who helped, to *Sea Sharp*, and to the Lord himself. I felt His hand on my shoulder many times."

Sharon Sites married her former sailing instructor Al Adams and left Los Angeles in mid-'66 bound around the world as mate of their 31-foot-LOA ketch *Maria.*

LOUISE MYERS

Louise Myers, owner-skipper of the 38-foot-LOA Angleman ketch *Porpoise*, is a former sailor of small boats who bought a copy of Bowditch—"the sailor's bible"—in 1961 and began studying navigation "for no reason at all." In 1964 she began crossing oceans for good reasons. An individual with a clean-cut way of doing things and of accomplishing what she sets out to do, Louise is also an amateur radio operator with enough skill at sending and receiving Morse to quickly copy weather code from a passing ship. With "MM" for marine mobile after her call letters, she is frequently in telegraphic contact with other operators around the world.

An all-around small-ship skipper who personally does much of her own work, including the copper painting of *Porpoise's* bottom during haul out, Louise Myers sails with a carefully chosen male crew that includes her eleven-year-old son. "We leave in a few days," Louise wrote in 1966 from Suva, Fiji, "for Samoa, Tonga, New Zealand, Australia, New Guinea, the Philippines, and Japan."

Lady Rozelle Beattie, who has cruised extensively in her Folkboat *Martha McGilda* on the German, Dutch, and Normandy coasts and in Finnish waters, most of the time singlehanded, and German yachtswoman Ingeborg von Heister, who has sailed her trimarans *Ultimo Ratio II* and *Nimble Jest* on long solo ocean voyages, are in the forefront of a small number of European women who skipper their own small vessels on ocean passages.

Sea-minded small-ship women who are good at the helm and understand sail handling, navigation, and all-around ship's work are far more numerous today than in the mid-fifties when Anne Worth circumnavigated with her husband in their aluminum-alloy cutter *Beyond*. Some, like Betty Nordlund and Jo Vancil, can caulk a seam, scrape and paint a mast, or mend a sail as well as a professional and when fitting out or cruising can visualize details better than some men.

With cruising ventures increasing yearly, it is impossible to mention more than a few of the circumnavigating women of seasoned good judgment who have a decent respect for the sea and have proven capable of looking after a small sailing vessel. Françoise Moitessier of *Joshua*, first woman to round Cape Horn in a really small vessel (see page 282), Janet Steele of *Adios*, a quiet and unassuming mate-navigator in the best tradition, Mary Kittridge of *Svea*, Dot Bradfield of *D'Vara*, and several wives who recently completed seamanly voyages around the world in well-found little vessels have done much to prove that well-planned and executed voyages are rarely spectacular.

Take Annie Van de Wiele of Zeebrugge, a Belgian girl of courage and a natural aptitude for the sea who has been cruising fifteen years and circumnavigated in *Omoo* (a 45-foot-LOA gaff ketch) with her husband and a friend, for which they received the "well done, sailor" award of a Blue Water Medal.

Sailing boats at an early age and dreaming of ocean voyages in small craft while still in her teens, Annie said, after her first circumnavigation, "My own peculiarity is to love the sea for itself. Crossings never seem too long. After 30 or 40 days at sea a port has never seen me in a hurry to get ashore. My home is *Omoo* and she is never as private or satisfying to me as when she is well out at sea."

In *The West in My Eyes*, one of the most interesting accounts to be added to the literature of small-ship voyages, Annie asked, "Why go round the world?" and answered, "It is difficult to explain but we had never thought of anything less. . . . We had always wanted to go as far as possible."

In 1966, Annie Van de Wiele arrived in the Caribbean from Belgium with her husband Louis in their new gaff cutter *Hierro* (32-foot LOA) on another properly fitted out, well-provisioned, carefully planned voyage.

"The art of the sailor," says Annie, "is to leave nothing to chance."

> *Cape Cod girls they have no combs,*
> *They comb their hair with codfish bones.*
> —*"Cape Cod Chanty"*

CHAPTER 8

Ocean-Cruising Junks

When one has good wine,
A graceful junk,
And a maiden's love,
Why envy the immortal gods?
—LI T'SI PO (A.D. 705–762)

~~~~~~

SINCE wind and water were always among the most important phenomena of nature to the Chinese and to this day junk sailors honor the deities of the sea, is it any wonder that the people of China, oldest people on planet earth, were among the first to venture to sea in small craft?

Junks claim a more remote origin than the oldest surviving craft in the Mediterranean or Norse seas, and because of their great antiquity much of the origin of the art of the junk is lost in the mist of time.

From the rectangular stern junks of Hong Kong and the cotton junks of Tsung-ming which sailed the Whangpoo for centuries to the red and white junks of Wenchow or the blue-pooped junks of Ningpo, China has always had a greater variety of sailing craft and more vessels used as a way of life than all the rest of the world together.

Today, in Hong Kong alone, over 200,000 people are living on junks and sampans, making a living with their boats and seldom going ashore. Most are Taoists and have candles and incense aboard to honor Tin Hau, patron saint of the *shui-jen* (water people). On Wu Yuen Chieh, Fifth Moon Festival, small lanterns made of oiled paper are set afloat so the spirits of the drowned may see their way.

Normally junks and sampans are run as a family venture. Whether working a large salt junk through the Yangtze narrows in midwinter, mudlarking on the Tung T'ing, or offshore fishing in a *ku chai* (purse seiner) out of Kowloon, everyone aboard—men, women, and children of as many as four generations—has always had duties according to the communal custom and discipline of generations.

The junk that so often appears to the unseamanly eye as lubberly and cumbersome is nearly a perfect ship in its own way and one of the most seaworthy ever built. (In 1938 off the Tungsha Banks I passed two fishing junks bound in for Woosung and the Whangpoo that had been through a typhoon and had most of their foresections gone but were still well afloat because of their watertight bulkheads.) Regardless of the superstructures required and preferred by a people with families who live out their lives aboard, the underwater lines of coastal sea craft, especially the South China junks, are surprisingly fine.

Contrary to what many think, the Chinese balanced lug is not a square sail. It is a fore and aft rig trimmed and handled on all points of sailing, including tacking or jibing, much as if it were gaff or Bermudian. A patched and repatched Chinese sail supported by split-cane battens can have half of its surface full of holes and still draw well. And for the swift squalls and diversities of the South China Sea, the junk master has the fastest-reefing rig in the world. With halyards slacked, sail and battens drop swiftly into buntlines, like a Venetian blind. Even on the largest junk one man can take in a three- or four-batten reef in seconds.

Having started over two thousand years ago the Chinese sailor added many artful refinements and arrived at a high degree of efficiency hundreds of years before the science of aerodynamics explored and pointed the way for modern Western sailors. It is entirely possible, though unlikely ever to be proven, that the fore and aft rig originated in the East, was brought West, and evolved separately to the gaff and the triangular headsail.

A thousand years before the European Age of Discovery, Chinese junks were crossing the oceans and ranging far and wide to trade with distant islands and continents. They visited India and Ceylon in the fourth century and by the first half of the fifth were mooring in the Euphrates.

The largest junks of the T'ang era (618–907) had a tonnage of 1,000 *po-lam*—about 200 tons—and were using the centerboard and the leeboard long before the Viking invasion of England. During this territorially expansive dynasty, sea travel to Western countries increased, with large junks sailing from Canton to the Euphrates by way of Malacca, Ceylon, Cape Cormorin, and the Malabar coast. Persia was made a virtual protectorate and Korea became a tributary state. Tonkin and Annam came within the scope of Chinese rule, and her influence was felt in northern India.

In the eighth century the Buddhist astronomer Yi-hsing mentions the polarity of the magnetic needle as well as its declination (not mentioned in European or Arabic literature before the end of the twelfth century). The scholar Shen Kuo wrote in 1086, "Taoist geomancers rub the point of a needle with a lodestone, so that it acquires the property of pointing south. But it always declines slightly to the east and is not due south. Some are magnetized to point north. In my family we have both the south- and the north-pointing needles." The governor at Canton told his son, "The shipmaster to ascertain his position by night looks at the stars; by day he looks at the sun; in dark weather he looks at the south-pointing needle."

Speaking of the high degree of ingenuity in design and function achieved by Chinese sampan and junk builders, Sir Frederick Maze, noted authority on junks, has pointed out that the Chinese have shown more originality than any other people in connection with shipbuilding. Long before the end of the twelfth century, the Chinese perfected hulls divided into watertight compartments and were using the windlass and the stern post rudder. They had cloth and mat sails and reputedly made 6 knots in a good following wind.

When Europeans were still fearfully hugging their coasts, Chinese sailors were out sailing to East Africa in four- and five-mast junks. During the Southern Sung dynasty (1127–1279), maritime trade continued to increase and the navy grew from a few junks to a large number of squadrons. With a force of more than fifty thousand junk sailors, China took control of coastal sea lanes, displaced the Arabs who had dominated the Indian Ocean trade, and carried on a lively commerce with the Malabar coast. Gold, silver, coppercash, porcelain, and silks were carried on the outward voyage to pay for the pearls, elephant tusks, rhinoceros horns, incense, and aromatics that were brought back.

A ship departing China in midwinter would arrive at Lambri (the northwest corner of Sumatra) in approximately forty days, spend the summer trading, and, the following season, would sail in the northeast monsoon to the country of the Arabs in sixty days. "All sea ships start in the eleventh and twelfth moon with the south wind."

The eastern part of the Pacific, dominated by the monsoons that blow from the continent of Asia out to sea in the winter and the reverse in the summer, is well suited to junk life. The three great rivers that divide China, her coastal topography, and the surrounding waters—the Japan Sea, East China Sea, Formosa Strait, and South China Sea—brought forward the more than three hundred different craft that evolved out of the practical genius of Chinese shipbuilding. And, as in England, Scandinavia, Brittany, and New England, their rugged, deep-indented coast lines developed a hardy breed of sailors.

At a time when European ships were driven by heavy, baggy flax canvas, the junk with its batten-stiffened lug had the best-setting sails in the world. The Malay sailors adopted the Chinese lugsail, and the perceptive Arab traders adopted many nautical devices used in junks. As late as the thirteenth century, China was still far in advance of the Western world, with compartments of watertight bulkheads, self-reefing battened sails, multiple sheets that trim the head as well as the foot of a sail, and the use of leeboards in the form of a long balanced rudder lowered or raised by a windlass. The Chinese junk was a finer ship at that time than any in medieval Europe.

When Marco Polo was in China, seagoing junks were making regular voyages around what is now Singapore, skirting India and reaching the trade ports of Arabia. Writing of Chinese junks, after sailing in several, the greatest traveler of the Middle Ages told his fellow Venetians, "These ships are of fir timber. They have but one deck with 50 to 60 cabins wherein the merchants abide greatly at ease, every man having one to himself. The ship hath but one rudder but it hath four masts and sometimes they have two additional masts which they ship or unship at pleasure."

When Marco Polo told his contemporaries that Chinese junks were in every way more seaworthy than the best Venetian ships of the thirteenth century and that their watertight compartments fore and aft made them practically unsinkable, he was laughed at and considered a liar by naval historians until centuries later, when he was proven right on every point.

Just as Roman, Grecian, Phoenician, and Viking vessels all had figures on their bows to drive off evil spirits, and some craft in the Mediterranean still have eyes painted on the bows, the decoration of junks has always been bound up with religion, mythology, and symbolism. Red is the prevailing color because of its evil-dispelling power. The Chinese, who consume nearly every living thing to be found in water, hold the fish in high esteem as a symbol of watchfulness because it never closes its eyes. Be his cargo vermicelli from Chinchew or coal dust from Pietieu—as the *loadah* (skipper) sees it, without eyes, how could his junk see? From the Yellow Sea to the Gulf of Tonkin, most cargo junks have eyes that look straight ahead to avoid distant perils invisible to mortals, and on fishing junks the eyeballs of the oculus are set low in the white to be alert to observe fish.

Though the eyes which decorate the bow of the junk are claimed to show Egyptian influence and reference to Osiris, many Oriental scholars are now convinced that Egyptian methods had nothing to do with the original Chinese sampans and junks. The Chinese, like the early Indonesians and the South Sea people, had great natural feeling for their tools and materials and intuitively created sea craft that were, unlike the conservative Egyptian forms, as beautiful as they were able and seaworthy.

A century before Vasco da Gama and Columbus, Chinese master mariners under the eunuch admiral Cheng Ho sailed in fleets of thirty to sixty or more junks on long transocean expeditions. They visited thirty countries in the Indian Archipelago and Ocean, cruised the Persian Gulf, traded in the markets of Aden and Mecca, and reached "Mu-ku-tu-shu"—Mogadiscio in Africa. Cheng Ho personally commanded sea quests totaling more than 75,000 miles to trade and spread the culture of the third emperor of the Ming dynasty throughout the Far East.

When the galleons arrived and Magellan, Mendaña, Le Maire, and Tasman were out scouring the Pacific with visions of spices and gold dancing before their eyes (but never realized), Chinese junk masters with ships that equaled and perhaps surpassed those of Magellan, Cabot, and Drake were quietly carrying on a fine trade in gold and silver across the China Sea.

As the ships of Tarshis brought ivory, apes, and peacocks to King Solomon, Chinese mariners brought peacock feathers, trepang, swallows' nests, and gold from the East Indies and junks from Canton carried ivory, buffaloes, geese, horses, mules, asses, "precious stones and birds which talk and sing" to the Spaniards at Manila in return for most of the silver that the galleons of Aragon and Castile freighted west across the Pacific from the slave labor mines of Mexico and Peru.

Proud Europeans, especially the Spaniards, who ruled Manila behind the strong arm of the church and the cannon, found it hard to understand how a "heathen race could be so advanced." In 1584 the Spanish factor at Macau wrote, "It is a cause for wonderment that this people, who had no communication with Europe, should have advanced almost as much by themselves." When the Portuguese found that junks easily outsailed their galleons, they adopted the Chinese rig and built two-masted, close-winded lorchas for the South China Sea.

Yearly, twenty to sixty Chinese junks, laden with silks, musk, brocades, porcelain, nuts, iron, cloaks, and the finest of hand-crafted vestments "made by the heathen" for Spanish churches and convents from Sonora to Chile, laid the foundation of the great Manila–Acapulco galleon commerce and fixed the course of the Spanish colony's economic life for over two hundred years.

Sea junks from Canton, Amoy, and as far north as Ningpo made the 650- to 1,000-mile passage yearly with the monsoon, generally at the new moon in March, making the voyage in fifteen or twenty days. After disposing of their cargoes to the best advantage in Manila, they made return passages "in good season" before the end of May.

Freebooting and privateering also played a prominent part in the story of China's sea craft, as it did in early British and American naval history. When Lin Taok'ien, the Captain Kidd of China's corsairs, sailed into Manila Bay in 1574 with a fleet of seventy large junks manned by four thousand men led by tough captains, the Spanish garrison suffered so heavily it was almost annihilated. Only the ninth-hour arrival of reinforcements saved Manila from being taken over by Chinese sailors, a blow to Spanish prestige not soon forgotten by the proud conquistadors.

In 1662 Chang Ch'eng-Kung, a keen naval strategist with a high-pooped armada of war junks, inflicted heavy losses on the Tartars and later drove the Dutch off the island of Formosa, set up an independent state, and demanded tribute from the Spaniards at Manila.

Despite the maritime ventures of her traders, the achievements of her far-ranging junk masters, and her many advancements and nautical innovations, China as a nation has neither greatly prized nor striven for naval glory and mercantile power as the aggressive Western nations have. The nonaggressive ethics of Confucius, with emphasis on the tranquility of the empire and self-fulfillment within classic traditions of their own society, was a strong deterrent. Feeling certain that outsiders who came to the Orient for mercenary gain had no real understanding of the essential qualities of truly civilized men, the ruling classes scorned contact with "foreign barbarians" and left trade and privateering to the lower classes.

While there were a few Europeans, like the Jesuit Matteo Ricci and the British diplomat Sir George Staunton, who did not make the mistake of counting as valueless everything that was not Christian, most of the Westerners, especially sailors and trader-adventurers, were a scornful, lawless lot, with contempt for Chinese traditions and respect only for force of arms.

Referring to Occidentals, the emperor of China once asked, "Why is it they are always at war or preparing to go to war with someone?" To the king of England he wrote:

The Celestial Court does not rate as precious objects coming from far away; . . . King, keep peace among your own people. . . . In future it is unnecessary to send further envoys by land or sea. Know only how to open your heart and study benevolence. Then will it be said that without sending envoys annually to my Court you progress in civilization.

All this was changed in the nineteenth century, when China became a pawn among nations reaching out for new resources and new people to exploit. In direct and flagrant defiance of strict Chinese laws against narcotics, hundreds of millions were made sailing contraband cargoes of illicit drugs into China from Turkey, India, and Persia—a sordid three decades of smuggling, bribery, corruption of port officials, and worse. Brigs, barks, and fast little schooners from Boston, New York, Liverpool, Cowes, London, and Aberdeen handled a major share of the narcotics trade. Owners and masters amassed quick fortunes and some became respectable merchant princes and leaders in the tea trade.

The Opium War, that ugly first page in the story of China's forced Westernization, was followed by a scramble for territorial encroachments. Wherever the traditional spirit and way of life interfered with trade profits, Western bullets and grapeshot decided the issue. Behind the polite patter of official idiom, special privileges, leaseholds, concessions, enforced grants, and contracts were extorted. What could not be had by threats and "negotiation" was taken by force. The guns—which forced the ratification of special treaties, crippled China with huge indemnities, and brought her independence to an end—increased the rivalry among the victors and brought on a long dogfight known as the "battle of 99-years leases and concessions."

With Britain in control of Hong Kong, the opium revenue, and a lion's share of the other trade, France fought and took Chinese Annam and Tonkin, and Japan fought for Manchuria, ending up with Formosa, the Pescadores Islands, and an indemnity from China of approximately $172,-000,000. The Russians took part of South Manchuria (Port Arthur and Dairen); Britain next acquired Wei-hai-wei; Germany took Tsingtao, Kiachow, and part of Liaotung; and the French, deciding on another grab as a *quid pro quo* for what others had additionally taken, took Kwangchowwan and two islands in Kwangchow Bay. Throughout this period of encroachment, the United States appropriated her full share of commercial advantages by extraterritoriality and other remunerative treaties with "most favored nation" rights.

In the early twentieth century, China's waterborne population greatly increased the percentage of her standing as the most amphibious people in the world, and she continued to build small, seagoing ships capable of sailing anywhere. Yet there has never been a Chinese Sir Humphrey Gilbert or a Dumas, a Le Toumelin, or a Chinese Slocum among the hardy breed of long-voyaging junk masters—perhaps partly because there has always been enough struggle, adventure, and maritime employment along their own far-flung coasts and in the South China Sea, where squalls swoop down out of a clear blue sky without warning, swiftly followed by high winds or typhoons.

Keying

The history of transocean junk voyages made by Westerners is a long one. Best known to early Americans and Europeans was the *Keying*, a three-masted, 750-ton Foochow trading vessel. First to make the voyage from China to America and on across the Atlantic to Europe under sail, the *Keying* was visited by Queen Victoria and other members of the royal family soon after her arrival in the Thames on March 28, 1848.

Keying (160-ft. LOA, 25-ft. 5-in. beam, 12-ft. draft) was purchased at Canton by twelve Englishmen, who manned her with the help of twenty-six Chinese under a Chinese captain. Her main deck "was arched," she had a raised quarter-deck, two poops, and a raised forecastle. Her foremast measured 75 feet, main mast 90 feet, and her matting mainsail was said to have a spread of 11,000 square feet. To avoid the Chinese law against the sale of a junk to a foreigner, at that time a capital offense, *Keying* departed quietly under Chinese colors, ostensibly for a coastwise yachting cruise. She carried the Treaty Port flags of Canton, Ningpo, Shanghai, Amoy, and Foochow, and at the masthead a long fish vane indicated "good luck to *Keying*."

The century-old junk cleared Hong Kong December 6, 1846, and had an easy passage to the Java Sea and Sunda Strait. In the Indian Ocean off Mauritius she weathered a severe southwesterly gale, the worst of the voyage. The Cape of Good Hope was rounded, and *Keying* made St. Helena April 17. Though bound for England, owing to strong head winds encountered after leaving St. Helena and to the mutinous state of the crew, course was changed for New York, where she arrived July 9.

After some months in New York and Boston, *Keying* cleared for England February 17, 1848. A hard passage was had all the way across. A very strong gale on February 28 washed her two boats away, split the foresail, and damaged the rudder. During the difficult job of repairing the rudder, the second mate was drowned while working over the stern. Weighing approximately 7½ tons, the hardwood ironbound rudder was hung in the Chinese manner without gudgeons or pintles. It drew 23 feet, required two men in fair weather, and in heavy weather had to be worked by a score of men on a luff tackle purchase.

Concluding sixteen months of ocean voyaging, *Keying* arrived off St. Aubin, Jersey, on March 15, having made better time on her transatlantic crossing than the regular steam packet. From Gravesend she went on up the Thames to London and later sailed to Liverpool and other British ports.

Whang Ho

In 1908 the *Whang Ho*, a one-hundred-year-old former pirate junk, made the crossing from China to San Francisco skippered by Mark Graham, who formed the Whang Ho Company in San Francisco and obtained financial backing to sail the Foochow junk to the East Coast via Magellan Strait.

After calls at West Coast ports she cleared for New York, but somewhere in the Roaring Forties a wave carried away her huge rudder. A jury rudder was rigged and she then sailed to Tahiti, where permanent repairs were made.

From French Polynesia, *Whang Ho* had a slow passage to Thursday Island and from there to Sydney, Australia, where her arrival late in 1908 caused a considerable stir in shipping circles.

Amoy

Among old China hands much impressed by the 1912 voyage of the junk *Ning Po* from Shanghai to San Francisco was Captain George Waard, a Dutch mariner who admired junks with carvel-built hulls, liked the use of heavy wales for longitudinal strength in place of keels, and had an appreciative eye for the square bluff bow and stern that reminded him of his native Holland. In 1921 he built the 65-foot-LOA three-masted junk *Amoy* at a small yard in Amoy, South China. The following year, with his devoted Chinese wife, his son Robert, and a Chinese crew of three, Captain Waard sailed from Shanghai to Victoria, B.C., taking eighty-nine days on the passage.

Cruising south from Canada, they called at several coastal ports en route to San Francisco. After a long stay up the bay at Vallejo, *Amoy* set out again, bound south, and in the following two years sailed to Balboa, passing through the Canal to visit many South American and island ports. After many months in the West Indies, *Amoy* crossed to the Gulf and cruised on up the East Coast to New York.

At Bridgeport, Connecticut, Captain Waard sold the *Amoy* to Alfred Nilson, who had come aboard in San Francisco as a member of the crew. Nilson and his wife Rita raised a family of three boys aboard and twenty years later were still sailing the *Amoy* in East Coast waters.

There is no record of a Japanese junk sailing across the Pacific in modern times, but for the past 250 years disabled craft have been picked up adrift in the great clockwise circle of the Kuroshio Current or found wrecked along the shores of the North Pacific.

The daimio Date Masamune sent a large junk from Japan that reached Mexico in 1614. After exchanging trade goods that included "fine woven silk goods of mixed colors, cutlery, finely wrought weapons, and suits of armor," the junk spent several months refitting, sailed from Acapulco in 1615, and had a slow passage home to Japan. A second junk sent by Masamune in 1616 had a very hard passage and lost a fifth of its crew on the long crossing to New Spain. Spaniards at Acapulco took a very dim view of rivalry in the Pacific trade and severely warned the junk master never to return on pain of death. The return voyage from the Mexican coast to the Orient was made by way of the Philippines, where the junk was sold to the Spanish governor. This voyage marked the end of direct Japanese intercourse with the New World until the nineteenth century.

Of one hundred disabled Japanese junks, in which several hundred sailors were found still alive, forty-four were encountered at sea and fifty-six,

Junk *Amoy* on arrival at Victoria, B.C., after an 89-day passage from Shanghai.

Captain and Mrs. Waard with their son and crew of the junk *Amoy*.

after floating helplessly for months, were stranded or wrecked on islands and coastal areas from the Aleutians to the Northwest Pacific Coast. Many of these well-authenticated records also provide ample evidence of the infusion of Japanese blood among the Northwestern Indian coastal tribes.

The strong northeast monsoons have blown scores of junks off the coast of Japan into the full sweep of the deep-indigo Kuroshio. Pushing north-easterly past the Kurile Islands, the warm "Black Stream," joined by the icy dark-green Oyashio sweeping down from the Bering Sea and the Sea of Okhotsk, moves steadily out past the Aleutians into an immense arc that brings rain to the Pacific Northwest, passes on along the coast of Oregon bringing fog to the San Francisco Bay Area, and from the south makes a 9,000-mile sweep back to the deeps off the Philippines.

Caught and dominated by this western limb of the North Equatorial Current—longest known east-west oceanic drift in the world—Japanese junks have been carried toward America at an average rate of ten to fifteen miles or more a day. Some have been found as far south as Mexico. Still others that fell into the equatorial western current have been cast ashore in Hawaii, Ocean Island, and on reefs, atolls, and other islands in the equatorial belt.

The following two brief accounts of Japanese junk drifts are more or less representative of many of the others.

Captain Alexander Adams, a former pilot at Honolulu, related that in latitude 32° 45′ N., longitude 126° 57′ W., when sailing master of the brig *Forrester* and cruising off Santa Barbara, California, he sighted at sunrise a Japanese junk drifting by with her rudder and masts gone. Although it was blowing a gale at the time, he boarded the junk and found fourteen bodies in the hold sealed in firkins ready for burial, as was the Japanese custom. The captain, carpenter, and one seaman alone surviving, he took them on board the brig, where by careful nursing they were well in a few days. They were on a voyage from Osaka to Yedo and were seventeen months out, having been dismasted in consequence of losing their rudder.

In November, 1927, the *Ryo Yei Maru* was found off Cape Flattery, rolling in the winter swell under bare poles. When seamen from the American liner *Margaret Dollar* boarded the 100-ton junk, they found the bodies of two of the crew dead in their bunks and nine skeletons lying about the deck.

A diary kept by Suteji Izawa and Genosuke Matsumoto until the day they died revealed that the *Ryo Yei Maru* was disabled December 12, 1926, while her crew was fishing within sight of the Japanese coast. Failing to at-tract the attention of several other vessels, they were blown steadily east in the winter monsoon and by the fifth day were caught in the "Black Cur-rent."

After attempting to make the Bonin Islands under sail but failing be-cause of unfavorable winds and the strong current, they decided to try for the American coast before becoming too weak to work the vessel. "We dared not express to each other our innermost thoughts," wrote Izawa.

New Year's Day, 1927, they prayed to "Konpira," the deity of Japanese sailors, and shared a few mouthfuls of dried bean cakes.

Only one fish was caught, and on March 6 with the last of the rice gone the crew began to fall ill. Three days later the first man died. A bird was caught and shared among the remaining ten, five of whom died during March. As they weakened they tried to sail out of the drift, but with a foul bottom and a poor sail rig the Kuroshio held them in its inexorable grip.

Three men died during April. On May 7 the captain died. Genosuke Matsumoto, the last man alive, wrote on May 11 that he was ill and felt that he would die very soon. There were no further entries in the grim log.

Six months later, the rudderless *Ryo Yei Maru* was found, with barnacles and weed two feet long, wallowing slowly southeast by south toward the Strait of Juan de Fuca, her dark sails long since torn to ragged shreds.

Fou-Po II

The ill-fated three-year cruise of the *Fou-Po II* is included here in some detail because it is one of the least known of the many long ocean cruises that have been made in ocean junks.

Eric De Bisschop, one of the most capable Western seamen to cruise extensively in junks, was a master mariner with considerable deep-sea experience before he arrived in China. He had held a commission in the French Navy, was captain of a mine sweeper, and commanded a passenger liner at the end of World War I. He owned and sailed a three-master in the African trade and was an experienced small-boat sailor who later devoted himself to maritime ethnology.

Following several years of sailing out of Ningpo and Amoy in the early thirties, the loss of the junk *Fou-Po I* on the reefs of Formosa in a hurricane brought Eric De Bisschop and Joseph Tatiboet, his friend and crew, back to Amoy, where they built *Fou-Po II*.

"The Chinese junk type of sail is, I believe, the best to be found for ocean cruising," said De Bisschop.

My reason for building another junk was that such a vessel embodies the knowledge of the ages, is extremely seaworthy, shipping practically no water, is roomy, easy to handle, and inexpensive to build. The length of the *Fou-Po* was forty feet, beam seventeen feet, draft three feet, or five feet, with the rudder which acts as a centerboard. Her ample breadth and high poop gave room for a large and comfortable cabin. Three huge bamboo poles were her masts and she carried lug sails with bamboo battens running entirely across. With her hull painted in red and gold Chinese designs from her bows to her overhanging stern, with two big eyes like Spanish onions on her square bow, she was reminiscent of the Middle Ages.

With the backing of the Société Française de Géographie, De Bisschop and Tatiboet sailed in the wake of the supposed early migration route from the south of Asia.

I had pondered over the early migrations of the Polynesians and resolved to follow the supposed routes studying and recording as we traveled. The course we sailed took us to the Philippines, the Dutch East Indies, the north and northwest coast of Australia, the shores of Papua, and the Solomon, Santa Cruz, Gilbert and Marshall archipelagos. After many long months at sea the hull was foul with growth and badly in need of cleaning and the rudder needed repairs. With her fine French flag flying above her sails and shrouds the *Fou-Po* arrived at the pass off Jaluit at dawn on the morning of July 22, 1935. About one hundred yards from the breakers we headed into the wind and awaited the inspector.

Despite the affability of the Japanese officials and friendly smiles of the natives, two hours after our arrival we had become suspects and, practically prisoners. The little Chinese junk had suddenly, in the mind of the governor, become a hydrographical boat disguised. The discovery of my papers with their graphs, the study of currents, my anthropological notes, and an imposing pile of notebooks (I took six or seven observations a day) were immediately interpreted as undeniable proof of guilt. Our damaged rudder and the barnacles and salads on the hull seemed to the governor only a clever pretext.

I was put through hours of questioning, the boat was ransacked and reconditioning of *Fou-Po* was impeded. We patched sails as well as we could and had to be content with only reinforcing the rudder. Finally, the intervention of an officer from a war transport who took our side and pointed out the irregularities of the governor's actions and the insult to the French flag enabled *Fou-Po* to put to sea again.

Tati and I were thankful to put Jaluit behind us and, when we were alone once more at sea, Tati shook his fist at the disappearing atoll and angrily said, "That pig of a governor! He seemed to want to know the route we were going to follow. Did you give it to him?"

I told him we should steer a course toward the north, into the trade winds.

Then I shouted to Tati, "Come about! Let us go south instead." Gently the *Fou-Po* pivoted and we headed southward into the depth of the night. As we sailed the breezes freshened from the northwest.

For 25 days we cruised about, battling winds and currents, while I continued my study of the counter equatorial currents, of which little is known in the West Pacific. When we reached 180 degrees longitude I felt my work was finished and we decided to make for Honolulu. This would mean two more months at sea, for although we were only 1,900 miles from Honolulu in a straight line, which would take only a few days in a steamer, in a sailing vessel which must tack and make allowance for the equatorial current throwing a ship from 15 to 50 miles a day toward the west, the straight line becomes a crooked one and the number of miles is trebled.

It was necessary for us to steer a north-northwest course until, between the latitudes 33 degrees and 37 degrees, we should reach a zone of variable winds dominated from the west; then it would be possible to sail east until we again met the northeast trade winds, when we should be in a position to sail southeast to Honolulu.

After turning northward we averaged about 110 miles a day. Not bad for a small ship like the *Fou-Po*. I looked at the map one day and remarked to Tati, "Another month and we shall be in Honolulu."

As the days passed I worked on my notes, classifying them and bringing up to date the scientific observations and the accounts of our cruise.

One day Tati came up from below grumbling, "It stinks in the cabin."

"Perhaps it is a dead rat," said I, but Tati reminded me that we had never seen a rat on board.

On opening up a partition a sickening odor reached us from the forward hold. Tati climbed into the hold and examined everything. With a curse he stuck his head up to say, "It is our emergency food supply!"

We had expected to call on these reserves in a few days. We always carried two big galvanized tins, hermetically sealed, containing two months' supply of rice, macaroni and flour. Now, two thousand miles from Honolulu, we found them a rotten mass of food.

"Those beastly officials at Jaluit!" exclaimed Tati. Undoubtedly during their search, our tins had been opened, the air admitted, and the heat and humidity of the tropics had brought this disaster upon us. We spread the rotting mass upon the deck, but it was useless, all had to be thrown overboard. We made an inventory of the food we had left and I wished to ration our meager store, but Tati could see no need for this.

I placed what provisions we had left upon the bunk in plain sight, ate very sparingly, and tried to make Tati see the desirability of his doing the same, by example, hints, and tact—but all to no purpose. Tati ate as usual and seemed to think I had placed the food on the bunk to keep my eye upon it, to his great resentment.

On October 15 our food gave out. There was nothing left to eat except a half bottle of curry powder and salt and pepper. That same day we discovered the rudder ropes had rotted. The rudder of the *Fou-Po* was an enormous wick, fourteen feet long, the size of a good tree, which reached down two feet under the keel. Deciding the work must be done at once before our strength gave out, we pulled the wick out of the water with great effort, hung it aft, and repaired it under a fiery sky. At four o'clock the work was finished and so were we.

A flying fish that came aboard was our last meal. Tati cleaned him carefully and fried him to a turn. Nothing was lost. With the fins, entrails, and even the scales I made a soup.

From that day on we lived on a diet of curry powder mixed with water and tallow from a box given us by the United States Navy for the purpose of greasing the masts. We never lacked for water, we still had a supply on board and were able to catch more in the frequent showers. How many times, hoping for the impossible miracle, did we turn the boat upside down searching for food, open boxes we knew were empty, and turn out the contents of the cupboards! And for the fourth time, at least, Tati put water in an old rusty tin which had formerly held sugar and imagined the reddish water contained some flavor.

We tried fishing without luck.

The good northeast trade winds on which we had counted to bring us in style to Honolulu turned to the southeast. The sky was black, and torrential rains and heavy winds, alternating with calms, compelled us to keep a continuous watch and to use our waning strength to work the ship. We were no longer able to find rest in sleep and would lie in a state of half consciousness when we were not on watch. My legs were lifeless, but my arms still contained some strength. Each day I would pull myself out of the cabin, drag myself across the deck, make my observations, and take our position. My eyes seemed covered with a mist which persisted in showing me food. Only with the greatest effort could I keep them open at all.

I have often observed that, given a thin nervous type of man and a strong phlegmatic one, the latter succumbs more quickly than the former. So it was with Tati and me. In two days after our food gave out, he was weaker than I after my many days of self-denial and fasting.

October 21 was my birthday, and Tati took out from the bottom of the cupboard a little piece of paper. In it, carefully wrapped, was half a cracker. "I had it in reserve for your birthday," said Tati. Oh, that half a cracker! With what sensations of delight we nibbled those last few crumbs of food, our very last. We made it almost a religious rite. We were not discouraged, however. Land was now only three hundred miles away in the south-southwest. Two days of good wind and then we should have steak and French fried potatoes.

Slowly our strength had been ebbing away. An atrocious gnawing tortured my carcass during the first week of starvation and then suddenly ceased. It seemed as if my stomach had finally tired of its useless revolt and had at last decided to accept the inevitable.

At last my observations showed that we were about one hundred miles from Molokai, and also that we were in the steamer lane. I lay on deck continually scanning the horizon. My eyes became so tired with watching that again and again I imagined I saw a ship. But finally a liner ablaze with lights did steam down upon us.

The battery of our flashlight was dead, but we lighted a kerosene lantern and this we waved. I was so weak I could not raise my arm sufficiently to make signals, but we called loudly, and were so near we could distinctly hear voices on the ship helloing to us. When we saw that our signals of distress were not understood and that the steamer was sailing gayly by Tati and I collapsed on deck. On arrival at Honolulu people from the steamer reported passing two men on a strange yacht northeast of Molokai who had waved greetings!

The next day we sighted Molokai and our courage somewhat returned. The prevailing winds of the Hawaiian Islands are the northeast trades. But for days we had encountered only southwest winds. These continued. That night we saw first the light at Kalaupapa and later on the lights of the city of Honolulu reflected in the sky. If the trades would only blow, we should be in Honolulu the next day. We tacked all the following day but at eventide the wind dropped and the currents pulled us back, so that the next day found us just where we had been on the previous morning. The wind persisted from the southwest, and for three days we tacked by day and drifted by night to where we had started.

When we were in sight of Kalaupapa, we flew the tricolor at half-mast, hoping someone there would recognize it as a signal of distress.

It was tantalizing to be able to see Oahu so clearly and not be able to make Honolulu. On the fourth day I was determined to make one more attempt, but Tati said no, that in another day I should be dead and that we must make for Kalaupapa, which was within our reach.

I had no charts of Molokai, and as we approached the reef-guarded island, about sunset, I saw a boat apparently riding at anchor. Believing this to be the anchorage, I steered in her direction, only to find the ship, a wreck, perched upon the reef. I veered off and although I do not know how I had the strength to handle the rudder, I instinctively guided the junk to a spot which I learned afterward was the proper anchorage. When I heard the anchor fall, I dropped to the deck as if dead.

We were quite near the shore, and Tati, though also in a state of total exhaustion, called for help and swung the lantern, but as it was raining very hard no one saw or heard us.

About ten o'clock, however, a canoe manned by four young Hawaiians came alongside. We told the Hawaiians that we did not wish to leave our ship but asked if they could bring us some food, as we were starving, having been without food for fifteen days.

The next thing I remember is awakening and finding myself in a nice white bed, surrounded by white walls, and attended by a blond nurse. The superintendent of the Settlement himself had carried Tati and me off the *Fou-Po* to the hospital, and, thanks to the kindly ministrations of the staff, we soon regained our strength.

Then, just as we were beginning to take an interest in life, we were brought the sad news that our little ship had been blown upon the rocks and pounded to pieces.

Not a thing on her was saved. When I thought of all my papers, records, and photographs—the result of three years' scientific research—the energy and privations spent to obtain them, and the material loss of the vessel, added to the natural affection a sailor has for his ship, tears filled my eyes.

After they fully recovered, De Bisschop and Tatiboet crossed to Oahu and in the two years that followed built the 38-foot-LOA catamaran *Kaimiloa* on a shady beach near Waikiki. With junk sails and rig they made a 264-day voyage from Hawaii to France via the Indian Ocean and the Cape of Good Hope in the interest of De Bisschop's studies of oceanographical data for the French Geographic Society (see Chapter 9).

Mon Lei

The junk *Mon Lei*, one of the oldest boats ever to visit the port of New York, has been a familiar sight there since 1947. A 50-foot-LOA, Swatow-type, carvel-built, short-keeled junk, she is believed to have been built about 1850 in central China. In 1938 *Mon Lei* was sailed from Hong Kong to San Francisco in eighty-three days with a crew of eight.

Sea Dragon

When the *Sea Dragon*, Richard Halliburton's 75-foot-LOA Ningpo-type junk, slid down the ways of a Hong Kong shipyard without observing the centuries-old launching honors traditionally given by the Chinese to the deities of the sea, veteran junk sailors and shipyard workers shook their heads.

Sea Dragon left Hong Kong with a crew of ten Americans and four Chinese on March 4, 1939. Twenty days out they were caught in a mid-Pacific depression approximately 1,100 miles west of Midway.

The last words from the junk were heard on March 24 through the static of a typhoon. "Lee rail awash," radioed Captain Jack Welsh. "We are virtually swamped."

After that, complete silence. The junk's position at this time was approximately 31° N. and 55° E.

The U.S.S. cruiser *Astoria* in command of Captain Richmond K. Turner searched 152,000 square miles without finding a single trace of the *Sea Dragon* or any of her crew. "Our planes and the *Astoria* combed a very large area," reported Turner, "but the Pacific is vast and there is a faint possibility the junk may still be afloat."

While junk masters of the *shui-jen* pointed out that the *Sea Dragon* had sailed without good joss, the general feeling of shipyard men in Hong Kong at the time was that the loss of the vessel was partly due to interior changes that greatly weakened the hull, including the removal of several orthodox compartments to make de luxe living quarters.

Some years later, marks of Oriental workmanship on the wreckage of a junk that washed ashore near San Diego during a gale evoked the theory that it was the remains of the *Sea Dragon*. K. M. Walker, marine surveyor and authority on Halliburton's travels, believed that the wreckage may have been carried by the Japanese Current to the North Pacific and on down the coast. "The keel of the wreckage," said Walker, "measured up to that of the *Sea Dragon*."

Tai Ping

In 1939, a few months after Halliburton departed Hong Kong in the *Sea Dragon*, John Andersen, a veteran merchant seaman, his wife Nellie, and four Europeans cleared Shanghai for a 6,000-mile passage to San Francisco in the 41-foot-LOA three-masted junk *Tai Ping*. They too planned to arrive off San Francisco's Treasure Island in time to see the World's Fair.

A few hundred miles out from the mouth of the Yangtze, sickness among the crew required a return to port. After their second start, an encounter with a pirate craft and a monsoon gale off the China Coast followed by calms and a shortage of water changed their destination to Victoria, B.C. Twenty-nine days out the liner *President Coolidge* was spoken. Captain Kohlmeister, a friend and former shipmate of Andersen's, maneuvered the 30,000-ton liner to provide a lee and the 22-ton *Tai Ping* came alongside to have her tanks topped off. Early in October skipper Andersen made a landfall on Quatsino Sound off the west coast of Vancouver, 108 days from Shanghai.

Hummel Hummel

When Dr. Allen Petersen and his young bride Tani found the junk *Hummel Hummel* (36-ft. LOA, 9-ft. beam, 2-ft. 5-in. draft) in the muddy yellow waters of the Whangpoo and bought her for $250, it took a lot of hard work to get her ready for a passage from Shanghai to Los Angeles.

Ballasted with three tons of iron, sand, and water, the two-masted former Ningpo fishing vessel departed Pootung Point April 28, 1938, with Dr. Petersen, his wife, and two Russians as crew.

Eight days out from the Great Yangtze Banks they raised the island of Oshima and late the following day put in to the Gotto Retto Islands off Nagasaki, Japan, where they remained several days. From Tamano-Uro *Hummel Hummel* cruised down the east coast of Kyushu through Van Diemen Strait and along the south coast of Japan to Yokohama, where they arrived thirty-three days from Shanghai.

Hummel Hummel had her seams recaulked and stripped with zinc, additional tanks installed, and for the long haul across the North Pacific took on 500 gallons of fresh water and six months' provisions.

Taking a departure from Nojuna Saki July 12, 1938, Dr. Petersen, remembering the warning of the chief of the secret police, set a course well clear of Japan's northernmost island. "Do not land on Hokkaido," he had been told. "If you do, the world may not hear of you again."

Variable winds were encountered the first week out, and as they reached up into the higher latitudes there were few sights to be had of sun or stars. Days and nights were thick with fog and heavy mists. The most northerly point reached was about 300 miles south of the Aleutians.

Fifty-eight miles a day were averaged during the eighteen days of July, and by the end of August they were midway across. The drinking water changed color and developed a very bad taste, but it was still potable without ill effects. When their eggs began to spoil Tani Petersen served them up scrambled with garlic.

On the fifty-fourth day they sighted a ship, which altered course to investigate the strange sight of a 36-foot junk flying an American flag in the mid-Pacific. It proved to be the Swedish tanker *Sveaborg*, and Dr. Petersen was able to check his position. Newspapers were tossed down and two burlap sacks that contained fresh fruit, vegetables, and two legs of pork. The master of the tanker told them that shortly after they left Honshu the worst typhoon in thirty years struck the Japanese coast.

On the seventy-fourth day out of Yokohama, Vic, one of the Russian crewmen, called down to Petersen, "I think I hear a cow."

The fog lifted shortly after, revealing breakers directly ahead and the outbuildings of a coastal ranch near Fort Bragg, on the Northern California coast.

"Hard over, Vic!" shouted Petersen.

Slowly the junk swung around and headed offshore. With the scent of earth and hay on the light offshore wind, *Hummel Hummel* was soon sailing

Dr. Petersen with Tani—mate of the *Hummel Hummel* and "one of the best deep-water sailors who ever swung aloft in a bo'sun's chair."

AL WOODBURY

Thirty-six-foot Ningpo junk *Hummel Hummel* arrives at San Pedro, California, 85 days from Shanghai

JIRO TA

south along the Mendocino coast. Anxious to reach his home port, Dr. Petersen sailed past the Golden Gate without putting in and on October 3 passed in through the San Pedro breakwater eighty-five days from Shanghai.

During a long layover and refitting in California, another ton of inside ballast was added. When *Hummel Hummel* cleared San Pedro December 3, 1939, with the Petersens and a crewman named Parky, she carried 150 gallons of fresh water and her provisions consisted mainly of rice, flour, and "salt horse"—beef and tongue in brine, dried onions, and garlic.

During the 3,000 miles to Panama, tidal races in the Gulf of Tehuantepec and a Papagayo that took half their sails and pushed *Hummel Hummel* four hundred miles offshore gave Petersen enough to think about.

At Balboa their crewman decided to remain in the Canal Zone, and the Petersens sailed on alone. With "joss sticks burning fore and aft to encourage benevolent spirits" *Hummel Hummel* cleared for Callao, Peru, in a driving rain squall and soon was bucking the strong prevailing west and southwest winds.

Having left too late in the season, Petersen reported

90 days of squalls and continual tacking against headwinds and current before reaching the equator. Twice the foremast carried away and although I was able to save the sail each time, I ran out of spare foremasts. An emergency fore staysail was then rigged up to enable the junk to hold her course. When the main gaff broke I had to splinter it as one would a broken leg.

In trying to fight our way out of the gulf we had to take advantage of every favorable wind. Sometimes we made short tacks of one hour, at other times every two or three hours, and at times I sailed for days on a course opposite from where I wanted to go hoping to find a better wind. During those trying months we rarely saw the sun or stars. Our life was sudden squalls, calms and heavy rain day and night until a greyish mold spread over the cabin walls. Then, on the ninetieth day out of Balboa, the junk crossed the equator! Here was a record of some sort that no one would wish to challenge.

Forty days after crossing the equator they were still bucking head winds and the Humboldt Current. So many long months in the water wore off their copper paint. The teredos (sea worms) were well at work in the bottom and the junk was beginning to leak badly.

At Pimentel, Peru, it was found that teredos had penetrated the hull so deeply that nearly all of the keel, a number of bottom planks, and the rudder had to be replaced.

Plans to sail to New York via the Strait of Magellan were given up, and *Hummel Hummel* sailed westward. During the first ten days the junk made 900 miles, and on the forty-third day from Peru the Petersens sighted Fatu Hiva in the Marquesas.

After a short stay they sailed late in May from Taio Hae Bay, Nukuhiva, and had strong east and southeast winds for a twenty-one-day passage direct to Pago Pago.

With war increasing over the Pacific *Hummel Hummel* sailed from Samoa to the Banks Islands in seventeen days. Thirteen days were squally and overcast with no sights at all, and for two days the junk lay hove to after losing a foresail in a southeast gale. A call was made at Rennell Island. After a grounding that nearly proved fatal on a coral reef off Sudest in the Louisiade Archipelago, *Hummel Hummel* was refloated, patched, and proceeded to Samarai Island, the port of entry for southeastern Papua.

When news of the attack on Pearl Harbor reached Samarai, Dr. Petersen promptly joined up with Australia's New Guinea Volunteers.

"After four years of sailing it is difficult to part with a ship that has carried you safely over 17,000 miles," said Dr. Petersen, as he and his wife Tani had a last look at the cradled junk under a canopy of palm fronds. (*Hummel Hummel*, his account of junk voyaging, is dedicated to: "Tani— one of the best deep-water sailors who ever swung aloft in a bo'sun's chair.")

Cheng Ho

A Rhode Island Irishman, Thomas ("Ted") F. Kilkenny, arrived in Hong Kong in the mid-thirties with a large roll of blueprints and the backing of a number of international sportsmen, including Count Ilya Tolstoy—grandson of the novelist—for an idea called the Ning Po Junk Expedition.

An adventurer who had sailed on square-riggers to Alaska, Kilkenny had sold several backers the idea of building a "queen of junks" with quarters subdivided into ten double staterooms with connecting baths, main saloon, dining saloon, galley with electric refrigeration, and forecastle quarters for twenty Chinese seamen. Plans were to sail from Hong Kong around Cape Cormorin, through the Suez, and up the Seine to the Paris Fair of 1937.

When backing for the Paris junk expedition fell short of expectation, Kilkenny received a commission to build the 70-foot-LOA gaff schooner *So Fong* in Hong Kong. With the owner and a crew of yachtsmen, he sailed the teakwood yacht to New York in 1937 via the East Indies, the Red Sea, and the Mediterranean. Returning to China, he turned to building small teakwood yachts for American buyers, including the now well-known "Teak Lady Class."

In 1939 Kilkenny was able to realize some of his long-cherished plans when Mrs. John D. Archbold, a wealthy New Yorker, commissioned him to supervise the building of a deluxe junk to provide transport for scientific expeditions in which she was interested. When the resourceful Irishman found that Chinese artisans build without blueprints as their forefathers have for centuries, and that in all of China there were no plans for a junk, he expedited his own plans and supervised building of the Archbold junk to Lloyd's specifications in the venerable yard of Ah King.

With the help of measurements taken from a century-old salt junk, the

89-foot-LOA 154-ton luxury craft with heavy, hand-sawn yacal frames, camphorwood knees, and three-inch planking slowly took shape. An ancient temple idol was placed on the stem during building to bring good joss, and there were appropriate ceremonies at "the marrying of the keel" and on launching day to drive evil spirits into the sea.

Across the stern of the large Ningpo-type poop, craftsmen carved a Holy Goose with wings spread, and directly below Seven Chinese Sages were seated to keep evil at bay.

With an "improved junk rig," three shrouds to each mast, a ship's rudder in place of the traditional one, and twin diesels, the *Cheng Ho,* named for the Chinese admiral who sailed to Africa in the fifteenth century, cleared Hong Kong in the northeast monsoon for a fast passage across the China Sea to Manila.

"At sea," said Kilkenny, a firm believer in tradition, "the British tar has his daily rum ration and the Chinese sailor has his ration of joss sticks." Aboard *Cheng Ho* each of the ten Chinese crewmen went daily, after each meal, to burn three joss sticks each in the dining saloon before a fireplace joss shrine. When the mizzen boom carried away in a gale that flung sheets of spray one hundred feet aft over the high poop, a dozen joss sticks were burned by some of the men in place of the usual three.

From Manila the owner of *Cheng Ho* and members of the Fairchild Tropical Garden Expedition cruised down through the Philippines, collecting rare plants and other specimens. From Zamboanga they cruised the Celebes coasts and then crossed to Surabaja in Java. Many calls were made at seldom-visited spots in the Malay Archipelago. When Germany invaded Holland, war conditions brought the Fairchild Expedition to an abrupt end at Amboina, where most of the original crew left.

Under Captain Ellis Skofield, the junk made her way slowly eastward through the tropics and against the prevailing easterlies to Suva, Fiji, where she arrived late in 1940. She then made a 5,000-mile plant expedition to the islands of the Central Pacific for the Arnold Arboretum of Harvard University.

Shortly before the attack on Pearl Harbor, *Cheng Ho* arrived in Hawaii and was "sold" to the U.S. Navy for one dollar to become patrol vessel 1X52 in Hawaiian waters during the war years.

In 1947, when she was returned to private ownership, the junk came under control of Otto Degener and Eric De Bisschop, who formed the Cheng Ho Trading and Exploring Company to operate between Hawaii and French Oceania.

Flying the French flag, *Cheng Ho* cleared Honolulu for Tahiti in January, 1948, with a group of adventurers and general cargo. Shortly after her return passage from Papeete with passengers and a cargo of vanilla beans, several libel suits were filed at Honolulu by crew members for back wages.

After months of legal maneuvers, *Cheng Ho* cleared Hawaii for an eighteen-day passage to Papeete and remained in the Society Islands to become a copra trader. Legal battles over her ownership were not resolved until 1955, when she was ordered sold by a Papeete court. Promptly bought by a French firm, she was put back in the interisland trade in French Polynesia.

Long a familiar sight in Papeete harbor, *Cheng Ho* was given two new diesels, renamed the *Hiro*, and set to carrying cargo between the Leeward Islands and Tahiti with occasional voyages through the Tuamotus.

When the yardmaster at Ah King's in Hong Kong was told that the *Cheng Ho* was still sailing after a quarter of a century in the South Seas, he attributed much to the fact that she was launched in the traditional manner, started her long voyaging in good joss, and that her eyes were focused correctly to avoid distant perils.

Free China

The 73-foot-LOA, 30-ton, former coastal trade junk *Free China*, reputed to have been sailed by a refugee family from the Fukien coast of mainland China to Formosa, was bought for $1,200 by five young Chinese employees of the Formosan Fisheries Administration with the intention of entering the 1955 Transatlantic Yacht Race from New York to Sweden.

With an additional shipmate—Calvin Mehlert, U.S. vice consul from Taipei—the *Free China*, under skipper Marco Yu-ling Ching, departed Keelung April 16, 1955, bound for New York via San Francisco. A few days out from Formosa the two-masted junk was riding out a typhoon from the East China Sea with a sea anchor made from her 35-foot mizzenmast. Considerable damage, mainly to tiller gear and to the 25-foot ironbound rudder, required a month's stay at Yokosuka, Japan, for repairs.

On June 20, during the night of the third day out from Japan, skipper Ching was swept overboard in heavy seas but, holding to a line, managed to pull himself back on board shortly after. The North Pacific crossing was made in good time, and the *Free China* sailed in through the Golden Gate on August 9 to tie up at Fisherman's Wharf fifty-four days from Yokosuka. The planned Atlantic crossing and world voyage had to be abandoned due to lack of funds.

A well-known addition to San Francisco Bay, the 90-year-old Fukien junk with her nine watertight compartments, $2\frac{1}{2}$-inch cypress planking, and ironbark mainmast was refitted by Harry J. Dring of the San Francisco Maritime Museum for sailing in local waters with a crew of sea scouts.

Rubia

Flying the Spanish flag, the 60-foot-LOA, 30-ton *Rubia* was the first junk to pass through the Suez Canal and cruise in the Mediterranean. Owned and skippered by José Tey, with a crew of five Spaniards and one Chinese, the three-masted, high-pooped *Rubia* had a diesel auxiliary and was fitted out

Junk *Free China* on arrival in San Francisco Bay from Formosa.

with a leeboard as well as the traditional rudder in Hong Kong at the yard of Yun See, where she was built.

Departing the Crown Colony on January 17, 1959, a boisterous passage was had to Vietnam and Singapore. Cruising up through the Strait of Malacca to Penang, *Rubia* went on to Madras and Bombay, crossed the Arabian Sea, and sailed up the Gulf of Aden to Djibouti on the hot, dry coast of French Somaliland.

Instead of the ten days "allotted for the Red Sea," forty-seven days were spent rounding Cape Ras Kasar, careening at the Bay of Mohammed Quol, and working up against strong seas and head winds to Suez. In the Mediterranean, *Rubia* made calls at Crete, Catania, Rome, and along the French Riviera before reaching Barcelona and the end of a 12,000-mile voyage on September 9, 1959.

High Tea

"There is no ideal sail for all conditions and I doubt whether there ever will be," said Brian Platt, who sailed his junk *High Tea* from Hong Kong to San Francisco.

Among most yachtsmen the jib-headed rig has become generally accepted. It is a good sail. But for all-round cruising ability in difficult conditions, I think the Chinese sail is unbeatable.

People seemed to think I was sailing a Chinese junk across the Pacific in a kind of *Kon-Tiki* adventure, trying to prove something. Indeed, one cannot make a trip like that without making some interesting discoveries, but all I wanted to do was to sail across the Pacific in a small boat—a desire that doesn't have to be explained to yachtsmen. And I didn't even start with a Chinese junk.

Brian Platt started from Singapore in June, 1958, with a modern 27-foot-LOA cutter, the *Chempaka*. By the time he reached Hong Kong via Borneo and Manila, he was convinced she wouldn't do for a long ocean passage in the North Pacific. Accordingly he sold the conventional yacht and had a typical Chinese junk built locally to his specifications by Chinese craftsmen. *High Tea*, a three-masted junk, was 32-ft. LOA, 24-ft. LW, with a 9-ft. beam, 4-ft. 6-in. draft with false keel, and 7.7 tons displacement. A 15 h.p. Enfield diesel was installed for auxiliary power.

On May 7, 1959, I left Hong Kong, bound north to Japan and the latitudes where I might pick up the westerlies. I should have had favorable winds to Japan but the northeast monsoon, which should have been ending, decided to stay on. Instead of trying to beat up through the Formosa Strait, against the current, I took one long tack across the China Sea to where the Kuro Shio [Japan Current] flowed steadily and predictably northwards. In that long beat I began to discover some of her qualities.

After a hard passage across from Hong Kong Brian Platt's 32-ft. LOA Chinese junk *High Tea* arrived at San Francisco February 10, 1960.

From the tip of Luzon, where I changed the water in my tanks, I picked up the Kuro Shio and sailed, still beating much of the time, past the islands that string up the Luzon Strait and on up the east coast of Formosa. I had one or two ideas for modifications, so I put in to have them done at Okinawa. All the time I was at Okinawa the wind blew from the southwest, but the day I left it was flat calm and then a head wind came in again. For all that, I covered in a fortnight the 850-odd miles to Yokohama.

The rest of the summer I stayed at Misaki, on Tokyo Bay. By September I was ready for the big crossing. A short shakedown cruise to Choshi on the Chiba peninsula, a few more days fitting out, and I was away. A couple of weeks later I was back again with a broken main mast. Ten days out it had snapped off at the top, without warning, and a passing Japanese fishing boat towed me into Hanasaki, Hokkaido. By mid-October I was off again with a spliced main mast.

It was getting cold and blowy, but the winds were favorable at last. I had been through the tail of a typhoon after leaving Japan the first time, and it was small potatoes compared to what I began to go through now. "Please wind," I would sometimes say.

"Let up just a little, just a day or so to let me dry things out and get on with some repairs." But it never did. In three weeks I was halfway across the Pacific.

Then one night, when for a change it was not blowing particularly hard, I was awakened by the main mast going over the side.

By morning the wind and sea had got up again but I was getting quite expert now in such situations. I got the wreckage of the mast and sail aboard and lashed down, set *High Tea's* course once more under foresail and mizzen, then huddled over the saloon stove and thawed my frozen bones. The main mast had snapped in exactly the same way as before, below the repair. I began to realize the true cause. Basically they arose from my more misguided attempts to improve the Chinese rig. Thinking to strengthen the masts, I had gone too far and destroyed their flexibility. What to do now? The nearest island for repairs was Midway, about 600 miles to the south. The main Hawaiian group was about 1,500 miles to the southeast, and the North American coast still stood 2,500 miles east. There were also the Aleutians, of course, but not at that time of year! I decided to carry right on for America, only keeping to about the same latitudes and making for Humboldt Bay instead of San Francisco.

It continued to blow, and even with the 100 square feet in my foresail and mizzen (80 per cent of the sail area had been in the mainsail) I averaged over 50 miles a day for the next 2,000 miles. My chief worry, now that I realized how weak they were, was that I would lose the foremast. I could carry on sailing without the mizzen, but not without the foresail. When the foremast did choose to go over the side it was again at night, during the last and perhaps worst of the westerly gales. Apart from getting the mess aboard next morning there was nothing I could do in the next two days except drift; it was blowing too hard, and was too rough, to try rigging a jury mast.

When the wind calmed down I squared off and re-tapered the foot of the foremast (it had broken at the base), pulled the stump and managed to re-step what was left. I carried old triangular sails for just such emergencies. My progress was down to about 30 miles a day, including four hours' use of the engine which until then I had kept in reserve. I seemed to have passed out of the area of strong favorable winds. Now they were fitful, often light, sometimes contrary, with a great deal of rain.

On Christmas morning, 1959, I was becalmed in a long swell about 20 miles from the entrance to Humboldt Bay. From the look of the sky I could stay there all Christmas if I relied on the wind, so I decided to risk my final reserve of fuel. Crossing the bar at the entrance to the harbor the engine stalled for lack of fuel. Nobody can really understand what that implies who does not know the entrance to Humboldt Bay with a Pacific swell breaking in. Fortunately the Coast Guard were on the alert and plucked me through.

High Tea had been 70 days at sea. She was dirty and badly needed repainting, and I had to replace the masts and patch up the sails and running rigging. After that I sailed the last lap down to San Francisco. The wind, back to form, blew against me all the way.

Comparing his modern Bermudian-rig cruising yacht *Chempaka* with the junk *High Tea*, Brian Platt said, *"High Tea* was the better rig. I do not know how *Chempaka's* rig would have stood up to the almost continuous winter gales of the North Pacific. Frankly I would not like to try, though I would not mind making the same journey again on a junk."

Golden Lotus

"Ocean cruising had been my lifelong ambition," said Brian Clifford, a young New Zealander who had sailed conventional small craft and had several years' experience as a licensed mate of Pacific freighters. "So I decided—why not cruise in a vessel that would introduce new ideas to New Zealanders."

After looking over dhows, Singapore junks, and Celebes trading schooners, Clifford decided on a Chinese junk and had the Golden Lotus (36½-ft. LOA, 13-ft. beam, 3-ft. 6-in. draft) built by Wung Kee at Pak Sha Wan near Kowloon for little more than what a good diesel auxiliary engine would have cost in New Zealand.

Following a shakedown cruise that was much too brief, Clifford and three friends departed Hong Kong December 2, 1961, for New Zealand. The first day out, part of the rigging carried away and the tiller broke and was replaced with a spare. A week of northeast gales and heavy seas further damaged their rudder and tiller gear. At Singapore, where they arrived December 20, repairs and several modifications were made.

The run down through Bangka and Belitung, across the Java Sea to Sunda Strait, and out to Christmas Island was made in the northwest monsoon. That island's main anchorage was closed to shipping due to gale winds, and the junk sheltered at Waterfall Cove for ten days before shoving off for Randja Island and on through the Savu Sea to Dili, Portuguese Timor. With Clifford and his mates anxious to make Thursday Island before the northwest monsoon gave way to the southeast trades, Golden Lotus averaged one hundred miles daily on the ten-day passage across the Arafura Sea.

"We lacked the funds and time to lay over and plot our courses to take advantage of prevailing winds and currents," said Brian Clifford. "For example, on our 1,800-mile passage from Thursday Island to Sydney, we battled against the wind most of the way through the tricky waters of the Great Barrier Reef."

After they crossed the Tasman to Auckland, completing a voyage of 8,500 miles on June 30, 1962, Clifford wrote: "Our Chinese craft taught us that however much we got to know about handling a junk at sea there was still a lot more to learn. In short, she trimmed us down to size. We are proud of Golden Lotus—she came from an ancient line of ocean thoroughbreds."

One Step

One Step (ex-Lorrie), a 63-foot-LOA Hong-Kong-built junk, was sailed from China to Australia in 1964 by Dudley Shuter, an Australian, with five Chinese sailors and two American missionaries as crew. After leaving the Philippines bound south, the junk struck a floating log at sea but suffered no damage. Later, in the Great Barrier Reef north of Cooktown, she grounded heavily on a submerged coral ledge but was winched off without damage.

One Step cruised widely in the Southwest Pacific, visiting many ports and outer island anchorages with a crew of Australian divers and underwater photographers. Under skipper-owner Noel Stroud, the junk was on a cruise from Sydney, Australia, to film underwater documentaries when she caught fire and sank ten miles off Trial Bay, northern New South Wales, on December 8, 1965. The four members of the crew were rescued by the Greek vessel *Cassian Mariner*.

Ying Hong

Often, while sailing in the South China Sea as a mate on merchant ships out of Hong Kong carrying general cargo to Far Eastern ports, Mike Briant, a sailor from South Africa, dreamed of owning and sailing his own small vessel on long ocean voyages. During these years he was able to observe Chinese junks at close quarters and to recognize them as seaworthy ocean-cruising craft. Much of his time in port was spent in crowded junk harbors and small-boat yards, consuming gallons of Chinese tea while discussing and comparing the skills and workmanship of different yards. During these years he learned much of how a junk is best handled under sail.

On one voyage, when his large Hong-Kong-bound ship was en route from Japan down through the China Sea and laboring heavily in a full gale, Mike was deeply impressed by three fishing junks that came by under a good spread of sail. The junk sailors waved cheerfully as they pressed along at a good clip through the heavy seas toward Amoy. When another officer, on the bridge at the time, remarked that "no European could handle a Chinese junk like that," Mike decided he would have a try. Soon after he resigned his mate's job and moved into Ho Sag's shipyard on Aplechan Island to supervise the building of a junk for ocean cruising.

The three-masted, 42-foot-LOA *Ying Hong*, with yacal keel and bulkheads, teak planking and decks, and five watertight compartments, was built without plans in five months by a temperamental Chinese artisan and his crew. From the well-rounded stern to the eyes at the bow and the windlass at the foot of the mainmast, everything was made by hand including the tools used to build the boat—fiddle drills, bow saws, chisels, and adzes. The 36-square-foot rudder had the usual diamond-shaped holes in the blade to prevent dead water along the after edge. A small diesel auxiliary was installed; gravestones were used for ballast. With Mike and a friend living in the boat-yard with a rucksack, sleeping on the deck of the unfinished junk, and making their own sails by hand, *Ying Hong* was launched complete with fire-crackers and proper joss for a total cost of slightly less than $8,000.

Skipper Briant, with shipmate Colin Ogg and Harold Hawthorne, cleared Hong Kong September 20, 1961. He had intended to sail earlier in the southwest monsoon season to be sure of following winds, as September is the transitional month. However, they made good progress and reached the

Hong Kong junk *Ying Hong* at Castries, St. Lucia, after a 35-day passage from Ascension to Antigua.

Skipper Mike, mate Patricia, and son John Steven Briant of *Ying Hong.*

south tip of Formosa in good time. Following is Mike's account of what happened next:

How we came to be caught so close to shelter and how we then happened to run, not away from a typhoon but right into its track, is a long story and all to do with the forecasts of a radio station. However, this is what happened.

Before we had even realized that we were experiencing the outer fringe of a typhoon we lost the top 8 feet of our mainmast. I would like to say that this was due to sheer force of wind but it wasn't. The mast was defective and we should never have allowed it to be stepped in Hong Kong.

Once having realized what we were in for we ran before it for about six hours thinking we were getting away from the track. The junk performed magnificently. With the wind well over gale force and increasing all the time and high following seas with breaking crests, she was safe and still easy to handle. She never once came in danger of broaching, mainly I think because of the high measure of control afforded by the huge rudder. With her high poop deck she was of course in no danger of being pooped. The impression that she might tend to stick her nose in when sliding down a large following sea due to her bows being so much lower than the stern is completely erroneous. Once on the face of a following sea, strangely she seems to stick her backside down, and comes down it like a duck.

We eventually hove to under the tiny mizzen alone and for the next 24 hours stayed below reading and sleeping. In this way she rode three to four points off the wind and although very uncomfortable seemed completely safe. To make progress around the deck one literally had to crawl around on all fours against the force of the wind but no seas came aboard at all. About six in the evening we found ourselves in the eye of the typhoon—dead calm but with a nasty, confused sea. We slept through the other half of it during the night and next morning the wind was dying fast. Under foresail and mizzen we eventually made Kaohsiung, Formosa, where we repaired our main mast and then set off round the south tip of Formosa again and up the east coast. Here we found the Northeast Monsoon had set in with a vengeance.

After a week of trying to beat up to Japan we gave up the idea altogether. We agreed instead to head for South Africa. From Formosa we sailed through the Philippines to Borneo and round the Borneo coast to Sarawak. Here we went 200 miles up a jungle river by way of exploring. Then down through Indonesia and out through Sunda Strait into the Indian Ocean. We stopped at Cocos Island and Mauritius on our way to Durban, South Africa.

At Durban, skipper Briant met, married, and signed on a wife-cum-mate for future voyaging. Following a long stay in that port, they had a very hard trip round Cape Agulhas and the Cape of Good Hope to Capetown. From Africa to the West Indies was all plain sailing with no major incidents. Calls were made at St. Helena and at Ascension Island, where a girl crew member from another yacht was signed on for the passage to Antigua.

In five years *Ying Hong* sailed more than 20,000 miles, visiting half a hundred ports and scores of islands. From the Windward Islands, the Briants with their two children planned to cruise up the East Coast to Canada. "We would like to visit England and Europe," said Mike, speaking of future cruises in *Ying Hong,* "and we would also like to cross the Pacific. We may do both."

A few of the advantages of a Chinese cruising junk according to Mike Briant are:

1. Low initial cost. 2. Seaworthiness. 3. Ample space and comfort for a cruising family. 4. If you use the rig as the Chinese do sails cost next to nothing. We make our own. 5. The right type of junk is important. Ours, a Har Gau Jai type, has a round stern instead of the usual large flat transom. This makes her a good boat in a following sea. 6. The sails are very easy to handle in many ways (not all). It is a 60-second job to put in a reef or shake one out, and my wife Pat can do it alone without calling anyone else on deck.

The Hong Kong Junk Club races on the Crown Colony's Gin Drinkers Bay have attracted international attention in recent years. Junk races have been held in Australia and Germany. In the United States, the Pacific Northwest has its popular North American Unlimited Junk Races near Seattle, Washington. With 35-foot junks completely equipped, including a diesel auxiliary, selling for $8,000 in Hong Kong, several yards in the Crown Colony are building and exporting them to Australia, the United States, West Indies, Britain, Sweden, Germany, Spain, and several other countries. Whether the widespread interest will last remains to be seen. Once the novelty has wore off many of the highly decorated junks have become little more than picturesque additions to bays and inland waterways.

Since Slocum's voyage in the *Liberdade*—his Cape Ann dory with sampan stern, rudder, and rig—a number of sailors on both sides of the Atlantic, who have made notable ocean voyages with junk rig on modified junk or conventional yacht hulls, have found that the balanced Chinese lugsail can hardly be bettered for simplicity and ease of handling.

Slocum proved what can be done with the rig, by a hard-pressed sailor short of cash, on his 5,500-mile voyage from Santos, Brazil, to Norfolk, averaging 100 miles a day or more with a best day's run of 175 miles in the three-masted, 35-foot-LOA *Liberdade*. "Her rig," said Slocum, "was the Chinese sampan style, which is, I consider, the most convenient boat rig in the whole world."

Commander Robin Kilroy spent twenty years considering and planning a perfect offshore sailing vessel and had long experience in sailing traditional craft from Bristol pilot cutters to modern yachts before he designed and built his 38-foot-LOA *Boleh* with the bow of an Arab dhow and the hull of a Chinese junk and sailed her across three oceans from Singapore to England via the Cape of Good Hope.

"What impressed me chiefly about Chinese junks," said Commander

Kilroy, ". . . was their carrying capacity, their speed before the wind, the ease with which they can shorten sail, and their ability to point high into the wind when necessary in narrow waters. I think the Chinese have evolved a better design for safe, comfortable, commodious and reasonably fast ocean or coastal cruising than has come from any Western nation."

Other modern sailors, like R. M. Ellison with the Chinese-rigged 36-foot schooner *Ilala*, have used junk rig to advantage on conventional yacht hulls. And the fine performance of H. G. Hasler's Chinese battened lugsail on his four solo Atlantic crossings and other ocean voyages has done much to show its capacities when handled by a competent sailor.

In Colonel Hasler's experiments toward an improved type of small sea-going sailing yacht, after seven years with a "Lapwing rig," he designed a pure Chinese lug rig in 1959 for his 25-foot modified-Folkboat *Jester*. The single, light (240 square feet) Terylene sail "retained ease of handling in all wind strengths and reefed in seconds, without touching the sail, by simply veering on the halyard. In a hard breeze," said Hasler, "the sail remains flat, and with the wind on or forward of the beam it can be feathered off for maximum drive with minimum heel. Under these conditions she is particularly fast."

Four years after his high-latitude passage that took second place in the first Singlehanded Transatlantic Race, Hasler sailed *Jester* from Plymouth to Newport, Rhode Island, in thirty-seven days, twenty-two hours, for fifth place among fourteen modern ocean yachts in the 1964 Singlehanded Transatlantic Race.

After his first two North Atlantic crossings in his junk-rigged Folkboat, Colonel Hasler had this to say: "The design of this sail and gear is extraordinarily subtle. The more I learn about it, the more subtle it seems. I suspect I am still missing certain points known to the Chinese, who started two thousand years ahead of me."

The emergence of Asia is the greatest historical fact of our era. Everywhere along the China coast, mechanization and modern co-operatives have vastly changed the old customs and taboos. To a sailor it is readily apparent in the white wakes of junks and sampans with auxiliary marine power devoted to what junk masters call the "new wave." The motorization of junks in North and South China has spread widely. Modern diesel-powered junks have supplanted sail and oar on many routes. But, while it is true that some types of small craft have vanished forever, the sailing junk by its suitability to specialized uses and to the Chinese sailor still holds its own. Wooden offshore sailing junks are still an important part of the Viet Cong and Vietnamese fishing industry. Each coastal province has its own large fleets. (Hundreds of these junks were taken over by the navies of both governments to patrol the waters of the Mekong Delta, the Gulf of Siam, and the Gulf of Tonkin.)

From the Yellow Sea south to Shanghai, Hong Kong, Mandarin Bay, and the waters of Vietnam, which curl through the South China Sea down to the Gulf of Siam, motley fleets of pure sailing junks in a wide variety of types still swarm the rich deep-sea fishing grounds. Thousands of weather-beaten offshore junk-trawlers and three-masted long-liners, foredecks filled with fine mesh seine, manned by men, women, and children who know no other life, remain dependent on hand capstans, hand lead and line, alarm clocks, primitive compasses, and a patchwork of mended and remended sails. With their junks already as functional as a boat can be they see no need for change.

Today South China's floating villages and closely packed small-craft towns have boat schools, clinics, stores, restaurant sampans, and market boats that sell rice, ginger, vegetables, and fruit. About half of the *shui-jen*—sea people—are fishermen and traders with their own strict codes and self-governing councils in an almost completely amphibious world from floating dry-docks and junk doctors to sampan postmen and coffin makers.

How many families can the reader think of in Europe or America who sail, work, and live aboard a 30- to 40-foot sailing craft for a lifetime?

The *shui-jen's* junk is his entire domain, the cradle of his family and his working home at sea. Even the smallest baby learns instinctively to spread its legs and sway to the motion of the junk, knows at about age five the best way to catch a turn around a bollard, and learns soon after to handle an oar, having picked up the rhythm while strapped to its mother's back.

Experts assure us that China will have more than a billion population by 1980. A large percentage of these people of tomorrow will be sampan and junk sailors dependent on pole, *yu-loh* (oars), hand capstans, and sail alone. "The wind and sail is our life," said the recently elected head of the largest Crown Colony junk master's guild, "for that is the way it is, and always will be."

Though today their fishnets may be woven from modern nylon mono-filament, much is still believed to be in the hands of the spirit of the sea. Each junk has its shrine and incense for Tin Hau. And in the South China Sea where the *tung shang fung* blows half the year from the northeast, the self-reliant junk sailor remains adept at making the best use of it—an art centuries old in those waters before the Viking Age began.

CHAPTER 9

Transocean Catamarans and Trimarans

~~~~~~

LIKE the tailor Blodgett who prophesied that "sewing machines will never come into general use," there are still those who hold that sailing vessels with more than one hull will never become popular and who decline to realize that modern ocean cruising in catamarans and trimarans is a part and product of a turbulent time, a mid-century period of multiple advancements in many fields—social, political, educational, mechanical—that future historians will consider the most revolutionary in the history of man.

Between this new and very old movement—from ancient Polynesian craftsmen to computer machines for calculating twin-hull lateral resistance, from twelfth-century double canoes to mid-sixties aircraft-type, semi-monocoque structured catamarans—eight centuries went by before aerodynamic studies and experiments enabled Westerners to make significant advancements in multihull craft.

When we recall that Leonardo da Vinci was designing helicopters and that flights to the moon were planned hundreds of years ago, we are reminded that basically little is new. A stone-, bone-, and shell-age people who knew nothing of mathematical balance, of lateral resistance, or of values squared to this or that but were born and bred to the salt sea and to their great catamarans voyaged for centuries over fifteen million square miles of the Pacific while Europe was still struggling to emerge from barbarism.

Seaworthiness and speed, the prime goals of most modern multihull sailors, were achieved to a high degree by South Sea Islanders long before the first Spanish caravel entered Oceania. Cook, Bougainville, Kotzebue, and Schouten all attest to the weatherly qualities of Tongan and Samoan ocean-cruising catamarans—which, as Cook put it, "outran our ships considerably." "The rig of these vessels is so excellent and they go so well under sail that there are few ships in Holland that could overtake them," wrote Schouten. "Though we ran seven or eight knots," said Bougainville, "they sailed round us as if we were at anchor."

In Micronesia, where the early sailing canoe reached a higher development than anywhere else in the world, large Gilbertese *bauruas* have been logged at 15 knots. The swift flying proas sailed at sustained speeds up to 20 knots. Because of weatherliness and fine cruising qualities, they voyaged widely and made thousand-mile passages with Spanish mail between the Carolines, the Philippines, and the Marianas.

Polynesian sea quests were not primarily for speed or for the sheer joy of sailing, as some twin-hull enthusiasts would have us believe, nor were they "accidental voyages," as a few tendentious theorists have claimed. The almost forgotten art of the master multihull builders of the South Seas and the lore of the weather-wise Polynesian catamaran sailor were combined with the classic need to wander, a compulsion to see what was over the horizon simply because the horizon was there, and later to transport people, animals, plants, and flowers between Tahiti, Hawaii, New Zealand, and the outermost archipelagos.

Under a top *faatere* (sailing master) a 40- to 60-foot double canoe sailed close to the wind with very little leeway and in moderate conditions maintained speeds up to 8 knots. With the wind abeam 6 knots were made or with the wind before the beam about 4 knots, depending on current and sea. Sailing north on the wind from Tahiti to the northeast trades, and from there full and by to Hawaii, or bound south close-hauled through the trades to the equator, and through the southeasterlies on a board to Nukuhiva or the Tuamotus, the two-masted, plank-built pahis with inserted ribs and V-shaped double keels could average 140 miles daily under favorable conditions.

Only a few of today's sophisticated version of the double canoe modified to aerodynamic standards do better than the early Polynesians under the variable conditions of transocean cruising.

Several times in the past century twin hulls have had a resurgence of interest—most notably by Sir Charles Petty in the reign of Charles II and by the "wizard of Bristol," Nathaniel Herreshoff, who experimented with 30-foot catamarans as early as 1876 and said, "It is my belief that a single-hulled sailing machine can not be developed that will have a higher average speed than the multihulled craft." Despite the faults of Herreshoff's catamarans, they proved so much faster than conventional keel craft that they were banned from formal racing.

Kaimiloa

In 1936 an early modern version of a Polynesian double canoe was being built on the beach at Waikiki that was to start more people thinking of the possibilities of long-voyaging catamarans for world cruising than any other twin-hull voyage up to the early fifties. But at the time when Eric De Bisschop and Joseph Tatiboet pitched their tent at a quiet Waikiki Beach spot, shaded by trees, and started to build Kaimiloa (Quest Overseas), they were laughed at and frequently referred to in the following months as the "mad Frenchmen," and as the craft took final shape it was predicted that they would never get as far as Samoa.

Few of those who scoffed knew that Eric De Bisschop was a master mariner of wide experience and an authority on native craft of the Pacific and Far East. Fewer still knew that he was a dedicated free-lance ethnologist who devoted over twenty-five years to research and long voyages in proof of his theory that the tough maritime ancestors of the Polynesians furrowed the oceans of more than half the world two thousand years before Magellan.

Carefully examining all the models in the Bishop Museum at Honolulu, including many said to be "ancient," De Bisschop concluded in 1936 that they were only "replicas for tourists." He felt that most academic authorities on Polynesia, being ignorant of the sea, were lacking in the knowledge of seamanship that would enable them to understand the construction, handling, and sailing qualities of Polynesian vessels. Failing, after much search and research, to find any accurate plans or reliable knowledge of the early Polynesian double canoe, he designed Kaimiloa on his own. "For such a vessel what could be learned from theoretical naval architecture?" he asked. "My opinion is, nothing. I follow my own instincts and seamanly judgment, trace my own curves, my imagination becomes reality modified—by following my nose. No mathematics in it at all."

Kaimiloa departing Hawaii March 7, 1937, on her historic voyage halfway around the world to France via the Cape of Good Hope.

Kaimiloa's two deep V-shaped hulls were joined by four heavy beams on which a 34-foot mainmast and a foremast were stepped. The two rudders were attached outboard to the stern post of each hull. Each of the hulls had a cabin nearly its full length, with ample headroom. The starboard cabin was the chartroom, and the port contained the galley and sleeping quarters. The completed 38-ft.-LOA, 17-ft.-beam, 12-ton catamaran had a draft of 3 feet.

Following a trial run off Oahu a number of adjustments were made, particularly to the steering rudders. On March 7, 1937, the two Frenchmen and their catamaran cleared Honolulu under schooner rig with a red-and-white battened junk mainsail and vermilion fore-staysail bound for Europe via Africa and the Cape of Good Hope.

Kaimiloa's narrow double-ended symmetrical hulls were like independent vessels joined together, and her over-all weight added much to stability and cruising comfort on the voyage south. By natural balance between hulls and sails she was, according to her skipper, largely self-steering, whether close-hauled, reaching, running free or even with the wind astern and was frequently sailed with the helm lashed "with some scraps of inner tubes acting as springs on the tiller tackles. Not a very sophisticated method. But it works. The boat steers itself alone without the least yawing. In a heavy sea with stinging rain and spray one appreciates being able to stretch out in one's bunk."

First call was at Futuna, a 3-by-12-mile island between Samoa and Fiji, about 2,500 miles from Hawaii. When the craft with bright vermilion twin hulls and bold Polynesian designs along her sheer strakes anchored off the village of Sigave on the west coast of the fertile copra island, De Bisschop and Tatiboet received a festive welcome. It was the first time in the memory of the several thousand Polynesians of Futuna and Alofi that "a great double canoe" had sailed into the tiny French dependency from a distant country over the sea. During their stay they were well supplied with island products, and on the hour of departure the shelter cabin on the bridge deck was filled with the choice fruits for which the island is noted.

Sailing on west across the Pacific, *Kaimiloa* rounded Papua, and, after an encounter with the sharp, jagged shoals of the Great Barrier Reef, passed up through Torres Strait and out into the Arafura Sea.

"The voyage goes well," wrote the skipper June 8, near Timor, "nothing to do but let her run. Nothing remarkable. Always from 120 to 140 miles per 24 hours—and the helm lashed."

By mid-June, De Bisschop and Tatiboet arrived at Bali and went on to Java. From Surabaja they set sail for the Strait of Sunda, passed dangerously close to Krakatoa Volcano, and headed out into the Indian Ocean for a 6,000-mile, fifty-nine-day passage to Africa. July 9 the skipper wrote, "Since July

Very few of those who scoffed at the ventures of Eric De Bisschop knew that he was a competent master mariner and free-lance ethnologist of wide experience.

2 we have averaged 130 miles daily. Our best day was July 7 with 165 miles. Yesterday we made 152 miles and today 150 miles."

Though *Kaimiloa* had an average noon-to-noon run of approximately one hundred miles per day on her long voyage across three major oceans, her skipper was not primarily interested in speed. As a sailor-scientist his main concern was seaworthiness and the ability of a catamaran to carry sufficient provisions, gear, and special equipment for long periods at sea in the pursuit of oceanographical data and observations. He felt that the prehistoric islanders of Oceania were the greatest sailors of all time. "Many men are on the sea but only those with intuitive seamanly sense live with it," De Bisschop said, referring to the early Polynesians. Convinced they had well proven double canoes could sail anywhere in the wide Pacific basin, he wanted to show that such craft could have sailed anywhere in the world.

Without calling in at Durban they rounded Cape Agulhas late in August, and the austral winter off the "Cape of Storms" gave their Indian Ocean passage a rough ending. Gale winds and heavy seas drove the battered vessel far south, and like so many other sailors of the past half century they took a dusting and had a difficult time rounding the Cape of Good Hope.

A falling barometer and a full N.W. gale that lasted two days was followed, after a few hours of calm, by a second gale with the sea "as ill-tempered as it could be." When a sea anchor "purchased from a marine supply store in Honolulu" collapsed and was a total failure, a small trysail hoisted near the stern kept the catamaran hove to and drifting comfortably leeward. Finally the wind shifted to the S.W. and they were able to run in to Cape Town with a fair wind, making 8 knots. Even at this speed and with a following sea they let her steer herself, and she did so "better than in the hands of the best helmsman." On arrival Tatiboet gave thanks to St. Anne, and Eric had a stiff toast to *Kaimiloa*.

Departing South Africa September 17, 1937, good time was made in the Atlantic in the southeast trades to the equator. With one day of calm, an average of 156 miles a day was logged on the 1,660-mile run to St. Helena. Landfall was made on the island but they did not stop because, as De Bisschop put it, "It was where the British imprisoned my good friend Napoleon."

Difficulty was experienced in the northeast and the Portuguese trades on a course that took them past Ascension Island and the Cape Verdes to Portugal. They kept to the westward of the longitude of Madeira, expecting to be able to bear down on the island in the North Atlantic Westerly. However, it was December and the Atlantic was contrary. After a severe buffeting by a series of winter gales that *Kaimiloa* weathered well off Madeira, Ponta Delgada, and Lisbon, a wild and contrary northerly off Setúbal sent them south to Tangier, Morocco, where they arrived January 3, having sailed more than 6,200 miles from South Africa in slightly more than a hundred days with forty days of contrary gales.

Departing Tangier after a long stay, some good runs were made and the vessel had a daily average of 140 miles for the first four days. In a mistral on the coast of France, with the lighthouses marking the harbor of Marseille in sight, De Bisschop had this to say:

The northerly gale is really blowing now; it could blow the horns right off the cows. No matter, I look at all above, the bamboos of the mains'l are groaning under the effort. We are making ten knots at times. I see Planier rise over the horizon. We sweep over the seas and it disappears behind us. What a grand sight *Kaimiloa* makes dashing towards port smoking with spray.

After 264 days at sea the little twin-hull craft arrived at Cannes, France, on May 20, 1938, during a heavy rain storm.

Only a few of those who saw *Kaimiloa* in the Riveria after she had completed a sixteen-month voyage halfway around the world had the vision to realize that she was the forerunner of a new era in small-boat voyaging.

(In 1939 De Bisschop left Bordeaux alone in the double canoe *Kaimiloa Vakea*, cruised to the Canary Islands, and was bound for Honolulu when war conditions put an end to the voyage.)

Fully waterproof glues that were developed during the war years made it possible to build strong, light hulls from veneers; with the post-World War II trend toward smaller cruising vessels attention was again turned toward catamarans, and individuals in many countries began experimenting with new designs, techniques, and materials—especially in smaller craft for smooth water. A number of offbeat experimenters in this period came up with some far-out but quite good ideas that were later accepted by others. A few men, remembering *Kaimiloa*, were designing, building, and sailing larger craft on transocean passages.

Ananda

In 1946 the ketch-rigged trimaran *Ananda* (43-ft. LOA, 34-ft. LW, 22-ft. beam, 4-ft. draft) was built by André Sadrin and launched in southern France at Sète in the Gulf of Lions. Following a shakedown cruise in the Mediterranean she was sailed to Casablanca. In Morocco, Sadrin was joined by Didier Petit and Nick Scherer as crew. Sailing south in strong, fair winds they made the 900-mile run to St. Vincent, Cape Verde, in ten days.

Departing Porto Grande in October for an Atlantic crossing to the West Indies, they made very good time in the trades until a depression of some severity (strong seas and force 9 wind) reduced them to storm jib and a lashed tiller. Two weeks out, a squall that broke their main boom was followed by a full S.E. gale with torrential rains and very heavy seas. On the second day *Ananda*, with low freeboard (2-ft. 7-in.), had a difficult time in seas "15 to 25 feet high," was swept frequently from bow to stern, and one breaking crest nearly swept Sadrin overboard. During the five days they were battened down and hove to, the three-hulled craft was blown nearly a hundred miles south. One of the short, beamy floats became logged with water that they were temporarily unable to pump out. When the gale passed the float was pumped dry and the craft put back on a S.W. course.

Built of oak and mahogany, *Ananda's* V-shaped, canoe-stern main hull was very heavy (8.7 tons displacement), and her floats quite beamy. With the wind free or astern, she was hard on the helm and in strong seas difficult to steer. In fair weather her 600 square feet of Chinese-junk-type, battened mainsail and mizzen gave her a daily ocean-cruising average of 125 to 135 miles.

While bowling along at 10 knots on November 7 they sighted the 4,800-foot peak of Mount Pelée, and in the late afternoon *Ananda* arrived at Fort-de-France, Martinique, completing a tough Atlantic crossing in twenty days.

Copula

In 1948 when Raoul Christiaen, a follower of Voss, Gerbault, and De Bisschop, an adventurer and businessman who had answered the call of the sea and worked on the Ivory Coast, became intrigued with the possibilities of twin-hulled craft for long ocean voyaging, he decided to turn his dreams to reality by building *Copula*—so named to symbolize the mating of her two hulls.

Patterned after the *Marie-Celine*, a 23-foot French catamaran that had sailed to Casablanca and cruised successfully in the Mediterranean, *Copula* had narrow asymmetrical hulls (less than 5-foot beam each at midships) that were tapered like sabers and built of welded steel joined by angle bars. Completed at Toulouse, France, she weighed 22 tons, was 47½-ft. LOA, with 17½-ft. beam and 4-ft. draft. Being an admirer of *Kaimiloa*, Christiaen rigged the 42½-ft. masts with Chinese battened mainsail and mizzen (total sail area with jib: 1,345 square feet). Accommodations included two heads, three double cabins, and wheelhouse on the bridge deck.

Newspapers acclaimed, as they have so often since, that "catamarans are the boats of the future" and that *Copula* was the forerunner of "a type that will revolutionize yachting." Others thought that the strange craft was a whaler to be used to catch whales between the two hulls. Monohull sailors sourly predicted they would never get across the Bay of Biscay.

All went well on the 1948 trials from Sète in the Mediterranean to Casablanca and back. Later *Copula* sailed from France to Spain, Majorca, Algiers, and return and was then pronounced capable of sailing anywhere.

In 1950 the crew on the outward passage from France included the owner, his wife, Jean Filloux, and Claude Graf. Bad weather in the Bay of Biscay gave them a slow crossing to the Spanish coast and around Cape Finisterre. Between Lisbon, Portugal, and Mogador, Morocco, 136 miles daily was averaged. After cruising in the Canaries and a long stay at Tenerife, the twin-hulled oceanographic cruiser departed for Martinique.

In the Atlantic observations were recorded for the National Meteorological Society, and specimens were collected and tests made for the Oceanographic Institute. Special equipment aboard included an air compressor to handle underwater gear, diving suits, a large generator, an automatic thermograph, a well-equipped laboratory, and a workshop. A fair passage was had with daily runs of 156, 150, and 138 miles and less on the thirty-one-day crossing to Fort-de-France, where they arrived January 10, 1951. Cruising up to Kingston and Port-au-Prince, they crossed the Bahama Banks to the Gulf Stream and on to Florida. After grounding on a sand bar off Morehead City on the North Carolina coast, they took the waterway to Atlantic City. *Copula*, looking like a prehistoric butterfly with her Chinese sails, coasted on up to New York, sailed under the East River bridges to the Sound, and anchored near Manhasset, having sailed 9,000 miles in ninety days at sea.

According to Christiaen, the steel-hulled, reverse-sheer catamaran proved swift and comfortable before a following wind and quite fast close-hauled in moderate seas. (Sailing to windward in fair conditions she made 8 to 10 knots.)

In his book *The Crossing of the Copula*, Jean Filloux, competent crewman and navigator, said of the Chinese junk rig, "Our sails pulled taut all the way up to the gaff, drew well over all without twisting. The aerodynamic principle involved was, I believe, one of the reasons for *Copula's* speed in every mode of sailing."

In strong seas *Copula* proved difficult to heave to in spite of her sea anchor and mizzen, according to one of her crew, who summarized succinctly, "In waves of 15 feet or more *Copula* would not heave to worth a damn."

Manu Kai

Much valuable information evolved from these early passages. A year after *Ananda* made her successful Atlantic crossing, one of the most important developments in multihull craft since Herreshoff's experiments came from Hawaii, where Woodbridge Brown and Alfred Kumalae designed and built the first Polynesian-type twin-hull craft utilizing modern materials and technical knowledge. As a result of "Woody" Brown's background as a glider pilot, his research among traditional island craft, and Al Kumalae's skill as a boatbuilder, *Manu Kai* (Sea Bird) embraced long-proven features from the Fiji and Gilbert Islands. Updated with aircraft techniques, deep asymmetrical hulls without keel or centerboard, a solid connecting wing bridge, and four watertight compartments in each hull, *Manu Kai* proved fast and sea-kindly in the lively waters off Oahu, went into commercial service, and was followed by *Alaii Kai* and other catamarans well suited to open sea sailing.

Tangaroa and Rongo

James Wharram left school with "the firm intention of following in the steps of Slocum, Pidgeon, and Robinson" but had to wait ten years before he had the experience and money to build *Tangaroa*, a Polynesian-type catamaran inspired by *Kaimiloa* and *Manu Kai* and named in honor of a Polynesian sea god.

In England, at the time, "catamarans were still regarded with the same kind of prejudice," wrote Wharram, "as were the first cotton sails, the first beamy centerboard boats, and the Bermudan rig."

Tangaroa, no doubt the only seagoing catamaran to be built in a rural English hayloft with the help of two German girls, was 23-ft. 6-in. LOA and had two cabins in each hull, one for the galley, one for a chartroom, and two for bunks. Completed in 1954 at a total cost of $420 and with the help of Ruth Merseberger and Jutta Schultze-Rhonhof, who shared Wharram's faith in twin hulls and his dream of ocean cruising, the flat-bottomed craft was transported from Manchester three hundred miles on a lorry to the Thames Estuary.

After a thousand-mile shakedown cruise, early in 1955 *Tangaroa* sailed from Whitstable to Holland and Germany, went up the Schelde to the Rhine, and from Düsseldorf back across the North Sea to Dover and Falmouth. The catamaran performed well, and for $7 a week the girls provided an adequate, interesting diet and "had money left over for kerosene and postage."

The following spring, after cruising the Spanish and Portuguese coasts to Cascais, *Tangaroa* was sent to Las Palmas.

Departing Gran Canaria at the end of December to cross the Atlantic, Wharram and his all-girl crew were soon driving before the trade winds with twin spinnakers boomed out and lashed to the tillers. *Tangaroa* steered herself well and "kept an accurate course in seas 10 to 14 feet high" until the port rudder broke from the strain of her constantly working spinnakers. She then swung beam on and took some water aboard before repairs could be made and she was put back on course.

Most of the way across, at a time when Atlantic tankers and freighters in the area were running three to four days behind schedule, *Tangaroa* continued to have trouble with her long, deep rudders that were used as much for leeboards as for steering. Instead of the expected thirty days, the smallest catamaran to cross the Atlantic took six weeks to Maracas Bay, Trinidad, where she arrived February 7, 1957. *"Tangaroa's* flat bottom was a mistake," Wharram concluded after 6,000 miles of ocean voyaging.

Twenty-four hours after their arrival, Wharram and the girls started looking for lumber to build a 40-foot deep V-hulled Polynesian ocean catamaran. Not primarily interested in speed because "speed is only achieved by reducing the living space, displacement and safety to a minimum," Wharram designed *Rongo* (32-ft. LW, 5.5 tons displacement) to carry enough provisions and gear for voyaging anywhere in the world without auxiliary power. With the help of Ruth and Jutta, the new craft was built in a year under three giant mango trees near a beach in Trinidad.

After seventeen months of ocean cruising in a 23-foot catamaran, *Rongo* seemed quite spacious. Each hull had four watertight compartments and a 14-foot-long cabin; one contained the galley, head, and bunks, the other was a combination chartroom with quarters aft. Storage space was fore and aft of the main cabins and beneath the cabin sole. Each cabin had headroom. "Cruising for me," said Wharram, "means comfort: a bunk that one can sit up in and read a book, a galley where one can turn out regular meals with the minimum of effort in all weather, a boat that handles well and has a bit of extra safety for the above-average storm."

Designed with a high bridge wing to prevent pounding, *Rongo* had a slatted deck between hulls, masts were stepped in tabernacles with lanyards and deadeyes on stays, and again fully battened Chinese sails were used. On her 600-mile cruise to St. Thomas in the Virgin Islands, an average speed of 6 to 8 knots was maintained. Going to windward she held a true course with the helm lashed and sailed within four points of the wind. From St. Thomas they sailed due north to New York, making the 1,500-mile passage in nineteen days.

For the first ten days of their crossing to Britain, light westerlies prevailed and they made 1,300 miles. South of the Grand Banks, *Rongo* drove before winds to force 9 and on occasion had warps over the stern. Her freeboard, flare, and overhangs gave ample buoyancy and lift with no water aboard. After the period of westerly winds, almost continuous easterlies kept her driving windward for much of the remainder of the passage.

Except for loss of a rudder, for which they had spares, Wharram and his two-girl crew arrived at Dun Laoghaire September 29, 1959, in good shape and went on to Conway, North Wales, completing the first round-trip crossing of the Atlantic by modern catamaran.

Rongo was refitted in 1960, her long rudders were replaced by shallow ones, a skeg was added, sail rig was improved, and the boat was made self-steering. After spending the winter in Ireland, the two girls and Wharram departed to sail around the world. From Cillero, north Spain, they cruised down the Spanish and Portuguese coasts to Cadiz and across to the Canary Islands. Late in 1961 Jutta met a tragic death ashore at Las Palmas.

On November 28 Jim Wharram and Ruth Merseberger left the Canaries for a twenty-seven-day passage in light winds to Trinidad. Later, from St. Thomas, they wrote, "Without Jutta we are not able to continue our voyage around the world. We miss her everywhere, and it is just too much for us."

Returning to England in *Rongo* in 1962, they steered only four days out of thirty-two days from Bermuda to the Fastnet and ended their passage sailing up the Irish Sea in a gale under bare poles doing 5 knots. In 1966 Ruth and Jim were completing their 46-foot Oro-class catamaran for future cruising. "I'm not particularly interested in racing or record passages," says

Jim Wharram, the designer of Britain's first transocean cruising catamaran. "After all, I go to sea to get away from the competitive rat-race, not to join it."

Among the many British multihull designers and builders, Roland and Francis Prout were outstanding. Starting experiments with catamarans in 1947, by the mid-fifties the Prout brothers had accumulated experience leading to a new concept and hull shape in their *Shearwater* and *Endeavor* that was lighter, broader-beamed for stability, with round bilge keels, centerboard plates for lateral plane, and rockered keels to come about more easily.

In 1956, proving the efficiency of the centerboard catamaran, *Shearwater III*, with a battened, high-roached mainsail, led the field in inshore racing catamarans and soon became the most popular design in Europe.

Day-sailing symmetrical catamarans from a number of British designers that proved seaworthy in the North Sea and the English Channel have evolved via broader underwater surfaces and large transom sterns into cruising craft.

From the *Shearwater* series, the Prouts went on to ocean-cruising catamarans and by the mid-sixties were building some of the largest catamarans afloat.

Michael Henderson, Hugo Meyers, F. H. Creger, Robert Harris, and a fairly wide scattering of others—British, Canadian, Australian, Spanish, Dutch, French, German, and American—both amateurs and professionals, were designing, building, and sailing catamarans during this early-1955-to-1965 decade of modern multihull history.

Waikiki Surf

In 1955 the appearance of *Waikiki Surf* (40-ft. LOA, 13-ft. beam, 3,000 pounds displacement, sail area 1,050 square feet) represented a considerable advancement in the design of oceangoing catamarans. Built to aircraft construction standards, hulls were deep and narrow with relatively short center uniting sections. With only about one-tenth the displacement of a 40-foot single-hull vessel, she carried nearly three-fourths of the sail area of a conventional craft.

Five days after the launching, Woody Brown and Rudy Choy, the designers of *Waikiki Surf*, cleared Honolulu with three friends for a passage to California that made multihull yachting history.

On the eastward passage, one-third of which was to windward, the first catamaran to cross from Hawaii to California and return averaged 180 miles per day, covered 2,800 nautical miles in slightly over 15½ days with variable weather and winds up to near gale force. On the return trip, with a green crew, she finished fourth in the Transpacific Race.

Aikane

Aikane (46-ft. LOA, 41-ft. LW, 16-ft. beam, 25-in. draft. 11,000 pounds displacement), an improved but direct descendant of *Manu Kai* designed by Rudy Choy and launched early in 1957, outran all single-hull yachts in two transpacific races and broke the ocean course record from Newport to Ensenada. Another deep, asymmetric-hulled cat, *Aikane* was given sharp, graceful lines, a 54-foot mast with roller reefing, narrow deckhouse so her big genoa could be sheeted in flat, 1,200 square feet of sail, and a 2,000-square-foot spinnaker.

Starting from San Pedro after the last of the thirty-odd ocean racing yachts had departed for Hawaii in 1957, *Aikane* soon passed all yachts up to 50-foot LOA and by the fifth day was leading the fleet including the 66-foot *Nam Sang*, the 56-foot *Jada*, and other Class A ocean racers. Her hull speed never dropped below 12 knots. On the tenth day, racing in to Oahu along Molokai's windward coast in following seas and a 25-knot catamaran wind, she arrived off the finish line at Honolulu twenty-six hours ahead of the 83-foot sloop *Barlovento*, the first official boat to complete the course.

Aikane has accommodations, provision, and gear capacity for extended cruising anywhere in the world. (With 6,000 pounds of supplies, gear, and crew she draws under 30 inches.) On long transocean passages she has logged many noon-to-noon runs of over 270 miles, has repeatedly made better than 290 miles a day, and on a 10,000-mile voyage from Los Angeles to Tahiti and return had a best day's run of 306 miles. Her many ocean records include a twelve-day run between Tahiti and Hawaii, close-hauled most of the way, and a sixteen-day, seventeen-hour passage from Los Angeles to Taio Hae Bay, Nukuhiva, in the Marquesas (3,000 miles). En route to Tahiti from Los Angeles her average daily run was 181.2 miles.

Although by the early sixties multihull craft had proven their ability as ocean-cruising vessels, there remained a strong difference of opinion regarding their use for transocean passages under all conditions. The early hostility of sailors and yacht clubs was not surprising. Almost every notable advance in material science has met with similar cynicism, skepticism, and opposition.

"Space travel is utter bilge," said the Astronomer Royal of England in 1956, only a year before Sputnik began orbiting the earth. The fourteenth edition of the *Encyclopaedia Britannica* (1929) labeled the two conditions then presumed essential for jet propulsion as incompatible and said, "All tests have been so extremely inefficient as to border on the absurd." In the late forties and early fifties, most traditional sailors felt that multihulls were absurd for ocean cruising.

Always, of course, the success of new experiences and experiments depends upon the common sense of man, which has often been lacking and has

Ken Murphy's cruiser-racer *Aikane* averaged better than 270 miles daily on long transoceanic passages and holds more records than any other cruising cat.

resulted in much bad press from multihull misadventures in the Pacific, Atlantic, and other oceans by a few who lacked competence in the art of seamanship. Experimentalists seeking spectacular bursts of speed and overenthusiasts under the banner of "taking the roll out of sailing" did as much harm by exaggerated claims as inexperienced multihullers who attempted difficult passages.

A recent survey of those who admitted to not liking multihulls gave the following main reasons: (1) instability—possibility of capsizing; (2) poor maneuverability; (3) awkward accommodations; (4) looks (as one of England's best-known sailors put it, "They are an anachronism and the ultimate in marine ugliness"; "Some look like half-submerged rocks," said another; "Just plain ugly," replied a commodore); (5) docking difficulties.

Stability: There was considerable capsizing in the early years. Some designers ballasted their cats to give stability by lowering the center of gravity. Buoyancy was also added to the masthead to offset the dangers of a knockdown. Centerboards or drop keels gained adherents. The tendency of some of the smaller cats toward pitchpoling when reaching at high speeds before a strong wind was largely eliminated by reserve buoyancy designed into the forward hull waterlines with relatively high bows. In Britain, Michael Henderson attained adequate stability with *Golden Miller* and *Misty Miller* by the use of ballasted fins, which he also considered essential for prolonged offshore cruising. The wide beam of the deep-water cat (usually nearly half the length) provides the stability to carry effective sail power. Today competent twin-hull sailors have safely handled cats under almost all conditions.

Windward Ability: While the principle of all catamarans is the same, different types behave differently. A bad cat, like a bad conventional keel schooner or ketch, is difficult to windward. But the good ones, usually with deep, rounded-V assymmetrical hulls or centered, semicircular hulls, are remarkably close-winded. More than a score of ocean records attest to the windward ability of catamarans against Class A ocean-racing keel craft.

Maneuverability: Sailing catamarans is a different type of sailing with a distinct technique, precision, and quickness of sail control; they tend to be more sensitive to maneuvering than other vessels. In the hands of an unskilled helmsman, a too rapidly turned rudder acts as a brake and turning momentum is lost by drag. Converted ex-monohull sailors have had to acquire new skills, the ability to feel at once the point of turbulence when the rudder blade begins a braking action, and have learned to ease sail pressure when the hull starts to lift since catamarans are less efficient when heeled.

Accommodations: Cruising accommodations and comfort have been much increased by design refinements.

Design: Because they improve the looks considerably, forward and after overhangs have been tried, but, as designer Dan Brown said of his *Anui Nui,* they also reduce the sailing length and hence the speed. Accustomed as he has become to symmetry, the traditional sailor has a natural aversion to asymmetry. With continuing improvements, most, if not all, of the early objections have been overcome. But what does or does not constitute a beautiful vessel (or an attractive wife) is a very personal matter. To a true multihull sailor, modern catamarans like *Aikane*, *Allez-Cat*, and *Iroquois* or trimarans like *Trice*, *Stiletto*, and *Toria*, are as pleasing to the eye as a lugger, an old straight-stemmer; or as a 20-ton gaff cutter with cumbersome gear once was to Claud Worth.

Docking: Docking problems remain and always will. The beam of most catamarans, approximately half their length, adds to the inconvenience of berthing at marinas—especially for those with 20 feet or more of beam.

Conclusion: No craft that floats on water is foolproof. Total safety, as Rudy Choy once put it, "comes only with a harp and a halo." Improperly handled, a multihull can be capsized in the same gale that will sink an improperly handled conventional keel boat. Despite broad claims for what an amateur can do and for how little experience is necessary, really high performance is attained only with a well-designed multihull and a good crew. Let it also be said that good twin-hulls and tri-hulls are not cheap. *Aikane* and her full gear would cost close to $50,000 today. (Robert Graham's 52-foot-LOA ketch-rigged, aluminum-built catamaran *Stranger* cost over $150,-000.) The cost of a trimaran like Dick Newick's 36-foot-LOA *Trice* is comparable to a conventional ocean racer of similar size and accommodations except that the single-hull vessel would cost many times as much to get equal performance. Close tolerance and high-quality work is never inexpensive. A well-designed 40-foot ocean-cruising catamaran built to Lloyd's approved specification with the hull sheathed in Dynel and finished with three coats of epoxy, fitted out with aluminum spars, stainless steel rigging, Dacron sails, and complete gear for extended cruising, would cost $30,000 today.

People who believe in catamarans don't necessarily believe in trimarans and vice versa.

When Victor Tchetchet, who did a lot with *Egg Nog* and *Flamenco* to introduce trimarans, showed at a very early date that an updated version of the Indonesian double outrigger could be faster than a similar-size catamaran, some interest in three-hulled craft was aroused, but it remained for Arthur Piver, Dick Newick, and others to design, develop, and demonstrate their true capabilities as deep-sea cruising craft. Despite his critics, and they are many, Piver, as a designer-sailor, can be said to have pioneered transocean crossings in modern trimarans. There is a vast difference between a costly Class A ocean racer-cruiser and a cruising vessel within the means of the average ocean sailor. In contrast to the $30,000 catamaran *Aikane*, Arthur Piver built his 30-foot-LOA sloop-rigged trimaran *Nimble* for $2,000 in 1960 and sailed from Fall River, Massachusetts, to England via the Azores —a total of 3,800 miles—in twenty-eight days, with ten days of gales and many days of almost calm and light winds, for a daily average of 135 miles.

A year later Piver's 35-foot-LOA *Lodestar* averaged 150 miles daily (under cruising canvas alone) for a fifteen-day passage from Los Angeles to Honolulu. Later, with two crewmen, Piver sailed south from Hawaii to New Zealand in *Lodestar.*

"First half of the passage to Tahiti was a close reach with particularly rough seas," wrote Piver.

The transition from NE Trades to SE Trades was accompanied by five days of vicious squalls—sometimes one after another—all day and all night. The wind was always from dead ahead. We did much of our sailing with only jib and mizzen—averaging about 140 miles per day for this leg of the trip.

The trip from Tahiti to Rarotonga (620 miles) took six days—in an almost endless calm. When light reaching breezes did appear, we were going just as fast as the apparent wind itself.

From the Cook Islands to New Zealand took another 18 days, with variable winds, although perhaps the roughest seas we have ever encountered were found off the New Zealand coast.

On one occasion we hove to for two days. It was quiet below, but every time we looked out of the hatch, we almost had our ears blown off. The boat hove to under just mizzen very nicely—but when we started navigating on the third day—found we had drifted 95 miles. So we lost three days instead of two. We determined that next time we would anchor to our 24-foot nylon cargo parachute.

In all of our trip we never had fair winds for any protracted period. Our last good day's run before reaching New Zealand was 215 miles. This 24-hour period contained: two hours of calm; six hours beating against light head winds; twelve hours under jib alone; four hours under genoa alone. Practically the entire distance was run under jib in a night-long frontal squall—fortunately from astern.

On her return passage from Wairoa, New Zealand, to Hawaii, a best day's run of 250 miles was made in the Roaring Forties. Nearing Rarotonga, *Lodestar* rode comfortably to a parachute sea anchor for two days in a storm that sunk three nearby Japanese fishing vessels with a loss of fifty lives.

Trimaran connectives are relatively simple compared to the critical strength of the catamaran wing. Light weight is essential for good performance. No ballast is required and plastic foam flotation is widely used. Most have divided rigs and because they are easily driven require relatively small sail for ocean cruising. In rugged going the mainsail is furled and the trimaran slogs windward or runs off before it under jib and mizzen. Now that modern craft with double outriggers have made long passages in all conditions the larger sizes are appearing in greater numbers.

Sixty-four-foot Empress
class trimaran designed
by Arthur Piver.

Arthur Piver's 35-ft.
trimaran *Lodestar*.

Vagabond AND Privateer

In Australia, Hedley Nichol's 35-foot-LOA *Vagabond*, 36-foot *Privateer*, and others have shown that a properly built trimaran is capable of hard ocean racing. In the 307-mile Brisbane-Gladstone Race, *Vagabond*, at times running on under jib alone, was fifty miles ahead of the fleet at Sandy Cape and beat the fleet home by an hour and fifteen minutes in weather described as the worst in sixteen years with "strong seas and wind gusting to Force 11 [60 knots]."

Trice

While *Vagabond* was winning top honors in Australia, Dick Newick from St. Croix, Virgin Islands, placed third with his 36-foot trimaran *Trice* against 143 entries in the Bermuda Race.

Trice, 36-ft. LOA, 20-ft. beam, 6-ft. 6-in. draft (with board down), displacement 4,400 pounds, sleeps four and can average a comfortable 10 knots at sea. Soon after launching she sailed 1,200 miles in ten and a half days to Newport, Rhode Island, so that she could sail along on the 1964 Bermuda Race. Starting ten minutes after the official fleet, *Trice* drew quickly ahead and to windward. By the end of the first day she had passed over eighty racers. Under unfavorable conditions, with winds forward of the beam most of the way, *Trice* passed 141 top racing yachts. An unofficial entry, *Trice* arrived in Bermuda only a few minutes behind 58-foot *Nina*, a Class A ocean racer nearly twice her size, and less than three hours behind *Stormvogel*, the 74-foot South African racing machine that has clipped the wings of many of the world's fastest ocean yachts.

Aikane, Trice, Snow Goose, Toria, Cosa Nostra, and others that have logged an impressive number of sea miles have shown their ability to keep the seas in any weather and have proven that, given reasonably competent handling, the best of the breed are able to keep to windward in force-7 winds in the modern ocean-racing manner.

Catamarans now reach high cruising speeds because their narrow hulls have less drag and they have achieved the stability to carry more canvas. "On all points of sailing," as Bob Bavier has said, "a good modern catamaran, foot for foot and sail area for sail area, is the world's fastest sailboat."

The multihull scene is changing fast. With problems of high torsional stresses overcome by modern materials, engineering, and refinements in design, bigger and faster ocean-racing cats and tri-hulls are in the works. (Present tendency is toward higher masts and more rectangular sails.) No less than three firms are designing what they hope will be "the fastest ocean sailing vessel." One will have two centerboards for windward performance and semicircular underwater sections for minimum wetted surface area off the wind. But whether Captain Charles Barr's twelve-day transatlantic record

Trice of St. Croix. Unlike many multihull sailors Richard C. Newick, noted designer of *Trice*, one of the world's top performing trimarans, has little to say about his designs, preferring to let their performance speak for them.

in the schooner *Atlantic* or the 400-nautical-mile daily runs made by several clipper ships will be surpassed by multihulls of the future remains to be seen.

It is enigmatic that one of the earliest prototypes of sea craft, used for centuries by sailors who lived without the neurotic fears that plague modern man, has become a craft increasingly devoted to reaching greater speeds at sea. With so much emphasis given to techniques of acceleration, one wonders why man is so obsessed with going faster and faster. What will be done with the time saved? What are the effects on the individuals involved? Will those who get somewhere faster be able to center down long enough to absorb something of the wonder, beauty, and uniqueness of wherever they may happen to be?

Contrary to those in a hurry who sacrifice everything for the endless details and pressures of racing at peak efficiency, a growing number of deep-water skippers who respond to other things prefer to sacrifice a few knots of speed for peace of mind and enough comfort and stowage space for extended global cruising.

Two-hull and three-hull long-voyaging craft continue to cross the oceans in many directions, and *Rehu Moana*, on her round-the-world voyage, has shown what a twin-hulled yacht can do in the Roaring Forties, crisscrossing the Pacific, and passage making in the Indian Ocean and the Atlantic.

Rehu Moana

Rehu Moana (40-ft. LOA, 34-ft. LW, 17-ft. beam, 3-ft. draft with the keel up), launched in the spring of 1963, was designed by Colin Mudie and built by the Prout brothers for Dr. David Lewis "as a serious seagoing catamaran fit to keep the seas in any weather and to carry my wife, Fiona, and I safely around the world with our two babies."

The hull was constructed of $1\frac{3}{8}$-inch plywood. Laminated frames and knees were massive at stress points with stems 18 inches thick. Two 8-foot drop keels ballasted with half a ton of lead each helped boost her weight (13 tons) to three times more than a normal cruising catamaran. With 10,000 pounds of buoyancy in expanded polystyrene behind watertight bulkheads, the vessel would float and could be sailed even if both hulls were stove in.

For a vigorous test of the design and construction, David Lewis and four companions made a shakedown cruise from Hole Haven, England, to Iceland. A gale north of the Faeroes sent the hollow, experimental wishbone mast overboard into the Greenland Sea. "Lying ahull with her quarter to the seas, moving downwind at about one and a half knots, *Rehu Moana* was dry and steady," said Lewis. "We could even cook." With a jury mast they made Seydisfjördur in Eastern Iceland, where a new rig was set up. Skipper and crew then took time to climb a couple of glaciers.

On the return passage to the Western Islands along a sea road of the Icelandic Sagas, while edging windward in a W.S.W. gale 250 miles west of

Rehu Moana bound south. (Helmsman steers beneath bubble dome.)

the Orkneys, *Rehu Moana* lost the top ten feet of her mast and put into Stornoway in the Hebrides to refit.

"The wishbone mast was a mistake," Lewis admitted, and rerigged the catamaran with a 47-foot metal mast and a Bermudian mainsail.

Fiona, the skipper's wife, and their two young infants came aboard in the Orkneys (with a supply of baby food) for the return trip through the North Channel and across the Irish Sea. In the western approaches to the English Channel when the baby food ran out, Vicky (three months old) and Susan (a year and a half old) thrived on mashed biscuit, eggs, and the gravy from meat pies. "The only problem," as Fiona Lewis put it, "was the lack of disposable nappies."

Tried and well proven in the far north, *Rehu Moana* rounded the Lizard and stood up for Plymouth Sound with guardrails festooned with diapers and her skipper convinced that she could sail anywhere in the world.

Under the new cutter rig with a stout Bermudian mast and with her original sail area—330 square feet in the main and 320 feet in the foresail—increased to 865 square feet plus a 720-foot square sail and an improvised steel bowsprit, *Rehu Moana* raced 3,000 miles across the Western Ocean from Plymouth Hoe to Newport, Rhode Island, in the 1964 Singlehanded Transatlantic Race.

Driven hard through days and nights on the northern route, with her skipper's determination stiffened by the need to know the vessel's limitations before his family embarked at Newport, *Rehu Moana* covered 800 miles the first week with two gales and eleven hours of calm. The second week, with two days of calm and a main boom that broke while close-hauled in a 45-knot wind, Lewis logged 728 miles. A few days later, in the center of a low-pressure area swept by bursting seas, *Rehu Moana* lay ahull while a force-10 wind gusted to 60 knots and swung from N.W. to N.E. and back. Week's run: 660 miles. Tacking hard on the wind for 162 out of 168 hours, with her mainsail set on a shortened boom, *Rehu Moana* ran 651 miles the next week.

With a broken boom, split headsail and overloaded with equipment and gear for her world cruise, the first singlehanded multihull to complete a transatlantic windward passage ghosted in through the mist past Brenton Reef Tower thirty-eight days and twelve hours from Plymouth for seventh place among the fourteen modern ocean yachts that crossed the finish line.

David Lewis was joined by his wife and their two infants. "Having sold our house and temporarily given up the medical profession—we feel confident and free, as never before in our lives. *Rehu Moana* is now the only home we have and we plan to live aboard for the next two or three years while making a circumnavigation."

With a new boom, recut headsails, and heavy cases of mountain-climbing gear aboard, *Rehu Moana* cleared Newport for a second Atlantic crossing on the second leg of her west-about route around the world—a 3,000-mile, thirty-four-day passage to the Cape Verde Islands. From São Vicente a third Atlantic crossing followed—this time 2,623 miles, on the wind most of the twenty-seven days to Salvador, Brazil.

During a rainy three-week stay at Rio de Janeiro, Lewis removed the pipe bowsprit and installed a third keel aft between the two hulls, to correct weather helm experienced in the South Atlantic.

Clearing Rio on November 8, 1964, *Rehu Moana* cruised down the coast of South America and sailed through Magellan Strait, and the Lewises spent several adventurous weeks exploring the bleak Patagonian bays and channels of Tierra del Fuego to within a few hundred miles of Cape Horn before working their way north to Valparaiso, where they were joined by Priscilla Cairns, an experienced small-boat navigator from Surrey, England.

Pushing on westward across the Pacific from Chile, on June 17 to 19, a three-day gale was encountered with northeast winds gusting to 60 knots. *Rehu Moana* lay with helm lashed and her quarter to the wind and 18-foot seas for fifty hours. The second week west of Juan Fernández, they had three days of gale winds and were hove to for twenty-five hours. From June 13 to 21 eight days of contrary gales and violent rain squalls kept them hove to for sixty-six hours, and they made only 100 miles. *Rehu Moana* kept sailing to windward in rough seas and force-8 winds. By the end of the fourth week, some easterly winds and some goose-winged sailing down wind helped to give them 500 miles for the fifth week.

During the night of July 10 they arrived off 5-by-12-mile Easter Island (Rapa-nui), the easternmost outlier of Polynesia, in a fierce squall and spent a difficult night hove to at the exposed anchorage of Hanga Roa, waiting for daylight. In the morning the wind was more favorable, they were able to anchor, and the skipper took the children ashore.

Hotu Matu'a, the first inhabitant of Rapa-nui, is said to have arrived in two great double canoes (90 feet long with 6-foot draft). And, though the memory of those great seafarers had already waned when Roggeveen discovered the island in 1722, the present islanders gave the modern version of a long-voyaging double canoe a great welcome. Half the population came to the quay. Whaleboats brought out bananas, pumpkins, chickens. Susan and Vicky were given an 18-inch-high Maoe Kava Kava (tiki) with a large nose and fierce grin that they named "Baby Doll."

Sailing briskly westward from Easter Island, *Rehu Moana*, with a remote control self-steering gear controlled by a lever that locked into the wheel itself, steered herself much of the 1,500 miles to Mangareva and from the Gambiers made the 900-mile run up through the Tuamotus to Papeete in ten days.

Departing Tahiti, Priscilla Cairns alone kept track of their true position while David Lewis, navigating without instruments in the ancient Polynesian manner, by observations of wind, sea, sun, stars, birds, and by estimating

Blue Crane, designed and built by Peter Spark at L'anse aux Espires, is one of the fastest cruising cats in the Caribbean.

Trimaran of tomorrow—the *Stiletto* (33 ft. by 19 ft. 6 in.) first of a new class designed by Piver as an ocean racer-cruiser.

time, sailed *Rehu Moana* from Huahine in the Leeward Islands to Rarotonga in six days and from the Cook Group on to New Zealand.

The first catamaran to visit Iceland, Magellan Strait, and Tierra del Fuego has been sailed hard in many seas. Heavily laden with provisions and much special equipment, *Rehu Moana* has made her crossings in good cruising time, performed well on long windward passages, and made 150 to 200 miles daily sailing down wind. This remarkable boat, its crew, and the skipper David Lewis—London physician, adventurer, and above all a sailor—have done a lot to prove the seaworthiness of a catamaran for world cruising.

When catamarans and trimarans first came to wide public notice it was frequently said that they would completely revolutionize sailing and ocean cruising. They haven't. They are still in the development stage and will continue so for some time to come. Many different designs claim the same advantages. Symmetrical—asymmetrical: arguments go on and proponents of both types have large followings. Potentialities have been clearly shown, problems have been solved, and new ones have come forward.

A number of multihulls have made transatlantic crossings in less than twenty-two days. (A Piver trimaran crossed from the Canaries to Antigua in fifteen and a half days.) Others have ridden out major storms drifting down wind or broad off before gale winds trailing anchor rodes, weighted lines, or parachute sea anchors. Several weathered hurricanes in the South Pacific and the Caribbean, and a 24-foot "Nugget" trimaran survived a typhoon in the Gulf of Siam. The question no longer is whether they are seaworthy. It is whether they are the best possible vessel for the purpose.

Experience gained from scores of long ocean voyages has done a lot to improve the breed, but if multihulls are to make the most of their promising future much remains to be done before the ideal craft is achieved for driving windward in a lump of a sea, for round-the-world voyaging, and for living permanently aboard.

Most of the facts and tendencies of today are those that nobody foresaw fifty years ago. As Robert Maynard Hutchins has said, "The world is getting newer every minute. Anything may happen, and what is most likely to happen may be what we least expect."

With the modern understanding and vast amount of data available on fluid dynamic theory, and with much of the world committed to a high rate of technological change, anything *can* happen. The problem of production is solved, in principle at least, and we can visualize revolutionary production methods and materials producing functional catamarans and trimarans with hydrofoils or outriggers in which stability is achieved not by weight, keel, or ballast but by lateral spread of attached hulls. Tomorrow's multihull with triple laminated hulls and glass outer skin will be cruising south with styrofoam radar reflector and wind vane at the masthead, space-age cruising gear, and a saberjet-type bubble top over the cockpit.

Though regarded only a few years ago as freaks and still considered by some to be offbeat, bastard craft, twin-hull and triple-hull yachts for ocean cruising will increase tenfold in the next decade. But against a monohull tradition that goes back to the Norse galleys and beyond, another quarter century of multihull cruising history with many competent circumnavigations and noteworthy ocean passages will need to be recorded before conventional prejudices against them are overcome.

Like it or not, traditional blue-water sailors who decline interest in any boat with more than one hull cannot ignore the fact that catamarans and trimarans are part of the mood and direction of a generation seeking fresh, yet hard-nosed, solutions to old problems. New forms and criteria contrary to designs that have been enclosed so deeply and for so long in the popular consciousness will continue to emerge, and the monohull cruising sailor will have to admit, at least, that there is room on the oceans for both types.

CHAPTER 10

Cape Horn Passages in Small Vessels

Indeed our sufferings, short as has been our passage, have been so great I would advise those bound into the Pacific never to attempt the passage of Cape Horn if they can get there by any other route.
—CAPT. DAVID PORTER, *U.S.S. Essex*

If the sea shouts an insistent challenge, a sailor can never be truly content until he has voyaged from Fifty South in the Atlantic to Fifty South in the Pacific in his own command. This is the ultimate test, given to very few to know.
—CAPT. WARWICK TOMPKINS, SCHOONER *Wander Bird*

THE currents, westerly gales, and bleak desolation of that classic sea reach, 50 south in the Atlantic to 50 south in the Pacific, that baffled prime seamen of all ages, has kept most small-craft voyagers away.

Harry Pidgeon, Alain Gerbault, Jacques-Yves Le Toumelin, and scores of other circumnavigators have passed west or east through the Panama Canal. And most of those who have sailed around South America in small craft have gone through Magellan Strait, or Beagle Channel and Le Maire Strait, to pass from one ocean to the other without rounding Cape Horn.

The sloop *Anahita*, the cutter *Waltzing Matilda*, Bill Tilman's cutter *Mischief*, and other small vessels that seek out remote and desolate places have sailed through Magellan Strait, and some have cruised in the waters of Tierra del Fuego archipelago. Though still but a handful, the number is increasing. David Lewis and his family, in the course of their westward passage from the Atlantic to the Pacific in the catamaran *Rehu Moana*, spent seven weeks among the bays and inlets of the western two-thirds of Magellan Strait and the windy channels of Patagonia.

A few persevering navigators of faith and fortitude, including Conor O'Brien, Vito Dumas, and Marcel Bardiaux, have sailed around Cape Horn in vessels less than 40-foot LOA. In 1966 Bernard Moitessier and his wife Françoise sailed their 40-foot ketch *Joshua* nonstop from Tahiti, round Cape Horn to Spain in 126 days, and the same year loner Edward Allcard doubled the great Cape the hard way, east to west, in his 36-foot ketch *Sea Wanderer*. Circumnavigators Bob and Nancy Griffith and son Reid—age eleven— crossed from South Africa in their ferro-cement cutter *Awahnee II* and rounded Cape Horn under a triple-reefed mainsail in snow squalls and a rising gale. South of Ushuaia the Griffiths met and passed *Sea Wanderer* as they cruised up through the channels of Tierra del Fuego to Magellan Strait en route to Valparaiso, the Marquesas, and Honolulu.

Four and a half centuries are not much as time goes in Tierra del Fuego. Little has changed there since the earth began and very little since Willem Schouten of Hoorn and his tough salted mariners from the Zuider Zee sailed the *Unity* around the southernmost reaches of the American continent and named the gray granite bastion at its icy tip Cape Hoorn.

Currents still flow continually west to east. Prevailing winds at almost all seasons are westerlies varying from about S.S.W. to N.N.W.—blowing gale force for days and sometimes weeks on end. Cape gales, especially from the southwest, come off the Antarctic laden with snow, sleet, and hail. Between False Cape Horn and the Ildefonso Islands the "ships' graveyard" is still there. Far fewer whales are seen today, but the blue-winged Cape pigeons, huge fulmars, and the great albatross swing in broad arcs across the sky as they did in the time of the Ancient Mariner. South of 56 degrees latitude, icebergs flow eastward before the Cape current, as when Dana sailed by, and in that unobstructed sweep the wind and sea reach ultimate force.

The prodigious stowaway Balboa and his ragged followers began the story of Cape Horn when they struggled across Panama and saw the ocean beyond. But it was an epic voyage by a Portuguese in the service of Spain and a reach into the unknown by an Elizabethan that led the way and gave impetus to the long procession of early ships—Spanish, English, and Dutch— that came that way, many to leave their names forever on its channels, capes, and islands.

Ferdinand Magellan's achievement can perhaps best be appreciated by small-ship sailors, for the high-charged, narrow-pooped caravel *Trinidada* and her escorts were quite small vessels. With a towering sterncastle and

Edward Allcard took his 36-ft. LOA *Sea Wanderer*, a 56-year-old re-rigged Bermudian ketch, around the Horn, east to west, from 50 S. to 50 S. in 1966.

Major Tilman's cutter *Mischief* at Peel Inlet in Patagonia.

shallow, round-bottomed hull, the *Trinidada*, about 78-foot LOA, was little more than the size of Warwick Tompkins' Cape Horn schooner *Wander Bird*. They were difficult to tack and under a square foresail, mainsail, and lateen mizzen made 4 knots at best. Iron-fastened and unsheathed, except for lead stripping, in a capful of wind they were kept afloat only by continuous labor at the wooden pumps day and night.

The punishing Antarctic gales tore at the tiny flotilla as it worked the unknown coast down to a bay in Patagonia. Frequently their food was a piece or two of dried fish with an onion or a handful of wormy raisins. After wintering at Puerto San Julian, a gale drove them into the long-sought strait past a promontory Magellan named the Cape of the Eleven Thousand Virgins. Probing into unknown waters through channels to the west, southwest, and finally northwest, it took five weeks to work the cranky fleet through the strait. With lookouts in the tops and leadsmen in the chains, hundreds of tacks were made against icy winds and treacherous crosscurrents. When squalls and williwaws struck, sheets were let fly. At other times they had to wait for favorable slants of wind. In five weeks they sailed five times the 310 miles from Cape Virgins to Cape Deseado before standing out to the northwest into the South Sea.

On leaving the land, sails were backed and a bombast fired to honor the discovery of an opening into the Western Sea. After the grace of Our Lady of Victory was invoked, Magellan addressed the officers on the poop of the *Trinidada:* "Gentlemen, we are now steering into waters where no ship has sailed before. May we always find them as peaceful as they are this morning. In this hope I name the sea Mar Pacifico."

Fine words but a vain hope to *marineros* who were soon reduced to a groaning, staggering remnant with gums puffed out, teeth covered with pulpy growth, some with ulcers all over, others with joints so swollen they screamed in agony. Nineteen were buried at sea. Others lay helpless about the decks until that ninety-eighth day from Tierra del Fuego, when the faint outline of Guam was sighted off the starboard.

At a time when knights, moneylenders, and kings looked on maps as glorified treasure charts and on papal bulls of demarcation as something to squabble about, at a time when archipelagos and whole oceans were transferred at the stroke of a pen and the discoveries of seamen of the world were giving a new orientation to the life of man, the post-Magellanic voyages attracted the greatest sailors of the day.

Sebastian Cabot, Pilot Major of Castile, tried for the Strait but like his predecessor, Amerigo Vespucci, failed even to find the entrance. Del Cano, Camargo, and Ladrillo—armored knights of Aragon, Leon, and Castile—felt the curse of the Strait but managed, at a high cost in lives and ships, to get through.

Cape Horn.

Cape Horner furling the mainsail.

Francis Drake and his men never ceased from handling their astrolabes and swinging the lead between anchorages, bays, and inlets. Though they were without charts and had only the reports of Pigafetta, they beat westward from Cape Virgins to the Pacific in the best time of all.

On September 6, 1578, the *Golden Hind* squared her yards and stood out into the Pacific with a fair wind from the southwest. After her came the *Elizabeth*, and close astern of her sailed the little 30-ton bark *Marigold*, rising and falling in the enormous swell of a heavy sea. After seventeen days of needling through the Strait, the *Golden Hind* was the first English hull to leave rocky Cape Deseado fading astern off the larboard quarter.

Shrouds were swiftered in. Double breechings were placed on the guns to prevent them from breaking loose. The waist deck was soon awash from the forecastle to the poop.

On the third day the wind backed round into the northeast. It came roaring out from the ice-covered blue peaks of the Andes in mighty squalls that hulled the tiny fleet. With only a few patches of canvas showing, they held head on in the heavy seas on the "steerboard tack" west-southwest, fourteen points from the wind. When forced to lay to under bare poles, their high poops held them in the wind as they were driven far off course into the unknown waters of the great South Sea.

September 28 in latitude 57 degrees south the *Marigold*, fighting for her life, was less than a mile leeward of the *Golden Hind*. During the night a grayback engulfed the little bark, and she disappeared with all hands; nothing, not a spar or a plank, was ever seen of the *Marigold* again.

Aboard the *Golden Hind*, four men were kept at the relieving tackles to ease the strain on the rudder and keep the ship from broaching when she fell off as a sea passed under her counter. Swifters were doubled cross deck from the lower shrouds. Rolling tackles and preventer slings were set up to steady the spars. The flagship continued to rise and fall off, to roll, twist, and shudder at times from truck to keel. But she stayed afloat. She did not lose her masts or rigging.

"Blood and wounds! I take God to witness," said Drake on the fourth day after the loss of the *Marigold*, "never hath there been a tempest so violent since Noah's flood."

The *Golden Hind* and the *Elizabeth* were driven south to 57 degrees, far below and west of Cape Horn, before the storm eased and they were again able to carry canvas. Over a month after entering the Pacific, both ships struggled back to the Patagonian coast seeking water. The *Elizabeth* drove back into the Strait and the *Golden Hind*, ratching offshore for five days, anchored finally about a hundred miles below Cape Deseado, where seven men were lost in a pinnace. Her cable parted and she was forced to beat off from that wild coast to the west-southwest, hauled as close to the northwest wind as possible.

She held for two days and nights on the starboard tack with her bowlines hauled out. The weather worsened, and on the third day she rode hulled. Under bare poles her high poop held her into the wind. In the full easterly set of the Cape Horn current she was driven south of the Cape over the edge of the known world into an area that was to be a graveyard for ships for centuries.

Lines and canvas froze hard. Spindrift was blown mountain high, like balls of snow, above the charging graybacks. The waist deck, slippery and slimy from so long under water, was impossible to cross without life lines. Men remained at the pumps day and night.

On October 24 during a brief lull the lookout sighted a cloudlike shape that became land. Rough bearings were taken as well as the swinging compass card would permit, and the discovery was plotted in 57 degrees south latitude. By nightfall a haven was found on the east side and the *Golden Hind* anchored in twenty fathoms "about the length of the shot of a great piece from land."

"We be at anchor, gentlemen, over the edge of the earth on the southernmost land in the world," Drake announced that night in the main cabin.

"Then, sir," asked Chaplain Fletcher, "where lyeth the great South Continent Terra Australis?"

"There is no great continent stretching south," replied Drake. " 'Tis but the clashing of two oceans in a most large and free scope." °

Wood, water, and "herbs of great value" were found, and the small refuge was named Elizabeth Island.

At the beginning of November the *Golden Hind* was able to sail northeastward and then northwest. Drake's luck held, and he made his northing to 45½ degrees south by November 15. From there the queen's "experte and valiant capitaine" cruised the coasts of Chile and Peru, captured a fortune in Spanish silver, and probed north to California and Oregon.

King Philip II, unaware of Drake's discovery of open ocean to the south of Cape Deseado, sent that able navigator and historian Pedro Sarmiento under command of a court politician with a cumbersome fleet to fortify and garrison Magellan Strait and prevent any further Elizabethans or other mariners from getting through. Most of the fleet and hundreds of Spaniards were lost, owing in part to the lack of resolution and the desertion of Don Diego Flores, the politician-commander. All subsequent attempts to fortify the Strait failed miserably.

A hard century and the bitter struggle against Spain bred sea enterprise among the Hollanders. Dutch masters were tough and had to be. A few, like Oliver van Noort, an ex-alehouse keeper, were merciless with their own men

---

° Dialogue and incidents aboard Drake's flagship are from the author's manuscript *Wake of the Golden Hind.*

and were notable for atrocious crimes against the native people of Patagonia even in those hard times.

Willem Schouten of Hoorn, as good a mariner as any of his day and better than most, was his own pilot, relying on no one but himself. He ran a taut ship. No clods were signed on the *Unity*. To sail with Schouten a man had to be a real sailor, as capable at fitting out and handling a swivel gun, carriage cannon, or a small boat as at traditional ship's work. But, unlike Van Noort, Willem Schouten was a humane commander with a decent respect for his men, for human life, and for the rights of other human beings white, black, or brown.

Seven months out from the Zuider Zee the *Unity* under Captain Schouten arrived off the southeastern tip of Tierra del Fuego on January 25, 1616, seeking a new sea route into the Pacific to circumvent the monopoly of the Dutch East Indies Company.

Well through the narrow strait that now bears the name of Le Maire, the *Unity* stood to the south and east under her lower sails in the full brunt of the "mighty waves that came rolling along before that fierce wind." Double lookouts were posted. Leadsmen were kept casting. Anchors were on the bow with cables ranged and ready. But there were no soundings to be had. They were in deep waters untouched by Drake and others, who had been driven far to the westward.

On January 26 they were "russeled mightily by a severe storm out of the West-south-west." From a course to the south they wore ship on the twenty-seventh and stood toward land on the larboard tack. The wind, accompanied by rain and hail, held westerly. Schouten wore ship, stood south again, and the following morning stood once more to the northward. During a lull in the weather on the twenty-eighth, topsails were hoisted and a course held to the westward. The following day two islands that they named the Barneveldt Islands were sighted off their starboard bow lying to the west-southwest.

With the Barneveldts abaft the beam, Schouten stood southwest and later the same day hauled his wind and stood northwest.

"Land ho!" hailed the lookout shortly before evening. "Two points on the weather bow."

All hands stared as a few details and the bold, snow-ribbed outlines of a rocky island came into view. They were the first Europeans to behold that granite promontoiy lying like a clenched fist sloping north from the cliffs (1,391 feet high) that mark the extreme continental reach toward the South Pole.

Leads were cast in a bottomless sea. And as the bluff-bowed *Unity*, forging slowly ahead against the current, closed with the great Cape shortly before dark, Willem Schouten, his brother John, and young Jacques Le Maire were convinced that they had discovered the last point of land between the two seas.

"Cape Hoorn!" roared Schouten, rejoicing at the moment and recalling the people of the little port of Hoorn who had invested in the venture. "Cape Hoorn. Rounded 8 P.M., January 29, 1616," he recorded in the log. Though off in his latitude like most pioneers of the day, stout-hearted Schouten and his men were the first to sail around that open sea at the bottom of the American Continent and note the pitch of the southernmost cape.

Ratching off from the land in the night, they sailed to the south of west and then to the north but were driven south to 58° 25′. Ratching back to the north against wind and current that set them inshore, they sighted Magellan's Cape Deseado on February 12. The first men in history to double Tierra del Fuego were well aware of what the new opening to Mar Pacifico could mean to little Holland and what it might do to King Philip's ambitious plans to keep the new ocean a Spanish lake. Off Deseado, all hands were piped to "splice the mainbrace," and a full cup of wine went three times around.

After refreshing north at Juan Fernández, the *Unity* sailed west on a wide traverse across the Pacific and out of the concern of this chapter.

The voyage of George Anson, who left England in 1740 with a small expedition to challenge Spanish power in the Pacific, was one of the hardest ever recorded in those waters. Wallowing north from Cape Horn, struggling for more than five weeks for westing, their rigging and sails froze until they snapped upon the strain. Main, mizzen, and futtock shrouds were lost in this way. The consort *Gloucester* sprung her main yard in the slings; the *Wager* lost her mizzenmast and main topsail yard when her chain plates gave way as she fetched a deep roll. The *Anna*, a pink, broke her forestay and the gammoning of her bowsprit. The flagship *Centurion* sprung her main topsail yard, and a "mountainous, overgrown sea followed by a most prodigious swell" snapped her shrouds, endangered the masts, and shifted the stores, heeling the ship "two strakes to starboard" until she rolled to her gunwales. With every hand working to save the ship, the admiral himself took the helm.

In squalls of thick mist and sleet, guns were fired on the half hour to keep the fleet together. The clacking and clanking of pumps never ceased. Wracked spars were fished, spare rigging set up, yards were lowered for repairs and swayed back up. After each disaster the fleet again "haled upon a wind."

Of her original five hundred people, the *Centurion*, after three months in Cape Horn waters, arrived off Juan Fernández with less than two hundred men, most of whom were near death. When the *Gloucester* made the island she was in an even more deplorable condition, with two-thirds of her men dead from scurvy, exhaustion, and the rigors of the long fight north from the Cape.

What can we say of Cape Horners like Anson and his men who, after a month to recover, went on to attack Spanish commerce in the Pacific, sought out and won a furious battle against the heavily armed, well-commanded, 36-gun great galleon *Nostra Signora de Cabadonga*, and, after extracting a fortune in bulk silver plus 1,313,843 pieces of eight, sailed out to China, forced their way into the Canton River, refitted, and returned to England via the Cape of Good Hope with the greatest fortune ever brought back in one ship?

Magellan's Strait was used for more than two centuries by windships, but the cost in lost vessels was high. Of those that weathered Cape Virgins many were lost in the narrows, and others on the Evangelistas at the western end. For over three centuries it was safer and sometimes faster for sailing ships to buck the prevailing westerlies, the swell, and the icebergs off Cape Stiff.

Pioneering small vessels like the *Columbia* and the 90-ton snow *Lady Washington*, opening a new trade route from the Atlantic to the Pacific in 1788, were the first New England traders to round Cape Horn bound north for Drake's "New Albion."

In that same year Lieutenant William Bligh was defeated by the Horn and forced to take the long way around to Tahiti. After twenty-nine days of beating to windward against the drift of the Cape Horn current, of tacking to the extreme south to wear northward on a larboard tack, hoping for a more favorable slant, the proud lieutenant with his first naval command gave up the struggle on April 22, 1788, and, ordering the *Bounty's* helm aweather, squared yards to run off into the South Atlantic and across to Table Bay. Years later Bligh still brooded over his failure and spoke bitterly of having been beaten by the Horn.

Before the fifties, vessels making the passage from the East Coast around the Horn to California in less than two hundred days were considered to have made a fair voyage. Matthew Maury's *Wind and Current Charts* and *Sailing Directions* were as effective as the sweet lines and tall spars of the clippers in reducing the average voyage to 133 days.

In 1857 Donald McKay's *Great Republic*, a four-masted bark 335 feet LOA under command of Captain J. Limeburner, who with his officers always went well armed, doubled the Cape with skysails set for a ninety-two-day run from Sandy Hook to the Golden Gate. Under Josiah Cressy the *Flying Cloud*, carrying sail to the utmost limit day and night, made the passage in eighty-nine days and eight hours. The *Andrew Jackson*, storming along under the hard-case Cape Horner Jack Williams, arrived at San Francisco

The four-mast bark *Flying Cloud* takes a long-rolling sea aboard.

March 23, 1860, from New York in eighty-nine days, four hours. On the east-about run, Freeman Hatch of the *Northern Light* thought enough of his seventy-six-day record passage from San Francisco around Cape Stiff to Boston to ask that it be chiseled into his tombstone with no other data except his name. And it was.

Fished masts, lost boats, and shattered bulwarks tell of the killing drive, and the wracked hulls, twisted spars, and wreckage on deck attest to what those long-rolling seas can do to a stout ship.

In an age of Negro slavery, shanghaiing crimps, and bucko mates, an age that saw at the same time the highest development in ship design and the poorest conditions for seamen, the ranks of Cape Horners had its share of hell ships, reckless drivers, and "belaying-pin soup." A few manic-depressives—"quarterdeck madmen," as they were called—were capable of hazing a man to his death or shooting a topman off the yardarm while praising the Lord, the rational, or the fact that the victim was better off dead. Richard Dana, who rounded the Cape in the Boston brig *Pilgrim,* and Herman Melville, who returned home as ordinary seaman in a frigate, remembered to speak out for those before the mast who shared in the misery but seldom in the profits or the glory.

In the post-clipper years after 1870 the long procession of whalers that rounded Cape Stiff and stood north dwindled. Long after the tall clippers, the slow, steel grain ships from Australia to the English Channel ran their easting down about the Horn, but there was a world of difference between this and beating around to windward. From the clippers that carried cargo at $50 a ton to the undermanned steel nitrate ships that carried guano around the Horn at 16 shillings a ton spanned a half century of diminishing returns, with the emergence of seagoing steamships and the gallant but hopeless struggle of the tall ships to survive in the last days of commercial sail.

Spray

Though vessels as small as Benjamin Pendleton's 40-ton sloop *Hero* were sailing in Cape Horn waters as early as 1821, Joshua Slocum was the first solo sailor to navigate Magellan Strait in a boat under 40 feet LOA. After sailing through the Strait from east to west, old Josh received a capful of wind off the west coast of Patagonia that nearly drove the *Spray* around to the Falklands.

On March 3, 1896, in the long swell coming in between the Evangelistas and Cape Pillar, one of the most storm-wracked areas in the world, *Spray* cleared the Strait before an easterly wind that shifted to southwest by the following morning and then went to a fierce northwesterly gale.

"No ship in the world could have stood up against so violent a gale," said Slocum.

The only course lay in keeping her before the wind. . . . She was running with a reefed forestaysail, the sheets flat amidships. In this trim she ran before it, shipping never a sea. The first day of the storm gave the *Spray* her test in the worst sea that Cape Horn or its wild regions could afford, and in no part of the world could a rougher sea be found than at this particular point, namely, off Cape Pillar, the grim sentinel of the Horn. . . . It was the fiercest I ever saw, and several large vessels that were in it were dismasted.

Spray was driven to the south and east under bare poles.

On the fourth day of the gale, rapidly nearing the pitch of Cape Horn, I inspected my chart and pricked off the course to Port Stanley, in the Falkland Islands, when I saw through a rift in the clouds a high mountain, about seven leagues away on the port beam.

Having lost the mainsail, during a lull Slocum set a reefed square sail in its place, closed with the rocky coast, and, wearing ship to avoid breakers, spent a hard night standing off land in hail, sleet, and fierce squalls. In the morning he worked up through a wild breaking sea to Thieves' Bay in Cockburn Channel.

Anchoring and weighing many times, twice knocked down by squalls and williwaws, *Spray* went round past Mt. Sarmiento and back into Magellan Strait by way of Froward Reach through the channels which connect it to Cape Horn. In Crooked Reach, where the tidal streams of the Atlantic and the Pacific meet, Slocum, like the Canoe Indians and sealers before him, moored to great, long streamers of kelp in 20 fathoms, waiting for the tide to change.

In the Strait he refitted, cut and sewed a peak and leech into the heavy square sail and bent it on for a mainsail, and, taking on a cargo of tallow that was found near a wreck on the beach, he weighed on April 13 for another try at the Pacific.

The stolid New Englander who was not averse to praying for a favorable slant got a fair southeast wind that day, "the first true winter breeze of the season from that quarter." By the next morning *Spray* was holding a course to the northwest with the sea on her quarter bound for Juan Fernández.

"Then was the time to uncover my head," said Josh, "for I sailed alone with God."

Fifteen days out, the *Spray* anchored near Robinson Crusoe Bay off the island that has succored so many Cape Horners, including the gloomy mate of the *Cinque Ports* Alexander Selkirk, who found sanctuary and a measure of fulfillment there piping and dancing with his cats and goats. Old Josh promptly brewed up a large pot of coffee and, as soon as the sloop was secured, gave the islanders of Juan Fernández free instructions in the art of frying Yankee doughnuts in hot tallow. His bulky cargo from the wreck was soon disposed of, part in barter and part for cash at "a reasonable profit."

Pandora

The yawl *Pandora*, first small boat to round Cape Horn, was built at Perth, Australia, and fitted out by owner-skipper George Blythe and his mate Peter Arapakis.

Built somewhat on the lines of the *Spray*, the *Pandora* (37-ft. LOA, 14-ft. beam, 6-ft. draft) was full-bodied with wide square stern, short main mast and bowsprit, and a 25-foot main boom. She carried two foresails, was gaff rigged on main and mizzen, and had $5\frac{1}{2}$ tons of iron and cement inside ballast.

Departing Bunbury, West Australia, May 3, 1910, for a voyage around the world by way of the Horn and the Cape of Good Hope, *Pandora* called at Melbourne and en route from Sydney to Auckland encountered a hurricane in the Tasman Sea. Stripped to bare poles, running off before a heavy sea, she was pooped and knocked on her beam-ends with the loss of port and

The Rudder

Pandora at New York after crossing the Pacific and rounding the Horn.

starboard bulwarks and much deck gear. When she failed to lay to a sea anchor, a close-reefed trysail was set that brought her under control.

A month's stay was made in New Zealand for repairs before Blythe and Arapakis headed E.N.E. across the Pacific. After a good passage to Pitcairn and a week at Easter Island, they cleared for a run through the Roaring Forties to the Falkland Islands.

On January 16, 1911, the *Pandora* had Cape Horn only three and a half miles off her port beam. Visibility was poor. It was bitterly cold with flying scud and sleet. Off the gloomy southern end of the continent, the wind hardened to a full gale and the seas rolled high.

"Somehow there came on me a sense of foreboding," Blythe wrote later to a friend in Perth. "We had bad days in the Tasman, but I never knew what the sea was till I came here."

A man may live his life out in small boats and never meet an ultimate sea—that is, if he is lucky and if he keeps away from Cape Horn and the high southern latitudes where, as Captain William Jones pointed out in *Cape Horn Breed*, "seas can be fifty feet high and can roll forward in endless procession with occasionally one sea of abnormal size towering above the others."

By January 22 the *Pandora* was under bare poles making heavy weather of it near the Falklands. Her wheel was lashed and both sailors were below when she was swept by a mountainous grayback and flung to starboard on her beam-ends. The two men fell against the bulkhead, then tumbled to the cabin top, as a second great sea hit the port quarter and the yawl rolled completely over. When she came up both masts were gone, the boom was smashed, and the dinghy missing.

Forcing their way up and out from below, Blythe and Arapakis managed to free the wreckage that was threatening the hull and lashed together a sea anchor of spars and sails that helped the vessel to survive the night.

Sea-swept and half foundered, they were drifting toward the rugged coast of West Falkland Island when sighted by a Norwegian whaler that towed them ten miles to the whale station at New Island.

With the help of the Norwegian seamen and the kindness of the whale station personnel, the *Pandora* was repaired, given new masts, and refitted for sea. On March 4, 1911, she departed the Falklands for an uneventful crossing to St. Helena and to Ascension Island. From there they made a 4,850-mile passage to New York in forty-six days.

Not content with having sailed 22,000 miles at an average of about 120 miles daily, the first small-boat sailors to round the Horn were determined to continue on around the world. On July 30 George Blythe and Peter Arapakis cleared New York for London and were never heard from again. No wreckage or trace was ever found of the *Pandora*.

Mary Jane

The first single-hander to sail a boat around Cape Horn the hard way—fifty south to fifty south from east to west—was Alfon Moller Hansen, a Norwegian from Forvik.

"I was not very old when I decided to make the ocean and small-craft voyaging my career," said Al, who became a seaman by trade to earn enough to buy, rig, and fit out the *Mary Jane*, a 36-foot-LOA, gaff-rigged Norwegian pilot cutter with 2-inch oak planking laid on 6- by 7-inch pine ribs.

The *Redningskjöite*, designed by Colin Archer, who built Nansen and Amundsen's famous polar ship *Fram*, was well proven by the Norwegian Coast Life Patrol and was, in Hansen's opinion, the best possible boat for a world cruise. With "Mate," a black dog from Skalvikfjord, and "Sailor," a gray cat from Bergen, as shipmates, Al left Oslo July 15, 1932, for a good passage to Weymouth, England. His auxiliary power was a large oar, "because I always think of an engine, despite its convenience, as somehow spoiling the pleasures on a voyage of this kind."

From England *Mary Jane* cruised to Gijón, Oporto, and Lisbon. Running short of funds but with the sailor's instinct to keep going, Al wrote, "Though my crew and I live comfortably on 4 to 5 dollars a week, at Lisbon I sadly parted with my sea boots to obtain a little cash for provisions."

Setting off down the Tagus on an ebbing tide, Al found that the cat Sailor was missing. When a thorough search of the ship turned up no feline

Al Hansen aboard *Mary Jane*.

Al Hansen in *Mary Jane*.

he returned to Lisbon, "for the value of friendship is something I have always understood." A search of the waterfront turned up the missing cat on a nearby tugboat. With Sailor back aboard, the skipper cast off for the Canaries and had a fair crossing from Las Palmas to Miami, Florida, with a daily average of approximately 100 miles and a best day's run of 176 miles on the forty-three-day passage.

Mary Jane went up the Mississippi, cruised the Great Lakes, and worked back out to the Atlantic on the St. Lawrence. While at Detroit, Sailor, the seagoing cat from Bergen with 8,000 miles of small-craft cruising to her credit, was run over by a car. Her place aboard was taken by one of her kittens, "Sailor, Jr."

Taking things as they went, Hansen cruised leisurely down the coast and across to Buenos Aires in his own good time. On long passages when he got weary he hove to. "It is best not to make definite plans," he told a former shipmate. "Fate may sometimes force one to abandon them or deviate. . . . My voyaging is not made in search of anything but contentment."

From the Rio de la Plata, the sailor from Forvik passed down the Atlantic and around the Horn to the westerlies and the long-running seas of Schouten and Drake with only his cat and dog to talk to and the fulmars overhead for companions. Making her westing in the Antarctic winter, the rugged little ex-pilot cutter arrived at Ancud, Chile, 110 days from Buenos Aires.

From the Island of Chiloé, Al Hansen set off for Puerto Corral and was never heard from again. For a long time his friends refused to believe that he was lost at sea. But months later, when wreckage from the *Mary Jane* was found on the rocky southern coast of Chile, there was no longer any doubt what had happened.

"What a loss," wrote Vito Dumas, "that Al Hansen with all his determination and enthusiasm should not have lived to round other capes and other seas."

Lehg II

"Cape Horn has been the reason for this voyage which has taken me, in 274 navigating days, from Buenos Aires across the South Atlantic to South Africa, the Indian Ocean and across the Pacific to Chile," said Vito Dumas at Valparaiso, while preparing his 31-foot-6-inch-LOA ketch *Lehg II* for the crucial last leg of his circumnavigation in the Roaring Forties.

"Dumas—go through Magellan Strait," urged Rear Admiral Gaston Kulcheski of the Chilean Navy, as he gave him daily meteorological reports of hurricane winds off the Horn. "I will give you a destroyer escort."

Loners are a tough breed; Vito Dumas, the hardiest singlehanded sailor of them all, was not the man to want an escort and had no intention of going through Magellan Strait. He wanted mainly to be left alone to make his own decisions.

Between voyages, while running furrows in the earth on his small farm near Buenos Aires, when the gulls swooped down after worms in the fresh-turned sod, Vito would imagine himself at sea bound for the tip of the continent. He considered that all of his previous long voyages were but preparations for a "run of the Horn. What I had dreamed of for almost 35 years now lay within my reach. Frankly, I was afraid to start. But I knew that if I was to live at peace with myself I must start soon. Time was short. During those twenty to thirty days when the sun is farthest north conditions are best for a small boat to round the Horn."

After an early Mass on May 30, 1943, Dumas departed Valparaiso, passing on the way out a battered five-masted Canadian ship with a cargo of lumber that failed in an attempt to round the Horn and returned to Chile in bad shape. By late afternoon *Lehg II* was well away from the coast.

After passing Juan Fernández, variable squalls were encountered on a board close-hauled to the southwest. The barometer went down, the temperature came close to freezing, and on the ninth of June the ketch was pooped by a sea that nearly washed Vito overboard. "The seas were constantly on deck and it was impossible to do anything without getting completely soaked. The boat was laboring heavily under the impact of the heavy seas."

At the end of six days of gales he was 600 miles north of the Cape and steered west for two days to avoid the coast. On June 21 he was 400 miles W.N.W. of Cape Horn, averaging 120 miles daily on a course to the south of Diego Ramirez. The next day, sailing due east in a 40-knot wind under mizzen, staysail, and storm jib, he saw Tierra del Fuego to the northeast and, off to the south, "shimmering whitely, the coruscating reflection of Antarctic ice."

As *Lehg II* closed to less than a hundred miles from the Horn, Dumas felt the awe that has reached deep into every small-boat sailor who has weathered the Cape. "Yet, here, hard by Cape Horn, that dim light of my compass on this dark Antarctic night made me look with tenderness on these wrought planks, flesh of the trees of my country, fashioned by human knowledge into a boat."

After a lull caused by the meeting of two storm fronts from the northeast and from the southwest *Lehg II* was hit by a fierce northerly. Heavy hail pounded the deck. The cabin thermometer read 5 degrees below zero.

At midnight according to my reckoning Cape Horn was abeam. I was squatted on a wooden seat alongside the bunk cleaning the mist from a compass set between my knees when the boat gave a sudden lurch to port. I went forward—hard. And with both my hands on the compass, my face struck a sidebeam. It felt as though the sharp edge had cut through the bridge of my nose and both eyes. For seconds I lay against the beam, blood pouring from my nose and eyes. Then I fell back upon the seat.

The Argentine-designed and built double-ended ketch *Lehg II* in which Vito Dumas circumnavigated and rounded Cape Horn.

I sat still trying to adjust to the situation. I was afraid to touch my face. There was a sinking in my stomach.

Swaying dizzily, I pulled myself up the ladder and thrust my head out into the open air. The cold clamped over my face, freezing the lacerated tissues and clumps of blood. I staggered back inside, still afraid to touch my face.

"I have one eye," I thought—whether I had the other or not did not seem so terrible at that moment.

The cold hung in the air like a lifeless carcass contaminating everything it touched. But I welcomed the cold then, because it numbed my face and eased the pain in my nose and eyes. I was able to peel off the blood in thin flakes.

At six A.M., I was moving about securing the sail to the yard, clearing the scuppers in the cockpit, without complete consciousness. During the morning the wind eased off and backed to S.W.

Now the *Lehg II* was coated over with a solid mass of milky-white ice in weird stalactite forms across the yard, over the housing and mast. The boat was riding low in the water because of the additional weight and I used an axe to chip off as much of it as I could. As I did my eye caught sight of a huge black mass ahead of me. I took it to be reefs and veered the boat off to the southeast. My face, swollen and distorted, was a mess.

By the following morning I was 120 miles out into the Atlantic, south of the Falkland Islands. Here, I changed my course, intending to sail between the islands and east of the Cape. But I was not certain how far I could keep going west before being caught up in the boiling sea and thrown against the coastal reefs.

The hours went by with apprehension. I peered ahead fixedly into the darkness. Then, on the evening of the 27th, about 25 yards off my bow, I saw something break the surface. A seal! I knew I was dangerously near land and I headed northeast on a course that would carry me beyond the islands.

I knew then I had made it and the sense of release was indescribable. I felt that I had thrown off a stone I had been carrying against my chest for more years than I cared to remember.

Forging on under mizzen, storm trysail, staysail, and jib, Dumas thought often of Al Hansen. (In February, 1934, on the eve of the Norwegian sailor's departure to double the Cape, Vito had had dinner and had spent the night aboard the *Mary Jane*.)

There was much fanfare in Buenos Aires upon my arrival 12 days later, 71 days from Valparaiso, but for me the great moment had come and was gone, until somewhere, at another distant point in the sea, I could find another Cape Horn.

Les 4 Vents

Marcel Bardiaux, the second small-craft sailor to round Cape Horn from east to west, doubled the Cape singlehanded in midwinter in the course of a solo voyage of circumnavigation to over five hundred ports and anchorages.

Following six years of preparation and fifteen thousand hours of hard work, Bardiaux completed his sloop *Les 4 Vents* (30-ft. 8-in. LOA, 8-ft. 10-in. beam, 5-ft. 9-in. draft, 4 tons displacement) in January, 1950. Built to be self-righting, with watertight compartments fore and aft, the little Bermudian-rigged craft, looking like a racing yacht with submarine lines, was virtually unsinkable and about as indestructible as possible for a wooden hull. Her frames, reinforced with bronze, made a complete circle over the cabin top. A waterproof cover extended over most of the cockpit so that Bardiaux could steer from inside the cabin.

Leaving Le Havre in February, Bardiaux cruised to Portugal, Casablanca, the Canaries, and West Africa and crossed from Dakar to Rio de Janeiro—the first yachtsman to sail singlehanded from Europe to South America.

Departing Buenos Aires and the Mar del Plata for "Cape Horn, the goal of my dreams," Bardiaux made a number of calls along the Patagonian coast, rounded Cape Virgins May 1, and pressed south against a head wind and current. Sails were hardened down stiff each night and often had to be dipped in sea water to unfreeze them in the morning.

On May 13 *Les 4 Vents* rounded Cape San Diego, the southeasternmost point of Tierra del Fuego, less than a hundred miles from the Horn, and stood out into Le Maire Strait to beat windward with the help of an 8-knot current against a 50-knot westerly gale. After several tacks were made across the 25-mile-wide strait, in wild seas raised by the opposing wind and southwest-moving current, the gale increased in violence and soon backed to southwest gusting to force 11.

Hove to by now, Bardiaux had slipped below to fetch a sea anchor to reduce sternway when the slim, deep sloop was caught in the trough of a swell and struck abeam by a mountainous sea that rolled her completely over.

Bardiaux was flung onto the cabin top half stunned but recovered quickly to leap up through the hatchway and close the hatch seconds before the vessel turned completely over again. "This time," said Bardiaux, "I seemed to be rather long under water and was about to let go, thinking it was all over, when the mast slowly emerged and so did I." The buoyancy of twenty empty five-gallon G.I. tins bolted to frames beneath the deck helped to roll her upright.

Foresails and storm trysail were gone, the cockpit shelter was reduced to a bent frame, and the boat had a bad list from the wash of sea water in the cabin. A long warp from the bow made fast to 15 fathoms of chains eased the vessel while Bardiaux pumped her out by hand.

With the temperature at 14 degrees below freezing, Bardiaux remained soaked for ten hours tacking west along the bold coast of Tierra del Fuego until he found shelter in Aguirre Bay anchored to 60 fathoms of chain. Thirty hours later he weighed for a hard slog to the southwest under storm staysail and a few feet of mainsail in a howling westerly gale. On May 12 *Les 4 Vents* came within a few miles of Cape Horn and, after doubling it in hail and snow, held on a starboard tack southwest to latitude 56° 20′ S., where flow ice was encountered and the sails were frozen stiff.

The skipper intended standing well off after doubling the Cape and making his next landfall on Chile. But faced with worsening weather and needed repairs, and not caring to strike farther south into an area of icebergs where storms last for weeks in the austral winter and where, if wrecked, there is no chance of survival, he decided to seek shelter in one of the fjords of the Patagonian archipelago—an area mentioned in the *South American Pilot* as "about as inhospitable a land as is to be found anywhere in the globe."

Weathering Hermite Island northwest of Cape Horn, *Les 4 Vents* worked north between bleak and unfrequented islands where the wind is a permanent feature of the landscape. A worsening gale that backed to northwest forced the sloop to drift eight hours under a bare pole across Nassau Bay to the southeast of Navarino Island, trailing an anchor and 30 fathoms of chain. After completing a 300-mile circuit of Cape Horn, she worked up into Beagle Channel and sailed close-hauled to Ushuaia, the southernmost town in the world.

A month was spent repairing the holes made in the hull by ice. Bardiaux then continued westward, entered the Pacific at Cooks Bay, and, passing through Barbara Channel into Magellan Strait, cruised north in the Patagonian channels and out to Valparaiso with many calls along that difficult 1,500-mile stretch.

Crossing the Pacific to Tahiti and New Zealand, *Les 4 Vents* was holed and nearly lost on an incorrectly charted reef near Noumea, New Caledonia.

Twenty-two broken ribs and four planks had to be repaired before the little Bermudian sloop pushed up through Timor Strait to Indonesia, crossed the Indian Ocean and the South Atlantic to Brazil, and sailed back to France via New York, Bermuda, and the Azores for a total of 543 landfalls in eight years of world voyaging.

Cardinal Vertue

Australian yachtsman Bill Nance from Wallaby Creek, Victoria, bought the noted 25-foot-LOA sloop *Cardinal Vertue* from Dr. David Lewis. Leaving Britain in September, 1962, he sailed singlehanded to Melbourne, Australia, via Buenos Aires and Cape Town—making the 6,800-mile Indian Ocean crossing from Africa in seventy-five days. The Laurent Giles-designed Vertue sloop arrived at Fremantle under jury rig with the main mast broken off sixteen feet above the deck.

On December 1, 1964, Nance sailed from Auckland for a passage down through the Roaring Forties and around the Horn to Argentina. Sailing mostly with the working staysail and main, often well reefed down, the fourteen-year-old British-built stock boat covered the next 2,000 miles in thirteen days with the wind vane doing most of the steering.

On December 30 at 51° S., *Cardinal Vertue* was running before a full gale under a bare pole with 30 fathoms of warp and a tire streamed out astern when "a sea bigger than any I have ever seen before" crashed aboard, broke off the tiller at the rudder head, and forced the little vessel to lie ahull.

"I have no great faith in lying ahull," said Nance, "and probably only survived because the weather eased and by the following day I was able to fit the spare tiller."

The barometer dropped to 28.73 with a leaden sky as the little 5-tonner approached Cape Horn.

On January 7 landfall was made on Diego Ramirez, and later the same day *Cardinal Vertue* ran close by the Horn in a rain squall thirty-eight days and 5,000 miles out from New Zealand. When the Horn was well astern, Nance felt such relief at having that crucial leg of the passage behind him that he wrote, "Though there were still 1,600 miles ahead to Buenos Aires I felt I was almost there."

After a struggle with the tide, Nance passed up through Le Maire Strait and kept well offshore in the South Atlantic to benefit from the Falklands current. Having had few gear failures other than loss of a main halyard and a main sheet fitting on the boom, the smallest singlehanded yacht to cross the Pacific in the Roaring Forties and round the Horn to 50 south in the Atlantic averaged 121 miles daily for the 6,500 miles of hard sailing from New Zealand to the River Plate.

With his east-about solo circumnavigation completed at Buenos Aires, Bill Nance made a fast run from the River Plate to the West Indies for a daily average of 123 miles and, from Antigua to Nassau en route to Florida, logged 180 miles, noon to noon, under a spinnaker, for the best single day's run of an epic 31,000-mile voyage.

Rounding Cape Horn for some is a quality of the human spirit. Each sailor, human and fallible, has his personal quest, and each solo navigator's lonely satisfaction is his own. To Vito Dumas, to Marcel Bardiaux, and to others, rounding the Horn was a fulfillment they otherwise might not have achieved in a lifetime.

"Lives there a sailor," asked Dumas, "who would not rather have made a Cape Horn passage in his own small vessel rather than any other voyage in the world?"

Apparently there are a great many. For, despite the accumulated knowledge of centuries, the latest wind and current charts, and the advantages of modern hulls and gear, most voyagers in southern latitudes omit the old windship route from 50 south to 50 south—an average sailing distance of about 1,500 miles.

Bill Nance aboard his 25-ft. sloop *Cardinal Vertue* after an epic 31,000-mile solo circumnavigation and west-to-east Cape Horn passage.

Elizabeth Island, the land discovered by Francis Drake south and west of Cape Horn, is long gone from the scene. Like Niuafoou, Tonga's often-disappearing island, Drake's discovery has sunk beneath the sea. But, except for the erosion of westerly gales and the grind of icebergs, Cape Horn and its companions Diego Ramirez, Staten Island, and the tideswept break of the Strait of Le Maire remain. Off that raw tip of the continent, where the oldest laws and the most enduring hold, it is as it was when the groaning hulls of tall wooden ships passed that way, storming along under close-reefed topsails, wearing around from one tack to the other and back, or lying to under a couple of storm staysails and a goose-winged topsail.

Round-the-world voyages by one or the other of three main routes are increasing yearly, but small-boat circumnavigations via the great Cape at the bottom of the world where the Forties roar eastward remain rare and always will be a unique achievement.

In this day of space explorations and the precedence of air power over the sea, little is heard of Tierra del Fuego or Patagonia as a small-ship area. Yet thousands of miles of fjords, inlets, and bays that reach westward from Cape Horn and from the blue-white mountains and the gray shore of Magellan Strait up the coast of Chile present a singular cruising ground. Men like

Pringle Stokes and Robert Fitzroy, who commanded the *Beagle*, spent many years there and in open boats sounded and charted various channels and anchorages.

Not everyone seeks quiet, remote places. But also, not everyone would choose to moor to the Quai Bir Hackeim at Tahiti or sail the tourist route in the Caribbean if offered the opportunity to cruise in Patagonia.

There is a breed of individuals, many of them loners, who will always seek the outermost parts of the globe. But in a shrinking world few areas remain where there are challenging regions almost unchanged in a thousand years. For navigators who prefer to leave Cape Horn, the Diegos, and the loom of the Falklands to the Cape pigeons and the albatross, the long reaches of Magallanes Province offer a labyrinth of channels, islands, and desolate grandeur.

Sailors have always been explorers, and today a surprising number are collectors and field specialists in many categories from geology to ethnology. Some, like H. W. Tilman, are noted mountaineers and glaciologists. A large number are free-lance naturalists, writers, and photographers.

There is much for field explorers in Patagonia and Tierra del Fuego. In 1955 a German naturalist and small-boat sailor discovered several extremely rare plant specimens, and recent surveys in southern Patagonia reveal the presence of vast, untapped mineral wealth. For those who find a lot in common between sailing and mountain exploring, there is the Patagonian icecap from the Pacific to the Argentine lakes. On the southernmost coast of Chile, where the high Andes reach down to the edge of the sea, a mountaineer-sailor, as Major Tilman has shown, can begin a glacier climb directly at sea level.

For those interested in human ecology, there is the tragic rape and slaughter of the ancient races of the Cape Horn region—a people framed by bleak topography and the terrible wind from the Cordillera of the Andes, who owned so little more than their life blood yet were able to hold their own in one of the world's most inhospitable regions with no clothes other than a patch of sealskin and no shelter other than rude wigwams until they were all but wiped out by sealers, otter hunters, and the scum of other adventurers. How thin a veneer upon the substratum of humanity must our culture be when marauding white men listed in the records of Europe and the Americas as civilized can so easily revert to savagery! Tuberculosis, measles, and white vigilantes nearly finished the destruction of a once-proud race. The pattern was repeated throughout most of Patagonia. In half a century the white population of Magallanes increased tenfold while the Indians decreased almost to extinction.

Early in 1966, Dr. David Lewis in *Rehu Moana* visited a Chilean government settlement of forty-eight Indian people—the largest surviving group of Alaclufe Indians, who once ranged the seas up to Cape Horn in birchbark canoes. He found their health restored and found, contrary to Darwin's descriptions, that they were handsome and alert. "As might be expected," said David, "their knowledge of tides and currents was encyclopedic and invaluable to us. Let us hope that the tide of mortality of this unique race is at last ebbing."

It is true that these mountain-islanded channels of unsurpassed beauty at the end of the world call for real sailoring and discourage all but the most able. But their worst is not too bad for competent skippers who seek areas of splendid isolation and love the wilderness enough to sail long distances to get there in their own small ships.

If the increasing numbers of small-craft owners to whom remoteness and inaccessibility are attractions is an indication of a trend, Magellan's Land of Fire may yet become a cruising ground for sailors who, like the Lewises, Smeetons, Tilman, and others, avoid traditional routes and shrink from ports with crowded marinas, noisy outboards, and native islanders with transistor radios.

CHAPTER 11

Ocean Cruising, Present and Future

Cruising is more than a sport. The mood of it comes over you at times, and you can neither work nor rest nor heed another call until you have a deck beneath your feet and point a bowsprit out to sea.
—ARTHUR HILDEBRAND

Surely the sailing yacht must survive, for in her alone will men find satisfaction of an instinct which drives them, regardless of progress and reason, to venture out to sea.
—E. G. MARTIN

SINCE we live in a cruising age we know, of course, that modern boats don't look like lima beans or gum drops and that ocean cruising has little relation to moon voyages. And of course we are wrong. The world has been proven wrong about many things in an era where we hardly learn what age we are in before another is named. According to aerodynamic theoreticians the bumble bee can't fly, but as Rimski-Korsakov noted and everyone with a garden knows it soars quite well.

The rules that govern the natural world, from the currents of the ocean to the jet streams of outer space, are much the same. Skimming along on undersea wings and air-cushioned keels, we already have the promising prototypes of a space age afloat: revolutionary oceangoing boats built of aircraft materials that look like miniature moonships, sailboats on stilts (foils) moved by a sail that is not called a sail but an air foil, amphibian earth-and-sea skimming ACV's (air cushion vehicles) that rise from several inches to several feet above the need for waterways or roads yet use both and can cruise along in the open sea.

Japan has an advanced-design hydrofoil that looks like a watermelon seed but maneuvers like a space ship. Britain has SR.N2, an ACV powered with gas turbines that skims over five-foot waves with ease and last year traversed Canada's Lachine Rapids at 50 miles per hour. The U.S. Army has a noiseless, solar-powered small boat that can operate entirely on power converted from sunshine. In the under 20-foot-LOA group an all-fiberglassed 10-horsepower air-cushioned boat called Air Dents is available that looks like a gum drop and sails along at 30 miles per hour four inches above water, snow, or land by forcing a thin layer of air down between two keels. Along the same line Japan has a 14- to 16-foot small craft with built-in surface-piercing foils called a Yodo-jet that sells for about $3,000.

Many vessels a decade hence will achieve stability without ballast or keels through aerohydrofoil—the air and water forces of hydrofoils and air foils acting in equilibrium through electronic controls. With refinements in the art of new material fabrication and, in some cases, with entirely new substances available, innovations by uninhibited designers, especially in the field of multihulls and hydrofoils, will shock conservative sailors of tomorrow. Beyond this, experts assure us, the design of seagoing yachts is still in its infancy.

Lightweight gas turbines with few moving parts and almost no vibration at all are now being used by the U.S. Coast Guard on 26-foot surfboats. The Maritime Administration's blue-water hydrofoil *H. S. Denison*, with retractable foils, gas turbines, and a cockpit like a jet plane, travels on her hull to 26 miles per hour before rising on foils and gaining speed up to 70. Built especially for ocean voyaging, the aluminum-hulled vessel has logged nearly ten thousand miles of open sea cruising, much of it at 40 to 50 knots foilborne in waves up to nine feet.

How about all this? What about the able, self-reliant sailor who takes serious account of the new but prefers cruising with traditional gear, under sail alone? Most of the new designs are for special purposes, and much new equipment is a question of convenience rather than necessity. There is still nothing wrong with a hand lead and line. As L. Francis Herreshoff has pointed out, the greatest small-boat voyages of all time were made by men who had everything to work with but money, speed, and special gear. Why then are such high speeds stressed for ocean vessels? Isn't seamanship and the art of ocean cruising more important?

It is. Naval designs and speeds for small seagoing boats are far from what the average ocean-cruising sailor is thinking about. Present trends will affect everyone, but space-age craft traveling at high speed through the water or skimming on top of it will never replace sail. So little has been known for so long about the aerodynamics of sails that a few recent steps forward have seemed like leaps. Though no one has yet made a sail more efficient than the Chinese junk's—wistful remembrance of things traditional won't help—the tides are running strong the other way.

In this period of transition, exotic aerospace materials such as Boron fiber composites have been adapted for marine use. New developments in light alloys are appearing with steel- and glass-reinforcing fibers running through them that will likely be used for future sailing spars. The unstayed mast is here to stay. (Planes did away with wires and spreaders years ago.) Unorthodox rigs are in the works that will be handled from the helm. Fully battened mainsails will become more widely used, as will instantly retractable fins, hydraulically operated retractable keels, and stabilizers for small craft. But the use of refinements in water-resistant glues, laminations, and other materials, and the fact that tomorrow's flowering of small boats will be made of many materials besides wood, doesn't mean that marine nails and screws will become museum pieces.

When we look at the whole sweep of man's history on the oceans of planet earth, we see that everything that deserves to be called progress has depended on new experiences in the shape of ideas tested and proved by questing sailors. Whether Leif's Vinland was at Tickle Cove or at L'Anse aux Meadows, or whether the Bahamas landfall of Columbus or the 300-mile Davis Strait hop of Leif Ericson receives highest honors, seems of small importance any more.

Today is the age of the non-hero. There is still enough chance and full adventure on the salt waters of the earth for anyone. While men are out reaching toward the farthest galaxies, much of today's exploration is still being done on foot and by individuals in small vessels. Almost every month brings an important new technical discovery of some sort in the laboratory, in naval research facilities, in towing basins and air tunnels, under the sea, or out crossing the watery skin of the earth in a small boat.

When the last blank places on the maps were filled, many thought it was the end of the age of discovery when it was but the beginning. Down to the present era of small boats voyaging around the world, sailors have been discovering things. Herman Melville found a great white whale and Robert Louis Stevenson found a home in Samoa. Ralph Stock found a dream ship and Michael Carroll found a perfect anchorage at Skopelos in the Aegean, where the quiet cove of Panormos put an end to his quest. In recent times the U.S.S. *Nautilus* found the Northwest Passage.

Great modern voyages have been made by sailors who found, beyond islands and remote anchorages, a profound certainty in their own destiny and accomplished something greater than they intended. Melville in his sometimes cryptic symbolism found and gave us a lot more than the *Pequod*, Ahab, and an ocean-cruising whale. Joshua Slocum, who, like Thoreau, went looking for a simple, quiet life and found the infinite, was well aware that he had sailed out of one way of life into another and that nothing again would ever be quite the same. For more than half a century his *Sailing Alone Around the World* has compelled others to dream of their own unlimited possibilities.

The sea, more than any other environment on our planet, is full of unknowns, and we still only know a fraction as much about it as we do about the land. Fuel cells and solar and nuclear systems will provide ample power for extended underwater as well as surface explorations and circumnavigations. The unconventional underwater yacht of 1984—a fast, two-man "Volkswagen cubmarine" of the sea—will have vista-view bubble ports and will go where no men have been before. Now undergoing design studies are underwater freighters and passenger submarines that may, among other things, open up the vast circumpolar Southern Ocean. Before the century closes, man's probing into the outer galaxies and beneath the sea will produce more than one saga surpassing that of Eric the Red.

With aquanauts already living under the sea, why should man not learn to live on the sea? Why not indeed? As terrestrial creatures we carry the ocean within us; there are many individuals who have lived almost entirely at sea for more than a decade and are now ocean cruising as a total way of life.

Small sailing vessels have been a source of inspiration and serenity since long before Noah's boat survived the Deluge. The long quest that has come down from Andean reed rafts and Irish curraghs to the modern search for a poor man's ideal ocean cruiser has included in recent times the smallest twin-bilge keel sloops, through the ever-popular Folkboats, Tahiti ketches, Vertues, up to the more sophisticated and considerably more expensive 30-foot-LW or more vessels. Whether they prefer a Red Sea dhow, a Chinese junk, or the latest Bermudian racing yawl, sailors have been faithful for centuries to a well-sprung sheer line unbroken from bow to stern.

Archeologists and sea historians a hundred years hence, if there are any left then to pursue their arcane calling, will find it hard to understand why Western sailors took five thousand years to move from the square sail and the gaff rig to the Bermudian and why the best designing talent took over half a century to get around to the small light-displacement sailing hulls that combine functional ability with form and proportion, can point high and foot fast, and are beautiful by most standards.

Perhaps it was because, as we have seen, a seagoing sailing vessel is many things to different people. Some want a small craft for living aboard that is also a good sea boat, others a vessel that can stay out in all conditions of wind and sea with a family crew. Mostly what is wanted is a small, easily handled boat designed for the lowest possible maintenance cost, built for and tested in transocean cruising to keep the sea in comfort and safety, that is smart in windward going, can run well with a fair wind, or will lie snugly hove to in a full gale.

In the decade since 1957, when *Bounty II,* the first molded-fiberglass ocean-cruising yacht made its debut, nearly a hundred different fiberglass cruising boats from 18 to 48 feet LOA have come on the market. Never before has there been so much tank testing of models and scientific investigation into the design and performance of sailing vessels. Midget-cruising sailing craft are increasingly popular in Scandinavia; in Britain, where anchorages are heavily populated with small cruising vessels less than 25 feet LOA; and in France, where today 20- to 30-foot-overall week-end sailing boats are to be seen everywhere.

In the evolutionary gulf stream of nautical history, man has spent the past five hundred years trying to sail closer to the wind in a vessel that would also perform well on other points of sailing. While lugsails and sprit-mainsails are nearly gone, gaff sails—though greatly decreased—appear to be holding their own in some areas and the fore-staysail, with 350 years of ocean passage making behind it, has come back into its own and now holds the limelight with the Bermudian mainsail. At the end of the span from animal skins and cocopalm matting through flax and cotton canvas to heat-treated man-made fibers, the nonabsorbent synthetics (Terylene in Britain and Dacron in the United States) quickly took the lead during the fifties as the best material for sailmaking.

The men aboard the simple gaff schooners who sailed to Bermuda in 1923 would not have believed possible what is accepted today as standard in a sport that looks up to its top designers of cup defenders and top helmsmen as honorary gods. The production of racing machines better able to thrust to windward typifies the spirit of our age. With the new designs slated for next year and the year after, it would seem that the wind tunnels are kept busy around the clock. In the next Singlehanded Transatlantic Race, larger and longer light-displacement yachts will be seen, and let it be said quickly that there is a vast difference between a specialized craft built to win a particular race and an honest ocean-cruising vessel owned by a small-ship voyager who has to make do with what he has.

No important changes have occurred in the proportions of advanced Bermudian rigs in the past quarter century or, more properly, since 1937, when the small-mainsail, big-fore-triangle cutter *Maid of Malham* first appeared in England. But the early beauty and simplicity of the Bermudian rig has given way to a multiplicity of large headsails that has turned many racing craft into oversize sail lockers. The small mainsail and numerous headsails on a 25-foot-waterline modern racing sloop or cutter often includes fifteen or more headsails from masthead genoas, Yankees, working and storm jibs to staysails, reaching Yankee ghosters, and spinnakers.

When properly used, the gaff, spritsail, and Chinese lug, though popularly displaced by the masthead fore triangle, are almost as effective and are often handier than many modern rigs. The dhow lateen, the oldest fore-and-aft rig, is nearly as efficient as anything we have today. French designer D. de Manfred, in a departure from orthodox rigs, designed, built, and displayed at the 1966 Paris boat show the 21-foot cruiser *Zaroug*, built for offshore sailing with a modern version of lateen rig having a L-shaped yard swiveled at foot of mast. H. G. Hasler, who tried an amalgam of East and West rigs, ended up using an almost pure copy of a Chinese junk sail for a double crossing of the Atlantic in *Jester* in seventy-one days both ways. "Every time I try to improve on the Chinese I run into difficulties and have to revert," said Hasler, stressing the need for comparative experiments at sea with small-ship rigs. "The truth is that we know hardly anything about the aerodynamics of sails."

We are only beginning to learn something of the role that sailors will play in the future. With today's rapid rate of change and space-age adaptations to sea use, the future of that special breed—known as ocean-cruising sailor— will depend a lot on his resilience and ability to adapt to many of the things that have broadened the horizons for all sailing craft. Even the conservative Hiscocks have added a Hasler trim-tab vane steering gear, an alloy boom, an echo sounder, and a plastic dinghy to the gear of *Wanderer III*.

The modern cruiser-racer is more weatherly, faster, and perhaps more seaworthy in some ways than the older craft, but when cost, real love for a beautiful hull, and respect for tradition are taken into account it is not hard to understand why there is a countercurrent in the United States—and to some degree in the Scandinavian countries and in Britain—toward designs based on traditional types in preference to standard production-by-automation boats that look almost exactly alike from the stemhead fittings to the taffrail. Today wood is boiled, steamed, baked, laminated, glued, and pressed, but there is still a solid demand for frame and plank construction and some yachts are still built of top-quality oak, mahogany, and teak by skilled craftsmen. R. M. McIlvide, a New Zealander who cruises in the South Seas, built his beautiful 48-foot ketch *Arita* from a single kauri tree which he bought while it was still standing.

A cruising boat can express a man's whole attitude, and many noted sailors are thought of in connection with a particular vessel. It is hard to think of Josh Slocum without also thinking of *Spray*, of Captain John Voss without thinking of *Tilikum*, of Tom Steele without his ketch *Adios*, or of the Peter Pyes without *Moonraker*. We know, too, as Theodor Reik has pointed out, that certain individuals cannot adapt to urban centers and standardized living. Listen to Tom Steele, who says after two circumnavigations:

It was only after the completion of my first voyage in June, 1955, that it occurred to me that here was a special way of life, precarious though it may seem by normal

Lee Graham aboard his sloop *Dove* at Honolulu with shipmates Suzette and Joliette.

standards, and not something to be put aside and renewed only sporadically. Everything is a compromise and I suppose we will always be making slight changes and improvements to *Adios*, but the thing to remember is that we are doing what we want to do.

In man's long march from the stone age down to the last third of the twentieth century, he has become increasingly intrigued with paths leading away from his cave. But only in comparatively recent times have his individual explorations in small vessels become global. With no more Vinlands or terra incognitas, the search today is for other things:

For solo voyager Lee Graham, who at sixteen years of age had sailed more than 20,000 ocean miles and in 1966 was sailing around the world in his 24-foot sloop *Dove* with a library of school books, maps, charts, and his cats Suzette and Joliette, it's a quest for a global education and an understanding at first hand of what the world is all about. Lee started sailing at ten, was a competent navigator at thirteen, and will be the youngest sailor to circumnavigate.

For Hella Jakubenko, seventeen-year-old capable navigator and ocean sailor in her own right, cruising in the South Seas in her father's 45-foot Bermudian sloop *Hella*, it is the achievement of a dream.

To Turkish sailor Sadun Boro and wife Oda, circumnavigating from Istanbul on their 42-foot ketch *Kismet*, it is to know the unknown and "the freedom of being a stranger."

For twenty-two-year-old Ann Brittain of Connecticut, sailing as master of her own 61-foot yacht *Valhalla* across the Pacific from Sydney to Panama en route to the Caribbean, it is a search to sustain an ocean-cruising way of life.

Swiss sociologist Michel Mermod, single-handing around the world in his 25-foot sloop *Geneve*, is seeking and finding some of the answers to people living together peacefully in social groups.

"Between the conception and the reality," as T. S. Eliot put it, "there falls the shadow." And for ocean cruising the shadow is finances. What do the circumnavigators and others who cruise as a way of life do for money?

"Live simply" is one of the answers and part of the creed of loners Edward Allcard, Marcel Bardiaux, and Peter Tangvald and his wife Simonne. Pierpont Morgan's oft quoted: "If you have to ask what it costs to run a yacht you can't afford it" is no more true now than it ever was. Those who don't have to ask the cost usually don't cruise very far very often. While ocean cruising is one of the last strongholds of personal freedom, most small-boat voyagers have to do more than know the costs—they have to somehow find the means.

The husky, well-found 45-foot schooner *Sea Wyf* from Vancouver, owned by German-born Canadian Bill Rudolph, called at San Francisco bound for the South Seas with three friends on a retire-now-work-later plan. "We have enough cash for a while," said Rudolph. "After we reach New Zealand the retirement will be over for a spell. Then we'll work." When heard from a year and a half later, they were doing well odd-jobbing around the Pacific.

Today the largest number who live permanently aboard and cruise as a way of life make a living by charter cruising for three or four months a year—an occupation that, under the right conditions, is little more than an extension of what they would choose to do if they didn't have to earn a living. Competent seamanship is of course essential, says T. Crichton, a British sailor who has chartered for many seasons in the Mediterranean, but "the patience of Job, a degree in psychology, or an amused resignation toward the foibles of mankind are better qualifications for a charter skipper than a master's license."

Charles Cottrill, a New Zealand chiropractor and ex-merchant seaman who converted a Guernsey lobster boat into the 45-foot yacht *Sarabande* for world cruising, raised funds in the Mediterranean and elsewhere en route from England to Panama and Tahiti by conducting a chiropractic clinic four hours daily in various ports. John Wiley of the ketch *Tane* collected rare butterflies and other valuable insects and did research work on insect migration. Others are malacologists (shell collectors), crocodile hunters, and biologists.

Humphrey Barton, a marine surveyor who has made ten Atlantic crossings in small craft and now cruises widely in his 11-ton Bermudian sloop *Rose Rambler*, formerly surveyed ships in the winter to be free to cruise during the best part of the year. Circumnavigator Bob Griffith, who has sailed over 100,000 miles with his wife and son in the past seven years and in 1966 made an east-to-west passage around the Horn in *Awahnee II*, a 52-foot ferro-cement cutter that they built in New Zealand, is a veterinarian.

Englishman Geoffrey Matthews, well known in the New Hebrides and Solomons for his crocodile-hunting exploits, crossed the Indian Ocean single-handed in his 52-foot ketch *Dida* with the aid of a self-steering gear that he built at Timor, and early in 1966 departed Durban to explore the crocodile-hunting possibilities in the Amazon. Tom Harrison, ex-captain in the Congo navy, explored the west coast of Africa en route to Europe in *Sundowner*, a 24-foot Australian ketch bought with the proceeds from crocodile hunting in New Guinea. Many are boatbuilders and work briefly in boatyards around the world; a growing number take and show 16-millimeter documentary films; others get grants to do oceanographic research or collect for museums.

Retired army dentist Bill Lee and his wife Gretchen, who cruised 42,000 miles from Hong Kong to Australia, India, the Red Sea, and the Mediterranean in their 33-foot sloop *September Song*, have fitted out a new vessel, the *Bee Bee*, with a dental office and lab in which they intend to cruise to the more remote settlements of the Bahamas, providing dental attention on an annual schedule.

With air liners taking a major share of travelers to and from major seaports, the Pacific is emptier now of commercial vessels than it has been since the early windships, and a number of Polynesians like David Fifita are turning to ocean cruising in small craft. Captain Fifita, Tongan hero of the Minerva Reef epic, who was a qualified master mariner at age twenty and cruised widely in the 42-foot Tongan cutter *Taufale* and other transocean vessels, is building a small cutter to tour the world lone-handed.

It is true that Tahiti is a booming nuclear and jet-age frontier, that Suva has a modern yacht marina, that there are now condominiums beneath the coco palms, and that islanders are dancing the frug in Fiji, doing the twist and watusi in Bora Bora, and producing abstract art for tourists. But the true South Pacific that has always remained an illusive goal for most travelers is still within reach of ocean-cruising sailors, from remote valleys in the Marquesas to Suwarrow, Fanning, the Australs, and other seldom-visited islands in Micronesia and Melanesia where Melville, Stevenson, Gauguin, Louis Becke, and Robert Dean Frisbie have left faintly glowing images that will be there as long as men remember to remember,

Only about thirty yachts a year call at the Marquesas, most of them bound to Tahiti or to Honolulu or the Pacific Coast. There are still no hotels, no restaurants, no bars or honky-tonks in the group. From Stevenson's favorite anchorage at Anaho Bay on Nuku Hiva to Hana Menu in Hiva Oa, Vai Tahu at Tahuata, and Hana Vave (Bay of Virgins) in Fatu Hiva, the valleys—with coconut groves, wild mangoes, limes, and bananas—are little changed since Gauguin and Stevenson were there. Sailors can still sail up Controller Bay and anchor in Melville's classic green valley of Taipi Vai, where they will find an abundance of nonos but no more lovely Fayaways.

Though it took all of history up to the 1840s for the world population to reach one billion, there is now an annual increase equivalent to another Great Britain or another France every year. Speaking of the automated age and of bumper-to-bumper, nose-to-nose man of tomorrow, the director of India's Institute for Population Studies warned that the United States needs a birth ban more than India and that "by 2000 A.D. the auto will have become man's greatest curse and will have to be cut back to one per family." Professor Chandrasekhar might have added that small boats will partly take the place of cars and soon will be considered a leisure necessity.

"Within the next hundred years man may work only three years of his life, retiring at age twenty-seven," industrial economics professor George Halverson told several hundred California educators at a recent symposium on the emerging affluent and automated society. "Machines will do the work, bringing to fruition the trend toward an abundant society of maximum productivity with minimum work. As a source of income, work may be outmoded. Just by being a human being, you will receive a guaranteed annual income. If the society can afford to, why not?"

Many will disagree with Dr. Halverson's conclusions, but one way or another we face a future in which a combination of circumstances and technical developments will provide men with fewer working hours and a way of life with much leisure. The unpredictable variant is man himself. He has become accustomed to noise and chatter; it is quietness that puts him to the test. What will he do when he can turn his nose to the sea breeze without having to worry about returning it to the grindstone? So far he hasn't done so well.

A generation raised on push buttons and on an amplitude of automatic *things* is leaning more and more on what is easily obtained and maintained, from apartments without upkeep to boats with automatic controls bought on credit in the carnival atmosphere of annual boat shows and department stores. Some of these sleek, shiny creations—mass produced with ersatz nautical decor, all-chrome trailer plumbing, and the latest in gadgetry for people in a hurry, seeking excitement in a sport that also conveys status— must make Lloyd's of London weep.

British economist Lord Keynes, looking forward to a workless West, once said he viewed the prospect with a certain dread. In a nation like the United States, that spends fifty times more on tranquilizers than the rest of the world and has more people in mental hospitals than in all other kinds of hospitals, recreation has certainly become a crucial problem.

Since the use of leisure cannot be solved by TV time-killers or at a ball park watching other people play games, a curious imbalance has developed between the increasing amount of free time available to many and their ability to know what to do with it. Put in another way—unless more and more people learn to like strawberries and cream, hiking, planting a garden, mountain climbing, ocean sailing, and other forms of first-hand engagement, they won't know what to do with themselves and may end up attempting to tear the house down.

The traditional scene of small craft swinging to their moorings in placid bays and coves is already almost gone in some areas—replaced by crowded marinas with recreation centers, trailer ramps, and loud-speakers blaring canned sea chanties. Some have been used as vast land-promotion schemes where people dress in the latest nautical fashion and live like goldfish in a bowl.

However limited man's choices may seem, there is still the open sea. Once considered a luxury, a small craft able to sail away from the ravages of roof-to-roof surburbia has become, for many, a family necessity, a part of the need to get away from banalities and hucksters out to where people are less articulate and life more meaningful. Husbands and wives, children, even cats and dogs are making coastal cruises. The thousands of families on both sides of the Pacific and the Atlantic and in other waters who now go ocean cruising will be followed in the next decade by ten times as many.

Freedom of travel is a natural law traceable to Socrates, Marco Polo, and Hugo Grotius, who knew better than most men how vital is freedom of movement to man's spirit and survival. Today more and more sailors have come to realize that though a nation may control the seas with the largest fleet it does not necessarily mean more freedom but quite often means less.

Three great nations that lived on the shores of the Mediterranean and denied freedom of the ocean to others have perished from the face of the earth. When Carthage forbade the Latins to sail west of the Laconian foot-hills, she was finally beaten. Genoa tried in vain to keep the Provençals away from Sicily. The Venetians wanted the exclusive use of the Adriatic and the Turks the Black Sea—both in vain.

When Portugal and Spain, by the Treaty of Tordesillas, divided the distant sea world between them, England and Holland ignored the papal ruling and, at a time when Pizarro was ravishing Peru and sending home the largest shipments of gold in history, made plans to enter the forbidden waters of the Indies via a northerly route. Before the end of that century did not England and tiny Holland vanquished the mighty powers of Spain and Portugal?

Long after the westward expansion of the United States, and the subjugation of the freedom and rights of the Indians, the present system of domination of the sea that Americans inherited from Europeans reached out across the Pacific for a "strategic annexation" that turned several million square miles of former Japanese Micronesia into a virtual American lake and added a new list of forbidden areas for ocean voyagers with official warnings of restricted waters not to be entered or sailed through.

All curtains that inhibit the right to move freely about the earth, whether of naval gold stripes, bamboo, iron, or plain red tape, erode a right as basic and crucial as the right to free speech or worship. A case in point is the skipper of the ketch *Phoenix*, intercepted on the high seas for penetrating a "forbidden area" and taken to Honolulu under arrest—a true David-and-Goliath case in which a dedicated, ocean-cruising family incurred the wrath of the Establishment, including the U.S. Atomic Energy Commission and the Defense Department.

On the last leg of a six-year, 54,000-mile voyage around the world in their 50-foot ketch *Phoenix*, Dr. Earle Reynolds, a mild-mannered, law-abiding American anthropologist accompanied by his wife, two children, and crewman Nick Mikami, the first Japanese yachtsman to circumnavigate in a small vessel, was arrested on the high seas for having sailed into a vast area of open ocean (390,000 square miles) that the U.S. Atomic Energy Commission had staked out and declared off limits to all sea traffic of all nations, an act that seemed clearly in violation of international law.

Reluctant at first to interrupt a quiet, dedicated way of life as an ocean sailor and top scientist in his field, Dr. Reynolds later became so convinced that the AEC regulation forbidding a yacht to sail in an area of open ocean was wrong and would never stand up in an honest court of law that he decided, with the brave backing of his wife Barbara and his two children Jessica and Ted, to defend to the best of his ability the concept of freedom of the seas.

At a time when E. B. White was writing in *The New Yorker*, "I hold one share in the corporate earth and am uneasy about the management," the trial was held in the jingoist atmosphere of a military town. The government's position was quite openly bolstered by the Honolulu trial judge, and the anthropologist-sailor was found guilty.

The subsequent appeal of Dr. Reynolds, widely reported in the world press, stirred the sympathy of thousands of Europeans and Americans, landsmen and sailors alike, who felt that freedom of the seas was more than a cliché and should be respected by all governments. Sympathetic editorials appeared in many publications, from the *New Republic* to the *Saturday Review,* and in Hawaii the *Tribune-Herald* editorialized: "Who is Uncle Sam

WARREN ROLL, OF THE *Honolulu Star-Bulletin*

The *Phoenix* sailed for those with less courage . . . less vision.

WARREN ROLL

Earle Reynolds, daughter Jessica, and Mrs. Barbara Reynolds discuss
school lessons in cabin of *Phoenix*.

to speak of freedom if he is to violate the traditional freedom of the seas himself?"

Months later the Honolulu judge was ruled in error by a higher court for not allowing the ocean-cruising sailor a proper defense, and a new trial was granted.

In his struggle as an individual against inequities of the lower court and the best talent and resources of the Justice Department, Dr. Reynolds won a battle for all sailors when, after months of expensive court procedure, the U.S. Court of Appeals at San Francisco reversed the Honolulu conviction and ruled that the AEC did not have the right to make up regulations roping off large areas of the high seas. The high court unanimously ruled that the AEC regulation forbidding entrance into a large area of the Pacific was invalid and held that "the conviction of appellant [Earle Reynolds] . . . is without legal authority and it must be set aside and the judgment reversed."

Vindication of the skipper of the ketch *Phoenix* was applauded by sailors of many nations, and the United States suffered a moral defeat in the eyes of much of the world for having denied the rights of a small-craft circumnavigator who had the integrity to stand up and fight for a cause, even when it meant proving a powerful government agency to be wrong.

At the 1964 U.N. Conference in Rome, the United States voiced strong opposition toward any act that would inhibit the right of man to move about. Many countries expressed the same sentiment. Yet less than a year later, in direct contradiction to the lofty statements agreed upon at Rome, it was proposed in Washington that an exit tax be imposed on both Americans and foreign visitors.

Regardless of treaties, the United States did as it pleased in the Trust Territories and refused to let the World Court give a decision in the matter. France does the same thing over a broad area in the Tuamotus, where the placid reefs of Fangataufa and Mururoa have resounded to recent nuclear explosions. Russia has restricted Pacific areas for rocket testing, and China will doubtless have its own sea area for testing. Japan has restricted travel by her nationals to protect the yen and still today makes it difficult for her small-boat sailors to go ocean cruising in international waters.

Stated bluntly, the freedom to sail around the globe at will—a freedom dating back to the Magna Carta and in recent years confirmed by the Universal Declaration of Human Rights, by the French Constitution, and by the U.S. Supreme Court—is a freedom not now fully enjoyed by any people, maritime or otherwise, whether in the "free world" or elsewhere. If the blue horizon is to remain a challenge and not become a limitation, the unrestricted right to sail the global sea regardless of race, color, creed, or politics needs affirming now more than ever before. No border or sea area need be a prison or a *verboten* wall among nations at peace, whether in Berlin, American Micronesia, the South China Sea, or French Polynesia.

Fortunately, many people today are coming to realize that equal fear, equally shared, is not progress; one hopes that enough mature thinking will prevail in maritime governments to abolish in the very near future all restrictive measures which affect freedom of the seas.

The eighteenth-century impact of sailors in the Pacific is still being felt from the Marshall Islands to Woomera, Australia, to Tahiti. There has always been something foredoomed about Polynesian loveliness. Even Captain Cook believed, "It would have been far better for those poor people never to have known us," and Diderot the encyclopedist warned the happy islanders against interloping whites: "Under their rule you will be almost as unhappy as they are."

And so it has come to pass: Tahiti is the center for General de Gaulle's thermonuclear test program, and in 1966, on the two hundredth anniversary of Bougainville's voyage to New Cythera, the French government sent greetings by exploding their first hydrogen bomb within a few hundred miles of Tahiti—at which moment there was loosed upon the seas another unmeasured, perhaps unmeasurable, radioactive threat to everything that lives in or feeds from the waters of a wide ocean area in the Tuamotu Islands. As a direct result of atomic testing in the Pacific by the U.S., the *Japan Quarterly* has pointed out that, in one year alone, Japan had to take 992 boats out of commission because of contamination of international fishing waters by radiation, and over a million pounds of contaminated fish had to be destroyed. The Monte Bello Islands, north of Onslow, West Australia, are still radioactive nearly nine years after the last British nuclear explosion there.

Again and again the hand of man has destroyed what even the worst elements spared. The other side of the romance of whaling, which made New Englanders swell with pride, was the wanton butchering of whales, seals, otters, walruses, and other creatures in Antarctica until some species are nearly extinct. Men like Charles Scammon, who turned refuge areas and mating lagoons and beaches into huge slaughterhouses until entire coves ran deep with blood, were followed by modern whalers that made even worse depredations until some species were so depleted there appeared little hope for their recovery. Only in the last few years have the gray whales been brought back from the brink of extinction.

History records the destruction of once-powerful civilizations that mismanaged their natural resources. Presently—by the billions of gallons monthly of industrial and human pollutants dumped into rivers and waterways (the Tiber, the Seine, the Potomac, the Hudson are all well polluted), by the pall and the black smudge horizons that now hang over most cities and environs, by the radioactive miscalculations and wastes that are dumped into the sea in large quantities—man has been risking, through ignorance, his ability to survive.

"The sea," as John F. Kennedy put it, "will ultimately determine conditions of life in the rest of the world." With cities and suburbs becoming self-defeating through smog, overpopulation, and congestion, there is more and more need for the best use of the world ocean—its resources and submerged lands, its anchorages, and its natural beauty, wild areas, and wildlife, which belong collectively to the community of nations.

Progress, as the English have learned, means preserving and cherishing, as well as using. Nature Conservancy in Britain makes it clear to sailors and others that they can live and travel on its waterways but should regard them as something inviolate, to be kept clean and free of pollutants. On the non-tidal Thames, which provides 60 per cent of London's drinking water, no waste may be jettisoned. On small cruising vessels making a river passage, wastes from galley and head drain into a bilge tank, emptied periodically or pumped out electrically at river depots managed by the Thames Conservancy.

The U.S. Coast Guard will have antipollution equipment on all its cutters by 1972, at which time pollution-control devices will probably become mandatory on all ships, freighters, and tankers as well as on all yachts, ocean-cruising and otherwise.

While space continues to beguile the public, many scientists now believe that man's future is in the sea. "If we are to survive on this earth," says Dr. Harris Stewart, Jr., chief oceanographer of the U.S. Coast and Geodetic Survey, "we must come to understand the intricate workings of the global sea and the role it will play in the future of the race." Question number one then for today and tomorrow is: What approaches can be taken on a global scale dedicated to the science, art, and philosophy of the sea?

Men are capable of care as much as they are of destruction. If conservation and freedom of the seas is made an international cause, generations ahead can learn that there must be left undisturbed wildlife sanctuaries, scenic areas, geological features, flora, fauna, and quiet coastal anchorages to counter man-made terrestrial imbalance and help heal the wounds of civilization.

After all, what is the sea? It is space. It is, or should be, wilderness uncontaminated with nuclear waste. As the root center of life and vitality, it is the hub of man's most adventurous dreams and achievements. While much, perhaps too much, is said lately about exploiting the oceans, its greatest resource is the inspiration, well-being, and freedom associated with its openness, where the only restrictions are a sailor's capabilities and his observance of the decent customs of mariners.

The need is for an interrelationship of man as a total human being with his total environment, and a new balance between humans and the sea through great oceanographical projects that will dwarf anything yet seen on earth. Leading marine biologists propose a world-wide federation to protect the oceans, with marine laboratories, stations, and research vessels, linked possibly into a huge network through a satellite orbiting overhead, to study and control ocean pollution and to investigate and protect marine animals and plant life.

Norway, Finland, and Sweden already have a co-operative program. In the Caribbean, the Association of Island Marine Laboratories unites oceanographic facilities of several nations; and in the Mediterranean, scientists of Greece, Italy, Israel, Turkey, Yugoslavia, Spain, and other countries share research facilities, ships, extend fellowships to graduate students, and exchange information on their findings through the Mediterranean Association for Marine Biology and Oceanography (MAMBO).

More important than the quest for the New World, the Spice Islands, or the Northwest Passage ever was—and more crucial than today's search for new life on Mars—is the need for a common meeting ground for the human community.

For generations the secrets of the sea have been shared by neighboring countries. Seamen share the same sea marks. The information on charts is freely exchanged. Fundamentally a seaman's interests are the same whatever his nationality. In another decade sailors will share the language of aerodynamics, will understand and speak the idiom of sea science and engineering. Perhaps a universal sea language will emerge, spoken and understood by sailors in addition to their native tongue.

Sailing academies, seagoing university ships, the East-West Center at Honolulu, sea grant colleges, and other farseeing measures mark the progress of the young sailor. Well over a hundred thousand boys and girls twelve years and older have taken sea-school cruises on Britain's *Dunera, Devonia, Nevasa,* and other ships. En route to Scandinavia, Russia, North Africa, and the Mediterranean, daily classes begin at 9:15 A.M. and include the background and contemporary life of the next port of call, understanding among people, and a voluntary daily navigation class.

Dartmouth and other universities in the United States, Europe, and the Mediterranean now have a fleet of sea training vessels. Graduate students in marine sciences are taking courses in biological oceanography while cruising around the world aboard Stanford University's 136-foot schoolship-schooner *Te Vega* as part of a fifteen-nation co-operative effort.

France has established a National Sailing School at Quiberon that will have a sailing fleet of sixty vessels, from Finns to ocean racers. Noted solo sailor Eric Tabarly, winner of the 1964 Singlehanded Transatlantic Race, was put in charge of the school syllabus. Britain has the 300-ton topsail schooner *Sir Winston Churchill* for the sail training of young boys. Argentina, Chile, Denmark, France, Portugal, Norway, Spain, and West Germany all have smartly kept, square-rigged vessels for training young sailors. In 1966, sailor-congressman Claiborne Pell introduced a bill in Congress to establish a novel type of higher education called Sea Grant Colleges for teaching and research in the field of marine sciences.

With other advances, habits of thinking change. Man is beginning to realize the interdependence of all peoples and all oceans. In addition to the Peace Corps, we may have a Sea Corps with multiple objectives for young people who feel the challenge of finding out for themselves about the human community around the globe.

Increasingly we live in the present of what the future may bring, and the broad outlines of the seagoing man's world of tomorrow are beginning to be clearly visible.

Just as plastic foam has become the universal flotation material in boating, light alloys have become the most widely used material for masts and spars. Other sophisticated jet-age materials including titanium and polyethylene have been adapted for marine use, and a new unicellular rigid vinyl plastic foam sheet that has the strength of wood and fiberglass but only half the weight is now available to boatbuilders.

There will be less sea roll, for those who prefer it that way, with a new British stabilizing system suitable for all size vessels down to the smallest yachts—controlled by a servo sensing unit that has been tested off the Firth of Forth to cut a 27-degree roll to 5 degrees.

Aquafoils are now operating year-round on open-ocean runs, and foil stabilized single-hull craft will be making transocean passages before long.

A new technique that enables a vessel to determine rapidly the changing pattern of the path of the Gulf Stream in order to stay in it will shorten passage time.

Unlike the Vikings, who victualed with dried fish and grains, the modern sailor already has dehydrated, freeze-dried, pre-seasoned, and pre-cooked foods available, and the ocean voyager of 1975 will be able to carry light, compact, unspoilable provisions for a complete world cruise, without need to replenish in distant ports, and a compact, self-operating salt-water distillation unit that will produce 3 to 8 gallons of distilled water per hour.

Thanks to pioneer weather satellites Tiros and Nimbus, world-wide weather forecasts will be made two to four weeks in advance by synchronous satellites that will photograph the cloud cover over the entire earth daily while their infrared sensors monitor the oceans and their currents. (Before Hurricane Carla, the all-seeing eye of Tiros III gave advance notice in time for 350,000 people to move to safety in the largest weather exodus in modern history.)

Navigation by "new stars"—space satellites—is already in full operation aboard a number of ships and will be available to ocean-cruising sailors, who will use simple receivers and digital computers for the necessary computations to obtain fixes to within a few feet in place of the traditional "within a few miles."

Let it also be said, slowly, that new advances and innovations of the space age will require far more wisdom than man has so far had in good supply.

Sailors and their backers have always had things to worry about. It seems there is no getting away from that. Before Columbus left Palos, the Queen of Spain said to him, "No matter what you discover, I am already worried about it." With a thousand times the knowledge possessed by the ancients, the electronic-age sailor is very little happier. Beneath his outer façade he is usually worried about economics, a way of life—often about the future and the unknown. His era is no longer so certain it can master anything that might be discovered in the laboratory or outer space, and he is no longer certain about the part he himself is going to play—tomorrow.

With all the electronics, sonar, and other latter-half-of-the-twentieth-century navigation and safety equipment, there is still uncertainty and mystery in the all-encircling ocean from the South China Sea to Cape Horn to the Devil's Elbow—that patch of wild water seaward from Cape Hatteras where the warm waters of the Gulf Stream collide with the cold waters of the Labrador Current. Rated by meteorologists one of the most unpredictable weather centers in the world, the Devil's Elbow is only a small part of that large section of the Atlantic known as the Deadly Triangle (an area of over 700,000 square miles) in which have gone unresolved some of the most puzzling modern mysteries of the sea, including the disappearance without a trace of the 45-foot yawl *Revonoc*, the 56-foot schooner *Windfall*, the 55-foot schooner *Evangeline*, the 58-foot schooner *Enchantress*, and the 36-foot ketch *Dancing Feather*.

As strange as the disappearance of the small ships mentioned above was the loss of John J. Pflieger, commodore of The Slocum Society Sailing Club. After a passage from New York to Bermuda in his 26-foot gaff cutter *Stella Maris* and a long stay at St. George's, John Pfleiger cleared Bermuda early in July, 1966, for a solo passage to St. Martin in the Netherlands Antilles and was never seen or heard from again. The sixty-eight-year-old commodore's cutter *Stella Maris* with jib set, her tiller lashed, and with no one aboard, sailed herself in through two treacherous outer reefs to arrive, safely and without damage, on a sand bar at Antigua. Everything aboard was shipshape. The skipper's pipe was in the cockpit filled with tobacco; a raft, safety gear, and enough food and water was aboard for a transatlantic passage. Last entry in the log gave only the ship's position (approximately 100 miles east of Puerto Rico on July 12). What happened to the much-loved commodore, who befriended many transocean sailors, and how long his cutter sailed herself with no one aboard will never be known. (Like Dante's Ulysses, many aged small-ship sailors have vanished with their boots on because they were determined to make just one more voyage.)

Edward Allcard, a very capable solo seafarer, once said, "How can mere words possibly exaggerate a great storm at sea?" Early in 1966 on the Pacific slopes of the globe, many lives were lost and several small ships foundered when the worst hurricane in seventy-five years ripped across the South Seas. In Alaskan waters, in the same year, several modern vessels fully equipped with the latest gear and electronics have completely disappeared without a trace. The 43,000-ton Italian liner *Michelangelo* arrived at New York with two dead and twelve injured after an Atlantic storm described by Captain Giuseppe Soletti as the worst in his forty-one years at sea. "At the peak of the gale a 60-foot wave swept away 20 staterooms and twisted steel plates at the bow as if they were tinfoil."

Among three small yachts recently damaged by whales, the 50-foot *Easterling* was badly holed between the Galapagos and the Marquesas; the trimaran *Highlight,* en route from New Zealand to Rapa in the Australs, had her port and starboard floats smashed by a whale; and in the Indian Ocean, the trimaran *Cosa Nostra* encountered a whale off Madagascar and had her rudder broken off but continued to Durban with a jury rudder.

Three modern, well-found ocean-cruising yachts skippered by experienced and able sailors were lost in the South Seas in less than six months. William Proctor, en route home to England, after sailing two-thirds of the way around the world solo from Portsmouth, disappeared somewhere between Honiara in the Solomons and Port Moresby. Wreckage believed to have been Proctor's 21-foot sloop *Popey Duck* was found near Bodi Bodi in the Laughlans. After an intensive air and sea search, all hope was abandoned for the safety of the 38-foot ketch *Marinero.* The American vessel, under Swiss registry, went down with her crew of five somewhere between Wallis Island and Apia in the fierce hurricane that hit that area late in January of 1966. Several months later the 42-foot catamaran *Hinano* of Newport, California, foundered in a violent storm en route from Tahiti to Hawaii.

More than others, the ocean-cruising sailor understands how little we know about the salt waters of the globe, a frontier whose topography has yet to be plumbed and whose secrets hold the key to the origin of man and very likely to his survival on planet earth.

Just as isolationism has become untenable, so too is chauvinism. Thomas Fleming Day, one of the best yachting editors and small-craft sailors of all time, put it this way: "If a man is a good sailor, I love him: I don't care whether he is black, white or yellow, what flag he sails under, or what God he kneels to." Fortunately the seas are vast and there is room for men of wide differences. Whether the U.S. Apollo moonships or the Russian Voskhod

Te Rapunga off Diamond Head.

George Dibbern's flag meaning good will among men puzzled officials
of many nations.

spacecraft land on the moon or get to Mars first is of small importance to the dedicated blue-water voyager.

Sailors, who seldom talk about brotherhood, practice it. Slocum, for example, the classic loner, was an honored citizen of the world and still is. George Dibbern, the sailor without a country, cruised widely in the 32-foot ketch *Te Rapunga* under his own flag, a square of white with a red cross in a blue circle meaning good will among men. (With the rise of Hitler's nationalism, when no one in Germany, it seemed to Dibbern, dared speak of understanding and peace, he "denationalized" himself, composed his own passport, and set out from Cuxhaven to search for a new way of life across many oceans and a quarter of a lifetime that led finally to New Zealand after 60,000 miles of ocean cruising in *Te Rapunga*.) "All good sailors belong to one large family," said Jacques-Yves Le Toumelin, one of the most perceptive of solo circumnavigators. "The foolish quarrels of nations are meaningless to us."

To the small boat voyager it is the sea which comes first: it is the supreme consideration, stretching to every shore, wind-cut and passionate, greater in breadth and loneliness, than all the deserts of the world together.

—*Richard Maury*

With most of his requirements increasingly fulfilled by machines and devices, the global-cruising sailor is one of the best examples of an individual seeking his *mythos* in the sea wind and the arc of a mast according to his needs and capacities. And it might just be that long after lunar landings in space caravels are routine, twenty-first-century man will come to realize that the greatest sea of all is right here on earth.

Beyond the vast range of what is known and all the latest expertise, it is good to think occasionally of all that is still unknown about the sea, small ships, and sailing that will perhaps always be unknown. In one way or another the sea has resisted man's efforts to rush over it even in this mechanical age. Many of the infinite possibilities which beguiled the first mariners across the Western Ocean are still there. Now, as then, they are part mirage and part truth. The ultimate horizon lies, as always, just beyond.

> *In the moods and the silences of a great ocean there lies an uncertainty, like a question mark, that is the reflection of life itself.*
> —PETER PYE

A Glossary of Sailing Terms

STRANGE and perhaps confusing as it may seem to landsmen, the distinctive language of the sea is beautiful, precise, and meaningful. After thousands of years of global usage, it is still undergoing changes, new words are being added, and many old words are no longer used. No attempt is made here to tell anything to sailors, and most certainly not to ocean-cruising voyagers. Sailing will always be more of an art than a science, and the aim of the following is simply to give as many concise explanations as possible—mainly those that need no explaining to mariners but may make the meaning of certain nautical terms clearer to the shore-side general reader.

ABAFT. Behind. On the after side of.
ABEAM. Right angle to a vessel's keel or course.

ABOUT SHIP. To change tack.

AFT. Near the stern.

AHULL. Hove to under bare poles and driven before the wind.

ALL STANDING. To turn in fully clothed.

AMIDSHIPS. A vessel's middle part.

ATHWART. Across. At right angles with a vessel's keel.

AVAST. Stop. To cease heaving.

AWEATHER. To windward.

BACK, TO. A wind backs when it shifts counterclockwise.

BACKSTAYS. Rigging leading aft from masthead to support a mast.

BAGGY WRINKLE. Sennit yarns or other material to prevent chafe.

BARE POLES. Without sails.

BATTEN. Flat stiffener fitted to after edge (leech) of a sail.

BEAM. Greatest width of a vessel.

BEAM-ENDS. A vessel is on beam-ends when hove over until her decks are nearly vertical.

BEAM, ON THE. In a direction abeam of the vessel.

BEAR A HAND. Assist.

BEAR AWAY. Move away from.

BEAR DOWN. To approach from windward.

BEAT. To sail to windward.

BEITASS. Viking term for a removable pole which acted like a spinnaker boom to keep a sail stretched and drawing on the wind.

BEND, TO. Secure a rope. To fit a sail.

BERMUDIAN (BERMUDAN). Modern rig with tall triangular mainsail without a gaff.

BOARD. A tack when close-hauled.

BOLLARD. Strong vertical post to receive mooring lines.

BOOM. A spar used to secure the foot of a fore-and-aft sail.

BOOMSPRIT SAIL. Ancient Tahitian outrigger sail (not to be confused with a spritsail).

BO'SUN'S CHAIR. Canvas or wood seat with bridle to carry a man aloft.

BOWSPRIT. Spar extending forward of bow to which headsails are secured.

BRAIL. A rope used to gather in sail and secure it to a mast.

BREAST-HOOK. Timber or plate across a vessel's stem for strengthening the bows.

BROACH TO. To swing round broadside into wind and heavy sea.

BULKHEAD. A partition below deck.

BULWARK. A vessel's hull planking that extends above the deck.

CAPFUL OF WIND. A light squall.

CARVEL-BUILT. Built smooth-sided wth planking edge to edge.

CATAMARAN. A twin-hulled vessel.

CAT'S-PAW. Very light airs rippling the surface of the water.

CAULK. To fill seams with oakum or other material.

CENTERBOARD. Plate lowered through bottom of a vessel to give keel area.

CLEAT. A fitting for securing a line.

CLEW. After lower corner of a fore-and-aft sail.

CLINKER-BUILT. Built with overlapping edge-on-edge side planks.

CLOSE-HAULED. Sailing as close to the wind as possible.

CLOSE-REEFED. Reefed down to smallest sail area.

COCKPIT. Open area near the stern where helmsman sits.

COUNTER. An overhang of the stern over the water.

CROSSTREES. Crosspieces near top of mast to spread shrouds.

CUTTER. Single-masted vessel with two headsails.

DEAD BEFORE. With the wind directly aft.

DEADEYES. Traditional circular blocks with holes for lanyards to set up rigging.

DEAD RECKONING. Estimating position of a vessel by compass, log, and calculation of wind and current.

DHOW. Lateen-rigged vessel common to the Indian and Arabian coasts.

DISPLACEMENT. The volume or weight of water displaced by a vessel.

DOLDRUMS. Windless equatorial region.

DOUBLE-ENDER. A vessel with pointed bow and stern.

DOWNHAUL. A rope for hauling down a sail.

DRAFT. Depth of water required to float a vessel. Measure of vessel from waterline to bottom of keel.

DROGUE. See sea anchor.

FATHOM. Six feet.

FID. A tapered wooden pin to open strands when splicing fiber rope. (Also a flat pin in heel of bowsprit or topmast.)

FIDDLEHEAD. Carved timber substitute for a figurehead on the bows.

FORE AND AFT. Lengthwise.

FORECASTLE. Forward compartment of a vessel.

FOREFOOT. Where the stem joins the keel.

FOREPEAK. A triangular area below deck in the bows.

FOREREACHING. To make headway when hove to.

FORESAIL. Principal sail set on the foremast.

FORESTAY. A wire from the masthead to the bow.

FORESTAYSAIL. Triangular sail hanked to a forestay.

FOUNDER. To sink.

FREEBOARD. Height of the deck from waterline.

FULL AND BY. Close-hauled on the wind with sails filled.

FUTTOCK SHROUDS. Iron rods that support a ship's top and topmast rigging.

GAFF. A spar that supports the head of a sail.

GAMMONING. Fastenings that help secure a bowsprit against pull of the forestays.

GENOA. A large overlapping jib.

GOOSENECK. A swivel fitting that secures the boom to the mast.

GOOSEWINGED TOPSAIL. Just showing to a gale a small area of canvas the shape of a goose's wing.

GUDGEON. Eye fitting into which the pintles of the rudder fit.

GUNKHOLING. Leisurely cruising to out-of-the-way places.

GUNTER LUG. A mainsail that is extended above the masthead by a long gaff lying nearly parallel with the mast.

GUNWALE. Upper edge of a vessel's side.

GYBE. See jibe.

HALYARD. Rope used for hoisting. (Sail, boom, flag, etc.)

HAND, REEF AND STEER. Term for seamanly competence.

HAND, To. To lower, take in or furl a sail.

HANK. Metal clip for securing a sail to a stay.

HARD CHINE. Hull with sides and bottom joining at sharp angles instead of curving round.

HAWSER. Heavy rope or cable.

HEAD. A vessel's toilet.

HEAD KNEES. Knee-shaped timber in bows of older ships.

HEADSAILS. The sails forward of the foremast.

HEAVE TO. To stop headway. Trim sails and helm so a vessel is best able to ride out a gale.

HELM. A vessel's steering device. Usually a tiller or wheel.

HOVE TO. See heave to.

HYDROFOIL. A boat with a hull that rises clear of the water and skims along on underwater foils.

JACKSTAY. Rod or wire on which a sail or anything may travel or be secured.

JAMBING CLEAT. Cleat with V-shaped jaws that "jam" and hold a rope fast.

JIB. Foremost headsail.

JIB BOOM. Spar extending beyond bowsprit.

JIBE. To change tack and swing off before the wind.

JIBSTAY. Forward stay on which jib is hoisted.

JURY. A temporary makeshift.

JURY RIG. Improvised rig to work a vessel to port.

JURY SPRIT. Improvised spar.

KEDGE. Auxiliary anchor for moving a vessel.

KEDGE, TO. To carry out anchor and haul or winch a vessel up to it.

KEEL. Fore-and-aft backbone and lowest part of a hull.

KETCH. Two-masted vessel with mizzenmast forward of steering position.

KNOT. Nautical speed measurement meaning one nautical mile in one hour.

LANYARDS. Small lines to make anything fast. Formerly rope rove through deadeyes to set up rigging.

LAPSTRAKE. See clinker-built.

LATEEN. Triangular fore-and-aft sail set from a yard and hoisted obliquely to mast.

LATITUDE. Distance north or south of the equator.

LEEBOARD. Large board that suspends over the side to lessen leeway.

LEECH. The aftermost edge of a sail.

LEEWARD. Down wind. Opposite from side on which wind is blowing.

LEG-O'-MUTTON SAIL. Triangular fore-and-aft sail set abaft mast in small craft.

LEVANTER. Strong northeasterly Mediterranean wind.

LOA. Abbreviation of overall length of a vessel.

LODESTONE. Piece of stone (magnetite) that seeks magnetic meridian (points magnetic north) when freely suspended.

LOG. Device which measures speed and mileage through water.

LOG BOOK. Concise daily record of things of seamanly importance aboard ship.

LONGITUDE. Distance east or west of Greenwich meridian.

LUFF. Forward edge of a sail. Bring a vessel closer to the wind.

LUGSAIL. Four-sided sail with head bent to a yard and set with tack well forward of the mast.

LW. Abbreviation for length of a vessel at waterline.

MAINMAST. Tallest mast of ketch, yawl, or schooner.

MAINSAIL. Principal sail set abaft the mainmast.

MAIN YARD. Lower yard to which mainsail is bent.

MAKE FAST. To secure.

MARCONI. See Bermudian.

MARLINESPIKE. See fid. Similar to fid, but of metal for splicing wire.

MARTINGALE. Short spar extending from bowsprit to counter pull of headstays.

MIDSHIPS. Midway between stem and stern. Widest part of a vessel.

MISTRAL. A cold northwest wind of the Mediterranean.

MIZZEN. Smaller sail aft on a ketch or yawl.

MIZZENMAST. The aft and shorter mast of a ketch or yawl.

MONOHULL. Vessel with a single hull.

MULTIHULL. Vessel with two or more hulls. Usually a catamaran or trimaran.

NAUTICAL MILE. 6,080 feet.

PAMPERO. A sudden and often violent wind which blows off the Argentine pampas.

PAPAGAYO. Northeast gale blowing off the coast of Central America.

PINK. An early double-ended (often schooner-rigged) vessel with blunt bow and sharp, overhanging stern that rose to a peak several feet abaft the stem post.

PITCHPOLED. Vessel lifted and thrown end over end by a huge sea.

POOPED. Heavy sea coming aboard over the stern.

PORT. Left side of a vessel when facing forward.

PREVENTER. Additional stay or extra rope to limit movement of gear.

QUARTER-DECK. Part of a ship's uppper deck abaft the mainmast.

REACH. To sail with the wind on the beam.

REEF. To reduce sail.

ROARING FIFTIES. Above the 50th parallel of latitude.

ROARING FORTIES. Boisterous westerly winds prevailing in the round-the-world sailing belt between 40° and 50° South.

RUDDER. Flat plate hinged to stern post by which a vessel is steered.

RUNNING. Sailing before the wind.

SCHOONER. Two-masted sailing vessel with mainmast aft.

SEA ANCHOR. A conical drag of canvas, timber, or of spars lashed together to keep a vessel's head to the wind.

SHEER STRAKE. The upper line of planking on a vessel's side.

SHEET. A rope, or tackle, used to trim sails.

SHROUDS. Wire ropes that give lateral support to a mast.

SIROCCO. A hot, south wind of the Mediterranean.

SLOOP. Single-masted sailing vessel with one headsail.

SNOW. A brig with auxiliary mast abaft the mainmast on which a fore-and-aft gaff sail is set.

SOUND. To determine the depth of water.

SPINNAKER. Large triangular sail boomed out on opposite side from the mainsail.

SPRIT. A spar which crosses a mainsail diagonally from lower part of mast to the peak of the sail.

SPRITSAIL. Quadrilateral sail with peak extended by a sprit.

STARBOARD. The right side of a vessel looking forward.

STAYS. Wire rigging giving fore-and-aft support to a mast.

STAYSAIL. Triangular fore-and-aft sail set on a stay directly forward of mast.

STUNSAILS. Extra sails run out on a ship's yardarms in moderate, steady breezes.

TACK, TO. To work to windward by sailing close-hauled alternating from port to starboard boards.

TAFFRAIL. Railing around the stern.

TEHUANTEPECER. Strong north to northeast wind from southern Mexico blowing across the Gulf of Tehuantepec into the Pacific.

TEREDOS. Sea worms that eat wood and damage unprotected wood hulls.

TOPGALLANTS. Sails set above the topsails.

TOPPING LIFT. A rope which takes the weight of a spar.

TRAMONTANA. Cold, dry violent wind blowing down the Adriatic Sea.

TRIMARAN. A triple-hulled vessel.

TRIM-TAB GEAR. Modern self-steering device.

TRUCK. Fitting at top of mast.

TRUNNEL. Wooden pin for securing timbers together.

TRYSAIL. Small storm sail set in place of mainsail in heavy weather.

VEER. To pay out rope or chain. Shift of wind clockwise.

WARP. Heavy mooring line.

WEAR SHIP, TO. To change tacks by going around stern to the wind.

WILLIWAWS. Violent bursts of wind that come suddenly off the mountains in Magellan Strait, Alaska, and elsewhere.

WINDLASS. Winch to haul up anchor and chain.

YAW. Vessel slews from side to side, unable to hold a steady course.

YAWL. Two-masted vessel with a short mizzenmast abaft of the stern post.

Notes on Blue-Water Voyaging Books

THOUGH many of our greatest books have been connected with small sailing vessels and the skin of water between the hot and cold edges of the globe, it is not the accounts of Pigafetta or Drake so much as the solo odyssey of Joshua Slocum, the first loner to sail in Magellan's wake, that continues to hold wide interest. That single volume, written by an uncommon Yankee original whose affinities were with the great sea wanderers and nonconformists, has been responsible for more boys (from seventeen to seventy) going to sea in small craft than any other book in all sea literature.

Called by Van Wyck Brooks the "nautical equivalent" to *Walden*, Slocum's *Sailing Alone Around the World* holds its place as a classic of pure narrative, not because of the adventure (scores of others have gone around the world) but because Slocum was broadly aware, had poetic sense of wonder, humor, and an original style—clear and unencumbered.

In a supersonic age that has annihilated time and distance, it is still not easy for the organized or overorganized individual to cast off moorings for a year or two on the open sea. Yet a phenomenon of the present decade is not only the growing number of global voyages being made under sail but the number of books that are being added to the literature on the subject. When a singlehanded sailor is made a knight of the Legion of Honor and his book about a transatlantic crossing sells over 50,000 copies in a few weeks, and another sailor, half the world away, becomes a national hero and best-selling author for a solo transpacific crossing, it can be said that the appeal of small-ship accounts is greater than ever before.

The processing of a cruising narrative into an absorbing book that reaches a wide audience and finds a place on most nautical bookshelves is no simple affair. More than a few with the salt beat in their blood have found that, while the art of ocean cruising can be difficult, the art of writing about it is even more so. Only two or three mariners have been able to write about the sea as St. Exupéry wrote about the air. But today's standards are high and a few who can handle a pen as well as they can hand, reef and steer have achieved an effective style through vivid, straightforward prose.

The most notable early small-ship voyaging accounts—Richard McMullen's *Down Channel,* a coastal cruising classic of charm and wit; Fiennes Speed's *Cruises in Small Yachts;* the buoyant camaraderie of E. F. Knight in *The Falcon on the Baltic*—and a scattering of others were written by sailors who knew their business, took pride in doing it well, and later wrote about it in a brisk, literate fashion.

McMullen and Knight, who loved small ships in the way some men love women, status, or money, were resilient individuals with a firm belief in their ability to do whatever they set out to do. Beyond a backbone of seamanly competence, their books reveal a lively turn of mind with sharp insight into people, places, and the many wonders of ocean cruising.

Other contributions to the literature of the sea, written by capable hands that were more at ease with a halyard, needle and palm, or a sextant, include the lucid, direct style of Conor O'Brien, the candor and laconic humor of G. H. P. Muhlhauser, both circumnavigators of note, and, of course, Commander Graham's *Rough Passage.*

Captain Voss with his hard-and-fast theories and the iconoclast sailor-writer-editor Thomas Fleming Day with his waspish and sometimes caustic prose had their share of followers. Small-craft classics like Harry Pidgeon's *Around the World Single-Handed,* Vito Dumas' taut and truly epic account *Alone Through The Roaring Forties,* and the honest, moving books of Jacques Le Toumelin retain their places on the shelves devoted to great solo navigators who, in writing as in voyaging, knew how to carry sail.

In the notable early accounts the same clear notes of men making competent passages are heard again and again. But, beyond what is learned about the way of a small vessel in the sea, only when such chronicles were charged with special meaning and with something of the deep inner satisfactions of sailing offshore have they reached a really wide audience, as did Ralph Stock's *The Cruise of the Dream Ship.*

When Alain Gerbault sailed his cutter round the world singlehanded, without auxiliary power, a seamanly feat that received the Blue Water Medal of the Cruising Club of America, it was not mastery of language but mastery of seamanship, of himself, and an endless extension of his capabilities beyond what he believed possible that enabled him to convey the fullness and roundness of his experience to a very large number of readers in at least nine languages.

Good books deserve good readers but even the most unresponsive cannot fail to get something of the rhythm of great waters from William Robinson's *Deep Water and Shoal*. Though he may never get there the reader hears the distant sea-drummer most sailors hear, stands watch at the wheel of *Svaap*, struggles with canvas in rain squalls, visits green islands, and shares in the balm of remote anchorages in quiet lagoons.

The voyaging books of men like Hilaire Belloc and Curtis Bok—who understood the art of finding the simplest things in life and enjoying them; who believed that the real significance of sailing is in those qualities that have to do with the human spirit— cut deeper than most and reveal harmony and reverence for life.

In Curtis Bok's *Maria*, a profound and beautiful sea tale that comes along once in a blue moon, truths ancient and ageless come alive. And in *N by E*, Rockwell Kent's sharp prose and superb woodcuts transmit something of the human spirit pushing out to where it has never voyaged before.

Richard Maury's *The Saga of Cimba*, a small-craft classic with a real and abiding sense of the sea, evokes much of the spirit of a little schooner and the visions of young men in a sea-wise balance of islands, taut canvas, and trade winds. Frank Wightman, an independent thinker with a lively observation and philosophy, has written good accounts in *The Wind is Free* and in *Wylo Sails Again*. Adrian Hayter is another who evokes life with clarity and vigor.

Suspenseful voyaging experiences can happen to anyone, but the best books are not filled from cover to cover with exciting adventures. Unexpected things come up that may tax a sailor's ingenuity, but it is the understanding and maturity of the skipper or his wife and their degree of aliveness that makes for good small-ship sea writing. The ambiance of new landfalls and a streaming in through the senses of the wonders of the deep sea give their words wings that reach sailors. A transocean passage with the Pyes, Hiscocks, Millars, or Van de Wieles in almost any boat would be memorable.

David Lewis, who is leaving his mark on modern sailing history and who always likes to have a lot of water ahead of him, is gifted with qualities of courage and quite extraordinary determination, generally hidden by unassuming prose. Beyond the willingness to try something new, to make a mistake occasionally and to be honest enough to admit it, there is a sense of breadth, inner depth, and probing in his books.

Most modern individuals who skipper their own small ships on long voyages and are able to write about it well reveal strong independence of thought. A few like Edward Allcard, Peter Tangvald, Colonel Hasler, and Major Tilman sail shorthanded by most standards and often discard things thought by most sailors to be essential. Their differences are many but they share two things: a high degree of seamanly ability with deep affection and respect for the sea. In Tilman's case the latter qualities extend also to mountain peaks and the writing of excellent books for those who respond to solitude and wilderness. After reading *Mischief in Greenland* for the second time, a friend said to me recently, "Major Tilman can get more out of an arctic voyage than other men could get out of a year in paradise."

The current narratives of remarkable ocean passages in small craft by modern individualists, determined to live the life they chose, may add little to the evolution of mankind but they work wondrous therapy for readers confined to the routine of making a living. According to Melville, every man is a mariner. However this may be, the unlimited possibilities of the voyager have long been a classic subject and the best leave the reader feeling that he might well be the narrator if only he had a suitable craft and didn't have responsibilities to consider.

Both in the sea and in outer space we are in the middle of a change in the conception of man's capacities and goals. A new vision is emerging. Sailor-narrators like Francis Chichester, David Lewis, William Tilman, and others, some presently sailing through regions (Cape Horn and Magellan Strait to the Arctic Circle) as strange as any Odysseus ever visited, prove that the human spirit is no less expansive or vigorous than it was in the Elizabethan or the clipper-ship days.

France's noted single-hander Eric Tabarly, author of *Lonely Victory*, will sail a 60-foot ketch across the Atlantic alone in the next Singlehanded Transatlantic Race. (Sir Francis Drake's 63-foot LW flagship *Golden Hind* had a complement of eighty men and the *Santa María*, 90-foot flagship of Christopher Columbus, required fifty-two men.)

With the same kind of faith and perseverance that brought him through a bout with near-fatal cancer a few years ago, Francis Chichester, sixty-six-year-old author of *Along the Clipper Way* and other well-written across-oceans accounts, is sailing his 54-foot ketch *Gypsy Moth IV* from Plymouth, England, 13,750 miles nonstop to Sydney and from there 14,750 miles on around the Horn and across the South Atlantic nonstop to Plymouth for a 230-day singlehanded voyage around the world—beating the time of the average clipper ships which followed the same course in the Roaring Forties.

A new type of sea book is emerging, written in the cabins of small vessels by those out probing the outermost anchorages, surpassing the bounds of the known and familiar. A few narrators have even become specialists in circumnavigation. Sailors of remarkable technical prowess like Eric and Susan Hiscock who have outsailed all other circumnavigators have found time to write four widely received books on their many voyages around the world.

Sailing off into the deep blue in a small vessel with sweet lines is one of the oldest dreams known to salt-water man but never before have transocean small-ship navigators and circumnavigators had the advanced gear, incredibly accurate instruments, and such well rigged-out masterpieces as *Wanderer III*, *Pen Duick III*, and *Gypsy Moth IV*.

H. G. Hasler's brilliant researches into special cruising rigs and gear have helped to make things better and a lot more is possible for the cruising sailor. But the art of writing words in the cabin of a small vessel remains difficult—words, that is, that creep into a reader's inner ear with a subtle and persistent persuasiveness that does its work at deep levels.

The latest wind vane self-steering gear is an aid to good seamanship but it cannot keep a good lookout. It cannot think, feel limitless vistas, or write tomorrow's blue-water voyaging books.

> All I know is that, for twenty months, neglecting the common joys of life that fall to the lot of the humblest on this earth, I had, like the prophet of old, "wrestled with the Lord" for my creation, for the headlands of the coast, for the darkness of the Placid Gulf, the light on the snows, the clouds on the sky, and for the breath of life that had to be blown into the shapes of men and women, of Latin and Saxon, of Jew and Gentile. These are, perhaps, strong

words, but it is difficult to characterize otherwise the intimacy and the strain of a creative effort in which mind and will and conscience are engaged to the full, hour after hour, day after day, away from the world, and to the exclusion of all that makes life really lovable and gentle—something for which a material parallel can only be found in the everlasting sombre stress of the westward winter passage round Cape Horn. For that too is the wrestling of men with the might of their Creator, in a great isolation from the world, without the amenities and consolations of life, a lonely struggle under a sense of overmatched littleness, for no reward that could be adequate, but for the mere winning of a longitude. . . .

—JOSEPH CONRAD

Reading List

~~~~~~

SMALL-SHIP OCEAN VOYAGERS

DURING man's movement from the oxwheel and early whale-hunter to modern global cruising sailor he has written a lot of voyaging books that vary greatly in breadth and depth. Some that deserved·to be widely known had a short in-print history in their original editions. In Britain Adlard Coles and Rupert Hart-Davis, with its excellent Mariners Library, and in the United States John de Graff deserve credit for keeping many of the best cruising accounts available in good editions at moderate prices.

In the Notes on Blue-Water Voyaging Books I've given a small indication of values the voyagers are best qualified to reveal and the following list, though in no way inclusive or definitive, is largely made up of narratives written by the voyagers themselves. Out-of-print books have been included only when still available in public libraries.

° *Indicates recipient of Cruising Club of America Blue Water Medal Award.*

ALLCARD, EDWARD. *Single-Handed Passage*. New York: Norton, 1950.

———. *Temptress Returns*. New York: Norton, 1953.

———. *Voyage Alone*. New York: Dodd, Mead, 1964.

ANDERSON, J. R. L. *The Greatest Race in the World: Solo Across the Atlantic*. London: Hodder & Stoughton, 1964.

ARROW, NEILL. *10,000 Miles to Boston*. New York: Stein & Day, 1964.

°BARDIAUX, MARCEL. *Four Winds of Adventure*. New York: De Graff, 1961.

BARTON, HUMPHREY. *The Sea and Me*. London: Ross, 1952.

———. *Vertue XXXV*. New York: De Graff, 1955.

BAUM, RICHARD. *By the Wind*. New York: Van Nostrand, 1962.

BELLOC, HILAIRE. *On Sailing the Sea*. New York: De Graff, 1951.

———. *The Cruise of the Nona*. Baltimore: Penguin, 1958.

BERNICOT, LOUIS. *The Voyage of the Anahita*. London: Hart-Davis, 1953.

BOMBARD, ALAIN. *The Voyage of the Heretique*. New York: Simon & Schuster, 1954.

BRADFIELD, S. E. *Road to the Sea*. London: Temple Press, 1964.

BRADFORD, ERNLE. *Ulysses Found*. New York: Harcourt, 1964.

CARLIN, BEN. *Half-Safe*. New York: Morrow, 1955.

°CHICHESTER, FRANCIS. *Alone Across the Atlantic*. New York: Doubleday, 1961.

———. *Atlantic Adventure*. New York: De Graff, 1963.

———. *Along the Clipper Way*. London: Hodder & Stoughton, 1966.

CLIFFORD, BRIAN. *The Voyage of the Golden Lotus*. New York: De Graff, 1963.

COLES, ADLARD. *North Atlantic*. New York: Norton, 1950.

CREALOCK, W. I. B. *Cloud of Islands*. New York: Hastings, 1955.

°CROWE, BILL AND PHYLLIS. *Heaven, Hell and Salt Water*. New York: De Graff, 1957.

DAVENPORT, PHILIP. *The Voyage of Waltzing Matilda*. New York: Dodd, Mead, 1954.

DAVISON, ANN. *Last Voyage*. New York: Sloan, 1952.

———. *My Ship Is So Small*. New York: Sloan, 1956.

DE BISSCHOP, ERIC. *Tahiti Nui*. New York: McDowell, Obolensky, 1959.

DIBBERN, GEORGE. *Quest*. New York: Norton, 1941.

°DUMAS, VITO. *Alone Through The Roaring Forties*. New York: De Graff, 1960.

ELLAM, PATRICK, AND MUDIE, COLIN. *Sopranino*. New York: De Graff, 1958.

FILLOUX, JEAN. *The Crossing of the Copula*. New York: Dodd, Mead, 1954.

GARLAND, JOSEPH E. *Lone Voyager*. Boston: Little, Brown, 1963.

°GERBAULT, ALAIN. *Fight of the Firecrest*. New York: De Graff, 1955.

———. *In Quest of the Sun*. New York: De Graff, 1955.

°GRAHAM, ROBERT DOUGLAS. *Rough Passage*. New York: De Graff, 1952.

GRIFFITHS, MAURICE. *The Magic of the Swatchways*. London: Arnold, 1949.

GUNN, JOHN. *Barrier Reef by Trimaran*. London: Collins, 1966.

°GUZZWELL, JOHN. *Trekka Round the World*. New York: De Graff, 1963.

HAMILTON, PETER. *The Restless Wind*. New York: St. Martin's, 1963.

HAYTER, ADRIAN. *The Long Voyage*. New York: Harper, 1959.

———. *Business in Great Waters*. London: Hodder & Stoughton, 1965.

°HISCOCK, ERIC. *Around the World in Wanderer III*. New York and London: Oxford, 1956.

———. *Voyaging under Sail*. New York and London: Oxford, 1959.

———. *Beyond the West Horizon*. New York and London: Oxford, 1963.

HOLDRIDGE, DESMOND. *Northern Lights*. New York: Viking, 1939.

HORIE, KENICHI. *Kodoku: Alone Across the Pacific.* Rutland, Vt.: Tuttle, 1964.
HOWARD, SIDNEY. *Thames to Tahiti.* London: Hart-Davis, 1951.
HOWELL, WILLIAM. *White Cliffs to Coral Reefs.* London: Odhams, 1957.
HOWELLS, VALENTINE. *Sailing into Solitude.* New York: Dodd, Mead, 1966.
KAUFFMAN, RAY F. *Hurricane's Wake.* New York: Macmillan, 1940.
KENT, ROCKWELL. *N by E.* New York: Brewer & Warren, 1930.
KILROY, ROBIN A. *Boleh.* London: Hodder & Stoughton, 1951.
KNIGHT, EDWARD F. *The Falcon on the Baltic.* New York: De Graff, 1952.
LA BORDE, HAROLD. *An Ocean to Ourselves.* New York: De Graff, 1962.
LE TOUMELIN, JACQUES-YVES. *Kurun Around the World.* New York: Dutton, 1955.
———. *Kurun in the Caribbean.* New York: De Graff, 1963.
LEWIS, DAVID. *The Ship Would Not Travel Due West.* New York: St. Martin's, 1961.
———. *Dreamers of the Day.* London: Gollancz, 1964.
———. *Daughters of the Wind.* London: Gollancz, 1966.
LONDON, JACK. *Cruise of the Snark.* New York: Macmillan, 1911.
LONG, DWIGHT. *Seven Seas on a Shoestring.* New York: Harper, 1939.
MACGREGOR, JOHN. *Voyage Alone in the Yawl Rob Roy.* New York: De Graff, 1954.
MANRY, ROBERT. *Tinkerbelle.* New York: Harper, 1966.
°MARIN-MARIE. *Wind Aloft, Wind Alow.* London: Davies, 1947.
°MAURY, RICHARD. *The Saga of Cimba.* New York: Harcourt, 1939.
MIDDLETON, EMPSON E. *The Cruise of the Kate.* New York: De Graff, 1953.
MILLAR, GEORGE. *A White Boat from England.* New York: Knopf, 1952.
MORISON, SAMUEL E. *Spring Tides.* Boston: Houghton Mifflin, 1965.
MUHLHAUSER, G. H. P. *Cruise of the Amaryllis.* New York: De Graff, 1951.
NICOLSON, IAN. *Sea-Saint.* London: Davies, 1957.
NUTTING, WILLIAM. *The Track of the Typhoon.* New York: Motor Boat, 1922.
O'BRIEN, CONOR. *Across Three Oceans.* New York: De Graff, 1950.
PETERSEN, E. ALLEN. *Hummel Hummel.* New York: Vantage, 1952.
°PETERSEN, MARJORIE. *Stornoway East and West.* New York: Van Nostrand, 1966.
°PIDGEON, HARRY. *Around the World Single-Handed.* New York: De Graff, 1955.
PIVER, ARTHUR. *Trans-Atlantic Trimaran.* San Francisco: Underwriters Press, 1961.
———. *Trans-Pacific Trimaran.* Mill Valley, Calif.: Pi-Craft, 1963.
———. *Trimaran Third Book.* Mill Valley, Calif.: Pi-Craft, 1965.
° PULESTON, DENNIS. *Blue Water Vagabond.* New York: Doubleday, 1943.
PYE, PETER. *Red Mains'l.* New York: De Graff, 1961.
———. *A Sail in a Forest.* London: Rupert Hart-Davis, 1961.
———. *The Sea Is for Sailing.* New York: De Graff, 1961.
RANSOME, ARTHUR. *Racundra's First Cruise.* New York: De Graff, 1958.
REBELL, FRED. *Escape to the Sea.* London: Murray, 1951.
REYNOLDS, EARLE. *The Forbidden Voyage.* New York: McKay, 1961.
——— AND BARBARA. *All in the Same Boat.* New York: McKay, 1962.
°ROBINSON, WILLIAM A. *Deep Water and Shoal.* New York: De Graff, 1957.
ROCKEFELLER, JAMES S., JR. *Man on His Island.* New York: Norton, 1957.
SEYMOUR, JOHN. *Willynilly to the Baltic.* Edinburgh: Blackwood, 1965.
SHERWOOD, MARTYN. *Voyage of the Tai-Mo-Shan.* New York: De Graff, 1957.
SINCLAIR, W. E. *Cruises of the Joan.* New York: St. Martin's, 1934.
SLOCUM, JOSHUA. *Sailing Alone Around the World.* New York: De Graff, 1952.

SMEETON, MILES. *Once Is Enough.* New York: De Graff, 1960.

———. *Sunrise to Windward.* London: Rupert Hart-Davis, 1966.

SMITH, STANLEY, AND VIOLET, CHARLES. *The Wind Calls the Tune.* New York: Van Nostrand, 1953.

STOCK, RALPH. *The Cruise of the Dream Ship.* New York: Doubleday, 1922.

°TABARLY, ERIC. *Lonely Victory.* New York: Clarkson Potter, 1966.

TAMBS, ERLING. *The Cruise of the Teddy.* New York: De Graff (2nd impression), 1950.

TANGVALD, PETER. *Sea Gypsy.* New York: Dutton, 1966.

TATE, MICHAEL. *Blue Water Cruising.* New York: De Graff, 1964.

TEY, JOSE MARIA. *Hongkong to Barcelona in the Junk Rubia.* London: Harrap, 1962.

°TILMAN, H. W. *Mischief in Patagonia.* New York and London: Cambridge, 1957.

———. *Mischief Among the Penguins.* Chester Springs, Pa.: Dufour, 1961.

———. *Mischief in Greenland.* New York: De Graff, 1964.

———. *Mostly Mischief.* London: Hollis & Carter, 1966.

TOMPKINS, JOHN BARR, editor. *A Voyage of Pleasure* [Log of Bernard Gilboy]. Cambridge, Md.: Cornell Maritime Press, 1956.

° URIBURU, ERNESTO. *Seagoing Gaucho.* New York: Dodd, Mead, 1951.

° VAN DE WIELE, ANNIE. *The West in My Eyes.* New York: Dodd, Mead, 1956.

VOSS, JOHN C. *The Venturesome Voyages of Captain Voss.* New York: De Graff, 1955.

WHARRAM, JAMES. *People of the Sea* [Catamaran Voyages]. Harrow, Middlesex, Eng.: Sun & Health, 1965.

WIBBERLEY, LEONARD. *Toward a Distant Island.* New York: Ives Washburn, 1966.

WIGHTMAN, FRANK A. *The Wind Is Free.* New York: De Graff, 1955.

———. *Wylo Sails Again.* New York: De Graff, 1957.

WILLIS, WILLIAM. *The Gods Were Kind.* New York: Dutton, 1955.

———. *An Angel on Each Shoulder.* New York: Meredith, 1967.

COLLECTIONS: VOYAGES AND SEA LITERATURE

ANTHONY, IRVIN. *Voyagers Unafraid.* Philadelphia: Macrae Smith, 1930.

BARTON, HUMPHREY. *Atlantic Adventurers.* Definitive work on Atlantic crossings in craft under 40 feet. New York: De Graff, 1962.

BRUCE, ERROLL. *Challenge to Poseidon.* Adventures in small craft. New York: Van Nostrand, 1956.

COLE, GUY. *Ocean Cruising.* London: Bosun Books, Adlard Coles, 1959.

DAVIN, TOM, editor. *The Rudder Treasury.* New York: Sheridan, 1960.

DE SELINCOURT, AUBREY, editor. *The Book of the Sea.* Comprehensive anthology of sea prose and poetry from Pindar and Vergil to Slocum and Marin-Marie. New York: Norton, 1963.

DEVINE, ERIC, editor. *Midget Magellans.* New York: Random House, 1936.

FREEMAN, IRA HENRY, editor. *White Sails Shaking.* Excerpts from sailing yacht accounts. New York: Macmillan, 1948.

GARRETT, ALASDAIR, editor. *Roving Commissions.* Annual collections of cruising logs by members of the R.C.C. London: R.C.C. Press, yearly.

HEATON, PETER. *The Sea Gets Bluer.* Selections from authors. London: Black, 1965.

KLEIN, DAVID, AND JOHNSON, MARY LOUISE. *They Took to the Sea.* Selections from authors. New Brunswick, N.J.: Rutgers, 1948.

MERRIEN, JEAN. *Lonely Voyagers.* London: Hutchinson, 1954.

PARKINSON, JOHN, JR., editor. *Nowhere Is Too Far.* Summary of Blue Water Medal Awards and cruising annals of the C.C.A. New York: C.C.A., 1960.

REMINGTON, CRITCHELL, editor. *The Sea Chest.* Selections from authors. New York: Norton, 1947.

SPECTORSKY, A. C., editor. *Book of the Sea.* Also contains large ship voyaging accounts but is included here because it is far the best of the anthologies of sea writing. New York: Grosset, 1954.

TAYLOR, WILLIAM B., editor. *Just Cruising.* Collection of yarns and articles. New York: Van Nostrand, 1949.

TELLER, WALTER. *The Voyages of Joshua Slocum.* New Brunswick, N.J.: Rutgers, 1958.

Index

Charles Borden in his sloop *Confucius III* returning to Spindrift from a coastal cruise.